Historical Documents
from
High Western Himalaya

Other Books by Tobdon

History and Religions of Lahul, (1984);

The People of the Upper Valley (The sTodpas of Lahul in the Himalaya), (1993);

Kullu: A Study in History (2000);

Cultural History of Western Trans-Himalayas, Bashahar-Kinnaur (2008);

Moravian Missionaries in Western Trans-Himalaya: Lahul, Ladakh and Kinnaur (Co-Author with C Dorje) (2008);

Exploring Malana, (2011);

Spiti: A Study in Socio-Cultural Traditions (2015);

Nathpanth in Western Himalaya (2015);

Bhoti Parichay: Grammar and Translation (2019);

Zong Gonpa of Village Tinno (2019);

Ancient Lahul and Himalaya (2021);

Buddhist Monumental Heritage of sTod Valley in Lahul (Co-Author with C Dorje) (2021);

The Brave Soldiers of Lahul: The Saviours of Ladakh in 19948 (2022);

Mahakappina: The King of Kuluta and the Kinnaras of the Himalaya (2023),

Historical Documents
FROM
High Western Himalaya

Lahul and the Areas Surrounding

Tobdan

Kaveri Books
New Delhi - 110002

Title: Historical Documents from High Western Himalaya: Lahul and the Areas Surrounding
Author: Tobdon

First Published in 2024

ISBN : 978-93-86463-25-8
Price Rs. 1800.00

Published by
Kaveri Books
4832/24, Ansari Road, Daryaganj,
New Delhi - 110 002 (India)
Ph. : 011-2328 8140, 4707 2321
E-mail : info@kaveribooks.com
kaveribooks@gmail.com
Website : www.kaveribooks.com

Typesetting at Creative Graphics, Delhi

PRINTED IN INDIA

Preface

The present work is a collection mostly of karchhags, a kind of document prepared at the moment of celebration of ceremony held in honour of some deceased person in a wealthy household. They record the salient facts of the occasion. Even though the documents are generally not dated but most of them contain at least a name of a prominent historical person, as such they are not less in importance in any way from any other kind of a historical document. Besides it also includes some other kinds of documents like decrees, inscriptions, etc. The documents being mostly under private ownership were collected mostly from the individuals or individual households. The original documents are in the scripts of Bhoti, Tankri and Sharda.

These documents cover the subjects of social, economic, religious, political, etc. kind, spanning a long period of about five centuries of the medieval and modern period. It covers uniformly the three valleys including all the four cultural zones of Lahul.

It has been over fifty years since the work of collecting the material began. I am aware that by now some of the original documents have been lost permanently. Some others may not be accessible or traceable any more.

Here there are some words used from vernacular languages. The same item is named differently in different cultures. The articles and the words are mostly not in use now. The words cannot be found in the lexicons. Only a few old men, who can be searched with much difficulty, know a few words concerning their own culture. The valuable knowledge will be lost along with them.

The attitude of the people towards the things relating to their past appears to be generally indifferent. I gave a copy of the gsol-

'debs, Prayer Book, to the monastery of mTsho Padma, Riwalsar, renowned as very rich. From the point of view of the monastery it is an extremely valuable property, like an object symbolizing their founding ancestors. It was delivered with the assurance of all needed possible help. On further enquiry even the whereabouts of the original was not known.

While arranging the material of the book it was found difficult to classify them in the usual manner like subject wise, script wise or to place them in chronological order. The easiest choice was found to place them in geographical order, to begin from one point and then to continue till the end.

The work being somewhat unconventional and of diverse nature some aspects of it were left loose. The originals are seen presented in several fonts in Tibetan and also in Roman transcription.

I have trimmed the documents but have tried to retain the essential facts contained in them and at places maintaining fully those with distinctive shape and form. No change has been made like spellings, etc. However, in the translations it has been followed as the meaning could be understood.

During the long course of the work some informed and cooperative persons came to help readily. They being large in number, I am not able to name them individually. I am thankful to them and all.

I am thankful to Sh. Rakesh Goel of Kaveri Books for accepting to take up the task of publishing this work.

Kullu, December, 2023 **Tobdan**

Introduction

(a) Karchhag: The tradition of writing karchhags existed in all the three valleys of Lahul since long past. Earlier ceremonies were performed in honour of certain worthy members of a few wealthy families at a much grander level. Preparations had to be made for it from long time before to gather and accumulate resources. This was presumed to be a great virtuous task. Those who had performed such a ceremony had attained and entered a class in the society more elite. There were only a few such households in a village or in the area. In the large village of Sindhwari, known as the village of Brahmins, there was one family who had performed the ceremony of Pung-ying and they were renowned as such. It was also an opportunity for the households to exhibit and establish the status of their prosperity and popularity in the area. A great number of people were invited to attend the ceremony. In the ceremonies it is said that people came from all over Lahul. Even though this is interpreted generally restrictively, there is an instance which authenticates the fact. In the ceremony performed by Thonu, the great Kharpon, in c. C.E. 1840, at Jahlma, it is recorded that valuable articles were distributed among the people and feast was given to all the people of the three valleys of Lahul to the full satisfaction of them all. According to the Census of 1901, the population of Lahul was near about 6,000.

The ceremony could be for one or more and could be both for male and female members. In the records these persons are known in relationship such as father, grandfather, mother, grandmother, etc. and many are found named. In the Brahminic tradition, followed by a class called as Soṅglā inhabiting more in the lower part of Pattan, it was called Pung-ying (Puṅ-yīṅ) a vernacular corrupt form of the Sanskrit word Punya. In Buddhistic tradition it was called dGe-ba,

Rab-gnas or mTshogs. Here dGe-ba is the proper term. Punya and dGe-ba both mean the same as virtue. In Pattan there is another class named as Garu, admixture of two sections of the society, Brahmins and Nangpa. They celebrated the ceremony in which features of both the systems were adopted. They invited both Lama and Brahmin priest for performing the rites. Such a ceremony was known as Ranah (Raṇāh). All the kinds of these ceremonies were very expensive.

In the Pung-ying no record was prepared. Description of the ceremony of Pung-ying performed, known as the last such kind of performance to have been held in Lahul, is given at (Tobdan, 2021: 249-266). The performance held in the household of Bir Singh, Shansha-1, it is Ranah of the kind of mixture of the two traditions of Pung-ying and dGe-ba. In the household of Thonu, village Jahlma, both the kinds of ceremonies were performed at the same time. The rest are dGe-ba, Rab-gnas or mTshogs, as each ceremony gives name to the performance. In the two kinds of performances of Ranah and dGe-ba an account of the ceremony noting the major and important facts was recorded and a document was prepared known as karchhag.

In Buddhistic culture there is a tradition that on the death of a person symbols representing the body, voice and heart (sku, gsung, thugs, in Skt. kāya, vāka and citta) are required to be raised at the time of celebration of the funeral rites in honour of the deceased. These symbols are raised in the form of statues, copying one or more sacred books and raising a chhorten, i.e. chaitya, respectively. Few people raised chhorten. Some people raised statues. Most of them raised i.e. copieda book or books. When a book was copied, in most cases they also prepared a karchag which either formed end portion of the book or could be a separate document. Both were called karchhag and the other one prepared separately was kept tied with the book copied at the moment. Dorchhod, Vajrachhedika, is the book most commonly found copied. We find the same practice being followed in the other areas also covered here.

Statues are generally of stucco and they are not known to contain any inscription. We know little about the contents in the chhortens.

The general contents of a good sized karchhag are that they begin with an eulogy by praising the Doctrine, mount Tise (Kailash), Gandhala, Drilbu, etc. They write, Jambudvipa, a part of the universe, the continent situated in the south, is the best among all. Tise (Kailash) is the living place of the Arhats. The Turquise lake, Lake Mapang (Manasarovar), lake of bathing, is the head of the four great rivers of the Himalaya. Mount Gandhala, prophesied by the Jinas, is the living place of the Dakinis, the Heroes and Heroines of the Doctrine, and it is connected through the unbroken chain of mountains with the mount Tise (Ti-rtse tī. = water, rtse = peak), (Kailash).

Further it records the name of the Raja of Kullu with the name of his capital and sometimes also the name of the local chief. Then comes the name of the person or persons in whose honour the occasion is being celebrated, name of the principal donor and the lady donor, description of the guest donors like their name, name of village, the kind and quantity of the articles offered, etc. It records the name of the deity whose statue has been raised, title of the book and the kind of chhorten raised. At some places item wise amount of expenditure made are also given.

They deal with a wide range of subject like social, economic, religious, political, etc. covering a long period of about five centuries of the medieval and modern period of Lahul upto the end of the British period.

Broadly we get a picture of the economic condition of the area. Despite the fact that the nature is so harsh that only one crop can be grownin a year and that also in small patches and slopy areas, everyone was fully fed and many also drunk.

The earliest of the karchhags belongs to the period of Bahadur Singh of Kullu (1532-1559). The latest belongs to the British period. It writes that the area is being ruled by the Phyiling, British. Along with it, they give the name of the Raja of Kullu and the Thakur of Lahul, with full date

We have already treated a set of similar documents but slightly of different type collected by A.H. Francke, (Tobdan and C. Dorje, 2008:73ff.), where the original writing has been reproduced photographically. The transcription and translation of the matter has been given in an earlier work, (Tobdan and C. Dorje, 1996).

(b) Inscriptions in Sharda: Sharda inscriptions are found in Lahul at four places. First is in Tindi, Pattan. Second at Triloknath. Third we find in Chhokhor gonpa in Tinan valley. The fourth inscription in Sharda is found at Margul-Udaipur, (Vogel, 1911-i: 249-251).

(c) Documents and inscriptions in Tankri script: Two documents in Tankri script have been found which belong to the period of Raja Tedhi Singh (1742-1767) of Kullu. The first such document is the inscriptions on three mohras, faces, of Naunath devata in village Rwaling. There is a small temple of one room in village Rwaling dedicated to the deity named Naunath. It is told to have come from a village in Lag valley in Kullu accompanied by the Gur, priest. He was also given a piece of land in the village. The family still exists in the village with the history accompanied. There is a small vehicle, rath, like those found in Kullu but not used presently. There are also some old musical instruments of the devata. It is known that till around 1960s it was taken on round of the villages. It has nine mohras of metal, silver and brass, but very small in size compared to those seen in Kullu. Three of them contain inscriptions in Tankri script. But they are difficult to read. Khub Ram reads the name Tedhi Singh. There are three dates written on two mohras. On one mohra we read sambat 12 and on another 22 which are equivalent to C.E. 1741 and 1752.

The second document is the title grant by Raja Tedhi Singh of Kullu to Rup Chand-Seva Dass, of Gundhla, C.E. 1760, in Tinan, (Tinan-b.iii,).

There is an inscription in Tankri written on a wooden board in the temple of Mrikula Devi at Udaipur. This document has not been treated so far by any scholar. Two references are found about Lahul in the Tankri work of an official of Kullu who was stationed at Tandi. Both are dated year 100 equivalent to C.E. 1824.

(d) Wood Block Engravers, Image makers, Painters and Scribes of Lahul: It appears that the class of wood block engravers got expanded after the advent of Tashi Tanphel of Ladakh to Lahul in c. 1880. During the period of his stay in Lahul for about two decades wood blocks for a number of books were prepared. Then it continued for sometime thereafter. The patrons were the Thakurs of Khangsar.

During the years 1883-85 wood blocks were prepared for the book Padma Kathang under the supervision of Tashi Tanphel at Tayul monastery. The engravers working there were as under:

(i) Engravers from outside Lahul: Mar-kha 'Um-lung-pa, sGrub-pa Paljor Phungtsog and Mipham of Chhushod, Ladak, and Pi-shu Tshering dBang-chhug of Zanskar.

(ii) Engravers from Lahul:

1. **Gemur monastery in sTod valley:** No-no Kargyud Rigzin, Tanpa Tshering, Nono Kongchhog Zodpa from village Tino, Tanzin Dondub from Yo-tse, Tanzin Chhosphel from Yar-gzhi of Jispa, a nun from the house of Bharong in Kolong and Lharje [doctor] Chhoskyid.
2. **Punan (Gahar):** There were the pupil-monks of Khedub Tshebang Rigzin and dBu-mdsab-phris, the two. Others were - Sonam Dorje from Bar-bKar-sdang, Lharje Tshering, Khyim-btses Tshering, Norbu, Mani, Dondub, Rigzin of Zholing, Paldan, Norbu from Beeling, Sonam Rigzin Anu-tse, Jigs-jed, Kyi-tsi, Che-pa of Lower Kyelang, Dug Dorje, Rigzin, Norbu from Upper Kyelang, Kyu-kar Rigzin and Na-mo of Bar-tsi house of Kyelang.

Tshebang Rigzin is the same as Tshang Meme of Tharbas, relating to Shashur Project.

Dondub, the engraver, from Punan appears to have been a good professional. His name is found in several works, at different places and for long period. We find the length of his working period from the earliest in 1892 to 1919 working at Tukiling and other places. He was also at Tayul. Mipham the scribe was also image-maker and Painter.

3. **Manchhad (Pattan):** Dug Tshering from Ghorom village.

(e) Khangsar Khar: Hari Chand, the Thakur of Khangsar, got his house, the Khar (mKhar) of Khangsar, constructed, which still stands in good condition. Meme Kasse of Jispa did the work of wood carvings here. He also built the masks of monkey and lion, of the mChhodpa dance of Khangsar. He also worked in building the Yarzhi gonpa of Jispa. He belonged to village Jispa, sTod, to the period 19th-20th century. The name Khangsar Khar, name of the castle of the Thakurs of Khangsar, Kolong, existed much before Tashi Tanphel gave the name Khar-gsar Khar after it was constructed newly. The family and the household is still known as Khangsar Khar.

(f) Kholl, name of an area: In an old document found in village Rhape there is mention of a geographical term Kholl (Khol) representing an area different from the name of the village and also from that of Lahul. The document is old. The sheet itself is broken on the right side. It has been dated roughly to the period of Raja Bahadur Singh of Kullu (1532-1559).

The document provides that, 'Lahul is prosperous and happy'. in the district of Kholl, here at [the village of] Yo-nam.

The statement gives that the village of Yo-nam is situated within the area of Kholl. Yo-nam certainly stands for the name of the village which presently is known as Rhape where this document is found, which name might have been lost later on. There are several villages in Pattan which have two names as Jahlma is also known as Yana-phel.Thus this appears to be name of an area smaller than Lahul but larger than the village. Yo-nam is definitely the former name of Rhape.

The owners of the household tell that this is the name of their deity who is propitiated by some other villages also. It is named as Khola-ṛu. The deity is supposed to be associated with a boulder situated at about six kilometers away from Rhape in the valley of Kugti. While going from Rhape to Kugti pass and Kugti village in Bhramaur the pilgrims going to Manimahesh halt here for one night.

The deity is also known as Kholaṛū Vāsī, inhabitant of Kholaru. This is in the style of the names of deities as is found in Pangi where for example Mindhal Devi is also known as Mindhal Vasini, resident in Mindhal. It is said to be the same as the deity named Khordev who is propitiated at several places in Pattan. The deity has a shrine at Sindhwari in Pattan.

The same term 'Khol' is found in two documents from village Wari. One is of the period of Tedhi Singh (1742-1767) and the other of the period of Raja Parbat Singh (1575-1608). In the document relating to Tedhi Singh it is written, "Under his reign is the prosperous Lahul. In the district of Khol, there is the [village] of Wari situated high." In the older document relating to Parbat Singh it reads: "While his kingdom is expanding, under his rule is the country of Lahul, the land of rules. and in the district of Khol is situated high (village of) Wari." Here Kholl stands for an area larger than village of Wari but smaller than Lahul.

The people in Pattan have no knowledge about the term. The village of Wari is situated, above Tandi, at one end of the valley of Pattan and Rhape is situated nearabout the middle of the valley but at an important place linking the village with Bhramaur. The term was not found at any other place. Thus we understandably take Kholl to mean the area between these villages. But as there exist signs of presence of the deity Kholl downwards beyond this we take the term designating the whole area of Pattan.

(g) Kharpon: an official of Kullu selected from Lahul and posted at Tandi: During the reign of the Rajas of Kullu there was an official from Lahul working under the Chief who came from Kullu and was posted at Tandi. He was designated as Kharpon as found written in the documents found in Lahul. It literally means Castle Officer/Authority.

Its equivalent in Kulluvi is not known. The household of Lhye-Thāling in Wari, the household from which came a line of Kharpons, know themselves also as Parshira. Satish Loppa tells that this is equivalent to the Kulluvi term of Palsara which is designation of an official of the Rajas in Kullu. He was an officcial of senior rank.

(h) Gandhala, Gandhola, Tinan, Nal-ze and Naltse: The two earliest karchhags of the Gundhla Kanjur write Gandhala for the sacred mountain situated at the junction of the rivers Chandra and Bhaga. Later documents write Gandhola. These early documents also write Tinan for the valley of Chandra and the village of Gundhla. The castle of the Thakurs of Gondhla or Gundhla built in the local style was first built by Dorje Pala and it was first named as Nalze. Later on it is found written as Naltse.

(i) Transcribing the word Tedhi, part of the name Tedhi Singh in Bhoti: There being no equivalent letters in Tibetan alphabets the scribes always found difficulty in transcribing the word Tedhi in Bhoti. So we find the name written in several forms like Trera, Tri-ri, etc. At one place it is even translated as mdses = beautiful. Also this is the name occurring the most among all.

(j) Notes: The following are explanations regarding descriptions of the offerings as found in the translations.

i. At the end of the karchhags there comes the names of the kins and the articles they offered. These have been summarized. Thus entries may be like: "uthi chhang, lagsha and one rupee (12)." It may be read that 12 persons made offerings each of the articles as given here.

ii. In the case of offerings of gold accounted in terms of coins, it may be understood like "gold 8 annas," as gold equal to the weight of 8 anna coin.

iii. One meal or drink means meal or drink given for one time to all the persons present at the time.

iv. In some old manuscript books we find one or two small circles kept blank and a point marked at the centre. Lama Rigzin of Jispa tells that this is kept to be pierced and then a thread is passed through them to join the pages, thus to bind the book. We find some books bound similarly kept in the libraries of old manuscripts in India.

l. Measures of volume and weight in Lahul

a. Measures of volume

Bre = 2 seers

Khal = 20 bre

Khari = 20 khal

b. Measures of weight

Seer = 8 chhatank

Bati = 2 seers

Maund = 40 seers

Contents

List of Plates

Book I
Translation and Notes

Part A - Lahul (Garzha)

1 Pattan (Manchhad), Chandrabhaga Valley

i. Tindi (Tīndī). Inscription on metal, Sharda script, Mushan Verman, Raja of Bhramaur (Chamba), c. C.E. 820.

In Tindi, near the border with Pangi, there is the temple dedicated to Mrkula devi, also designated as Bhavani and Mahakali. The building has been renovated recently. The deity is in possession of a dhol (ḍhola), drum, said to be made of gold dust and weighing about 3 kgs. An inscription is shown over it in Sharda script. The surface of the dhol is worn out due to age and continuously long use. The words were not legible except one letter and remains of some effaced letters in a line. Chattar Singh, the Pujari, tells the following legend as the reading of the inscription.

मूसावर्मनराजाभ्रमौर; ऊग्रुभंडारी; ठाकरू ठठियार।

mūsāvarmanrājābhramaur, ūgrūbhandārī, ṭhākrūṭhaṭhiyār.

Translation: Musa Varman is Raja of Bhramaur. Ugru is storekeeper or treasurer and Thakru is goldsmith.

This may be explained as that, the drum was manufactured in gold which was donated by Musa Varman, the Raja of Bhramaur (Chamba). The material, i.e. gold, was supplied by Ugru the Storekeeper or Treasurer and it was manufactured by Thakru, the goldsmith.

Vansavali of the Rajas of Chamba states that Bhramaur was once invaded by the Kiras (Tobdan, 2023: 79-101) and killed the then Raja Lakshmi Vamman. The Rani fled and gave birth to a son on the way. They went tunder the protection of the Raja of Suket. He protected and nourished the son well. When he came of age he married his daughter to him. He gave wealth and the village of Pangi. He also gave army. Then the prince regained his kingdom.

The king came to be known as Mūṣāṇa Varman, C.E. 820, (Vogel, 1911: 92).

The temple is also told to be in possession of a bell which, the Pujari tells, was gifted by Sahilvarman, the Raja of Chamba (c. C.E. 920-940).

ii. Margul (Udaipur). Inscription on stone, Bhoti script, c. 17th-18th century C.E.

The inscription was found written on a round riverside stone of about 15 kg. in weight. Its surface was smooth but undulating. In around 1973 it was placed in a small stone shed of around eight cubic feet (2′x2′x2′) above the road at about 200 meters before reaching the bridge at Udaipur from the side of Thirot. The stone has now disappeared.

Translation: Sin

I pay reverence to Avalokitesvara the god who is white in colour, devoid of fault, crowned with the Perfect Buddha, and looks upon the world with compassionate eyes. He having one face and six arms sits on the clean and faultless cushion of lotus with his right leg in dancing posture. I pay reverence to the self-born image of Avalokitesvara who draws six kinds of beings from the world.

The godess Vajravrahi represents the excellent mother of the Jinas of the three times in its fierce form, who kindly grants two kinds of boons to conquer completely those creating darkness, arrogance and madness. I worship and bow to her.

I, a nun, endowed with control over my fleeting mind, have got engraved in the beginning, middle and end, thousand manye mantras unalterable on stones in order to completely exhort the others for the sake of their happiness. E ma ho!

Still more, on the circumambulation paths of both Re-phag (Triloknath) and Margul, complete manye wheels have been raised again. At the monastery of Margul xxx has been constructed again. The benefit of these virtues should go to all those who have not yet achieved the Buddhahood. Manglam!

Note: Refer to Vogel (1911: 267) and Tobdan (1984: 97-98). The form of Avalokitesvara is known as *'gro-ba 'gro-drug 'dren* (the god who withdraws six kinds of beings from the world to liberation). There are similar images of Avalokitesvara at Gandhala-Tubchiling of c. 1840 and Chhukutsi.

For the Markula Image Inscription in Sharda script refer to Vogel (1911: 249-251). The inscription in Tankri of much later period on a wooden board has not yet been read.

iii. Triloknath (Rebāg)

a. Triloknath temple. Inscription on stone, Sharda script, c. ninth century C.E.

An inscription in Sharda script is found on the temple structure of Triloknath. It is written on the surface of a stone block in the wall just at the level of the plinth on the left side at the entrance to the antechamber. This was read by Diwakar Nath Acharya. Below is given his renderings in Devanagari and Roman transcriptions along with translation and comments:

"The Inscription:

1. ॐ नमः श्रीमदवलोकितेश्वराय ।।
2. अतुलविमलवीर्यः त्यक्तधेयोपरागः परहितनिरत [त्वान्नि]
3. र्ममेनिर्विषङ्कः (!) प्रबलगुणशताढ्योमूर्त्तिशःद्वंग्रराना प्रव [रशिख]
4. रकम्वः लाहुणस्यामहत्वंबदि 2

Transliteration

Line 1: [the sign of siddham] namaḥśrīmadavalokiteśvarāya/

Line 2: atulavimalavīryaḥ tyaktadheyoparāgaḥ parahitanirata [tvān] ni

Line 3: rmamenirviśaṅkaḥ prabalaguṇaśatā (ḍhyo) mūrtiśaḥ dvaṃgrarānāpara (va) [raśikha]-

Line 4: rakam(vaḥ) lāhuṇasyāmahatvaṃ (badi) 2

Translation: 'Success! Reverence to the glorious Avalokiteśvara! (This sign looking like capital 'G' of Roman alphabet stands for the sign of siddham).

'Because he is intent upon others' benefit, a man of incomparable stainless vigour, who has given up the slightest passion for belongings and is rich with hundreds of powerful virtues, Dvaṃgra Rānā in person has built an excellent towering temple for you, without hesitation, as high as the importance of Lāhuṇa.

'The second day of the dark half.

'Comments: After the invocation, the actual inscription is written in Mālinī metre. Two and three akṣaras are missing in the second and third lines, and I have guessed at them based on the context and metrical condition and placed them inside square brackets [ ]. There is one case of confusion of two sibilants: it reads *nirviṣaṅkaḥ* instead of *ni* the fourth line the akṣara *mvaḥ* is doubtful, particularly the *va* part.

'The reading *mūrttiśaḥ* is not so much fitting in the context. Still, we can interpret it together with *dvaṃgrarānā* and say that the described man in his person was called Dvaṃgra Rānā. However, we can consider that *mūrttiśaḥ* is a mistake for *mūrttipaḥ*, which means 'the caretaker or priest of an image.' In that case, we can identify Dvaṃgra Rānā as then priest of Avalokiteśvara image. So, the man who built the temple is named here as Dvaṃgra Rānā. He is either an influential man such as a petty king from this locality or the priest, if not both. The place name here is spelled as Lāhuṇa. After the verse, the inscription records just the day of the fortnight, which should be the day this temple was consecrated.

'It appears to me that the script used here retains some features of late Gupta script. So, I would call it proto-Sharada and date around the end of the ninth century," (Courtesy: Ane Nawang Jinba).

Note: The line of family of Dvangra Rana, the builder of the temple, appears to have become extint after sometime, (Refer. To Punjab Govt. 1918:16). It writes Lāhuṇa for Lahul. It coincides with Lo-u-lo of HieunTsiang and the present nomenclature of the region as Lāhul.

b. Karchhag from mDo, Bhoti script, Lal Chand, Thakur of Triloknath, c. C.E. 1900.

Translation: Aum swasti siddham!

Hello! Jambudvipa in the south is excellent among all the continents. 'Phags-pa where the Excellent Doctrine has spread is an Excellent holy place. Ri-'phags-gling [Rebag], the capital place, is a high raised land on the earth. The great ruler Thakur Lal Chand (bla'-la spyan-dha) and the priest-Manager (rkor-gnyer) Jams-pal Chhos-gyal('Byams-dpal Chhos-rgyal), the two for the benefit of the beings brought the sacred writing, mdo-mang, from Ladakh.

Note: This writing is contained at the end of the book mDo which was brought from Ladakh. Lal Chand of Triloknath belongs to the last quarter of the nineteenth and first quarter of twentieth century, (Panjab Govt., 1918:17). Thus the document may be placed in c. C.E. 1900.

iv. Household of Gyamzo, village Rhape.

a. Rhape, Gyamzo. Sonam Pal De of Gundhla, c. C.E. 1400 (?).

Text: *sku mmkhar nal-rtse nas no'o bsodnams dpal lde. mkhar ko skum mchhed steng zhal rnams dang b-hud kyi 'dir xxx dge la zong srong byed pa a-la-la. 'dor na sha-pa chhang-ma la sogs rnams. tshe 'dir bde skyid dpal xxx 'jal bar shog.*

Translation: From the castle of Nal-tse, Tinan, Gundhla, came No-'o, younger brother, Sonam Pal De (bSod-nams dPal-lde). mKhar-ko (brother and sister), husband and wife and ....

Note: Here younger brother for the former and brother-sister for the latter are the respectable addresses by the scribe. mKhar-ko here comes with the Thakur of Tinan, therefore is an important person. mKhar-ko again appears in a document from Tinan Khar of Tinan at a. iv.

b. Rhape, Gyamzo. Raja Bahadur Singh (1532-1559), c. C.E. 1550.

Text: *rgyal-tshan tog ltar mtho-ba'i ti-se'i .... mkha' 'gro'i 'du gnas ri-bo gan-dhal-la. der bzhugs bsod-nams dpal gis bskrun pa'i xx brung-pa dpal ...... L-9 lha-yul mtshungs rgyal-sa ma-gar-bsang. lha dbang dang mtshungs rgyal-po bha-dar sing. yab-sras dpal-'byor.........*

Translation: Mount Tise is high like the flag of victory. Gandhala is the place where the dakinis assemble. There lives Sonam Pal producing the ... Secretary (Drung-pa)...dPal.... The capital Makarsa (Ma-gar-bsang) is like the country of gods. Bahadur Singh (Bhadar Sing) the king is like the god Indra. Father and son, enjoy the life ....

Note: This is a one page document pasted on the cover of the book. This is the first page of the document, the rest are lost. About one fifth part of it on the right side is broken and missing. Otherwise the quality of the paper and particularly the ink is extremely good. Even though so old the ink still gives shining remarkably. The writing is so fresh and clear that it is better than most of the later writings.

c. Rhape, Gyamzo. District Kholl, c. 16th-17th century C.E.

Text: L-1 .....*yul-la g-yangs chhags gar-bya skyid-yul 'dir.* ..... L-2 *yang yul khol du skyid pa'iyo-nam.*

Translation: Lahul is a prosperous and happy country. It is under the kindness of the Great Compassionate One [Avalokiteśvara]. ....Here lives the family having origin of the lineage from mtsho-brjed clan, ... lde, by the three brothers. ..... in the [village of] Rhape (ya-nam), district (yul) of Kholl (Khol). The lady donors are: daughter-in-law (gna'[+ma]), mother-in-law (rgyug[+mo]) and [daughter, bu-mo?] the three.

The donors are: Son-in-law Dung-nge 'Zompa, husband and wife, the two. Bir-ma Khye-su.......... From lDan husband and wife. Ngu-rub Sonam, No-motse Mo-den and Ma-gu the three. Phetse Dolma, husband and wife. From Yobrang Mug-ru-nu Sonam, Mi-dpon.......

d. Rhape, Gyamzo. Raja Tedhi Singh (1742-1767), c. C.E. 1750.

Translation: Sultanpur, the capital, is a self-erupted, situated high on the earth. The great religious king Tedhi Singh (Trira-tri Seng-ge) conquers the external enemies and protects the subjects like his own sons. While his crown is held high and the territory is expanding, there lives the queen, the queen of Jammu ('Jam-mo), the emanation of Tara. The great teacher, lama Lozang Gyaltshan, whose crown of knowledge is held high, resides at Chhos dKor

Othang (Au-ta-mar). Lahul, the land of dakinis, is prosperous. The ten virtues have accumulated here at the happy village of Rhape.

There lives the family originating from the lineage belonging to the clan of rgyal-rgyud thod-dkar. The faithful donor Nga (Ngang)-dbangr Dorje,..... for clearing the path of emancipation of the deceased grandmother Zom Buthid, were raised the image of Shakya Muni Buddha for the support of body and the [book] Bardo Thodol for the support of voice.

The donors were wonderful. Nor Palmo was the faithful lady donor. The three excellent sisters are Malti, Palkyid and Lekyid. May they also be favourable to the Doctrine like their parents. Gur Nath, the excellent son, and his spouse, and the excellent daughter Tshering Buthid, the three, may they also be favourable to the Doctrine like their parents.

Summaries

Offerings received: Arag and sha lagpa (1). Arag, tsagmo and khura (1). Arag, chhang and sha lagpa (1). Chhang and lagsha (1). Arag and sha lagpa (2). One chhang (1). Chhang and tsha-sha (1).

The guests came from: Rangbye, Shansha, Garang, Othang, Yobrang and Wari.

v. The Household of Bhaḷhe Koḷhah, village Jahlma (Ya-na-phel). Tho-nu, the great Kharpon, and Raja Jit (Ajit) Singh, C.E. 1816-1841.

Text: gnas ri gtsang (rtsva) ri ga shes dril-bu-ri. ..... gu-lu dang ma-lu-ta. sa-gzhi bsil-ba tshal gyi gnas. phag-mo'i mar-'gul phyag 'tshal bstod. ga-sha'i mkha'-'gro'ichhos-gling na skal du. ..... ga-sha lha-yul gling gchig-po. .....

rgyal-ba'i lung bstan ri-bo gandhola. ..... gdan-sa chhen-po ao-thang dgon-chhen na. ..... da lta'i bla-ma bsod-nams dpal chhos-gtsug mtho zhing. .....

bstod kyi khang-gsar lhamchhod rgyas-murmgon. 'dren mchhog dpal-'byor chhos gtsug tho-ba'i dus. sa la 'bur mtho rgyal-khab sul-ldan bur. chhos-rgyal chhen-po rbrjid-ste seng-ge'i zhabs. dbu-rmog mtho zhing chhabs dbang sdar ba'i de'i mnga' 'og bzang-po'i chhab srid du. dpal mkhar gung-rang lha'i pho-drang der. tshe-dpal seng-ge'i dbu-rmog mtho ba'i dus. khang-gsar dpal-gyi sku mkhar na. chhos-blon ta-ra seng-geyab sras dbur mog mtho-bzhing chhab srid-pa'i dus. ga-shas khams gsum mi-dbang kun gyi sbdag. mkhar dpon chhen-por chhos-blon mtho-nu yis. dge-ba'i las bsgrubs mchhog la dad la shin tuchhe.

..... dang thog gsung rabs. mdo mangs rtag ldan dang. sangs rgyas rang nyid rnam-thar rgya chhen rol-pa dang. gsung rab rdorje gchod-pa'i sku par dang. de rnams khang-pa bstod kyi gzhis pa'i dkar sgona. sku rten shakya thub par nang rten zil gnon bzhugs. gzhan yang byin brlabs khyad chan sku rten mang rnams bsgrubs. 'og gi sya-nam-phel du. ..... bod lugs bzhin gyi rabs-gnas chhen-po dang rgya-gar bram-ze lugs la bun-brnyes bza'-btung chhen-po'i tshim mdsad nas. chhos blon mtho nus thog drangs. .....

khong yon gyi bdag-po yab sras gsum gyi pha-ma'i don dang don chhen tshe 'di-kar..... rigs rus khungs btsun kapur kha-tir rgyud. .....

dge bchu 'dsom-pa'i ya-rnam-'phel gyi yul dbus na ming chhen mtho-nu'i gzims-khang 'dir bkra-shis don rnams grub pa'i rab-gnas dang bu-nya bram-ze lugs gyi dge chhen dpag med ga-sha ral gsum la rin chhen nor dang bza'-btung chhen po'i gang 'dod tshim par mdsad pa nyed chag dpon mi re rnams la yang yon 'bul rin chhen grangs ga'i dul drug g-rgyas ya-shes bkur-ti dang mdsad nas thar-pa'i yon bgyid gsal ba bkrin chhe lags a-la-la ho.

..... rgyu song la. dngul skyang gyir mo nyishu bdun song. .....

gsung rten chhen po 'di la dge rtsi rtag pa'i mtho grangs la. dang-po khang-gsar mkhar nas skyem a-u-tri ra-po. .....

Tanslation: The sacred mount Drilbu Ri in Lahul is a place of pilgrimage. ..... Ku-lu-ta and Ma-ru-ta i.e. Maru or Margul. This is a sacred place of cool land. ..... I revere and bow before Varahi, the goddess in the emanation of Soar, of Margul. ..... Lahul has been the religious land of dakinis. ..... Lahul is singularly the land of gods. .....

Mount Gandhola was prophesied by the Jinas. ..... His living place is at the monastery of Othang. ..... Presently Lama Sonam Pall possesses the high doctrinal crown. .....

The village of Khangsar and the monastery of Gyemur, in the area of sTod, are the places of worship of gods. Paljor with high religious crown is excellent leader. ..... Sultanpur is the place grown high on the earth. The great religious king Jit (brjid-ste) (or Ajit) Singh whose crown is held high and the kingdom is expanding, under his rule [is the territory of Lahul]. At the prosperous castle at Gungrang resides Tshe-dpal Seng-ge, father and son, and his crown is held high. In the prosperous castle at Khangsar resides the religious Minister Tara Chand (Singh), father and son, whose crown is held high and the territory is expanding. Thonu, the religious Minister and great mKhar-dpon, the Lord of the three divisions of Lahul, accomplished the virtuous task of performing the auspicious task wonderfully.

The scriptures in the beginning. ..... The universal Domangs. Lalitvistara, the namthar of the Buddha himself, print of Vajrachhedika. These were (obtained?) from the household of Kara-gongma (dKar-sgo) in the village of Jhis (in sTod). The image of Shakya Muni is placed for worhip. Many other auspicious works were accomplished. At Yanam-phel the great show was done. ..... The great ceremony of Rabnas of the Tibetan system and Pu-nya of the system of the Brahmins of India were performed under the leadership of great religious Minister Thonu. Besides he arranged a great feast.

He is the Donor. The father and sons, the three, for the benefit of the parents so that in this very life, ... Belonging to the clan of Kapur-khatir having great origin. ..... Tho-nu, the famed, performed at his residence in the central village of Jahlma (Yanam Phel), where the ten virtues have assembled, the great ceremonies...... and valuable articles were distributed and a feast was given to all the people of the three valleys of Lahul to the full satisfaction of all of them. We the scribes were provided - with love, regard and pleasure - the gift of rupees six hundred.

The expenditures in pure cash were: rupees seven twenties. .....

The offerings for the ceremony were received firstly from Khangsar Khar as one Uthi of chhang and a goat, ...

Summaries

a. Expenditures made in the ceremony

i. Items and Amt. (Rs.) of Expenses:

1. Gift to the scribes = 600-00. 2. Cash, 7 twenties = 140-00. 3. Cloth for head dress = 140-00. 4. Ghee 20x4 = 80-00. 5. Honey = 8-00. Total Cash expenses = Rs. 968-00.

ii. Other items of expenditure

1. Flour of buckwheat and wheat = 9 khari. 2. Barley for chhang = 2 khari. 3. Sheep = 40.

b. Offerings received

Arag and lagsha (2). Rabo (19). Rabo and 'don-rag or arag (11). Tea 4 pieces (2). 'don-rag or arag (3). One rupee (1). sKyem or chhang uthi and rabo (2). Utthi chhang and lagsha (7). Arag and lagsha (7). Rabo and arag (4). Uthi and rabo (6). One rupee and uthi chhang (1). Phyemar and arag (2). Chhang pitcher (3). Chhang shunara and rabo (2). Rabo (3).

c. These villages gave one goat each

Gushal, an unknown village, Yobrang and Ranige.

d. Villages from where the guests had come

sTod: Khangsar, gZhis and Srangbar.

Gahar: Gungrang, Kardang, Barbog, Kyelang and Yo-rog.

Tinan: Draling, Ranglo, Tinan/Gundhla, Thorang and Khyinang.

Pattan: Rwaling, Mooling, Bargul, Gandhola, Tandi (Dang-ti), Wari, Rangbye, Lote, Ranige, Yobrang, Gorom, Phurah, Lindoor, Rapling, Othang, Jahlma, Tibog, Lomtsa and Kamring (Gomri).

e. The three Thakurs of Khangsar, Gungrang and Tinan, who is mentioned in the list of donors, participated in the ceremony.

f. Lambardars (nang-blon), heads of cluster of villages, had joined from these areas:

Kardang and Kyelang of Gahar. Ranglo and Thorang of Tinan. Gushal, Ranige and Jahlma of Pattan.

Note : See Household of Melag, Jispa, sTod, a.ii.

vi. a. Household of Lhye Koḷhah, village Jahlma (Ya-na-phel). Raja Vikram Singh, C.E. 1806-1816.

a. Lhye Koḷhah, village Jahlma (Ya-na-phel). Raja Vikram Singh, C.E. 1806-1816.

Text: bka'-'gyur sdus-pa'i gzungs bzhugso.

yul-la dbyangs chhags gar-gzha' mkha' 'gro'i gling. sa la 'bur mtho rgyal-sa sur-stan puri. chhos-rgyal chhen-po bhi'-gim sings-ga bzhugs. ..... yul las dge-bchu 'zoms-pa'i skyid-yul yam-phel 'dir. bla-mes ldan-sa chhos-'khor ao-btang 'dir. mtshan-ldan bla-ma slob-bzang stshe-ring grags. ..... skyid-yul ya-nam phel. ..... yon gyi bdag-po le-yi rang sems dkar-po'i dngang nas mus-gus skyid. me me'i rus khung tsun dar-ba gling-gi rgyud. dad-ldan yon gyi bdag-mo mtho-ba dang. bu-mo'ichhog-gyur nor dpa'-mo dang tshe-'ng dbang-mo gnyis. de-la smag-pa phe-le yi. tshe'i 'das byi'i po sa-zi ra-ma dang. 'dsom-pa gnyis. bhing-ka dang. tshe'i ring ga gzhi'i sgongs-pa gzogs phyir dang. ..... dam-chhos rdo-rje gchod-pa ma-bu gnyis. sdigs-shegs lug gzungs-ba gzungs-ba lnga bzhangs. bu'i mchhog-gyur smang-sngan mda'-sa'i. zhabs-stogs legs-par grub ngo-mtshar chhe. ..... rgya'i sitho la. ..... ya-nam phel nas dkog-dri ma-bu gnyis lag-sha chhang za-ma rten. .....

Translation: Lahul is prosperous country. Sultanpur, the capital, is a land high raised on the earth. There lives the great religious king Vikram (bhi-gim) Singh. Here at Jahlma (Yam-phel) is the land of pleasure and the ten virtues have gathered. The famed Lama Lobzang Tshering resides at Chhoskhor Othang (Au-btang). Jahlma is a prosperous village. The donor Le whose mind is clean and happy, having the clan of dar-bagling originated from the ancestors and spread. The lady hostess is the faithful mTho-ba and two daughters Nor-pamo and Tshe-'ang dBangmo.

Phe-la, the son-in-law, for the sake of the four deceased: Saze Ram and Zompa, and Bhering and Tshering raised Vajrachhedeka, small and large, Digshag, etc. Five works were raised. Mandas, the son, served well. The account of receipt of the offerings is as under. Kog-dri, mother and son, from Jahlma the two gave lagsha, and a pitcher of chhang. .....

Summary: The relative-guests came from the villages of: Phurah, Othang, Tandi, Krozing, Rapding (Ra-pe-gling), Shansha, Zasar, Goram, Kothi, Lomtsa, Wari and Lindoor (Ling-tod).

They offered: Chhang pitcher and phye-mar (1). Lag-sha and chhang pitcher (1). Lagsha and a-rag (16). Arag (2). Lagsha (4). Lagsha and phyemar (1). Arag and phyemar (1). One chhang and phyemar (2). Arag and phyemar (1). One pitcher of chhang and ghee one ball (tob) (1). Arag and snacks (1). Arag and one seer of ghee (1).

b. Lhye Koḷhah, village Jahlma (Ya-na-phel). Raja Hira Singh (?), British period, c. C.E. 1880.

Text: gser-'od dam-pa'ibshags-pa zhesbya-babzhugs-so. dge-'o.

'ri mtho sa gtsang gangs dkar ti-rtse yis. ri rgyud ma-chhad gnas chhen dril-bu ri. phu na gnas-bdag lha-mo rang-byon bzhugs. 'ada' nardo-rjephag-mosmthe-bong bzhugs. bar na rang-'byon 'phags-pa spyan ras-gzigs. rdo-rje gdan mtshungs ri-bo gandhola. ..... bdud-rtsi sman gyi chhu-gdong yod. rgyal-sa chhen-po sur-brtan puri zhes. sa skyong mdung 'dsin hi-ra seng-ge bzhugs. deng-sang sa la dbang bsgyur phyi-gling-pa. ..... de-yi chhab-srid bzang-po'i mnga' 'og 'dir. yul la g-yang chhags ga-sha mkha'-'gro-'i gling. ..... bu las phyi-ma tshe 'das me-me nis. bha'igra a-phi bsod-nams chhos 'dsom yang. .....

dad-ldan sbyin-pa'i bdag-mo yang-'dsom gyis. .....

Translation : gser-'od dam-pa'i.....

The pure land and high mountain of Drilbu Ri is the great holy place being connected with the white snowy high mountain of Kailash by the unbroken chain of mountain ranges. At the head of the valley resides the self-born goddess of the holy place. At the end of the valley, the holy place equivalent to the thumb, resides Vajravarahi. In the middle of the valley resides the self-born Arya

Avalokitesvara. The mount Gandhola is like Vajrasana, Bodhgaya. There is the medicinal water pit from where comes out the nectar.

Sultanpur is the great capital. There resides Hira Singh (?), the ruler, who holds a lineage. Presently the land is being ruled by the British (Phyi-gling-pa). ..... Lahul, the land of the dakinis, the prosperous land, is under his good rule. ..... Grandfather Nis Bhai Dra and grandmother Sonam Chhoszom, the two, were deceased after the son. .....

The faithful donor got raised the volume nya of the bigger 'Bum, and Vajrachhedika in gold. The faithful donor Lady Yangzom....... the loving sister Sonam Kunzom, daughter Norzom, son Phuntsog Tshering. The Thanka of Avalokitesvara with the three peaked crown was raised.

The account of receipt of the offerings for these excellent works are like this. In the beginning sister Sonam Palzom and son-in-law Pasang gave one rupee, arag, lag-sha and an authi of chhang. .....

Summary : Villages from where the guests had come:

Srob, Tandi (Dang-ti), Krozing, Phurah, Gushal (Gus), Marbal, Gharang, Tholong (mChhod), Bharing, Rangbye, Shansha (Shang), Lindoor (gLing-bstod), Kothi (Gothi), Jahlma (Yanam-phel), Rasrel, Haling, Taljoni, Lhom-tsa, Tibog, Othang, Kamring(?) (Gamir).

Offerings received: One rupee, arag, lagsha, au-khri (1). Au-khri chhang, anna 4 (1). Arag, lagsha (1). Arag, phyemar (17). Au-khri chhang, ra-pho (1). One rupee, arag and lagsha (1). Arag, rapho (1). Chhang one shunor (1). Arag bottle (2). Chhang alto (halto) (3). Tea (1). Rapho (1). Arag (7). One rupee (4). Four anna (4). Three anna (1). Two anna (5).

Note: The document gives the name of the Raja as Hira Singh. As his capital is given here as Sultanpur he certainly is a Raja of Kullu. But the name does not appear in the list of the Rajas.

vii. Village Shansha (Śānśā, Shang)-1, Household of Bir Singh. Rai Dilip Singh (1869-1892), c. C.E. 1880.

Translation: May there be auspiciousness, accomplishment and welfare. Here begins the Register.

Sultanpur is great capital of the kings. The lord, Dharamraj Dilip Singh, Raja of Kullu, resides here. May his dominion flourish like the waxing moon. Now a days the land is being ruled by the English. .....Chhoskhor Othang Gonpa, the monastery of Othang, is adorned with the three kinds of teachings. [Many scholars holding the tradition of sutra and mantra come here continuously like the garland of pearl]. Presently Lozang Nyima resides here. May the Doctrine of the Yellow Cap expand and progress. In the prosperous village of Upper Shansha (Shang) in his auspicious dominion, the laymen express happiness in the religious work and the women are faithful knowing that this world is impermanent and is like an illusion. Their family have origin from the ancestors of Tho-su.

The faithful Donors Mani and her younger sister Soni, the two, pray for the progress of the Doctrine of the Buddha, expansion and progress of the kingdom, repulsing the armies of the enemies, fulfillment of the wishes of the leading lamas, cleansing their kind parents of their sins, and for attainment of the perfect knowledge by the innumerable beings.

Dile (Dhill-li) Ram, the husband of the two humble beings, has expired and has gone away from this world. Raghu (Rag) Dass is father of Dile Ram who also has passed away from this world. The present ceremony was held for the same purpose. Raghu (Rag) Das, father, and Kishan (Gyishan), the latters' uncle, both have survived longer than their son Dile Ram.

For crossing the sea of the world by the path of the great liberation the following auspicious acts were performed so that they could cross the sea of the world and get the path of liberation. From among the heap of 80,000 sermons the condensed collection of the excellent Doctrine, Vajrachhedika, was raised. As a receptacle of speech, Papadeshna, the heap of dharni, holdings, was raised. As a receptacle of body, idol of Amitabh in the form of dharamkaya and of Avalokitesvara, and many tshva-tshva were raised. The wise and helpful relatives lent protection from all the sides. Many activities of openness has unlocked the knot of misery. The faithful Donors Mani and her younger sister Soni mixed the nectar of the gods in the meal: prepared delicious meal. The Teachers and scribes are filled with wonder. There is all environment of wisdom and friendship. The hosts worship the god and show happiness in the good work. They worship the Doctrine and feel merry with faith. May they have long life, have no sickness and be in pleasure! How wonderful!

Summaries: The villages from where the relatives had come: Wari, Gozing, Bha-da-ra, Lote (Lod), Rangbye, Tholong (mChhod), Shansha (Shang), Gorom, Lindoor (Ling-stod), Phurah, Tshogs-zing, Yobrang, Monastery (dGon-pa) (of Shansha?), Rwaling (Raling), Ghaling and Jahlma (Yanam phel).

Offerings received: Uthi chhang and lag-sha (1). Sha lag-pa and a-rag (1). A-rag (4). Half rupee (2). A-rag and phye-mar (5). Two annas (5). A-rag and half rupee (1). Four annas (4). U-thi chhang and goat (2). Al-to chhang (1). Uthi chhang and phye-mar (2). Ra-pho (1). One rupee (4). Four annas, a-rag and phyemar (1).

Items of expenses: Fifty khal of grains of Ne for chhang, thirty-two khal of wheat flour for fried cakes (khu-ra), nine khal of Ne given to the Brahmins, twenty khal of Ne used for tsampa (sattu), ten khal of wheat flour used for cakes (roti), one khal of wheat flour used for small khu-ra (snacks), nine and half maund of oil, eight sheep, and cloth (cotton cloth) costing two rupees.

The cost of preparation of the books of Vajrachhedika and Papdeshna was rupees three and half. Fifty-two rupees were spent for the statue of Avalokiteśvara. Seven rupees were spent as expenses for the consecration of the ceremony of Rab-gnas.

Sukh (Suku) Ram of Wari and Nor dPal of Othang worked as Nang-pa [manager]. Sukh Ram from Wari and Urgyan Chhering were in charge of meat (Sha-pa). Hasa Ram from Wari, Tsherring Buthid and younger sister were in charge of chhang (chhang-ma).

viii. Shansha-2, Household of Khinu, Karchhags.

The following karchhags belong to one household named Khinu of the village Shansha. Here in these documents it is named as Shang (śāṅ) sTod, Upper Shang. Locally, in Pattan, it is known as Srang-me (ṣāṅ-me) and now in official and general dealings it is called Shansha (śānśā). In sTod it is still known as Shang. The large number of documents evidently reveal that the household remained prosperous for quite sometime in the past. They have conducted so many ceremonies, largest in number among all, in whole of Lahul, in our collelction. Such kind of ceremonies are very expensive.

a. **Shansha (Shang), Khinu. Rai Dilip Singh (1869-1892), c. C.E. 1880.**

Translation: The great capital is named Sultanpur. There resides the great righteous king Dilip Singh. Presently the land is ruled by the English (Phyi-ling). Hari Chand [Thakur of Khangsar] is the righteous Minister. At the monastery of Chhoskhor Othang there resides Lama Nawang Damchhos (Ngag-dbang dam-chhos). May the Doctrine of Yellow Cap spread and expand. Bhayi and his son Gur Tshering are donor-landlords. The all accomplished Gyalba Gyatsho raised the fully accomplished mDo-mangs in the fully accomplished village of Shang sTod.

Note: Here the name of the village where the monastery is situated is named as Othang. In some other documents it is named as Au-ta-mar. No distinct name of the monastery is known.

b. **Shansha (Shang), Khinu. Thakur Hari Chand and Rai Megh Singh-i, (1892-1921), C.E. 1885.**

Translation: The great capital is named Sultanpur. There resides Megh Singh, the king, the lineage holder. Presently the land is ruled by the English. Hari Chand is the great Kalon, Minister. Lama Lobzang lives at Chhoskhor Othang monastery. Dom-dpal is the donor. Uncle Bhata (younger brother of the deceased) and the sons (of the deceased) for the sake of the deceased father raised this (book) of mDo, of deep meanings. The ceremony of Rabnas was held on the tenth day of the eleventh month of wood-female-bird year of the fifteenth cycle (C.E.1885).

c. **Shansha (Shang), Khinu. Thakur Amar Chand and Rai Megh Singh-ii, (1892-1921), c. C.E. 1910.**

Translation: Sultanpur is the great capital. There resides Megh Singh, the king, the lineage holder. Presently the land is ruled by the English. Amar Chand is the great Kalon, Minister. Lama Lhundub Tashi resides at the monastery of Chhokhor Othang. In the prosperous village of Upper Shang live the donors Dho-bhala and his son Sukhi Ram.

Account of the expenses incurred in the ceremony of this Rab-nas is: barley five khari; oil (mustard) eight maunds; ghee one maund; cash rupees fifteen; cloth worth rupees twelve; rice three khal; tea worth rupees four, and sheep five.

d. Shansha (Shang), Khinu. Thakur Amar Chand and Rai Megh Singh-iii, (1892-1921), C.E. 1921.

Translation: Sultanpur is the great capital. There resides Megh Singh, the king, the lineage holder. Presently the land is ruled by the English. There resides the great Kalon, Minister, Amar Chand. At Chhoskhor Othang monastery resides lama Lozang Dundub. Dho-bhala is the donor. This ceremony of dGe-ba was performed on the eighth day of third month of iron female bird year of the 15th cycle, (C.E. 1921).

e. Shansha (Shang), Khinu. Thakur Abhe Chand and Rai Bhagwant Singh-i, (1921-1947), C.E. 1924.

Translation: Sultanpur is the great capital. There resides Bhagwant Singh, the king, the lineage holder. Presently the land is ruled by the English. Abhe Chand is the great Kalon, Minister. Lama Tshering Dondub resides at the monastery of Chhokhor Othang. May the Doctrine of Yellow Cap spread and prosper. The donor Sukh Ram and his son Sobha Ram live in the village of Upper Shansha. Their origin is from lha-be, the lineage of their parents. The ceremony of Rabnas was held on Friday, the 15th day of tenth month of wood-mouse year of the 15th cycle (1924).

f. Shansha (Shang), Khinu. Thakur Abhe Chand and Rai Bhagwant Singh-ii, (1921-1947), C.E. 1928.

Translation: Sultanpur is the great capital. There resides Bhagwant Singh, the king, Vinaydhar. Presently the land is ruled by the English. Abhe Chand is the great Minister. At Chhoskhor

Othang (Thang) monastery, adorned by the three kinds of teachings, presently resides Lama Yishe Zangpo. May the sect of Yellow Cap spread and flourish. Here at the joyous village of Upper Shansha (Shang) live Sukh Ram and his excellent son Sobha Ram, of the pure lineage of lha-be, the faithful donors. The ceremony of Rab-nas was performed on the 10th day of 10th month of the earth-dragon year of 16th cycle, (15th), (C.E. 1928).

g. Shansha (Shang), Khinu. Thakur Abhe Chand and Rai Bhagwant Singh-iii, (1921-1947), c. C.E. 1930.

Translation: Sultanpur is the great capital. There resides Bhagwant Singh, the righteous king, the lineage holder. Presently the land is being ruled by the English. Abhe Chand is the great righteous Minister.

h. Shansha (Shang), Khinu. Thakur Pratap Chand and Rai Bhagwant Singh-iv, (1921-1947), C.E. 1933.

Translation: Sultanpur is the great capital. There resides Bhagwant Singh, the righteous king, the lineage holder. Presently the land is being ruled by the English. Partap Chand is the great righteous Minister. Lama Lozang Dondub resides at Chhoskhor Othang monastery. Sukh Ram, the donor, resides in the village of Upper Shang. Sobha Ram is the excellent son. The ceremony of Rab-nas was performed on tenth day of tenth month of water-bird year of the 16th (15th) cycle, (C.E. 1933).

i. Padma Thangyig copied from the wood blocks made at Tayul monastery, Tashi Tanphel, C.E. 1885, Karchhag.

The following is a Karchhag composed by Tashi Tanphel found at the end of the copy of the book Padma Thangyig in possession of the house of Khinu, Shansha. The document relates the story of preparation of wood blocks, among others, of Padma Thangyig, the Namthar of Padmasambhava, at the monastery of Tayul in Punan, Lahul. Another copy is found with the household of Barma, Jispa, sTod.

Translation: Title of the book: *au-rgyan ghu-ru padma 'byung-gna skyi skyes rabs rnam-par thar-pa rgyas-par bkod-pa padma bka'-i' thang-yig.*

The Buddhas in a gathering explained the infallible merits of [recitation of] the Namthar, Life Story, of Guru Padmasambhava.

The highborn Sonam Lhundub, Treasurer (mdsod) of Hemis monastery, Ladak, and his younger brother Sonam Dorje, the two brothers, the beloved sons of father Yang-zin and mother Tsho-mo, had strong desire to prepare new wood blocks of gSung-bum, etc. many books, specially the Namthar of Guru Padmasambhava.

Sonam Lhundub, the Treasurer, himself came to Lahul in the eighth month of the water-sheep year of the fifteenth cycle (1883). He requested the three leading Thakurs [Gundhla, Khangsar and Gumrang] of Lahul for the prepration of blocks which do not exist elsewhere. The leader among the prominent persons agreed that it should be executed in Lahul. For execution of the work for preparation of the wood blocks Vazir Thakur Hari Chand of the house of Khang-sar-khar (mKhar-gsar-mKhar) made initiation and arrangement of provisions.

Contributions were received from Thakur Lady Maan Dasi (man-dhas-si): rupees twenty-five, one rupee as cost of pho-la(?), for the sake of those preparing the blocks, feast to the workers, rice one khal, two sha-khog, onion one *bati,* and grain [Ne?] three khals. Norzin, Thakur Lady of Khangsar Khar, gave grain three khals. Nono Devi Chand, Thakur of Gumrang, gave tea one *bati*, ghee one *bati* and four seers, oil [mustard] two *bati,* sha-gog two, flour (phe) [buckwheat] thirteen khal, wheat flour two khal and ten bre, rice two khal, and lhum [of Ne] one khal and ten *bre*. The elder Lady, [of Gungrang] Tshering Palzom, gave ghee two *bati* and three seers. Elder sister (Jo-jo) Pal-zom gave phe [buckwheat flour] three khals. Tshering Sonam gave ghee four seers.

Hari Chand, Thakur of Tinan [Gundhla], and Thakur Lady Tshering Dolma Lhyas gave ghee one *bati*, wheat nine khal, phe [flour of buckwheat] three khal, one sha-gog, and rice six khal. The queen of Ladakh Tshe-zin Pal-zes Dolma Buthi Wangmo gave grain [Ne] and one spa [one time meal of tsampa with some liquid].

Lama Tashi Tanphel gave twenty five rupees. Pal-zang of Guskyar gave two and half seers of tea. Tug-tug of Upper Kyelang gave ghee one *bati*. Nono Hrijod of Mang-gon (Ma-dgon) and Thakur Lady Palzom Buthid gave *tsampa* two khals, chhang (skyem) of one khal grain [Ne]. The Nun (Jomo) Namgyal Buthid of Mangon gave *lhum* of one khal grain. Tsho-byed Pal-zang of Gungling one khal grain. The Nun Chhoskyid of Kyor lhum of two khal [Ne].

Chhoskyid, the cook, one *khal lhum* [of Ne]. The Nun Sonam Dolma of Chhiling gave *lhum* of fifteen *bre*. Wangchug and Dolma of Lapchang gave wheat three khal and grain three khal. Wang-drag Dorje of house of Pangrong and Sonam Chhos-phel of the house of Nang-tshang [insider] of Karing village, wheat two khal. Chhos Dag of Bushod [?] one rupee. The Teacher (Moshi = Munshi] Dya-lu one rupee. The residents of Kyor, Mangon, Gungling, etc. did excellent service to the engravers.

The responsibility of preparing the blocks was taken over by Lama Tashi Tanphel, born in the clan of mar-kha-ba-me-nyag gdong-dmar-po, a monk of Hemis monastery and Lama of sTagna monastery, the carver. He did the work of engraving beginning from leaf one to 171 and from leaf 281 upto the end. Engraving was done from the leaf number 172 to 280 by Tshewang of Tharpa [Tharbas] tsug-shi of Lower Kyelang.

The work of melting of the letters was done by Phuntsogs, the priest, of Ka-yabtag-btsun. The engravers were - Mar-kha 'Um-lung-pa, sGrub-pa Paljor Phuntsog, Mipham of Chhushod [Ladak] and Pi-shu Tshering dBang-chhug of Zanskar. From Gemur monastery in sTod valley No-no Kargyud Rigzin and Tanpa Tshering. Nono Kon gchhog Zodpa from Tino village. Tanzin Dondub from Yo-tse. Tanzin Chhos-phel from Yar-gzhi of Jispa. The Nun from house of Bharong and Lharje [doctor] Chhoskyid. From Punan [Gahar] valley were the pupil-monks of Khedub Tshebang Rigzin and dBu-mdsab Phris, the two. Others from Punan were - Sonam Dorje from Kardang (bar-bKar-sdang), Lharje Tshering, Khyim-btses Tshering, Norbu, Dondub of house of Mani, Rigzin of Zholing, Paldan, Norbu from Beeling, Sonam Rigzin of house of Anu-tse, Jigs-jed, Kyi-tsi, Che-pa of Lower Kyelang, Dug Dorje, Rigzin and

Norbu. From Upper Kyelang Kyu-kar Rigzin and Na-mo of house of Bar-tsi. Dug Tshering was from Ghorom village [Pattan].

The work of grinding the materials for ink and paper was done by Ku-lu, dKon-gnyer, of Tayul (Te-yur) monastery. Dam-dub-pa was manager. Sonam Chhoskyid the nun, was cook.

Others from among those engaged in the monastic profession from Tayul monastery were: Dugzom the Nun, the cook and Ane Palzom of Ma-gon, the two, Urgyan Dolma and Tashi, etc. They served the engravers and others. They did the work of arranging wood, water and looking after other necessities. We bow thrice.

The great work of engraving was accomplished at the holy place of Tayul (Te-yur) monastery named Urgyan Chhos-khor-gling, in the year of wood-bird year of fifteenth cycle [1885].

Since the parinirvana of the Perfect Leader, Shakya King, in the monastery of the world, 2786 years [965 B.C.E.] have elapsed. Since Siddha sTag-tshang Raspa (sTag Ras) was born it has been 311 years [C.E. 1574]. Since the foundation of Hemis monastery was laid it has been 266 years [C.E. 1619]. Offering from Nawang Chhos-bzang occupying the throne of Hemis 21 rupees were received.

Fifty-one years elapsed since Ladak came under the Singpa [Dogras, C.E. 1834]. May the reign of Shri Maharaja Ranbir Singh [1856-1885] expand. Sonam Namgyal Dorje is the protector [king] of Ladak.

During the year 1942 [C.E. 1885] according to the Indian (Aryadesh) system of reckoning Hindustan, etc. is being ruled by 'Queen Victoria, Kesari-e-Hind'. Lahul is being governed by Vazir of Khangsar (Kharsar), Thakur Harichand. This Kar-chhags was written during this period by Tashi Tanphel. May the devotees become practictioners of ten virtues.

Note: Tashi Tamphel, who was author of the major part of the whole work, is, in his own words, here addressed as a monk of Hemis and a lama of sTagna. This part of the work, called 'Kar Chhags', is part of the main book Padma Ka'i Thangyig. This work of preparing the wood blocks of the book was started in 1883 and completed in 1885, in about two years. It is told by the people that the wood block prints and many other items were taken away from the monasteries like Gandhala, etc. to Ladak loaded on the ponies. Tashi Tanphel was later on Rinpochhe.

The monastery of Ta-yul as is known today, where all this work was conducted, is written here as Te-yur and named as Au-rgyan Chhos-'khor gLing.

ix. Village Rwaling (Rāliṅ, Rwāliṅ), Household of Srangpa (Ṣāñpā).

a. Rwaling, Srangpa. mDo-mangs, c. 17th-18th century C.E.

Translation: Ka-na, the husband and wife, the two, the donors, for cleansing their own impurities of sin completely, and thinking for return of the kindness of their kind parents, for the deceased mother Bhagula and Nub-skyid, the two, [father and mother?], may they be lead to the land of the great pleasure, Sukhavati.Got raised (copied), the works of the well developed Doctrine viz.: snang-rgyad, kun-tu bzang-po'i smon-lam, gtsug-gtor nag-mo, sdig-shegs ser-gyi spu-gri, dbyangs-yig, etc. Offerings made for the accumulation of the merits were wonderful.

b. Rwaling, Srangpa, c. 17th-18th century C.E.

'phags-pa 'jam-dpal gyi mtshan yang dag par brjod-pa **(manjusrinamsangiti).**

Translation: The offerings received for (raising the above named) sacred writing is enumerated as under - Grandmother Zhun-nu gave one vessel (of chhang), bKa-achhen Lozang Khe-grub gave a big vessel of tea. Monk Konchhog Rangdol gave tea; monk Manju-shi one *debs*(book?); elder sister Nun She-rol one chhang and lag-sha, etc. Moreover she served the scribes well. Wonderful!

Summaries

The relatives had come from the villages of - Rha-pe (Ra-pe), Ra-srel, Lindoor (Ling-thung), Yobrang (gYo-brang), Malang (Mang-lang), Lote (bLod), Rangbey (Rang-bhey), Ke-lang, Wari and Othang ('Od-ma-na).

The articles offered are - tsho-ba gdan-non (one meal?), chhang, arag, cakes cooked in oil (khu-ra), ball of ghee (mar-ril), sha dal-mo, sha lag-pa and nang-sha.

Note: The monks performing the rites are perhaps pilgrims from Spiti or Tibet. They have written the names for the local items in literary forms.

c. Rwaling, Srangpa. mDo., Raja Tedhi Singh (1742-1767), c. C.E. 1760.

Translation: The Kargyud sect removes the darkness of the beings of Hiamalya. ...Lahul is the prosperous holy place of Dakinis. Sultanpur (sur-tan-pur), the capital, is an engraving on the earth. Here resides the great religious king Tedhi(?) (mDses= beautiful) Singh and the reincarnate queen Shakya Devi (dheb), who subdues the external enemies and protects his subjects like his own sons and servants.

While his crown is held high and the kingdom prospers, here under his good rules, resides lama Ye-shes Paljor whose seat is Chho-skor Othang (Auo-ta-mar). The crown of the Dotrine is held high. I bow to his attendants and the monks. Hello! Yobrang is a happy and prosperous village. (Next page is missing).

Note: The name of the king of Kullu is given in the form of translation as 'Beautiful'. The king is named with the name of his consort. The vessel of tea as an offering in a ceremony in the household points to an older tradition.

x. Village Lindoor (Linḍūr) (gLing-tud, gLing-stod).

The village, situated above Jahlma, is presently named as Lindoor. It is found written in more than one form as Lingthud, etc. Here it is written as gLing-stod which is meaningful as High Place.

a. Lindoor, Raja Pritam Singh-i, (1767-1806), c. C.E. 1780.

Capital Magarsa, the palace there, is like the castle of the gods. There lives the incomparable king Pritam Singh, father and son, and the royal Law spreads. Under his rule is the lawful land of Lahul. In the specially developed village of Lindoor there lives the family having lineage from their ancestors. The donor Sonam Palde, for the favour of his kind mother, got copied Vajrachhedika of the excellent Doctrine, seven times.

Sherab Nying-po, Jang-chubl Tung-bshags, mGonpo gLu-brugs Monlam, rDorje, Nam-chom Joms, Zamgpo Chhodpa and sDig-shags gSergyi sPudri of thirteen kinds of the works of Sutra, got copied. The lady donor Phag-kyid... Zompa Zangmo.... Tshering Zompa, son-in-law, daughter, relatives.

Summary: The donor guests had come from the villages of Lindoor, Malang, Haling or Hal-ling, Othang, Jahlma, Yobrang, Shansha, Malbar, Lote and Hupuling. The two servers were Shapa and Chhangma.

Note: The name of the old capital of Kullu as Makarsa is still retained in Lahul. It was shifted to Sultanpur in the time of Raja Jagat Singh (1637-1672). This document was found in the monastery of Gandhala-Tubchiling. Recently many families from Manchhad have been depositing books and statues here.

b. Lindoor, Raja Pritam Singh-ii, (1767-1806), c. C.E. 1800.

Translation: The Lama resides at Chhoskor Autamar, Othang. Sultanpur, the capital, is like a high eruption on the earth. The great religious king Pritam Singh, his crown is held high. Reverence to Miyan Charan Das, the great Minister.

Under his rule is the prosperous and happy country of Lahul, the land of Dakinis. Here in the village of Lindoor (Ling-tud) there has assembled the ten virtues. Here lives the family with the rgyan-shing clan of the ancestors. The faithful donor, Nanda Kumar (Kubi) and the lady donor Serzom, the two, hosted this ceremony in the memory of the deceased father Tshering Legspa and mother Sam Buthid, and Yangzom who passed away with 33 sheep on the top of the pass to Kullu [Rohtang], and raised the works of the well developed Docrtine: Dorchod, Digshags, Bardo, etc.

Note: Miyan Charan Das here designated as Minister is perhaps the chief representative of the Raja of Kullu posted at Tandi.

c. Lindoor, Rai Megh Singh (1892-1921), c. C.E. 1910.

Translation: At the great capital Sultanpur lives the righteous king Megh Singh. Now a days the Land is being ruled by the English. Amar Chand, father and son, resides there following the orders of the Lord. Lindoor is the joyous village. Here lives the family of gya-shing clan of origin from the ancestors. Urgyan Tshering, the faithful donor, for clearing the path of emancipation of the deceased grandfather Nandi Ram, father Bhagman, mother Tshering Kunzom, younger brothers Dhongru and Suntha, and the daughter in-law, Sezom, raised the book mtshan-'bum of the good Doctrine. Ghara of Othang, Shibu of Malang and Gurdas of Kothi, the three were Managers. Tshering Zompa and Tshering Kyid were Chhangma. Bhim Chand was Shapa.

The expenses were: Ne (barley) one khari and 5 khal. Ne for chhang 3 khari and 10 khal. Rice of 10 rupees. Additionally Ne of rupees 8 were spent. Ghee of rupees 30, Oil, mustard, of rupees 200, 10 sheep and tea of one rupee. Manglam.

d. Lindoor, Reconstruction of the Kankani Chhorten, Chaitya, 2023.

In the village of Lindoor there is a chhorten of the kind known as Kankni. Its body stands on two side walls and there is a passage between the two. There is a similar one at Kolong.

It is told to be of about six hundred years old. The legend is that it was built in memory of seven brothers who perished all together. It may be estimated to be about two hundred years old. There is a monastery in the village and also a small shrine dedicated to the folk deity named Buhaari devata. The decaying chhorten was reconstructed in the months of October-November, 2023. There in the gzungs, of the chhorten there were several items. Some articles could not be seen. Among those lying in the open were about fifty earthen balls like mtshogs, known as tsha-tsha, of white colour, of the weight around 250 gms. each. There is a book of 100 sheets, loose and unmbered. The written area of each sheet is about nine inches long and four inches wide. It is written on both sides covering full page. The matter is only prayers and some parables. It was placed in a wooden box. It was made of two sides, one piece each, cut off from a tree trunk. The two pieces were dug out equally. The book was encased fittingly. The papers were not harmed by water even though the chhorten was unplastered from outside. The gzungs did not contain any tsha-par or karchhag.

The book is untitled. The first sentence of the first page reads as: sangyas dang byang-chhub sems-dpa' la phyag 'tshal-lo. At page fifty the first sentence reads as de-bzhin gshegs-pa 'od-stong la phyag 'tshal-lo.

xi. Tholong (Ṭholoṅ, mChhod), Household of Som Dev, Karchhags.

a. Tholong, Raja Pritam Singh (1767-1806), c. C.E. 1790.

Translation: The Teacher resides at Gandhola. It is the holy place where there gather the goddesses and dakinis like clouds. mNgag-dbang .., the Teacher and his pupils, are sitting firmly on the lion-throne of the Virtuous Dugpa. The capital of Sultanpur is like the Upper Castle of Sar-Ling. The virtuous king Pritam Singh is like Gesar.

The village of Tholong here is ..... The faithful donor Sukhdev ... and the excellent Khyini, daughter Sukhi who is adorned with thousand lotuses, Phagspa Dondub, the young son, is like the son of god. The mother, sons and the other members of the family, the holy assembly... The two deceased Surthan and Surthani, brother and sister, may they be born in the world of Sukhavati heaven.

Summaries

The guests came from the villages of: Khyinang (Khyim nang), Triloknath, Tholong (Chhod), Lote (Lod) and Wari.

Kinds of offerings and their quantities are as follows: One rupee (1). 1 Goat (1). Chhang 1 uthi and 1 lagsha (1). 1 Lagsha (1). Chhang 1 pitcher and 1 lagsha (7). Chhang 1 ptcher (17). Chhang and phyemar (2). Arag 1 tsoli and phyemar (1). Arag 1 tsoli and sha ku-dal (1). Arag 1 tsoli and lagsha (3). Arag tsoli (3).

b. Tholong, Raja Vikram Singh (1806-1816), c. C.E. 1810.

Translation: The place of residence of the teacher Malig is like Gadan, the residence of the gods, which was not constructed but was self-born. The great castle is situated at the capital Sultanpur. The great religious king Vikram Singh, his crown is held high and the kingdom is expanding. Lahul the holy valley is under him.

Here at Tholong where there is assembled the enjoyment, the land of pleasure, the faithful donor Khintu and the lady donor Pomi, and the younger sister, the excellent sons Sukh Ram, Mansa Ram and Suku Nanda, the three; the son (grandson?) Rup Chand, Khim Das, Jag Deva, Bhimi Ram and Khigutu, the five, and (their sister) Padma Doma, and daughter-in-law Thobili, Tsherkyid, Nor Pamo and her daughter-in-law Tan Doma and the deceased grandfather Phagtse, and father Sukh Deva, mother Norzom, elder brother Kinu.

Summaries: The relatives had come from the villages of: Wari, Khyinang, Tandi, Garhang, Sumnam, Jahlma, Gushal, Khangsar and Krozing.

The offerings were: Arag and lag-sha (11). Arag and phymar (7). Arag and lagsha (1). Chhang and phyemar (1).

c. Tholong, Raja Ajit Singh (1816-1841), c. C.E. 1830.

Translation: The village of Tholong is well developed place of joy, under the reign of the great king Ajit Singh (Jit Singh). In the ceremony of Chhodpa, worship, the host is Khyindu and hostesses are Tsher-skyid, her younger sister Nor Pamo, and the excellent sons Mansa Ram and Sukhnand, the two, their sons Rup Chand and Khyimdas, and their younger brother Jagdev and Vidhi Ram, their younger brother Dilli Ram, the excellent daughter-in-law Tanzin Doma, and sister Surati, younger sister Tshe Pamo. These hostesses made the occasion of dGe-tsi enjoyable.

Summary: The account of receipt of the offerings in the ceremony is like this: From Khyinang (Khyimdang) a tsoli of arag and lagsha; from Gus Sonu gave lagsha and arag; Suki of Wari gave a uthi of chhang; and Sudarshana lagsha and arag; Majana and Soni gave sha lagpa i.e. lagsha and 1 ja-oo (a brick of tea); Pranpara Saje Ram sha lagpa and arag; Chandi gave Chhang one uthi; ...

Specially for the support of the body of the deceased companion Sukh Ram the statue of Amitayus, and for support of the voice Vajrachhedika, twice were raised. For the support of the heart Jangchhub Chhorten was raised. For the cause of the deceased Tsherkyid gave twenty khal of Ne and for the Arya Avalokiteshwar (Rebag) seven hundred lamps were offered.

The relatives had come from Khyinang, Tandi, Gushal, Sumnam, Mooling (Phooling), Krozing and Lote.

d. Tholong, Rai Gyan Singh (1852-1869), c. C.E. 1860.

This independent document consists of 14 pages with the title page reading as: *dkar-chhags dgos 'dod kun 'byung bzhugs so.*

Translation: The Karchhag fulfilling all wishes.

The great religious kings are some English and the king of Kullu Gyan Singh (Dhe-wan seng), the land is under their rule, happy and prosperous. The faithful host, having great origin, Rup Chand, Khyim Das and Jagdev and the hostess Tan Doma, and the excellent sons Tshepa Ram, Shiv Ram and Shiv Das, the three, and the excellent daughters Sonam Zom, etc. and daughter-in-law Tshering Buthid and the deceased Sukh Ram, Mansa Ram and Khyikutu, and younger sister and Surti for their benefit this ceremony of Tshogs (collection, the ceremony) etc. of the great offering was made. As required the statue of Amitabh was raised.

For the favour of and for cleansing of the dirt of sin of Tsher-skyid, mother of the three donors Rup Chand, Khyim Das and Jagdev, and wishing that she may get merit of virtue, for this purpose the statue of Jinputra, the well developed Amitabh was raised. For raising the statue of Amitabh the account of the donors of theofferings is given as under: Firstly Nor Pamo and Sukh Nand two gave one uthi of chhang and one tsoli of arag and sha lagpa..........

Summaries: The relatives had come from the villages of: Tandi (Tangti), Phurang, Yombhe, Ngang, Wari, mChhod, Kyelang, Tinan, Thorang, Mooling, Gus, Sumnam, Kozing, Malang and Malbar.

The articles received and their quantities are: Chhang uthi, arag tsoli and sha lagpa (1). Four paise (1). 1 uthi (4). Chhang 1 shunor (1). 5 paise (2). Arag tsoli and sha lagpa (2). Arag tsoli and phyemar (14). Arag tsoli and sha lagpa (4). Arag tsoli (3). Ja-oo 1 (6).

Note: In Pattan there were monasteries at Yobrang which was founded by Nawang Tshering of Zanskar, Shansha, Gushal, Lindoor, Othang, Gandhala, etc. Tandi, Tholong, Sumnam, etc.

were served by Gandhala. Shansha and Rwaling were served by Othang. Gushal by Gushal and Lindoor by Lindoor.

xii. Village Wari (Wārī), Household of Lhye-Thaaling (Thālīṅ).

a. Wari, Lhye-Thaaling. Raja Parbat Singh (1575-1608), c. C.E. 1600.

Text: .....lha-yul dang mtshungs rgyal-tse ma-gar-sang. lha-dbang dang mtshungs rgyal-po par-pa-ta sing-gh'i dbu-rmog mtho-ba'i dus. de'i mnga' 'og chhen-po yangs pa'i dus. yul la g-yang chhags gar-bya khrims kyi yul. yang yul khol du thon-pa'i wa-ri ru. .....

Translation: The capital Magarsa is like the land of gods. Raja Parbata Singh (par-pa-ta sing-gha) is like the god Indra. While his crown is held high and the territory is expanding, under his rule is the prosperous land of Lahul, the land of rules. Again [the village of] Wari is situated at a high point in the district of Kholl (Khol). The inhabitants here worship the 'Three Rare Ones' and give gifts. Dung-gu (mDung-gu) is the donor and the lady donor is Zang-xx. For clearing the path of emancipation of the elder brother and the companion the book Vajrachhedika, small and large, were raised.

From Wari came Lambardar Tshewang Dorje and Noo-tse, husband and wife. Others came from the villages of Rangbye, Lote and Malbar.

b. Wari, Lhye-Thaaling. Raja Tedhi Singh-i, (1742-1767), c. C.E. 1745.

b.i. Text: .....lha-yul dang tshungs rgyal-rts su-tan-pur. lha dbang dang tshungs rgyal-po krir seng-dge bu-mog mtho-ba'i dus mchhos-lon chhen-po gyi-pa ram la stod. de'i mnga''og chhen-po yangs-pa'i dus. ...la g-yang chhags gar-bya mkh'a-khro'i lings. yang yul khol du thon-pa'i wa-ri ru. .....

Translation: The capital of Sultanpaur is like the land of gods. The king Tedhi Singh (Krir Seng-dge), is like the god Indra. While his crown is held high, there lives the great religious Minister Kirpa Ram (Gyi-pa-ram). I bow to the king. Under his reign is the prosperous Lahul. In the district of Kholl, there is the [village] of Wari situated high. There is Konchog Chhod and other donors.

Drug Dargye is the Khar-pon. The lady donors are Nga Buthid and Drug Buthid. For cleansing the evil deeds raised the [book] named na-rag dong-srug.

b. ii. Wari, Lhye-Thaaling. Tedhi Singh-ii, (1742-1767), c. C.E. 1750.

Translation: Sultanpur the capital is an eruption on the earth. I bow to the king Tedhi Singh (dre-sa sing-ge) and the ministers. Here in the prosperous and happy village of Wari, lives the family having origin of the lineage from the ancestors with the clan of "tshangs mi-chhen." Tshering Gyatsho is the donor. Drug Dargye, the son, is Kharpon. mDomangs was raised.

Tashi is the faithful lady donor. The lama Gedun Palbar lives at the mount Gandhala. May the sons Mani Ram, Saha Nanda and No-tse be favourable towards the Doctrine like their parents. The daughters-in-law Drug Buthid and Ngang Buthid served well. The daughters Manaki, Chhonzom, son Buthid, Manzom and Azhiya, all helped the donors well.

The donor offered meal. Bhagi and Paljor Tashi from Shansha gave a meal. Dhani Ram Dhibu and Chhonpa Rago and Sonam Tshering gave arag tsoli and khura. Sanga Tashi Tshomo gave Khura and Chhang. Ngang Tashi and Tashi Buthid gave chhang. Others came from the villages of Rangbye, Marbal, Malang, Karozing, Lower Kyelang, Kothi (Go-dri) and Yobrang.

b. iii. Wari, Lhye-Thaaling. Tedhi Singh-iii, (1742-1767), c. C.E. 1760.

Translation: Drilbu Ri. ...Gandhala. ... Lahul the land of dakinis, is a prosperous land. Sultanpur is the high place erupted on the earth. Tedhi Singh (Dri-gru Seng-dge) is the great religious king. I bow to the king and the ministers. The teacher Tshering Sang Grub lives at the mount Gandhola. Reverence to the monks who form his associates. Under his, the Raja, good reign is the prosperous village of Wari. The family belonging to the clan of pha-ma tshangs-chhen [one having both parents living] having origin of the lineage from the ancestors, lives here. Drug Dargyas, the Castle Officer (Kharpon) is the donor. For the sake of his own parents and for cleansing of the dirt of his deeds, the Namthar of Avalokitesvara was raised. There were innumerable donors.

The lady donor and her brothers and sisters are Drug Buthid, sons Mande Ram, Ram Sen and No-tse; daughters are Ma-ti, Chhos-zom and Muni; and others. Grandsons are Ram Sen, Khyendu; grand daughters are Ma-zom and Surab Dila. They all served well.

c. **Wari, Lhye-Thaaling. Raja Thakar Singh (1841-1852), c. C.E. 1850.**

Translation: Drilbu Ri is... mount Gandhola.... Lama Tshul Thim Dan-zin is renowned whose fame of the tuft of the religious knowledge is heard afar. Sultanpur, the capital, is a place erupted on the earth. There lives the religious king Thakar Singh. Under his rule is Lahul, the land of dakinis. Wari is a village prosperous and happy. There lives the family of the clan of Tshang-chhen having origin of the lineage from their ancestors. The donors are Nanda, Leburu and Khi-drug. The lady donors are Dung Gyi-li and mother Thung-gi.

The sons are Sukh Ram, Tashi Ram, Ling-ga and Sukh Nanda, and Kon-ni is the daughter. For the sake of the deceased father Sukh (Su-du) Ram, Khim Das (Tas) and Bhag Datt (Bag-rdat); and mother Sazini, elder brother Bu-chung, sister-in-law (elder brother's wife), Tsher-kyid and daughter-in-law Bes-di, for the benefit of them all, the Vajarachhedica, small and large, three copies were raised.

From Rangbye was received arag and phyemar. From Drangra Asa and Voti arag and lagsha. Kunzom gave a uthi. Man-nu from Rangbye lagsha and uthi. Pichepa and Khini uthi and phyemar. More donors had come from the villages of Lote, Shansha, Labshak and Wari.

xiii.Tandi (Tandī, Tāṅtī), Household of Shanshi (Ṣanśī), Karchhag, British period, c. C.E. 1900.

Kar-phyag sal-bas me-long. **Karchhag – The Clear Mirror.**

Translation: Sultanpur is the great capital. This is the period of the reign of the British. The residence of the teacher, Namgyal

Chhodan, is at the mount Gandhola. May the reign of the Auspicious Dukpa sect (Paldan Dukpa), expand. Lahul is the prosperous land. Tandi is the prosperous and happy village. There lives family belonging to the clan of Hir-dha-pa. Bhosa is the faithful donor and lady donor is Urgyan Buthid. The two excellent sons are Prabh (Bra-ba) Das and Dharmudas. Nor Buthid is daughter-in-law, Padma Tshering grandson, Sonam Dolma grand-daughter. For the sake of the deceased Rup (Ru-ba) Das, [a section of] the excellent Doctrine Vajrachhedika was copied. This was also done for the expansion and progress of the Doctrine; and for the sake of the parents and the beings of six kinds, for repaying their kindness, and for cleansing the dirt of sins of self.

This is the account of receipt of offerings for dge-rtis. In the beginning Manak and Norpee, husband and wife, from Tholong (Chhod) gave two uthi, one tsoli arag and lagsha. Nordan and Urgyan each gave an uthi, a tsoli arag and lagsha. Ghanga Nandh a uthi, tsoli arag and phyemar.

Note: The document writes that it is period of the reign of British. But it does not name the Raja of Kullu, although it refers to the capital Sultanpur. There was a translater, who might have been an employee of the Raja of Kullu working at Tandi.

2 Gandhala

Gandhala-Tubchiling monastery, Register (tho-yig), c. C.E. 1830.

The following is record of the activities concerning the construction of the statue in c. 1840 of Avalokiteśvara as like as it is at Rebag.

Translation: P-1, l.1. Account of the offerings received for construction of the image of the great Merciful Arya Avalokiteśvara.

From Tinan Khar (Thakur of Gundhla) two rupees. Yangshan, lady Thakur, one tea. Tashi Yangzom, lady Thakur, one tea (both of Gundhla). Tsi-li from Go-ra (?). Buthid and Tshang Lamo one tea each. From Khyimnang one rupee.

l.2. xxtu from Khangsar (Kolong) one rupee. Dorje Namgyal of Ghurla and Tshering Sonam from Dalang (Draling) one rupee each. Dhu-dhu-tse two tea. Ane (Jomo, nun) one tea. Tashi Kunzom of Go-ra one tea. Namgyal Buthid of Hur one tea. l-3. Nomo, younger sister, from Yotar four paise. From Yonsar xxtu Ram [household named Yosar in village Thorang] half rupee. Tashi Tshering from Diling (Tiling), E-ta Manu from Thorang, Ghuru from Phugthal, Tshering Namgyal from Thorang, Karma Tshering and Sonam Tashi one tea each. l-4. Lama Tshulthim Tanzin one rupee and wine.

Nyer [Nyerpha= manager] Phuntshog served all one thugpa in the morning and one tea, one meal each for lunch and dinner and one shunar of chhang. The monks gave one rupee and arag. l-5.Dhanu gave one rupee. From Labrang received one rupee. The Smith gave one basket full of cakes of buckwheat and one rupee for mchhodme, for oil for worship lamp.

One tsoli chhang from Palzom. One tsoli arag from Lhundub Lama of Silla gonpa. Moreover Chandha, the Lambardar from Tandi one piece of cotton cloth and one rupee.

The Khampa doctor one tshal (colour?). Chhuru of Tandi gave five ta-ka. Rub Dass one rupee, bheri and a-rag. Mani Ram of Gongma cotton cloth worth one rupee. Tiling two rupees. Kunna and Las Mani each gave cloth of the kind of chhi-ta [of colour by spray] worth three rupees. Sonam Tshering of Sumnam gave cotton cloth worth one rupee.

Phags Tshering gave Ne half khal. Yeshe Buthid from Jahlma, three corals and one turquise. l-8. Again Smith from Lote gave cotton cloth of two rupees. Tse-ni, mother Gho-gri and Khyi-ni the three gave half khal of Ne. Bhusa one rupee. Bhagnandi from Rangbye one rupee. Chi-na from Lote gave three bricks of tea. Sukhdev from Rangbye gave three fractured trurquises.

p.-2. (1-1) Bherli from Brang-tang(?) two bricks of tea and xxx two. Churung of Wari gaveone rupee, two coral, one jewel and one turquise. Two young girls from No-tse of Krozing gave thirteen rupees. Dhompar from Malang one rupee. Chhepa, Doctor (l-2) one rupee. Bhirpal gold worth half rupee. Tanzin from Tholong one rupee. Tashi one rupee. Bhuchung one rupee.

Bali Ram, the Kharpon, gave two rupees as the carriage of paper worth loads of two men for the manye. Sukhdev, the Hakam, one rupee. l-3. Chepa, the Doctor gave twelve khal of Ne for the cause of manye. Saman from Marbal two bricks of tea. Mani Ram, Lambardar from Wari, one rupee. Bhuse from Lote one rupee and one shunar. Smith gave one tolpho of three. Khu khu one rupee. Tshering one metal plate. Chheylud from Wari gave rice and one rupee cash. Namdhol rice of one rupee. Man Dass from Brang-dar rice of one rupee. Hassan rice of one rupee.

Phe-le from Tozing one rupee. Medhan eight ta-ka. l-5. Dhonpar from Malang one rupee. Bhilbhar the Gur one rupee. Chandhe from Tandi for the cause of manye two rupees. Mani Ram of Gongma one rupee. Mani Ram of Yogma wool of one rupee. Sonam Tshering of Gongma of Sumnam one rupee. Zanskar Bho'i from Mooling two khal of wheat flour. Mandass one rupee. Mandass from Tholong for the manye, one rupee. Be-da [a musician] gave Ne worth one rupee. Tashi, 1.7. Mangdhe, Chepa Tshering, Tshe-kru and Ma-zhan from Gha-rang each gave one rupee.

The Khampas (kham) from Kullu for the necessary articles of manye and the initial prayer one rupee. Dug Phuntshogs, Dundub, Rigzin Dolma, Old lady Lozang and the Nun from Pangi each gave one rupee. Tsang-zom two tea. The (on behalf of) deceased Kan-chun three rupees. Three rupees were offered as cash.

Note: This document called Tho-yig was prepared at the time of construction of the statue of Avalokiteśvara (of the form 'gro-ba'gro drug-'dren, withdrawing the six kinds of beings from the world) which was installed at Gandhala. It is like that of Triloknath. Presently the monastery has been brought down and a new monastery has been constructed just below it nearer to the highway and the river which place is called Tubchiling.

Here Bali Ram is designated as Kharpon who had been in the employment of the Raja of Kullu, stationed at Tandi, ranking next to the Hakim. Bali Ram was the first Negi of Lahul appointed by the British upon the take over of the area of Lahul in 1846. The two must be the same person. Thus the event of construction of the image may be placed in the first half of the nineteenth century, c. C.E. 1840, before the take over of the area by the British. Bali Ram is said to have belonged to village Goram according to Satish Loppa and his household was named Hakim. The scribe of the document here was a well informed person but not trained like a lama. He was very well conversant with the local terms used differently in the three valleys. The contributors belonged to all the three valleys but most of them are from Manchhad and Tinan. The monastery of Gandhala is managed by the villages falling in Pattan nearby it. Hassan was a Muslim perhaps from Baltistan as they used to be there in Lahul and other places.

3 Tinan-Chandra Valley

i. Chhokhor gonpa

Chhokhor is a small village. At about two kilometers before reaching Sissu from the side of Khoksar, the road branches off to upwards and after winding round for about three kilometers one reaches the village where there is situated the old monastery named Chhokhor gonpa.

The monastery in the look of Tibetan Buddhism inherits in the worship room important artefacts of ancient Indian Buddhism. The principal statue is of Tara of metal quite heavy. It has some small statues of stone, marble and metal all belonging to the same aspect. The Bodhisattva statue of stone of about the height of six inches contains on its back a deeply engraved inscription in Sharda script and Sanskrit language. It was visited by G.C.L. Howell, the Asstt. Commissioner at Kullu with A.H. Francke and was examined by J. Ph. Vogel.

Francke traces its origin to the time of Atisha. He writes that, "but the chronicles of the country do not tell us anything about them, nor do they contain the date of the erection of the stately castle of Tinan by a Kulu king, as tradition has it." He further writes that, "there is a somewhat indistinct inscription in Sharda character on a boulder about a mile below the present village of Tinan. Another Sharda inscription on a stone idol in the Chhoskhor (probably Stod rgyal-mtshan Chos-'khor) monastery near Si-su which belongs to the Tinan district, contains nothing but mystic syllables. It was discovered by Mr. G.C.L. Howell and myself, and examined by Dr. Vogel,"(Francke, 1926-II: 218, Notes.). Vogel only informs, "Stone image slab inscription at Chos-skor near Sisu in the Chandra valley, British Lahul," (Vogel, 1911-I: 259).

The monastery was also visited by Rahul Sankrityayan. He writes that, the main statue is of Bodhisattva in lalitasana, of bronze. It is good and is about one cubit high. Then the Pujari, who was also a vaidya, physician, showed the image containing the inscription. It is made of stone more than eight fingers high, say about six inches. The image is of the Buddha having crown, in the mudra of turning the Wheel of Law. It shows influence of Vajrayan. Letters are engraved on the back of the statue. There is a mantra in the inscription. The words which can be read clearly are: 'Hum Phat swah!' From the inscription it can be proposed to belong to around the tenth century C.E., (Rahul, 1956: 30).

The inscription in reverse letters is a sacred formula like to be used by stamping it on a material like the kneaded dough, etc. but from the condition of the object it appears that it was perhaps used very little. A photograph of the stamp showing the letters in obverse shape obtained by C. Dorje is given in the plates. There is another small statue of marble. On the back of it there is written by scratching in Sharda. Prem Lal Yotarpa also tells that while constructing road to the village there came a large stone slab on the way near the village. When it was removed by JCB there was found a large skeleton, about six feet long, which was thrown into the river.

ii. The Household of Yangling, village Yangling, Raja Raj Singh, C.E. 1719-1731.

Text: ..... sa las 'bur mtho sur-brtan spur der. ..... chhos-rgyal chhen-po ra-dsa sing-ghzhes. dbu-rmog mtho zhing chhab-srid dar rgyas dus. de'i mnga' zhabs gar-zha'i gnas lung 'dir. bkra-shis mthongs mon rgya-bod gnyis kyi mtshams. yul-la dge bchu'i khrims ldan rang-lo zhes. yar-'dren bla-ma'i gdan-sa shel-tring du. bstan-'dsin rgyal-mtshan chhos-btsug mtho-ba'i dus. phun-tshogsdpal-'byor 'dsom-pa'i g-yang-gling 'dir. rigs rus khungs brtsun ha-si-ra' yi sbrgyud. dad ldan dkon-mchhog mchhod dang sbyin stong dge sbyin-bdag grong-dpon tshering bsam-'grug dang. sras mchhog dam-pa dpal dan blo-bde dang. rdsang-drung mdses ldan na-ma nor bu-khrid. ...... bsam don sgrub phyir dang.

lhag-par 'jig-rten 'di nas pha-rol du tshe 'das nag tsel 'byor-skyid dhala'-tu dang. bsod-nams blo-bde tshe-ring bstan-'dsin sogs. ma-bu lnga-po thar-lam bsgrod phyir du. dam-chhos theg-chhen rdo-rje gchod-pa dang gang de'i phan-yon gter-chhos sdig-bshags dang. snang rgyad la sogs pa'i sna bzhi tsam bzhengs. gzhan yang dge-rts rab-gnas yang dag sgrubs.

...... 'jig-rten pha-rol tshe 'das bu gsum dang. grogs gnyis zhabs-tog legs sgrub ngo-mtshar chhe. sras chhog bskal-bar ldan-pa'i blo-bde des. drin-chan a-ma gnyis dang nu-bo yis. drin-lan tshul bzhin 'jal-ba shin-tu legs. .....

nye drung rnams kyi dge-rtsi'i byung grang la. thog-mar bla-grang nas bla-ma rgyal-mtshan gyi dge-rtsi gnang. sra-sren nas jo-bo rgyal-po dang. jo-jo bstan-'dsin bu-khrid steng zhal gnyis. .....

Translation: ..... Sultanpur is like an eruption on the earth. ..... There lives the great religious king Raj (ra-dsa) Singh whose crown is held high and the territory is expanding. Under his sway is the holy valley of Lahul which is on the border between India and Tibet. The valley of lawful Ranglo is a land possessed of the ten virtues. The residence of the leading lama Tanzin Gyaltshan is situated at Shelting [Gundhla village]. Here at prosperous Yangling (g-Yang-gling), belonging to the clan of Hasira, having noble origin, live the faithful Konchhog Chhod, the donor, the Village Chief, Tshering Samdrug, the son Paldan Lo-de and the daughter-in-law Nor Buthid; the father and son. ..... For the fulfilment of the desires of......

Specially for the deceased Nag-tsel Jorkyid Dhalatu and Sonam Lo-de Tshering Tanzin, etc. mother and sons, the five, so that they may pass through the path of liberation, the Vajrachhedika, Digshag and sNang-rgyad, etc. about four works were raised. Moreover the auspicious Rab-nas was accomplished well. .....

The kinsmen from whom the offerings were received are: Firstly the offerings were received from Lama Gyaltshan from Labrang (Shelting). Jo-bo Gyalpo and, his spouse, Jo-jo Tanzin Buthid, husband and wife, the two. .....

Summary: The villages from where the guests had come: Sissu (Sra-sren), Yang-kar household of Sissu (Sra-sren), Shur-thang, Kastal, Ratil, Shag-dangs, Kha-yar, Srob, household of Yo-tar of village [Ropsang], She-go, Shi-ti, Yung-ling, Yobar, Tarkyi and Bogtse. It does not give the names of the articles offered by the guests.

Note: The village of Yang-ling is situated about a kilometer above Sissu-1. Here is situated the original residence of Gepang, the god of Lahul and the family named Yangling. It was originally the family from where the priests of the deity came. Originally there was one household which has now expanded to about half a dozen. Here the head of the family is designated as grong-dpon, Village Chief.

Here is named a village as Shi-ti [= white water]. Shi-ti and Du-ti were two villages situated on either side of a small nallah on the left side of Chandra, opposite to Sissu, slightly towards Khoksar. The two villages were washed away in the flood caused by the breaking away of the glacier of Shigri (shig = louse, ri = mount) in 1836. There is a saying about the village as:

Shi-ti Du-ti nau ṭol.

Dalang Titsang chaudah ṭol.

Translation: There were nine households in the villages of Shiti and Duti, and fourteen in Dalang and Titsang. Shi-ti and Du-ti are lost. Dalang still exists across the nallah of Gundhla. Titsang, which might have been situated below the highway towards Tandi, between Dalang and the river exists no more.

iii. Village Shashin (Ṣa-ṣin, Sra-srin), (Sissu-2).

Sra-srin: The place presently known as Sissu consists of two traditional villages which are separated by the stream traditionally namedas Nīśaltī Lumpā, Nishalti Nala. During the period when Lahul was with Punjab a hydro-electric generation plant with the capacity of I KW was established here which was later on abandoned.

The village on its left towards Khoksar is known as Khwagling (here Sissu-1) and that on the other side as Sra-srin, Shashin. towards Tandi, (Sissu-2).

iii. Village Shashin (Ṣa-ṣin, Sra-srin), (Sissu-2).

a. Shashin Jo (The Household of Thakurs of Shashin).

a. i. Shashin, Shashin Jo, Silla gonpa, 17th-18th century C.E.

Translation: Lighting of prayer lamps at Sil-la [dgon-pa], the Buddha knows.

Note: Silla gonpa is situated near Gundhla about two kilometers from it towards Tandi above the highway.

The above sentence forms title page of the matter given below at a.ii. Its matter, if there was, is lost. This title is inappropriate for the matter given below. Its language, wordings and the style are entirely folk, non-literary. It is not a work of a religious person but of a layman. For the words dug-pa and gshes honorifically it could have been 'bul-ba, and mkhyen, etc. The spelling of the word mchhon, written as is spoken, should have been mchhod. Sometime late an attempt has been made to shorten the title. Four words in the beginning and the last word 'gshes' have been blotted with white fluid with the objective of erasing. The first two words could not be deciphered.

a. ii. Shashin, Shashin Jo, Ka-ka Gyatsho, c. C.E. 1750.

Translation: Garzha (Gar-chhag), Lahul, the country of dakinis (mkhan-'gro yul), is enriched by the practice of the principles of the ten virtues. The mountain behind appears like a lion sitting in a stately posture. The collection of mountain peaks in the front look like a heap of jewels. Above the river Gung-gul [Chandra], is situated the well developed village of Shas-shin. There lives the family belonging to the lineage of well developed clan of 'byam-shes.

Ka-ka [elder brother] rGya-mtsho, the faithful, laborious and wise, performed the ceremony of worship of the [Three] Jewels and raised the concise form of *mdo-sde* book. The offerings made for the accumulation of the merits was wonderful............

[*de-ltar*]... In this manner, the father, mother and children for the prosperity of the precious Doctrine of the Buddha and specially for their long life the book, the well developed mDo, an abstract representing the whole mDo, was raised well. Those offering for the accumulation of the merits were many, wornderful......The hostess Lodos Mann .... Tashi Zangpo, the daughter, and Batsa Shunbi and the daughter-in-law Shibili did service like sheep, wonderfully. Dorje Semspa was the scribe.

The relatives giving offerings are: sDron-ma Tshe-bstan and bZang-mo, husband and wife; Yung-srungs Kyid, husband and wife, from mGon; A-jo So-nabs Kyid, husband and wife; bZungs-skyab and dKar-ru-skyid, husband and wife; from Ma-Chho-ge, mother and son; Seng-si-so and bSod-namss Kyid, husband and wife, and 'Di-ris Kin-dag, husband and wife.

Note: The document belongs to the Thakurs of Sissu, in Chandra valley. The family was a leading family in the area around the village but subject to the Thakurs of Gundhla. They are so far not recorded in the history of Lahul. Locally they are known as Sra-srin Jo, Thakurs of Sra-srin.

Gung-gul: The name apparently applies for the river Chandra. This is a rare instance of its kind in Lahul. In Lahul no local name is known for Chandra, Bhaga and Chandrabhaga. The form of the word 'grug-pa for 'brug-pa, current rg-yug-pa to mean to flow for the river is indicateive of the document being quite old. There are some other signs. This is a karchhag prepared on a death ceremony.

b. Shashin, Shashin Jo, Lhun-grub of Shashin and Raja Tedhi Singh (1742-1767), c. C.E. 1760.

Translation: The capital Sultanpur is like an eruption on the earth. May the crown of the great righteous king Tedhi Singh (Tre-dru seng-ge) be held high and his kingdom expand. This Rang-lo (the valley of Chandra around Sissu) of Lahul is under his rule. The residence of the Lama is at Shel-spring [Shel-ting = Sheltu of Gundhla]. The Teacher, a great scholar, Rabjam Lozang Dondub (Rab-'byam bLo-bzang don-grub), may he become the crown of the Doctrine.

Here at Yangling [just above Khwagling] prosperity has gathered. May Tashi Palbar (bkris dpal bar) the Lambardar (nang-blon) and his brother be healthy and their life strong. Tashi Palbar, the Lambardar of the area, and his brothers [rjed = mchhed], may their life be healthy and strong. Here at the prosperous Sra-srin, where the [ten] virtues have assembled, [the donors] belonging to the pure lineage of the clan 'Od-gsal, having origin to the gods, performed the worship of the [three] Excellent Ones and made donations in generous manner. May the life of Lhundub (Lhun-grub), younger brother, the faithful donor be strong. May the life of Nono Tshewang (Tshe-dbang), like the son of god, be strong.

The Lady donor, elder sister Namgyal Tshomo [rNam-rgyal mTsho-mo], may her life be strong. The excellent sons, like the sons of gods, Nono Jog (mjo-go) Ram, and Nono So-rnams rGyal-mtshan, may their lives be strong. ... ...The excellent daughters, as like the flower of Ser-chhen (a small yellow flower found at extreme heights, highly valued) Gyal Chhos Zom, Yeshe Chhos Zom, Padma Chhos Zom and Nyima Dolma, the four, honour to them. The excellent mothers Lagzom and Chatiri, honour to them. Honour to the daughter-in-law Kunzom.

The donors Nono Lhun-grub and elder sister [wife of Lhun-grub, sister address by the scribe] rNam-rgyal Tsho-mo, the two, got the wish fulfilling book *mdo-dmangs* of the well developed Doctrine raised for the sake of the deceased father [of Lhun dub] and for fulfilling the wishes of Lhundub, ... and for various auspicious reasons. ....

The account of the offerings made by the kinsmen for the sacred task of Ge-tsi is as under: In the beginning offerings were received from Lozang Dondub, the Lama of Ranglo. Then sNgags-ram (practitioner of mantras) Ye-she Chhos-phel, Lambardar [nang-blon] Tashi Pal-de [bKrshi Pal-de] mother and son; Tshering Paljor and Lags sKyid, husband and wife, from Shurthang.

Others came from the villages of .Kothal. Tinan Khangsar. Hurpa. Yang Kar. Hudun and Jor Buthid, husband and wife, from Tarki. bZhin Rogs. Purad Pharma (other side). Purad Tshurma (this side). Yarki house of Khyinang (Khyimnang). Margyad. Yos of Margyad. Phugtal. Yangling Pharma (other side). Srob. Shuling gong (upper) and Kyebag.

The service providers Nang-pa, Chhang-ma and Sha-pa served chhang and meat with variety of tastes and the guests were satisfied and pleased. Due to these merits may all the beings get the stage of the Sambuddha.

iv. Khyinang (Khyīnaṅ), the Village and Household.

Khyinang: The village named here in the text as Khyi-'dang situated in Tinan valley, is presently known as Khyi-nang. In some documents it is also found written as Khyim-nang.. There lives one family famous as the family of 'On-po [Astrologers]. The family was famous throughout Lahul for the profession. The origin of the family appears to coincide with that of the family of the Thakurs of Gundhla. These documents belong to the same family.

a. Khyinang, Nam-kha rGyal-po, the Thakur of Gundhla, c. C.E. 1350-1375 (?).

Translation: (This document has no title page.). Khyinang (Khyi-'dang) is the place where [the Doctrine] has spread. Following is the list of the guests making offerings for the ceremony.

Thakur Nam-kha' rgyal-po [of Tinan Khar] and his spouse (bag-ma = bride) Nyi-zla-skyid, the two honourables; elder sister Zangmo and Ti-ba-go-go, the two, wife and husband; uncle gSang-rdor; lama Ghi-gung-pa'; astrologers Norbu and sKa-rang-nga. Padma Zang-po and Srong-po the two from Chhoskor; rDe-re Tsun-chhung; Sonam sKyid; Tu-tu and Tsho-khum, the two husband and wife; Bir-mi of Margyed and Sonam Sing of Po-se; Gang-la sKyabs of Shi-go; Nor-zang of Tir-ra-ling (Tiling); Ta-la-ga of Purang; Bi-la-gon, the minister of Gundhla (Gudla); Tashi Zangpo; Jo-bo-tsa; Zangpo Jopo; Zangpotsa of Puradta; Ga-dun-bum of Khar; Nga-ko-'o Tsa-nu of Mooling; they, like the flocks of sheep, made offerings wonderfully in abundance.

Daughter Lha-mo Sar-kar-Go-na-tsa and others like her made offerings in abundance like the herds of sheep.

b. Khyinang, 16th-17th century C.E.

Title of the Book: The book of bigger dhārṇī [mantras] of five branches. He, He! May there be joy and happiness.

Translation: Drilbu Ri is the developed great pilgrimage place, the neck of the mountain. Tinan, well developed, is the righteous country. The castle of high Nal-ze, is like an engraving on the earth. The well developed place of Khyi-nang (Khyi-'dang) [here lives the family] of the lineage of dol-chhen nyi-ma-ris clan originating from their ancestors. With the accumulation of merits by their former deeds and being loving and kind, are leaders of the people. They protect them as like their sons and pupils. Drung-pa Sonam Zangpo and Onpo Sonam Drags-pa, the two brothers are donors.

Giving thought well they differentiated between the virtue and sin. In order to attach essence to the illusionary wealth, father Dungpa Khanpo and uncle Jampal, as the symbols of the body, speech and mind (of the diceased) raised wonderful image of the Teacher, the present book of *bzung-chhen gral-lnga*, and a chaitya.

The Lady donor Jo Cho rGyal-mo.... Those who brought articles for mchhod-me were praised wonderfully. On-po lTog-ldan and Thakur sBa-chan, the two, were the scribes of this wonderful document (book). The works of manufacturing the statues of the deities and constructing the chaitya and the writings were done well. The services provided by the two daughters of the house Mi-grub-pa and bZang-mo to the artists was wonderful.

c. Khyinang: Vajrachhedika 16th -17th century C.E.

dKar-rgyud Phun-tshogs and 'Dsoms-skyid, the two are donors. Dam-chhos dBang-po and sKal-bzang Tshe-ring did the task of engraving well. dKar-rgyud Phun-tshogs was scribe.

v. Tinan (Gundhla)Khar (mKhar), the House of the Thakurs of Gundhla (Gundhlā).

a. Tinan Khar, Karchhags of Gundhla Kangyur.

The following are karchhags from the set of books known as Gundhla Kangyur which were mostly copied here at Tinan.

a.i. Tinan Khar, Gundhla Kangyur, 2/12, 3/3, p. 685, Ra-na-pa-la of Gundhla, c. C.E. 1275-1300 (?).

Book: Title lost. ['bum]

Translation: Ghandhala, related to the mount Kailash, is the source of knowledge. There is no suffering of hunger and thirst here as there flows the river with eight wings. There is no fear of enemies and robbers anywhere here. One can experience as if one has got liberated from the world.

The owner, donor, Ra-na pa-la, [whose residence is] situated on the left side of such kind of holy place, possessed of faith and devotion, got the excellent book of 'Bum, mother of the three times, raised.

This was written by rGya-brag, the elder, the scribe, who follows the lineage of the intelligent Phag-pa-rje, the source of knowledge of Guge. .... There were two scribes to write this book. The former part was written by Zims-mal sNyil-phrug Dsl-ba-phye, and the later part by me, rGya-brag.

a.ii.Tinan Khar, Gundhla Kangyur, 6/12, 1/2, P. 533, Dorje Pala, c. C.E. 1300-1325 (?).

Book: *Kon-tsegs.*

Translation: The mountains are high and the land is clean in sPu-rgyal Tibet. Gandhala is one of the eight sacred places. Here at Tinan, which rests on it, was born Dorje Pala, of good character, the protector of the Doctrine. The subjects live in peace and are loved. The kingdom is strongly fortified by the chains of mountains. Worshipping the stage of the Triratna, may he attain the stage of Bodhisattva in his next life.

Considering the wealth and goods as illusion he got a copy of the book of the class of mDo-sde, Sutra, made. The Lord and the subjects, the two, who uphold the objects of worship, and rDo-rje rtse, the scribe, who made the Doctrine expanded, may they all attain the stage of the Perfect Bodhisattva; just like dGa-bo, Nanda, who was explained about the worldly enjoyment by the Buddha and Nanda attained the stage of Arhat, similarly the Buddha explained the Doctrine to the Donor and the devotees, may they also attain the stage of the Perfect Bodhisattva. [rje.x. bzang = rje-'bangs (?)].

a.iii. Tinan Khar, Gundhala Kangyur, 1/7, 6/6, p. 492, Dorje Pala, c. C.E. 1300-1325(?).

Book: *sa'i snying-po 'khor-lo bchu-pa'i mdo bzhugs-so.*

Translation: Gandala, immutable and permanent, is connected with the unbroken chain of mountains with the mount Tise, Kailash. At Tinan, which rests on it, there has been built the castle named Nal-ze, on a small piece of land, by Dorje Pala, who was born here, is like its jewel. His body is filled with bravery and luster. His shoulders are impressive. Being learned the kingdom is filled with devotion. Being greatly powerful he has brought the people under his reign. Being of good character the subjects are pleased to serve him. Being clean and pure he is like a King. His memory is like the lightning. .... (scribe) rDorje-rtse.

Note: It reveals that rDor-je-rtse was scribe, or the chief scribe for quite long time.

a.iv. Tinan Khar, Gundhla Kangyur, 1/12, 6/6 p. 6, 1 De-ljam rGyalpo of Tinan Khar and Raja Parbat Singh (1575-1608), c. C.E. 1590 (?).

Book: *chhos-rgyal chhen-po rgyal-po srong-btsan sgam-po'i 'phags-pa nam-mkha'i snying-po sogs phran 'ga' bzhugs-so.*

Translation: Gandhala, the great pilgrimage place, one among the eight holy places, and the Bell-mountain (Dril-bu Ri) where the Dakinis assemble, are situated in the West of Tise, Kailash, the king of the snowy mountains, and lake Mapang, Mansarovar, where the wish fulfilling water is accumulated, and on the northern side of the river Ganga, i.e. Chandrabhaga.

The castle of Nal-ze which is like an eruption on the earth, is situated in the prosperous and joyous village of Tinan, which is like a sea of wealth. The family of the Thakurs residing here belongs to the good lineage having origin from the clan of buram-shingpa. The great religious king Parbat Singh, the great religious king bDe- 'jams rGyal-po, the great minister Ra'u-la; and the donors Kharko and Sonam Gya-mtsho; and Tashi rGyalpo and (further page lost)....

a.v.i. Tinan Khar, Gundhla Kangyur, Miscellaneous 1/12, 1/6. Tashi Paljor of Tinan Khar and Raja Pritam Singh (1767-1806).

Book: *au-rgyan gu-ru pad-ma 'byung-gnas kyi skyes-rabs rnam-thar rgyas-pa gser-gi phreng zhugs-so.*

The crown of the great religious king, Pritam Singh, possessed of the qualities of being learned, handsome, youthful, brave and powerful, is held high. Here at the castle of Nal-tse, the donor, Tashi Paljor, son of god, of pure origin of the lineage of 'Od-gsal, and who is handsome, learned, brave and powerful, possessed of the qualities of ten virtues and practicing the two Laws, served well for raising, with his kindness, the articles of symbols for fulfilling the wishes of his (deceased) father.

Nangka Palmo is junior grand-mother of the owner. The lady donor, for fulfilling the wishes of her departed spouse got raised as the symbols of body, voice and heart respectively the image (vihar) of Padmasambhava made of gold and copper, the book of Padma Thang-yig and Jangchhub chaitya. The merits accumulated by raising such useful objects is wonderful. Hello! The younger sisters Mumpa and Lo-gros, the two, served well in raising these symbols.

Pa-di, the handsome son of god, and the excellent son Tira-ti, may they also make the Doctrine endearing to themselves like their father and grand fathers. Tashi Palmo, the excellent daughter, served well in raising these symbols.

The participants in the funeral ceremony (dge-ba) assembled like birds in the lotus garden. Hello! A kyog [vessel, pitcher] each was offered by the Khar from Kyelang, mother Gyal-mo from Mang-gon in Gahar, the lama from Khyi-nang and Khar of Barbog.

Others who joined the ceremony are: Tshering-rgyalpo husband and wife from Pyukar (Chug-dra); Lord Tu-bu husband-wife, and Thakur Paljor husband-wife from Sra-sren (Sissu); younger Thakur husband-wife from Tiling; Padma husband-wife, and younger brother Hi-ti husband and wife from Thorang.

Note: The above matter is found written on a sheet separate from the book as a Karchhag prepared on the occasion of celebration of death ceremony of the father of Thakur Tashi Paljor. The fact is repeated in the colophon of the book at the last page. [spar-tsal = dpa' dang rtsal. mo-me = mes-mo, grandmother.].

a.v.ii. Colophon to the same book: p. 754.

By the merits of this task of making arrangements and meeting the expenditure for raising the articles of symbols of the body, voice and heart, elder brother Tashi Paljor and the Lady owner Nang-ka Palmo, son and mother, the two, descending from the famous godly lineage of 'Od-gsal, and others of the class of Thakur, the scribe Dondub, and the innumerable beings, may they all attain the status of Padmasambhava, fulfilling their wishes.

a.vi. Tinan Khar, Gundhla Kangyur, 1/12, Book 2/6. P. 3-4. Pārī and Sinsaus Kum-mjed of Gundhla, and Raja Pritam Singh (1767-1806) of Kullu, and King Sing-ge Namgyal of Ladakh, c. C.E. 1790.

Book: *'drom-ston-pa brgyal-ba'i 'byung-gnas kyi skyes-rabs bka'-bsdams bu-chhos le-'u nyi-shu-pa bzhugs-s-ho.*

The following text is contained in a separate sheet forming pp. 3-4 of the book as Karchhag.

Translation: Hello! The religious king Pritam Singh resides at the great castle at the capital of Makarsa (Ma-khar-sā), and his crown is held high.

Sing-ge Namgyal resides at the castle in the great capital of bLe and his crown is held high and his kingdom is flourishing. Although the country and the holy place Leh in Ladak, were not visited but the work and objectives being related, relied on his name as heard. The sun and the moon adorn the space between the earth and the sky like in the amulet box. Pray, this is in the practice of exchange of love and friendship between the two.

The red path for the mules like the great red lightning has been constructed on the pass of Baralacha, the border. The white hard and rough path like ribs of the spine has been constructed for the sheep. The sons and servants gathered like the planets and stars and travelled happily.

Thus the reign of the father and son was flourishing. They lived in the worthy castle of Tinan, which is an eruption on the earth, in the prosperous country of Lahul, the land of Dakinis. They are like the great gods and they belong to the good lineage, famed clan, originating from the god 'Od gsal. No-no Pari and Sinsaus Kum-mjed, father and son, the two possess miraculous powers of bravery and skill.

The two for repairing the kindness of his (deceased) kind father, for subduing the causes of difficulty in their life and for attaining the pure status in the next life, raised works of the well developed Doctine, the Ka-bam Lags-po and books of the class of son and father, larger and smaller kinds of books. The great merit amassed due to this is here praised by all. Hello!

Moreover, the Lady Donor, Grandmother, sister, Nangka Palmo, for raising the holy books did wonderful service. The excellent mothers Sonam Palmo and bLo-gro, the two mixed the god's nectar in the meal of men, served nice meal.

Note: No-No Pārī and Sinsaus Kum-mjed, the two, father and son performed the ceremony on the occasion of the death of Tashi Paljor. Grandmother, Nangka Palmo, wife of Tashi Paljor, is still live. The important guests are: From the house of Labrang of Khyinang, Pad-dkar, the religious Lord of the siddha lineage, and Padma Senge, father and son; Thakur Padma from Thorang Ling; Thakur Paljor and wife sNum-chol husband and wife from Sra-sren; Thakur Sonam dPal-lde and Mugulu father and son; Tashi rGya-mtsho and sister Dolma husband and wife from Bar-bog Khar; Nono Sonam Rgyalpo and sister Tashi Palmo, husband and wife from Magon.

gNyer pa, the manager, Jogi Chand and Logro husband and wife from Gunla; Phagspa Tashi and Sonam Dsom pa husband and wife; Zang-skyab and Le husband and wife from Shuling. Alam the Lambardar and sister Bhelmo, the two from Lod, Lote.

Note: Seng-ge Namgyal whose capital is situated at Leh and who belonged to the first half of seventeenth century, lived earlier than Pritam Singh of Kullu.

b. Tinan Khar, manuscripts containing genealogical lists of the Thakurs of Gundhla.

b.i. Tinan Khar, The Chronicle called Golden Mirror, Raja Bahadur Singh (1532-1559).

"While the exceedingly lofty palace of the capital Ma-gar-sa was held by the great religious king (Dharmarāja) Bi-dhur-siṅ (Bahādur Siṅgh) with his helmet high, [there lived] in this castle Nal-rtse, the most eminent in the country – all hail! – a family of undefiled origin called H̱od-gsal; ('Bright Light') which was descended from the gods. It originated at Lcags-mkhar in Gun-de (Guge). [Its members are the following]: -

The Great Lord of men, Ra-ṇa-pha–la.	His son
rDo-rje-pha-la.	His son
Ñi-ma-pha-la	His son
Naṅ-ka-rgyal-po.	His son
bSod-rnams(nams)-dpal-[sde?].	His son
bSod-rnams(nams)-rgya-mtsho.	His younger brother
Bkra-śis-rgya[l]-po.	His younger brother

Tshe-riṅ-rgyal-po.

His son Bkra-śis.

His son Pa̱ha-ri-mkhan.

His son Bha-gha- man-rta.

His son Ha-ri-ya.

His younger brother Rgyal-po.

His son Dpal-ẖbhar.

'[May their life time become as firm as the mountains] and may their government increase like the fifteenth of the waxing moon! All hail! By the donors (214) Rgyal-po and Blo-dros-skyid, both, and Ṅaṅ (Ṅag-dbaṅ-gro[l]-ma, the best of mothers, by these three, at the death ceremony of Ha-ri, a Byaṅ-chub mchod-rten (stūpa) was erected for his soul. And as a verbal record, this chronicle called 'The golden mirror', was written. [It is astonishing how much was gathered and given for the sake of religion. All hail! The number of what was presented according to the word....

And the others, who brought flesh and beer for the benefit of men, were ... (c. 40 names)...like nectar of the gods.

May all the partakers in this sacrifice meet later on in Mṅon-dgaẖi-zhiṅ (one of the heavens).... the red colour of idols .... (be blessed!]

"[The chief of Tinan says that Gun-de is situated in Bir-Banghal (Baṛā Baṅgāl, a province in Kulu), and that his ancestors came from there.]" (Francke, A.H., 1926-II:213-214).

b.ii. Tinan Khar, Tshe-dbang Rabtan, death ceremony, Raja Tedhi Singh (1742-1767), c. C.E. 1760.

Translation: At the mount Dril-bu and Gandhola there is a deep pit of medicinal water of nectar of Tara [a rock carving of Tara, named so]. There is a gently descending river with eight branches, heads. E ma ho!

Specially at the excellent castle of Nal-tse, there is a bugle made of elephant tusk and a nail of sow. This is only a fraction from the guidebook to the holy place given here. Sultanpur is like the holy place of Gadan.

Whle the crown of the great religious king Tedhi (Tre-ra) Singh is held high, under his subjection is Tinan, in the Land of Law. Self-created, erupted from the earth, beautiful to look at, high and strong, such like is the great castle of Nal-tse. Here resides [the family of the Thakurs] well inheriting the lineage of bu-ram-shing-pa from the ancestors who descended from the god Abhasvara ('Od-gsal lha). The manner of origin from mChags-mkhar Guge is like this.

This is the manner in which the origin spread from the root Guge.

The Great Lord of men, Ra-ṇa Pha–la.

His son rDo-rje Pha-la.

His son Nyi-ma Pa-la.

His son Nang-ka rGyal-po.

His son bSod-nams dPal-bde.

His son bSod-namsbr Gya-mtsho.

His son Bkra-shis rGyal-po.

His son Bkra-shis dPal-'byor.

His son Pa-ri Khan.

His son Ha-ri-ya.

His son Bkra-shis dPal-'bar.

His son Chhos-bzang dBang-po.

His son Tshe-ring Dar-rgyas.

His younger brother Tshe-dbang Rigs-'dsin.

His excellent son is Tshe-dbang Nor-bu.

May the kingdom of the father and son expand like the bright part of the month. Tshe-ring Dar-rgyas and Tshe-dbang Rigs-'dsin, the two, are the faithful hosts. Tshe-ring Chhos-'dsom is the hostess.

The three, for assisting the deceased Tshe-dbang Rab-stan for emancipation from the path of liberation, raised as the stake of the body the images of Tshe-dpag-med, Vajrasttva yab-yum, the Vir, hero, Tamdin, six-armed mGon-po; and as a stake of the voice, twenty two copies of Vajrachhedika, and as a stake of the heart, the jangchhub mchhod-rten were erected with rich gzungs, relics.

With the strength gained by raising the stakes of body, voice and heart, may the father, mother and children, and the near ones remain strong in the time of hundred kalpas; and the deceased Tshe-dbang Rab-stan be born in the land of pleasure.

Summaries: Villages from where the kinsmen had come:

Pattan: Sugnam, Tholong (mChhod).

Punan: Tshul-khrims from Barbog khar.

sTod: Nono Sonam from Khangsar Khar.

Other Areas: Zanskar.

Tinan: Srel-tu, Purad, Chhokhor, Khangsar, Hurpa, Phugthal, Tiling, Shooling, Khyinang, Yotar, Dhigo, Khale, The Cave monastery of Ranglo, the small monastery of Khyimnang, Jyinsa, Thorang, mDsodpa, Gundhla ('Gul-la) and Margyed.

Articles received: Meal and drink (2). Arag and phyemar (1). Big tsoli of arag and lag-sha (1). Meat and 'don-sing (1). Tsag-mo and sha lag-pa (1). Tsag-mo and srum (1). Tsoli arag and lag-sha (1). Gsol-ja, tsagmo and lag-sha (1). 'don-sing and srum (1). arag and srum (1). Tsag-mo za-ma and lag-sha (2). Tsoli of arag, za-ma of dangsma and dgu-'da (1). Tsoli of arag and lag-sha (1). Dangsma and srum (3). 1 sheep (1). 1 seer ghi and 1 alto ru-ma (1). Alto of dangs and srum (1). 1 alto of tsag-mo (1). 1 za-ma tsagmo and srum (2). 1 za-ma tsagmo and lagsha (1). 1 alto tsag-mo and srum (2). 1 za-ma and lag-sha (1). Tsag-mo and srum (1). Dangs-ma and lag-sha (2).

b.iii. Tinan Khar, Document in Tankri script, Title Grant to Rupchand-Sevadas, Raja Tedhi Singh (1742-1867), C.E. 1760.

Title grant by Raja Tedhi Singh to Rup Chand-Seva Dass of Gundhla, C.E. 1760.

This document is in Trankri script. This is a copy prepared from the original and authenticated in the court of the Assistant Commissioner at Kullu in 1849. Here below is given the transcription of the text in Nagari.

नकल

(गोल मोहर।) साहब असिस्टैंट कमीश्नर साहब बहादुर कुल्लू सन् 1849 ई० की मोहर। (उर्दू और देवनागरी लिपि में)।

(पंक्ति-1) गऊग श्रीमाहाराजाधराजा श्रीमाहाराजा श्री टेढ़ी सींघेजी दे(पं-2)वस्य लाहुड़े द्रोगे गधलयाड़ ठाकोरा रूपचन्दा (पं-3)सेवादासा जोगसमाद कागद दीता ऐहाजे ऐ (पं-4) हे रूपचन्द सेवादास लाहुले द्रोगा रखया लाहुड़ा (पं-5) री चोउदाकोटाड़ी ऊप्र हुकम इसदा चउदा को(पं-6)टाड़ी रे वतुगरूए कामदारे राऐ भी इसरे हुक (पं-7) मे माफक चलणा होर अठदठइए हेनेतीन्ना (पं-8) भी इस द्रोगे खे रूजु रेहणा तीन्नाभी इस कने (पं-9) आऊणा होर भारी भी आऊंदे जांदे इसकी दे(पं-10)णे लाहुला बजीरा चेले क्रीपेरामा सरदारा (पं-11) रामधना दी से इस कागदे माफक तुसेभी ठी(पं-12)क करी देणा दठइऐ भी रूजू कराई देशो भा(पं-13)री भी देयोणे सं० 36 हा०प्र० 7 हाजर हुकमे माफक (पं-14) लीख्या रघुनाथपुर अस्थाने लीख्या की सारघे (पं-15) असोअर 23, नगारे जोडी़ 2, हेसी 2, बालती 2, (पं-16) रयय हत्येला 1, नगारा 2, श्रीबीजादसमीरे (पं-17) उछवा की पारढालपुरा तंबु आगे लेई आउ(पं-18)णे होर इनी गणयकरी दी अरज कीती ता दुही (पं-19) ठाकुरा जोग

हाजरा खे गणयकरहा बगसीजे ए हे दो (पं–20)हे ठाकर गुठ नज़र करदे जीस दीन द्रोगा भी (पं–21) ठाकुर पार गुठ नजर करगे तीस दीन गणयक(पं–22) र इसकी भी छड़ी दीघे होर त्रह टोल (तोह) पाहते से द्रोगे के हवाले हुइए कठ होइ कीण त्रे री टोला पेसे जे (पं–23) कठ हे न से त्रे ही जणे कठ होइ श्रीबीजादसमी की लेई ओणे।।

Translation

Copy

(Round Seal with the legend in Devnagari and Persian scripts): Honourable Court of Assistant Commissioner, Kullu, 1849.

(Lines – 1 to 3). Om. This message given through this letter from the great King Tedhi Singh – Raja of Kullu- is addressed to the Daroga [Superintendent] of Lahul, the Thakar of Gondhla (Gadhlyal), Rupchand-Sevadas.

(L.4). The message is like this that Rupchand-Sevadas has been appointed Daroga of Lahul. (L.5). His authority extends over all the fourteen kothis (Kotyad), circuits of administration, of Lahul. (L.6-7) Batugru [Messengers], Kamdar [Assistants] and all the subjects of the fourteen kothis will act according to his orders.

(L.8) The eight dathiye - collectors of grain received in levy- they will also remain under the authority of the Daroga. They will also come–to Kullu- with him [Daroga].

(L.9) The Bhari [carriers, the forced labourers] will also pay [attendance] before him while coming and going.

(L.10 & 11) The Vazir [Minister] in charge of Lahul, Kripa Ram Sardar and Ramdhan and their pupils will also correct their records according to this order. (L. 12) They may direct the dathiyas also to work under the Daroga. (L.13) They should also provide him (Daroga) with bhari.

It was written on the 7th of Ashadh in the year 36, (accordingly C.E. 1760) by order [of the king] in his presence.

(L.14 to 17) It was written at Raghunathpur that the Daroga will bring alongwith him 23 horse-riders, two kettledrums [with players], two professional singers and dancers (hesi), two men of Baltistan (balti), one rayaya hatyela(?) and two–players with-trumpets –narsinga- (nashan) on the occasion of Vijay Dashmi,

Dussehra, before the tent -of Raghunathji- in the ground in Dhalpur, opposite to Sultanpur.

(L. 18 & 19) The Honourable [Daroga] has been requested that the two Thakars have been exempted from appearance for attendance before him. On the day on which the two of them will come to offer ponies to the Thakur at Dhalpur, Daroga will also offer ponies on this day. On this day the Honourable will also present stick (Chhaḷī) on their behalf. All the three getting together headed by the Daroga will come on the day of Dussehra to pay attendance.

Note:

i. **The Document:** The present document is a copy of a document issued in 1760 by Raja Tedhi Singh of Kullu (1742-1767) to the Thakars of Gondhla, Lahul. The document was re-written and attested in the court of Assistant Commissioner, Kullu, in 1849. It is written in Tankri script and is principally in Kangri-Mandyali language.

According to the document Raja Tedhi Singh issued orders appointing the Thakars of Gondhla as Daroga, Superintendent, of whole of Lahul which constituted fourteen kothis, excluding Chamba-Lahul. The name of the Thakar in the document is given as Rupchand-Sevadas from which it appears that the name denotes one person. Practically they were two brothers. Rupchand was elder and Sevadas was younger. This fact is corroborated from other documents from the same family. They also had Bhoti names. According to the document by Bilchung below (b.iv), Sevadas died in the same year in 1760.

ii. **The Body of the Document:** Whole text of the document can be divided into three sections. The first section containing the main subject, or the original subject, of appointment of the Daroga ends at line 13. The concluding sentence makes the closing statement by mentioning the authority under whom the order was issued and then it gives the name of the place and date of construction of the instrument.

In the second part of the text, lines 14-17, it directs the Daroga to bring certain objects during the time of his attendance in the

Dussehra festival for inclusion in the performance of the mela. The figure of 23 horse-riders looks odd. Jhabe Ram [an informed local person tells that earlier Polo game was played in Kullu during Dussehra. We have no knowledge if it was played in Lahul. But the Thakars have been directed to bring 23 (aswār) horse-riders, which may be interpreted as horses with riders. According to Jhabe Ram it forms two teams (11 x 2 + 1 = 23), with one spare. The game used to be played at Dhalpur, at the upper part of the lower ground between the existing main road and D.C. office, where the *rath* of Ragunath is kept for seven days during Dussehra till 1948-49 which he had witnessed himself while he was still a child. According to him the players were not local and there also played a team of European players.

The subject in the third section, lines 18 to 23, highlights the relationship of the Daroga with the other Thakars, in the changed situation who have been made subject to him.

***iii.* Appellations and Designations:**

The name Lahul: The term Lahul is written in the document as Lāūḷa. It is colloquially pronounced in Kulluvi till today in the same manner.

The Thakur and Thakars: Here in the document the term Thakar has two connotations. Raghunath, the chief deity of Kullu, resident at Sultanpur, in the local usage is addressed as Thakar. The ruling chiefs of Lahul are also called Thakar. Here the two subjects have been differentiated by using the term Thakur for Raghunath.

Vazir: During this time one of the Ministers, Vazir, of the Raja, was assigned the charge of Lahul. He was also designated as Lahula Vazir, Vazir of Lahul.

Cela: The term in the context is difficult to understand. Jhabe Ram tells that Mahants and Vairagis, who might have been Ministers here, did not marry and their assets were inherited by their adopted pupils, who were known as 'cela'.

Chhari (Chhaḷī): Chhari literally means stick. Raghunath and every devata in Kullu possess sticks about slightly longer than a meter coated with artistically worked silver foil. It is one of the symbols of the devata.

iv. The officials referred to in the document are: Daroga, Batugru, Kāmdār, Daṭhiya and Bhāri.

v. **Presents:** All the three Thakars of Lahul were required to present gūṅṭh, ponies, to Thakur, i.e. Raghunath, on the occasion of Dussehra.

Two important developments took place at the moment. Firstly whole of Lahul was brought under the authority of a single local ruling family. This is the only known moment of such an instance in the history of Lahul. We don't know whether this system was introduced at all, if yes how long it remained in practice. Secondly, the Gondhla Thakurs changed the tenor of their pedigree by adopting the Hindi names with surname of Chand, starting from Rupchand. This continued till the last.

The text in Tankri has been read and translated with the help from Khub Ram Khushdil. Further valuable clarifications and suggestions were received from Jhabe Ram and Hira Lal Panthla. I am thankful to them all.

b. iv. Tinan Khar, Gundhla–Sultanpur document written by Bilchhung of Barbog Khar, c. C.E. 1900.

This document consists of two parts: 1. Genealogical list of the Thakurs of Gundhla, and 2. Land Record of their territory.

Section 1 : Genealogical list of the Thakurs of Gundhla.

Title: According to oral information and sample number 2, regarding the land of the Garpana, the Chief Landlord, kothi Gundhla, the area of Gundhla.

Ra-tana-pala.

rDo-rje-pala.

Nima-pala.

Nag rGyal-po. Caste Thakur,

Clan Gu-ram Shing-pa.

So-rnam Pala-de.

So-rnam rGya-tsho.

i. Krashis Gyal-po (died).

ii. Tshe-ring Gyal-po.

Krashis Pala-byor.

Pa-ri Kh'a.

Bhag Man-ta.

Ha-ri-a.

Pal-bar.

i. Chhe-rds'a' On-po.

ii. Tshe-ring Nam-gyal.

iii. To-dug rNam-gyal.

iv. Tshe-ring Gyal-tshan.

Tshe-ring l Dar-gye.

i. Rub-cand'da. ii. Se-ba 'Das (died).

Bhag Chan-'da.

l Dar-ma Chanda-'da.

i. Du-mo-dar Chan-da (died). Hir Chan-'da.

Gyan Chand (Dsyan Chand).

At the end of this part of the document on the right corner is written in Urdu giving the date of birth of Thakur Hira (Hir) Chand as June 5, 1852.

Section 2 : Land Record of territory of the Thakurs of Gundhla.

It is a long sheet of local hand made paper spreading in breadth one page and in length about ten pages with the matter in seven columns written in cursive Bhoti. The column headings were first prepared in Urdu and then were scripted in Bhoti, without translation. Of this the first page comprises the genealogical list, the part 1 as given above.

This part contains simply the land record of the cultivable land situated in whole Tinan valley comprising three kothis. The column heads of this part is difficult to read and also to decipher meaning. The author of the document was Bilchhung, Nono, the young Thakur of Barbog.

Gundhla Khar was the sole and direct owner of the lands in whole valley of Tinan. There is no mention of any kind of revenue cess collected.

Column heads from left to right with the meaning or explanation:

1. nai mal-k. [= nām mālik]. Name of the owner.
2. nai T-khra-yi-y-j-gir jo ji-min kh-t-hi. mi si–mat-phid m. [nām T-khrayiy jo jagir khatahai mi si–mat-phid m.] Name who enjoys the jagir.
3. nai b-r kh-s-ri-b naikh s rikyi s g 'u k hi. Name of the Area.
4. naiphyog-ma. [phyog = mchhog?=good.]. Name of [good] land
5. nai rig-mi-t-ld-r-mun-tsi. nām rig [= land] x x mun-tsi [= small piece of land]. Name of small land.
6. rag-s-b-bh-h-sb-l-kh-s-b [rak-baba-hisab lakh s-b. = Area according to the rate of seed (s-b= sa-bon, Bhoti, seed) in the measure of lākh]. Area according to the amount of seed used measured in lakh.
7. kas-yi-phid-t. [kai-fi-yat]. Description or Detail.

First entry below the column heads as above, right to left:

1. Hir-chan-ldkhra-kur. Hari Chand Thakur. The same name is repeated throughout the document.
2. khud–kas-t. Self cultivated. The same statement repeated throughout the document.
3. gun-ld-l. Gundhla. This column contains the names of villages.
4. Li-kyir-chhog. The big or good fields named Likir(?). This column contains the names of fields of one kind, i.e. good.
5. Li-kir pi-ri. The small uncultivable parts round the fields named as Pi-ri. This column contains the names of fields of the same kind but of left out and of inferior quality.
6. 1/10 zhingsa-gon. 1/10 land seed [land requiring seed equal to 1/10]. This column contains the seed required.
7. This column is left blank from the first to end.

Below at the end of the long document is given as: This document was written by Audi and Bilchhung, Nono [young boy] of Barbog Thakurs, the two.

A brahmin of Sultanpur, Kullu.

Signed in Tankri, Urdu and Nagari by Roliya Ram.

c. Tinan Khar, Karchhags, Records, prepared at the time of celebration of the social functions in the household.

Below are given four documents constructed at the time of death ceremonies and some social functions at Tinan Khar. The records are unlike those read above because here the authors belong to a different class. As we understand by reading these four documents, they were constructed by the scribes who were literate in Bhoti script but were not formally trained and experienced like the monks. These writings are devoid of eulogies or the kind of ornate sentences.

c.i. Account of receipt of offerings at dge-rtsi, a death ceremony, at Nal-tse Khar Tinan c.C.E. 1860.

This is a Karchhag prepared on the death of certain member of the family. It makes no mention of the religious supports prepared at the moment like copying of books, etc. It records only receipt of the offerings and has no other kind of information. This also indicates to the cultural changes taking place. This is a critical point of socio-economic changes taking place. Some old traditions are seen here in their vanishing phase and others in the beginning. About one and half decades of the British period has passed till now.

Translation: White, auspicious, Ge-tsi. Account of the receipts in the 'White Ge-tsi of Tinan Nal-tse (Nas-zes) castle', family of:

Twelve taka from Barbog Khar. Singe Ram ten taka. From Yotar ten taka and ghee one togor. The Insider Nyukur one tsoli a-rag and one togor ghee. Tshering Tobdan of Yonsar a meat one limb and one tsoli a-rag. Phugtul Insider one bottle a-rag and one togor ghee. Tshering Dugge of Tilling six taka. Ram Buti four annas. Purad insider gave one tsoli arag and one sha lagpa. Namgang Tshering of Sumnam one rupee. Khar of Gungrang one tsoli of arag and sha lagpa. Srangbar-pa one tsoli of arag. The Lambardar from Gushal twelve taka. . . . .

Here some of the old items and the related terms have become obsolete.

i. Villages from where the guests had come.

sTod: Srang-bar and Dartse.

Punan: From the households of 'Bar-bog Khar and Gumrang Khar, and villages of Mangon and Kardang.

Pattan: Sumnam, Tholong, Gushal and Mooling.

Tinan: Yotar, Nyukur, Yonsar, Purad, Tilling, Tarkyum, Thorang, Gundhla Khyinang, Phugthal, Hurpa, Manepa, Yangkar, Ralling, Shooling, Srob, Khangsar, Sra-sren Jo, Shu-gu-pa, Jagle, Margyad, Yangkar and Khyang-tse.

Presents made in the ceremony

***a.* Articles:** Tsoli arag and sha lag-pa (6). Tsoli arag (4). Za-ma chhang and tsha-sha (2). Tsoli arag and togor mar (3). Tsoli arag and togor phe-mar (2). Za-ma chhang and togor mar (1). Tsoli and sha lag-pa (1). Tsoli arag and tsha-sha. (1). Bottle arag and one togor mar (1).

***b.* Currency:** One rupee (3), all three from Pattan. 4 anna (1). 16 taka (1). 12 taka (2). 10 taka and 1 togor mar (1). 10 taka (1). 9 taka (1). 8 taka (1). 6 taka (3). 5 taka (1). 4 taka and 1 paisa (1). 4 taka (4). 3 taka (1). 6 paine (= paise) (2). 5 Pai-na (2). 12 paise and one togor mar (1).

Note: We find that of the 48 contributors 21 gave offerings in traditional items, two gave mixed both an item and currency, and 25 persons gave their contributions in currency. Thus more than fifty percent of the guests preferred to give their contributions in the form of currency. They belonged to different geographical-cultural divisions of whole Lahul as Gahar = 4, sTod = 2, Pattan = 5 and Tinan = 29. Unspecified = 8. These 8 unspecified persons are individuals like a lama and not representing a household-family. From sTod out of 2 one gave cash and the other as traditional article.

Similarly in Gahar out of 4 it was fifty-fifty. In Pattan, which here is represented only the tip, out of five, four gave in currency and one in traditional items. In Tinan out of 29 ten persons gave in cash, two mixed both cash and article, and 17 gave in traditional articles which works out to more than fifty percent. All this shows a trend towards the monetization of the economy in Lahul. Prosperity and advancement is observed more in Pattan. Here two persons gave bottles. This is introduction of a new item in the culture of Lahul.

c.ii. Karchhag prepared on the occasion of celebration of a death ceremony, c. C.E. 1880-85.

Villages from where the guests had come :

Others: Tashi Tanphel, the renowned scholar and artist from Ladakh.

Punan: Gungrang Khar, Kardang, Kyelang, Beeling, Barbog, Bokar, Zholing, Labjang.

sTod: Khangsar Khar, Sarang.

Tinan: Sissu (Shashin), Srob, Yotar, Shooling, Tinan Khangsar, Tilling, Hurpa, Khoksar, Korpa, Murtitsa, Yangpa, Thorang, Tarkyum, Purad, Yosar, Khyimnang, Phugthal, Ranglo.

Articles received: Bheri chhang and 1 bottle arag. (1). Tsoli arag and sha lag-pa (3). Phyedpa chhang and togor ghee (1). Tsoli arag and phye-mar (1). Bottle arag and tsha-sha (2). Bottle arag. (4). Bottle arag and sha lagpa (2). Tsoli arag and 1 togor ghee (3). Bottle arag and one sha-brang (1). [brang = chest. phyedpa = half, pitcher.].

Currency: Rupee one (8). Half rupee or 8 annas (7).5 anna (1). 4 anna (11). 2 anna (3).

c. iii. sha-kan ki dha-nā. Offerings received at the Auspicious [ceremony], c. C.E. 1940.

Here a new phrase with new terms has been introduced for the kind of offerings as 'shagun kā dāna' (shagun ki dha-nā)= (gift of auspiciousness).

The guests came from the villages: Khyinang, Khangsar [Tinan], Gungrang Khar, Purad Outsider, Purad Insider, Purad

Dagthungpa, Gunla Tarkhyangpa, Gunla Insider, Gularkyi, Tilling, Yotar, Cheschhung, Sissu (Shashin) Thakur, Korapa of Gunla, Gungrang Khar Upper, Dolma, Peon (Chobrasi), Srobpa, Yosarpa, Barogpa, Gungrang Chechhung, Khangsar Khar (sTodpa Khar).

Offerings received: One rupee (12). Half rupee or eight annas (5). Four annas (7). Two annas (1).

c. iv. Tinan Khar Ge-tsi, c. C.E. 1950.

c. iv.i. sha-kan ki dha-na, c. C.E. 1950.

Register of tea (gSol-ja, hon.): One rupee each from Tanzin Rabgye of Khyinang; Khangsarpa [Tinan]; Tagthumpa of Purad; Purad Insider; Purad Outsider; Sonam Tanzin of Tilling; and Younger sister from Shashin. Half rupee from Sona of Kyelang. One rupee (7). Half rupee (1).

c.iv.ii. *bartana.* Receipts of Exchange, c. C.E. 1950.

Bartana: Here a new term of Hindi has been introduced in the social dealings as *bartana*. The word literally means utensil. Here it means exchange. It means the contribution received from a kin or friend like on the occasion of marriage notionally has to be returned to the extent of equal in amount or value. The term comes from Kullu with the same connotation.

The Relatives came from the villages of:

Pattan: Jahlma, Kirting.

Gahar: Kyelang, Barog, Kardang.

sTod: sTodpa Khar, Zhis, Kolong Khar.

Tinan: Shashin, Purad, Gyera Thang, Nyukur, Srob, Ralling.

Offerings received: 5 rupees [1]. 4 rupees [1]. 3rupees [2]. 2 rupees [1]. 1 rupee: [13]. Half rupee [1]. One anna: [1].

Note: The name of Kolong Khar alongwith that of Khangsar Khar appears here for the first time.

These documents throw light on the trend and evolution of cultural and economic systems taking place in Lahul. Introduction of coins and currency, bottles and new terms in social dealings like shagun, bartan, etc. are examples.

In Lahul all the households in a village have names. On division the two may be named, according to the position of location of residence of the family, separately as insider and outsider; upper and lower; or of this side and the other. Thus Puradpa Nangma and Purdpa Phyima are Purdapa insider and Purdpa outsider.

d. gZungs-yig, dharni formulas

The residential building of the Thakurs of Tinan Khar were built in two differennt traditions. The one built in the local style of Lahul was first built by Dorje Pala of the family and was named Nal-ze which later on came to be written as Nal-tse. It was demolished partly in around 1973. It has now disappeared completely.

In it was found an earthen pot called gzungs-rdsa, ḍhāraṇī pot, a pot, of a capacity of about two-three litres. It was filled with grains of Ne (local huskless barley), shugpa (leaves of juniper) and kindney-beans (moong dal), etc. and some kinds of precious materials. The precious materials were pearls, coral, turquise and a piece of gold or some item of mixed metals.The grains of pearl were thin and small like the seeds of *til*, sesame, not usable for necklace. So were all the samples of precious materials. The vase was painted from outside in vermillion colour. Eight auspicious signs were painted around the middle in white colour. At the bottom were painted lotus petals all around.

In the pot were also found two narrow and long stripes of paper on one of which was written a formula and on the other a prayer. The same two prayers were found inscribed on stones at two different places on the wayside between Margul and Triloknath.

d.i. The first part, the mantra, which possibly is a quotation from some literary work, is incomplete. It is wholly in Sanskrit language written in Bhoti script.

d.ii. The second part is a prayer which follows the folk tradition and does not carry impression of the Doctrine.

Translation: May all our wishes be fulfilled. May we with all our members of the family be granted wealth, offsprings and prosperity. May there be blessings of the gods of the country and of the Manor.

4 sTod, Upper Bhaga Valley

i. Gonpa monasteries

a. Chhu-ku-tsi (Chhos-sku-tse) Gonpa, Khangsar.

The Chhukutsi Gonpa, monastery, is situated in the village Khangsar. Presently it is managed by Gemur gonpa. There were found three books in the monastery. One is Padma Kathang, the other one is mDo-mangs and the third could not be known. Main part of the book of Kathang is missing. The other two books are in much worse condition. Evidently the books had come from Zanskar.

There were found two documents with two different books, in the form of Karchhag, both concerning Zanksar. Of Kathang there is found the pre-title sheet and another sheet attached to it which is karchhag.

a.i. Padma Thangyig, bDe-mchhog rNam-rgyal, king of Zanskar, c. fourth quarter of 17th century C.E.

The page before the title page is decorated with the paintings of five figures with their names given below them. From left these are: Chhos-sku kun-tu bzang-po (Samantabhadra), Man-dha'r-ba, dBu-rgyan (Urgyan) padma, Ye-shes Tsho-rgyal and Chhos-sku sNang-ba mTha'-yas (Amitabh). The two great Bodhisattvas are in the aspect of Chhos-sku, Dharmakaya. This is another attempt to give ground to the name of the monastery. Chhos-sku-tse is its literary name. Its folk form is Chhu-ku-tsi. There are two households of the name Chhu-ku-tsi, divided from one, located near the monastery. One of them is the caretaker of the monastery.

In the centre in the picture Guru Rinpochhe, Padmasambhava, is sitting on a lotus throne. Left palm is open and rests on the lap in the centre. The right hand is on the chest in preaching aspect. He wears a single cotton cloth and a cap much like those worn by the lamas on ceremonial occasions called in Lahul as sgom-zhva. He has no other object of symbol. The ear rings are large. All the five figures have halo round their heads.

There is another sheet, in one page of it is given the occasion on which the book was copied and on the other side is given the story of origin of the book. The written part of this second page is framed in by another sheet and pasted around it. This signifies the importance of the matter given here.

Translation: In the west of the white snowy mountain Tise, where the Arhats inhabit, and on the left side of the slowly flowing river Sindhu, is situated in the centre of the earth the country of Zanskar where the Law of the Doctrine has spread. Here at Padum, situated at a high place, an eruption on the earth, where the king shines with the lustre of prosperity.

Hello! While the crown of the great religious king bDe-mchhog rNam-rgyal is held high and his kingdom is expanding, the prince, son of god, and the excellent mother, the Queen, the two are adorned with the three kinds of knowledge of the Doctrine. She possesses the treasure of discourse of the core of the secret path. We adore Khri Rgyal-mo possessing such a powerful mind. This region is under her good rule. The mountain on the backside is like the heap of precious jewels. In the front it is like the lake of turquoise slipping down from the sky. On the sides there flow many streams of water from the springs. At the head (of the valley) is situated the well developed great holy place of Kanika. In the happy village of Sa-ni there is assembled the ten virtues. Having amassed the merits in the former lives the impurities of the man has been removed and has received the blessings of purity. We adore the Excellent Doctrine with ten fortunes. The origin of lineage of the parents is from the clan of Kab-chhar. Dolma Dondub and the sons Dolma Paljol and Ngagwang Tson-drus, the three for the return of the kindness of the kind parents, for removing their own sins totally, and for the benefit of the six kinds of beings that they may get the path of liberation, the well developed work of Padma Kathang of the Excellent Doctrine was raised.

Beautiful! The faithful lady donor Tshewang Ghuru Buthid the two mixed the elixir of the gods in the meals of men. The enumeration of the presents received for the discourse is as under: Lama Dorje Zin-pa gave three chhang. (There are others who presented chhang and some others gave chhang and gifts).

b: Guru Sangs-rgyasg Ling-pa brought the larger form of the Namthar of Urgyan Guru Padmasambhava, the so called Golden Rosary, from the cracks of the rock called Shel (Crystal Rock), the treasury of the great cave of Jari (bya-ri = Bird Mount). Others could prepare none like this. This was made the original. There are different kinds of fifty-five kinds of Namthar of Urgyan Rinpochhe, besides that of Mandarva, Akashgarbha and Ye-shes Tsho-rgyal, etc. Moreover there are many legends. It is heard that a new book has become famous in bLo-bo and in the valley of Shangs but it has not reached us. There are different books famous in different areas. According to some responsible people there are three kinds of the Namthar - large, medium and short. The readers may see and examine themselves. This inexhaustible larger rendition of the Namthar composed by the great uncles and ministers begins here. May the virtues and happiness spread!

a.ii. mDo-mangs, Zanskar, king dBang-chhug rNam-rgyal, first quarter of eighteenth century C.E.

On the west of white snowy Tise (Kailash), the king of the mountains, and on the left side of the river Sindhu, as it falls gently and flows, on its left, is situated the country of Zanskar, the well developed religious country.

At Padum situated high, an eruption on the earth, resides the great king dBang (ang)-chhug rNam-rgyal, whose crown is held high and the kingdom is expanding. Under his good rule is the excellent pilgrimage place of bZang-gling Phugthal. Rinchhen Chhos bZang, the great mKhanpo, while his crown of the Doctrine is held high, is present here at Ang-mu-ru, the prosperous place where the ten virtues have gathered. The origin of the clan and lineage of the forefathers, the mantradharas, holders of the mantras, is 'Ug-pa. Hello! The faithful donor Dorje Tshering and Kachupa and Ka bTashi....

The wise and heroic lady, as if supernatural, mixed the god's elixir in the meal of men. The objects of worship, the presents, brought by the guests are wonderful.

The Lady donor Guru Buthid, and grandmother bLo-bzang 'Dsom-pa, for the fulfilment of the wishes of the father and uncle, for removing own dirt of sins, and for the benefit of the falling six kinds of beings, as a support of the body the statues of the Buddha, Manjushri and Tsongkhapa were raised, and for the support of the voice the book of mDo-mangs was raised. Everyone praises the accumulated merit. They consider that there is no essence in the illusory wealth. E-ma-ho! As a result of the amassed virtues in the former lives we received the Excellent Doctrine. Below is given the list of the guests who brought the auspicious presents in the sermon. The Manager (gnyer-pa) of monastery of (bLa-brang) of Phugthal gave four chhang and effigy of dough (gran-rgyas).

The guests were: The Manager of the monastery (bLa-brang) of Phugthal; bLob-dpon of Mune; grung-pa; dge-slong; Grub-chhung of Mune; Onpo of Shila-gnas; Grong-dpon of Da-ru Gnas; Mdor-zong 'On-po; Khar-pa from Cha-'a; ga-g'an Gag Chhos-'bel from sTes-ta Khar. Mon-mo Tshering, the lady perhaps from Pangi, Ka-bchu-pa.

The guests offering the presents had come from the villages: [Mune, Kha-sar, Sani, Shila, 'I-chhar, Mdor-zong, Cha-'a, Phug-thal, Shun, Yil (gYil), sTes-ta Khar, Ghu-ru, Grang-ze, Kar-rgyag, Surla and Snyu-ru.

The kinds of presents and their measures are as follows:

1 Chhang (13). 1 Chhang and rten (3). 2 Chhang (7). 2 Chhang and an article (rten) (29). 3 Chhang (2). 3 Chang and rten (6). 3 Chhang, a jug (chhab-rkyen) and rten (1). 4 Chhang and grang-rgyas, ball of tsampa (2). Paper 1 load (ḍag). Paper 2 loads (grag) (2). 3 Chhang prepared with the yeast of Phab (Phab-chhang mtshod gsum) (1). 1 Thung, drink, measured 1bre (Thung bre gang) (1). 1 Sbyor tea (1). 1 Meat (1).

Note: The measures of chhang in number and rten cannot be explained. From the second part of the name rNam-rgyal of the ruler of Padum it may be presumed to have had connection with the family of the kings of Ladakh.

b. Gemur Gonpa, Gemur (Gyemur).

b.i. Fresh site for construction of the monastery of gSam-btan Chhos-gling, Gemur gonpa, c. C.E. 1887.

This document was obtained from the family of Tanzin Paldan, of the eighteenth century, of village 'Bog, the household named Gemurpa, whose statue with the inscription of his name is found placed in the Gemur monastery. It was written by Tashi Tanphel in C.E. 1887.

Translation: The site for the construction of the monastery named bSam-gtan Chhos-gling has been selected at the source of water. It has been demarcated and the boundary pillars have been raised by the important, annual and regular caretakers. The land from this place, the point of source of the water, down upto the original land, the land which is being cultivated, should be irrigated intensively. As much as water is given here, it will be beneficial in the long run for the [construction of the] monastery. Brother Gelong, the monk, has been advised to irrigate in order to convert the land and making it capable of constructing the monastery over it. As he will irrigate the land it will get changed with good growth of grass. He will keep on doing so till he remains healthy and fit, untill he becomes too old. Anybody may remain caretaker of this common crop of grass. It should be left as it is. No turn of the villagers should be fixed for looking after and regular irrigation of the grassland. This document was written by Tashi Tanphel on 22nd day of the 6th month, year fire-pig, of 15th cycle [= C.E. 1887].

b.ii. There is a book entitled: *grub dbang shvamonatha'i khrungs-rabs rnamthar gsol-'debs dpag bsam khri shing bzhugso.* "The so called wish fulfilling Tree, the prayer for the Birth Story and Namthar of Shyamonath, Lord of the Siddhas."

Note: sTag-tshang Raspa received the name Śyāmanātha during his visit to Uddyana. At the monastery at Gemur one day in a year the said book is recited in honour of the Teacher.

Translation: This prayer, so-called wish fulfilling Tree, for the Birth Story and Namthar, of the virtuous Teacher, god of the siddhas, Nawang Gyatsho Uddiyanpa, on the initiation of the great monk Nawang Kargyud Gyatsho, was completed by the good friend Nawang Kargyud Gyatsho at Hemis Jangchhub Ling. Moreover the monks of Hemis like the disciples of Nawang Gedun Kyabgon thought that a small prayer to the Namthar of the above named Rinpoche, sTag Tshang Raspa should be composed. I undertook the task. Sonam of the Hemis gave the expenses. Tashi Tanphel, the monk of Hemis, happy to write and engrave, accomplished the task.

b.iii. There is another book similar to the above. The following is the colophon to the same.

Translation: This work of multiplication [engraving the wood block prints] of the work was the thought of Tashi Tanphel. He wrote it and corrected himself. Wangchhug Jordan did the work of engraving. Thinley Kunzang was the chief scribe. Others were Kargyud Rigzin Konchhog Zodpa and Paldan Dondub Tanzin Chhosphel. Those reciting the scriptures were the nuns Chhoskyid Dolma Yangchan and Tshering Buthid Chhoskyid. Chhos-zin Wangmo was also among them. The peripheral works were done by Rinchhen Seng-ge. The work was accomplished at Santan Chhosling in Lahul. The flag of virtue of this task of the Doctrine may fly in the ten directions and may get the stage of the Sambuddha soon.

Note: A handwritten sentence in the book at the end of it writes, "This work of the 'Birth Story' was dictated by sKyab-rje mYang-skyid sPrul Rinpochhe."

It has no date. The block was prepared in around C.E. 1880.

ii. Karchhags.

a. Household of Tengkhang (sTen-khang), village Khangsar. Tashi Wangyal and his son Tashi Wangdag, the Thakurs of Khangsar; Raja Pritam Singh (1767-1806) and his son Bikram Singh, c. C.E. 1790.

Translation: Aum svadhi sidham!

I salute bowing down to the three Excellent Ones. The Revealer Buddha, chief among the human beings; the spotless Protector, the Excellent Doctrine and; the Arya Sangh, excellent among the assemblies, by the Body, Voice and Heart. I bow to the lineage of the root teachers, whose knowledge of the Doctrine spread reaching the expanse of the sky. The kindness of love spreads like the light of the Sun and the Moon.

The web of the external world is supported by the wind. Over it is set the sphere of the water. Over it is set up the three cornered sphere of fire. Over it is set up the four cornered sphere of the earth. The Meru mountain of the hierarchy of originations was founded like this. The lotus was born well on them like a jewel. The internal world of the beings originated from the god Abhasvara. Externally the snowy Tise (Kailash) is the living place of the Arhats. There is also situated the incomparable palace of Chakrasamvara. This is the holy place where the beings obtain the armour for removal of the sins. The obscurities of sins and impurities are all washed without any remainder. The chief lake, Turquise lake, Lake Mapang, lake of bathing has been founded. This is the head of the four rivers having eight heads. The mountain Dril-bu-ri is connected with the Tise by the unbroken chain of mountains. The mountain Gandhola is a place prophesied by the Jinas. This is the wonderful place of gathering of the dPa'-bo and dPa'-mo, the Heroes and Heroines, of the Doctrine. In the interior of the valley resides the Guardian goddess Paldan Lhamo (Lhamo), riding a mare. She is wonderful guardian of the Doctrine subduing those leading to the opposite Doctrines. At the end of the valley at the nail of hand resides Vajravarahi. This is the wonderful place of meeting of the Proginators and Dakinis. In the middle of the valley resides Arya Avalokiteśvara, the liberator of the six kinds of living beings.

Lahul the Land of Dakinis, is wonderfully prosperous land. The high palace of Sultanpur (sur-tan-pu-ri) is an eruption on the earth. The king conquers foreign enemies and protects his subjects like his own sons and servants. The great righteous king Pritam Singh (Pir-tim-seng-ge) and his son named Vikram Singh (bhir-kim ra-rji seng-ge), father and son, holding the crown high may their kingdom expand. Hello!

At the self-born incomparably great house, Khangsar, (in the village of Khangsar), there live the great righteous minister Tashi Wangyal (bkra-shis dbang-rgyal) and his son Tashi Wangdag, (bkra-shis dbang-drag) father and son. May their lotus feet become steady and may their kingdom expand. Hello!

Having the bestowing (byin-rlabs) sprouted from the soil, here at the house of happiness, the house named sTeng-khang, here lives the family of the origin of the lineage, of the clan named 'bru-sha. The donor Phrinle bsTan-skyong and lady donor Tshering Angmo, the two mixed ambrosia of the gods in the meal of men. They are pleased to give offerings in worship to the Three Jewels and in bestowing gifts. The excellent sons Phagspa Tharchhen, Tshering Sonam Tanzin and Urgyan Kunga Tashi, and daughter-in-law Sonam Lagszom, and excellent daughters Padma Chhoskyid and Sonam Chhonzom, they offered gifts wonderfully for amassing the merits.

For the favour of the deceased Tashi Paljor, for support of the voice, na-rag skang bshags and narag dong-sprugs, the two works, were raised, copied. For the support of the body the images of Rigzin Tshe-dbang Norbu, Gyur-med Yung-'brug Dam-chhos-Nyi-ma of the lineage of rGyal-dbang 'Brug Padma-dKarpo (pad-dkar), prince Bhilbar Dorje, Tshering - the five brothers, and the three mGonpo brothers, were constructed.

For the support of voice: Na-rag sgang shags and Narag dong sprugs were copied. For the support of the heart Jangchhub Chhor-ten was raised. Reverence to the Idols, books and the Teachers.

The account of the offerings received is enumerated as under:

In the beginning Ga-ga bKrashi dBang-rgyal and Tshe-dbang dYangs-skyid the two from the Khar (Khangsar Khar) gave meal, tea and chhang. More from the Khar: one pitcher of chhang and one tsha-sha. The old man Grubpa from Gemur (rKe-mur) gave tea and a meal. Ga-ga Kargyud gave tea and cakes (roti). Sonam Zangmo from the house Bung-nad (gZhis) gave one tea.

The following gave chhang one mas-ta (pitcher) and meat a lag-sha. Tshedbang Damchhos; Rinchhen from the house of Pang zhi (village gZhis); Urgyan Tshering from Sarang; Ga-ga gnyer-pa (of

Gemur gonpa?) from 'Bog (Phog); Padma from Chugtha (Pyukar); Tshewang from Tshar-zi; Mipham Chhozang; and Kyid Tshering from Srangbar.

Tshering Sandub gave one pitcher chhang and one tsha-sha. Rinchhen gave one chhang and tea. Old lady Sonam Buthid gave one tea. Palzang gave one pitcher chhang. Tanzin Wangchhug, the dBonpo from Sarang gave one pitcher chhang and one lag-sha. Drug Phuntsog from Kyelang one ja'u. Chhonzom of house of Gungrang from village Tinno gave one pitcher of chhang and tsha-sha. Tashi Gyamtsho of the house of Karpa gave one pitcher of chhang and lag-sha.

Title of the book with which the document was found: "na-raga ngan-song dong nas sprugs-pa'i chho-ga bshags 'bum rin-chhe spungs mdos na-mang bchu-bzhi bzhugs s-ho."

Note: The Raja of Kullu and the Thakur of Khangsar are here named both father and son together. The prince Vikram Singh (is here named as Bhir-kim Ra-rji Seng-ge. The document in the later part uses fully the local dialect. The present author is grateful to his ancestors for the document they have left.

b. Jispā (gZhi, gZhis) household of Melāg, Thakur Tara Chand of Khangsar, Raja Ajit Singh (1816-1841), c. C.E. 1840.

Translation: The number of holy places is innumerable. Drilbu Ri is like Tsari. This is ideal place of residence of dakinis, the tutelary deity. Gandhola is a holy place prophecied by the Jinas. During the time of lama Gragspa rGya-mtsho the doctrine of Dugpa sect is being followed and is held in high esteem. Three rivers join here at the great holy place through which passes the Mother Dakini. This is the ideal place of residence of the saint dakinis Kuluta and Maluta.

Lahul, full of green forests, is a joyous country. The well developed wish fulfilling jewel, the self-born 'Phagspa, was born really. I go to the refuge of the wonderful place where the Buddha of the three times lives.

The great Merciful One, Avalokiteśvara, kindly bestows continuously the blessings of light rays like lamps in the land of darkness. I go to the refuge of the land of the Perfect Buddha. In the interior of the valley resides Lhamo, the goddess, the flesh eater dakini, with attendants, riding a mule. There are other innumerable holy places. I go to the refuge of all these holy places also.

The capital (rgyal-khab) Sultanpur (gSul-'than-pur) is like a high place erupting from the earth. The religious King Jit (Ajit) Singh (dse-bde = Jit), his crown is held high and the kingdom is expanding. Hello! At the auspicious castle in the blessed Khangsar village, there resides the great religious minister Tara Chand (Taar Seng-ge), whose crown is held high and the kingdom is expanding, along with the mother (wife of Tara Chand, and their) son the three. Under his good rule is the auspicious and prosperous house of Kara Gongma (skar-sgo) in the village of Jispa of the well founded lineage of ga-pur kha-tir.

Thakur, the great scribe, appreciating the religious work and doing it like a legal duty is wonderful like a Bodhisattva, with the strong desire for amassing unlimited amount of merits. For the tradition of the root teachers coming from Tibet, and he himself generating desire to serve well, bowed thrice. Thus a task of virtue was accomplished as prophecied by the Jina. Doing the great task of emancipation is wonderful.

Tho-nu, such like faithful leader, for the fulfillment of his own wishes got the first page of the mDo-mang written in gold. There are nine great scribes who are the leaders of love. Nono De-chhog completed Kathang De-nga. Jampal Gyatsho completed Padma Thangyig; rDor-gchod five times; a person in two years completed mDo-sde five times.

Thus Tho-nu, being of religious minded and doing effort with great faith, the donations received for the sacred works, is enumerated as under. A sum of rupees six hundred and fifty was offered for the religious purpose without pride. Thonu did great effort......Amassing merits of virtue without tiring in this life for the next life, is great and wonderful.

The great scribe Mang-stabs, even though ignorant, took up the work of copying this book of mDo-mang in his hand. The learned ones had no leisure to attend to the work. The humble scribe did not follow the directives. But he did according to his own will even though having no word or books to copy from. Those looking carefully may not kindly scorn the scribe.

Summaries: The donors belonged to: Gung-rang mKhar, Khang-gsar mKhar, Shug-gling i.e. Tashi Shug-ling i.e. Sha-shur gonpa, Bog, sPrang-bar (Srang-bar), Sarang, gZhis, Tinno, Karing, gSumdo and Rangyo.

The kinds of offerings made were: Tea, chhang one pitcher, sha dal-mo, lag-sha, me-ta, one rupee, meal and rice four bre. The first page of this book, a volume of mDo, is written in gold ink. See: Upper Kolhuh, Jahlma, Pattan.

iii. Inscriptions

a. Khangsar (Kolong), inscription on manye stone, Manye-Ringmo, Srangbar, Khangsar c. C.E. 1800.

The [image of the] god is white, devoid of any fault and is adorned with the ornament of prosperity of the Sambuddha. He looks at the world with compassionate eyes. I bow to Avalokiteśvara. Lahul, the land of dakinis, is prosperous. Khangsar is a place erupted on the earth. The faithful donor Hod-zer, belonging to the clan having origin and expanded from the ancestors, for the support of the voice he got raised many hundreds of [manye inscriptions on stone?].

b. Gemur, inscription on stone, Raja Bikram Singh, (1806-1816), c. C.E. 1810.

Mount Gandhola is .... Drilbu Ri is wonderful. The river is like the Great River blessed by the Buddhas. This is possessed with everything needed like Tsari. If we look at the sky it looks like the wheel with eight spokes. ..... While the crown of the great king of Sultanpur Vikram Singh, is held high, Lahul, the land of dakinis, is prosperous.

c. Gemur Gonpa, Thakur Dharm Singh of Khangsar, c. C.E. 1820.

Dharam Singh, in the great palace at Khangsar, and the mother and son, while his crown is held high and the dominion is expanding, the Law of the ten virtues is being followed. The donor Dug Gya-tsho and lady donor Gan-zom, the two, son Tashi Samxx ... dBang and [daughter] Padma Buthid, the two, all the members of the family think of the virtues, the essence... did unlimited merits, specially they raised one thousand manye-stones [inscribed] and one hundred.

d. Gemur-'Bog, inscription on stone c. C.E. 1850

The king, the special palace, ...while reigning over the subjects. Removing the sins ... under his reign is the good village of 'Bog... ra and 'Brug-Tshewang, the two, their wife Tanzing-'da and younger sister Anu, the two, moreover a son named Tanzing Tshewang (Tsh...), with the strength of the virtues earned in the former lives and endeavouring limitlessly in this life also, for the sake of the next life, for the removal of all the sins, acted wonderfully.

iv. The Revenue Settlement Report of Kothi Kolong, 1868

The Regular Settlement of revenue in district Kangra of which Lahul formed a part was conducted by J.B. Lyall, Settlement Officer, District Kangra, from 1865 to 1872 and the report was published in 1874.

The task in Lahul was allowed to be done according to the administrative system existing there. British Lahul traditionally was administered in three manners. Pattan, the whole of Chandrabhaga valley, was directly ruled by the Raja of Kullu through an officer appointed by it and posted in Lahul. The Kothis, revenue circles, in Pattan were termed as Khalsa Kothi. Settlement of the area was done as was done in Kullu and similar other areas, of the district. Lyall writes, that the papers regarding administration for Khalsa kothis in Lahul were made on the same model as those for Kulu.

The valleys of Chandra and Bhaga were administered through the Thakurs, the Jagirdars, and the kothis were known in these areas as Jagir Kothis. The whole of Chandra valley was administered by the Thakurs of Gundhla. The arrangement of revenue collection from Gundhla by the Rajas of Kullu was slightly different. In tradition it was assumed that the Thakurs of Gundhla were a kind of shareholder and they paid half of the produce of his jagir area to the Raja.

Bhaga valley was administered in two parts. The Upper Bhaga valley, named as sTod, comprising Kothi Kolong, was administered by the Thakurs of Khangsar, Kolong. The lower part known as Punan, comprising three kothis, was administered by the Thakurs of Gungrang. These three Jagirdars were allowed by Lyall to accomplish the task in their own traditional manner. They were given guidance and also proforma for conducting the survey and preparation of the records.

The nature of the holdings in Tinan: Layall writes that, there are three jagir kothis in Lahul: Kolong (or sTod), Gungrang and Ghondhla. Of this last named territory a half was described in former Settlement papers as resumed. One of the last Rajas of Kulu did in fact resume half, but practically the whole remained undividedly in possession of the Thakur who accounted to the Raja for half his collections of all kinds. After Regular Settlement he continued in the same way to exact the old dues and services from all the landholders, and to pay the Government the land revenue for half the kothi, plus nazarana on account of the other half. The whole of his payments may be considered to have been of the nature of nazarana, (para 136, Lyall).

The document of Gundhla was prepared perhaps by some local persons and it is very brief. The Thakur was considered as the owner of all the fields. The list, although prepared on the lines of guidelines, contains the names of fields and some other data about the land. The farmers, the tillers, do not appear in the picture here at all. We have already dealt the subject above. The Thakurs of Khangsar had perhaps employed for the task a person trained in revenue administration. The document is very comprehensive. The document of Gungrang was also prepared perhaps on the same lines. Information from this document has been used by Lyall for the purpose of explanation, in his report. Below we give extracts from the report on Kolong.

Land Record of Kothi Kolong, according to the Settlement Report 1868.

Column Headings and their explanations: There are nine columns, the seventh is subdivided into five parts, thus there are thirteen in total. There is one entry for each household which is also known as family. It covers all the households in kothi Kolong.

1. **Khata i.e. Account number**: The serial numbers of the entries is assumed as khata, account, number of the concerned household.
2. **Name with father's name and detail:** Here is also given the name of class of the household like Thakar, Kanait, etc.
3. **Name of the Household**.
4. **Name of land as famous in kothi Kolong**: Here is given the class of household to which it belongs like Garpan, tax payer (khralpa), chhagshi, etc.
5. **Number of kila (acre, a term from Punjab), land**: Here is recorded the number of pieces of land owned by the household.
6. **Area of land as per custom as is in memory:** The size of land is measured in the quantity of seed applied. Here is given the total quantity of seed applied by the individuals in lakh and patha.
7. **Rent paid.**
   i. **Cash.**
   ii. **Makar (?) or blanket (phari).**
   iii. **Grain, barley (Ne).**
   iv. **Ghee.**
   v. **Rent for Watermill.**
8. **Tax or Local Rate as proposed in the Settlement of 1868:** This column is left blank in all cases.
9. **Notes or Remarks.**

Below are given some samples of statements contained in the remarks column.

1. He left the land after the Settlement. The Jagirdar cultivates himself. Three daughters of Chhering Norbu have been accepted as owners.

2. He serves as Khangchungpa. But after the Settlement he left his land. Jagirdar is himself cultivator.
3. He died issueless. The allottee has absconded. Jagirdar has given this to the holder of khata number 8.
4. He discarded the fields after Settlement. Jagirdar has allotted to khata holder no. 8.
5. He has one watermill. For this and for service of Dothi he pays rupees 21.6.00 cash yearly. Total Rs. 28/-.
6. In lieu of chhagshigpa service he pays rupees 9 cash. He cultivates khata no. 18 for which he pays one rupee separately.
7. In lieu of service of khangchung he pays Rs.6/- cash. For nautaur land he pays Rs. 3/-
8. He serves as khangchungpa. His holding has been recorded less.
9. He pays 5 rupees and a blanket separately and one person remains for service as Dothi with the Jagirdar.
10. Now he has become khangchungpa and serves as such.
11. During Settlement one *pau* (acre) of land was not written in his name. Corrected.
12. Blanket not entered.

There are remarks stating that lagan, i.e. cess has been assessed less, he owns land in excess. Some such remarks are given below:

1. Some farmers left their tillage. The land was then taken over by the Jagirdar and allotted to some other person on the payment of agreed amount of rent in the name of the jagirdar till some regular arrangement was done.
2. For service of Dothi one had to pay rupees 21.00 and 6 annas cash yearly.
3. In lieu of chhagshigpa service one paid yearly rupees 9.00 in cash.
4. In lieu of service of khangchungpa one paid rupees 6.00 in cash.

5. Some rates were enhanced after the Settlement.
6. There were some conditions which converted one into the class of Khangchungpa, meaning 'small house' i.e. 'small householder'.

Khangchungpa was an economic class. Chhagshigpa and Dothi were hereditary social classes, (Tobdan, 2021: 238-248).

The Deserters

There is observed general trend in deserting the cultivation of the land. Most probably it could be due to the high rate of cess. The number of deserters from different classes of the society were as:

Nautor = 5

Chhagshi =2

Thralpa = 7

Khangchung = 6. **Total – 20.**

Out of the twenty, two are partial deserters. They have left either nautor land or a cultivated piece of land. The deserters belong to all the classes of the society. But they make a class in themselves: they possess small land holdings.

Below is given classification of the households as different kinds of tax paying and non-taxpaying as revealed from the document, with their numbers.

1. Gharpanh, the Jagirdar – 1
2. Dothi= 3
3. Chhagshi = 6
4. Khangchung = 17
5. Thalpa = 35
6. Freeholds = 4+(1)
7. Nautor = 9

The Freeholds are: 1. Gharpanh, the Jagirdar. 2. The monastery of Gemur. 3. Zong Gonpa, the monastery of Tinno. 4. Kyelad bLa-zhing, i.e. the field of the temple of the folk deity in village Kyelad. 5. Gar-zhing (mGar-zhing), i.e. the field tilled by the smiths.

There are total number of 72 living households of which the two (Jagirdar and Garzhing) are freeholds and the rest are tax paying families. Thus the population of the Kothi at the time may be estimated with an average number of 5 persons per household as 360. In the report, however, the village of Karing is not included except one household.

Karing, although geographically and culturally is part of sTod. But for all administrative purposes it is included in Kothi Gumrang and it still continues to be so. One household named Hayarpa of the village had land in village Sarang, so it might have been included in kothi Kolong.

Below is given names of the households with the name of the village as they fell in the village. Traditionally each household has a name.

1. **Khangsar:** Khangsar (Thakur) Khar, Srangbarpa (now village), Tengkhangpa, Tengkhang Gongma, Chhukutsi Yogma and Tagpapa.
2. **Chhika:** Chhikapa 3 households.
3. **Rarig:** Rarigpa 7 households.
4. **Rangyo:** Rangyopa 3 households, and Rangyo Gongma.
5. **Lingkyum:** Lingkyum Gongma and Lingkyum Yogma,
6. **Sumdo:** Sumdopa.
7. **Jispa (gZhis):** Barma, Melagpa, Karagongma, Yarzhipa, Karayogma, Tholagpa (perished) and Pangzhipa.
8. **Gemur:** Bogpa Yogma, Bogpa Phyima, Bogpa Nangma, Bogpa Gongma, Gemur Nangma and Gemurpa.
9. **Meh:** Gonpapa (two households), Mepha Gonpapa, Mepha Gongma (3 households) and Mepha Yogma.
10. **Sarang:** Sarang Yogma, Barzhigpa, Sarang Pagpa, Sarangpa and Bangchepa (perished).
11. **Kyelad:** Kyelad Yogma and Kyelad Gongma
12. **Rangrig:** Rangrig Pharma and Rangrig Tshurma.
13. **Kolong:** Sharnapa, Karpa Gongma, Yargong Yogma, Kolong Tholagpa (perished), Yargong Gongma, Gongpa (not known), Kolang Pharma (not known) and Pangkharpa.

14. **Tinno:** Bokarpa, Sarkhag Yogma, Yolagpa Phyima (now Phyima), Yolagpa Nangma (now Nangma), Melagpa, Gumrangpa, Gonpapa, Thahapa, Kyelangpa, Hayarpa and Kyelang Garzhing.
15. **Karing:** Karing Hayar.

The total figures of revenue and other data:

Number of fields: 1185

Area of the fields: 1593 lakh, 2 patha. (One bigha of land requires seed of Ne or wheat about one khal or lakh).

Cash collected: Rs. 367-9-00

Blankets: 1

Makar **(?):** 221.

Grain **(Ne):** 31 lakh, 4 patha.

Ghee: 105 seer.

Rent for watermill: Rs. 11-00-00.

Movable assets like sheep, goat, ponies, cattle, etc. are not seen here in the account. The highest landholding with 67 lakh and 3 patha and paying annual rent of rupees 28-00-00 was the household of Pangzhipa of Jispa, a kind of Dothi family.

5 Punan (Gāhar), Lower Bhaga Valley

a. Household of Tharbas, Kyelang.

a.i. Household of Tharbas, Kyelang. Rana Prayota, Capital at village Kardang, and Raja Parbat Singh (1575-1608), c. C.E. 1590.

Translation: Aom swasti siddham! Lahul, possessed of the ten virtues and the two kinds of Laws [sacred and secular], is wonderful and this is the place of meeting of the Heroes and Heroines, of the Doctrine.

The religious king is wonderful. The crown of Parbat-Singh (Par-ba-ta Sing-gh), the Lord of the Himalaya, and his brother is held high. Pra-yo-ta is powerful like him. The two religious kings, the two rare ones, possess incomparable desire to protect the [subjects like their own] sons and servants. May there be auspiciousness! Wonderful!

Kardang, the capital, is the place grown high on the earth. The clan "Ra-na of Kardang" has origin from their ancestors. sKyab-tse, greatly courageous, is the host. He for the fulfilment of the wishes of his kind father [deceased] got raised the book rDo-rje gChod-pa, Vajrachhedika, larger and smaller vesions, of the deep and the well developed Doctrine.

Note:

i. This is the only document found in Lahul referring to Kardang as capital. There lived a ruling family of Rana and the existing Rana was named Pra-yo-ta. Presently no family is known as Rana living in Kardang. There is a household named Kyelye who say that they were earlier known as Rana. They play the leading role in the Losar, New Year Festival, of the village.

ii. The document does not make mention of the Thakur of Barbog or Gungrang or any other in Gahar.

iii. It enumerates the names of the kinsmen who joined the ceremony, with the name of their household and the village, but does not name the presents they offered.

a.ii. Tharbas, Kyelang. Raja Pritam Singh (1767-1806), c. C.E. 1790.

Dril-bu Ri is the great pilgrimage place which is connected in unbroken chain [of mountains with Tise]. The mount Gandhola has been prophesied by the Jinas. It is wonderful place where the Heroes and Heroines [of the Doctrine] meet. Obesience to the king Pritam Singh (sPri-tim Seng-ge) who resides at the well developed capital of Sultanpur (Su-stan-pu-ri).

Under his sway is the valley of Punan. At the well developed castle at Gungrang there live the Astrologer Tshe-dbang, the father, mother and the son, the three, obesience to them.

In the prosperous village of Lower Kyelang there resides Pho-tu, the donor, having good origin from the ancestors of the clan of Che-pa. His excellent son Domba Tshering and daughter-in-law 'Brug Zom Buthid, may they remain favourable towards the Doctrine like their ancestors. The grandson and grand-daughter, may their life be long, have no desease and have the blessings of prosperity. Pho-tu, the donor, for the sake of his deceased companion raised the rdo-rje gchod-pa. For the purification of the self from the sins he got raised Dri-med Kun-ldan, the Namthar, and Srong... Obesience to all.

b. Household of Thaas (Thāsa), Kyelang, Raja Pritam Singh (1767-1806), c. C.E. 1800.

The capital of Sultanpur (Sur-rtan-puri) is very famous in the world. There resides the great religious king Pritam Singh (Pir-rtim Singh-'ga'), his crown is held high and the kingdom is expanding. Here at Lower Kyelang, the joyous village, there resides Pal-bZang, the donor. In the lower side of the happy valley of Punan at Gung-Rang there resides No-no Tshe-dbang belonging to the prosperous country and unmistakably to Lonchhen clan. The two donors Pal-bZang and (his) younger brother Dug Samtan, the two [and the lady donor Phe-tse Kyan] got the Namthar of Mila Repa and of rGod Tshangpa raised.

Note: Here there are two books of Domang in the family. One of them is called Balti Domang, tells Nawang, the owner of the household. It was copied by a lama from Baltistan. Both the books contain karchhag and both mention the name of Raja Pritam Singh.

c. Shashur gonpa, Kyelang, Karchhag with Domang written wholly in gold ink, c. C.E. 1900.

Shashur: The place where the Shashur gonpa is situated is known as Shashur. It lies about two kms. and by vehicle 5 kms., above Kyelang, the district head quarters.

Shashur Gonpa: The monastery of Shashur is commonly known as 'Shashur Gonpa' and in the literature as Tashi Shug-ling (bKra-shis Shug-gling). The word 'Shug' in the phrase is translated as shug-pa i.e. juniper. Shug is sometimes also written as 'Shugs'. The monastery is situated amid the forest of juniper. It is also told that there were seen some remains of old structure.

The central statue of the gonpa is of bDe-bar Gya-mtsho, to the residents of Kyelang, according to Urgyan Tshering, is known as Gyalwa Gya-mtsho [rgyal-ba rgya-mtsho]. It is flanked by two statues of the Buddha, in its two different aspects as Shāk Thub-pa and Sangs-rgyasg Tsug-tor chani. Shakya Muni and the Buddha with the Crest, as is explained in the present document. It is told, and also apparent from the central place given to the statue of siddha, that bDe-bar Gya-mtsho was the founder of the monastery. He belonged to Zongkhul gonpa in Zanskar. We know that sTag-tshang Raspa met him there and he was served there while coming from Kishtwar in 1613-14. Thus the monastery was founded after 1615, the year of departure of sTag-tshang Raspa to Urgyan from Lahul. We may suppose it to have occurred in around C.E. 1620. Donyod Dorje writes that it was founded by Deba Gyamtsho in 1610.

mDo, the Book: The gonpa is in possession of a book entitled, "'phags-pa bskal-pa bzang-po zhes bya-ba theg-pa chhen-po'i mdo." In short it is known as "mDo-sde bsKal-bzang." It is vol. I of mDo-mang of 16 volumes. The book is wholly written in gold. It is heavy, said to be more than ten kilograms. Its paper is hand made locally. The surface of the paper is well smoothened, unlike those of the commonly found other books, and is coloured shining dark blue, with pink border lines.

Nawang Norbu Kukuji who belongs to Kyelang, is a learned person in Bhoti, whose father Lama Domba remained Umzad [dbu-mdsad], the Chief Lama, of this monastery, in around middle of the twentieth century for nine years, for three terms of three years each. He tells that 15 tolas of gold was used for the ink which was contributed by the lamas of the gonpa by donating their chhag-tse, ear-ring. It is told that the book was used to be read once in a year on the day of Dark Moon, of the second month of the Tibetan Calendar.

Karchhag: The book mDo-sde bsKal-bzang contains two Karchhags. The first is a separate document of six sheets which describes the whole process of preparation of the book and then records the contributions received and used for meeting the expenses solely for the purpose of preparation of the book and the related works. The karchhag has two parts. The size of the papers of the karchhag is equal to that of the main book but the letters are distinguishingly smaller.

The second karchhag forms part of the main book and is given at the end of the book in its last page. It is written in letters smaller in size than that of the main book, as is the tradition, to distinguish the subject. It gives description of the contributions received for celebration of dge-rtsi, the occasion of completion of the whole work.

Tshang Me-me: The person who gave birth and lead to the project and got it executed, is not named here expressly. Nawang Norbu Kukuji tells his name as 'Tshang Me-me' [Tshang the Elder] whose real name was Tshe-dbang. He belonged to the household named Tharbas located in Lower Kyelang. The first two documents as above come from the same household perhaps forming part of the collection of Tshang Meme. He studied at Zongkhul monastery in Zanskar. He held the position of Umzad of Shashur monastery, for about thirty years. He is said to have been having very beautiful handwriting. After him Meme Karpo of Barongpa household took over the post. On the basis of the circumstances mentioned above the work might have been completed close to around C.E. 1900. We have no direct evidence for proposing the period of execution of the work. His full name was Tshewang Rigzin (Tshe-dbang Rig-'dsin).

c.i. Shashur, Karchhg No. 1, section i

The Document: This document is entitled as 'dKar-chhags me-long kun-gsal zhes bya-ba,'- 'The Epilogue called the All Clear Mirror.' The first page forms the title and the last page is blank. We divide the whole content of the work into four sections as follows:

Page 1(b) contains eulogy, introduction and brief history of Buddhism, etc. This part has not been treated here.

Page 2(a) gives some information about the present work and is like an introduction. The text of this part has been given fully. Pp. 2(b) to 5(b) contain the list of the donors for the construction of the book and the statues, etc. The data in this part has been abstracted and is given analytically in tabular form. This is a long list of about 520 or more donors. The donors are mostly individuals, in addition to the households. It gives full description of the article and its quantity, offered. A few donors are named, as is the practice, with the name of their household and village. Almost half of the donors are women.

They come from all the social classes of the area viz. Thakur, the ruling Chief; mgar-ra, the smith; and the common people, the bulk part of the society. There are the office holders, both religious and secular. They come mostly from within Punan i.e. Gahar, but also from Manchhad, Zanskar, Jangthang, and Khunu [Kinnaur]. There are Khampa also. Contributions are also found made on behalf of the deceased persons.

The last page of the document contains a separate paragraph which first mentions some honourd guest donors from outside

Lahul and then it provides the details of items of expenditures. This has been given fully, the text and in translation.

This Karchhag mentions the local chief, the Thakur of Gungrang as Tshe-dbang.

Tshewang of Tharpa tshug-shi, Lower Kyelang, the same Tshang Meme, had engraved the Padma Thangyig from pp. 172-280 at Tayul with Tashi Tanphel from 1883-1885.

Translation: mNgari-skor-gsum is identified as the land of origin of dakinis. Lahul is pure land where the ten virtues have assembled. This land has been travelled by many scholars and siddhas like Urgyan Guru Padma and Mahasiddha Ghantapad. This is the place of the learned persons who hold the two forms of the Doctrine: the explanations and meditation.

This is the place filled with the teachers and siddhas belonging to the two schools, and the scholars and siddhas possessing knowledge of the five classes of science.

Here at the great Vihar of Tashi Shugs-ling (bKra-shi sShugs-gLing), while the Doctrine of the Buddha is growing and expanding, the well-wishing friends Tshewang Rigzin and Thinlye, the two, are encircled by many learned persons. As such they look like the Moon so charming as encircled by the stars. All [the knowledge] have converged in you and there is no rival. At Gungrang, the high erupted excellent place, No-no, the great religious Minister [Tshe]-dbang, at the time when his crown is held high and the territory is expanding, protects [Punan] wornderfully with the Laws of the ten virtues.

The scribes who have excelled in lettering are Sangs-rgyas Don-grub, gChepa, Tshe-dbang and Nor-bu. The four brethren with the dance of their fingers acted wonderfully.

Lama Tshe-ring, Tshe-dbang and 'Brug rDo-rje, the three put off their ear-rings [and gave in offering]. In this manner they acted as the chief initiators. Because of this the wealthy persons became donors.

In the beginning Ga-ga Tshe-dbang of the castle of Gung-rang gave gold worth rupees five. The bChes-ma, lady, dPal-'dsom gave one rupee.

Note: There are four scribes named in pair as: Sangs-rgyas and Don-grub, the two, and Tshe-dbang and Nor-bu, in all four. We know Dondub from the colophons of other works of the same period as a famous engraver of wood blocks for books. Tshe-dbang is the same the Chief executor of the project and his name comes below again.

Chhag-tse: Chhag-tse is name of an ear-ornament which used to be worn by men. It is in shape like the finger ring of gents, in weight one of the pair is equal to about half a tola or less. But it is generally heavy. It is simple in design and no precious stone is used in it. It is also noteworthy that monks generally don't wear any ornament. It was worn by the common people of my previous generation. I had pierced my ears for the purpose but were not used and they then got filled up.

Tshang Me-me, the Chief Executor of the Project: The Karchhag, describing the gonpa states that at the great Vihar of bKra-shi Shugs-gling there live two great monks, Kalyanmitra, well wishing friends, Tshe-dbang Rig-'dsin and Phrin-las, the two. Here the Chief Executor is named fully as Tshewang Rigzin (Tshe-dbang Rig-'dsin). Thinlye belonged to Beeling. Among the three chief lamas offering their ear-rings Tshang Me-me is named in the middle.

Below is given details of the kinds of the donations received and the number of the donors of the particular item and its quantity:

(a) Contributions received in Gold: Lamas gave rna-rgyan, one each (3). Gold to-ra 2 (1). Gold to-ra 1 (1). Of rupees 9 (1). Of rupee 1 and ja-'u(?) 1 (4). Of ja-'u 1 (1). Of rupees 8 (1). Of rupees 5 (1). Of Rupees 3 (1). Of rupees 2 (1). Of rupee 1 (17). Of rupee 1 and paisa 5 (1). Of anna 12 (1). Of anna 4 (1). Of rupee ½ (2).

(b) Contributions received in Currency:

i. **In Rupee:** Ja-'u(?) 1 (15). Rupees 4 (1). Rupees 3 and ½ (1). Rupees 2 (6). Rupee 1 and 1/2 (1). Rupee 1 and anna 4 (2). Rupee 1 (85). Rupee ½ (25).

ii. **Annas:** Anna 6 (5). Anna 4 (61). Anna 3 (1). Anna 2 (106). Anna 1 (56). Anna ½ (8).

iii. **Ta-ka:** Taka 1 (13). Taka ½ (1).

iv. **Paise:** Paise 11 (2). Paise 7 (2). Paise 6 (12). Paise 5 (10). Paise 4 (3). Paise 3 (18). Paise 2 (41). Paise 1 (8).

The Donors: Names of the households and the villages to which the donors belonged.

a. Names of households of Kyelang. **Upper Kyelang:** Bar-tsi, dKar-pa, A-ta, Lhag-'dzom.

Lower Kyelang: Rdos-sku-pa, Pa-na-zhi, Bha-rong, Bha-rong yog-ma, Khu-ku-zhi and mGar-ba (blacksmith).

b. **Other Villages:** Ga-ri-mas-pa, Gung-rang, sKyor, Yur-nad, Tho-pa Tsugs-shis, Yo-lag-pa of Gung-ling, Mi-ya-pa of Gus-kyar, sBho-kar, Chhe-ling, Pyu-kar (Pu-kar), Me-lag-pa of Gus-kyar, Pas-pa-rag, Bhar-bhog, Bhi-gling, sTeng-rig, Gho-bzang Gong, Zho-ling, dKar-dangs, Bhar-bhog, Char-tsi and Lhab-chang.

c. **Villages or households not Known:** Tha-ma, Yar-lag, Me-ya, Yo-rog, Tha-ha, Tha-ma Gong-ma, Thar-pa, Pang-lag, Yo-ba and Tho-ba.

d. **Other households:** Yo-ba-pa, Tho-lag, sTag-pa-pa, Yag-thog-pa, Tho-ba-pa, Tho-lag Gong-ma, Tho-lag 'Og-ma, Yo-rog, Me-ya-pa, Yor-rdzong-pa, Gu-ru-gzhi, Yar-pa, Tho-lag-pa, Ti-mor-pa.

Unknown: Pang-rong, bar-zhig-pa, Za-mi-gling bzhi. Some of these households appear to be from sTod.

Spiti: Ma-ṇīpā means the Bu-zhen (dbu-chhen) actor-players of Spiti.

Manchhad, Pattan: Tholong (mChhod), Garhang (ghar-pa), Yobrang (Jo-var-pa), Lindoor (gLing-'thud), Sum-nams, Hrob and Tandi [Tāṅtī].

Tinan: Shi-la.

Others: Jangthang, Khampa, Zanskar, villages of Ropa and Asarang of Kinnaur.

c.ii. Shashur Karchhag No.1, section ii

Below is given a part of this Karchhag-1 which is shown as a separate paragraph in the last. It mentions the contributions received from some honoured guests and then it provides items of expenditure and the amount.

Translation: dBang (Ang)-rgyal and 'Byor-dhasa, the two, of village Ropa (Ropag) of Kinnaur gave one to-ra of gold. Dharampura of village Asarang (Hasarang), of Kinnaur, gave one rupee. The above are the receipts.

Now here is given the account of the expenditure. Fifteen to-ra of gold was spent. Six rupees were spent on *ram*. One rupee was spent on *tshal,* colour. One rupee was spent for glegs-thag, strap. Rupees four were spent for chhab-ma, buckles. Rupees three and half were spent on the three pieces of cloths, for wrapping. The cover boards were prepared and carved by the carpenter Tshe-ring dBang (Yang)-'byor. This is the fruit of the efforts of Phun-tshogs bsTan-'dzin.

May see carefully. For the support of the body the images of Shakya Muni [and] Buddha with the crest [were got raised], may they protect all. For the support of the words was raised bskal-pa bzang-po'i mdo. Rin-chhen 'khor-lo [precious wheel = manye wheel ?], was constructed well for the first time.

c.iii. Shashur Karchhag, No. 1, section iii

This book of mDo-sde bsKal-pa bZang-po was damaged. Offerings were made by the two nuns dPal-li and Tshe-ring kLan (Kran)-'dsom of the two households of dKar-pa of the Upper Kyelang for meeting the expenditure of its repair.

iii. d. Shashur Karchhag No. 2

Translation: This is the account of receipt [of the contributions] for the celebration of Ge-rtsi, the occasion of completion of copying the work Do-de Kalpa Zangpo.

Gungrang, etc.: In the beginning Gaga Tshewang of village Gungrang gave one rupee. Kushog Padma Thinlye Dadul one rupee. Lama Tshewang Rigzin one rupee. Elder Geshe Abhi one meal, drink and one bottle of wine. Younger sister [of house] of Bartsi one pitcher of chhang. Anu [of house] of Bartsi one seer ghee.

Guskyar: The house of Meyapa of village Guskyar one meal and drink. House of Tagpapa one pitcher of tsag-mo.

Gungling: Yolagpa house one meal and drink. The house of Kyangtsi chhang, one small pitcher. The house of Tholag rice, one man's load.

Lower Kyelang: Norbu of the house of Phaylang of Lower Kyelang one meal and drink. The other house of Tha-ha one meal and drink. The house of Yo-rog one meal and drink. The house of the other Yolag meal. House of Dusku one meal and drink. Daughter-in-law [same household] one bottle of wine. House of Panaji one meal and drink. Tshang Chhonzom, daughter-in-law [same household] one pitcher of chhang. House of Barong one meal and drink. Zompa Tshering of the other house of Tha-ma one meal and drink. The other house of Tharpa one meal and drink. Pangla [= Panglag.] the divided lower house of] Barong one meal and drink. Ngodub one meal and drink. Kyamo, daughter-in-law, one pitcher of chhang. Dondub one small pitcher chhang. Tashi one meal and drink.

Upper Kyelang: From the Upper Kyelang the village chief, the senior, one meal and drink. The junior [village chief] one meal and drink. The house of Chutapa one meal and drink. Tshering of the house of Karpa one meal and drink.

Beeling: The house of Yurnadpa one meal. Tolo, the doctor, one tea. The Elder Tshering and Tshering Palzom, the two, one meal and drink.

Kardang: The village chief one pitcher of tsagmo. The house of Dangrapa one meal and drink. Norbu of the house of Abhi one meal and drink. Gulu of the house of Meya one meal and drink.

Chepa, the senior manager of the great monastery of Tashi Shug-ling [Shashur], one pitcher of chhang and one bottle of arag. Urgyan Tshering, the kon-nyer, and his younger wife, the two, one meal and drink. Bhomting, of the house of Yobapa of village Lapchang, half seer ghee.

Rupee 1 (2). Ghee ser 1 (1). Ghee ser ½ (1). Arag bottle 1 (1). Meal, drink, wine bottle 1 (1). Meal and drink 1 (14). Meal 1 (1). Tea 1 (1). Rice, man load (1). Chhang pitcher 1 (1). Tsag-mo pitcher 1 (2). Chhang, small pitcher 1 (1).

6 Ye-shu (Moravians) Inscriptions, c. C.E. 1900

a. Kyelang. This inscription was found in Kyelang inscribed on a boulder near the Mission house and now this rock has been broken for construction of a building at the site.

Translation: Ye-shu, the Lord, said: "Just as the others do good unto you, you too do like the same unto others."

b. Inscription below Baralacha Pass: This inscription was discovered by Ms. Elizabeth from Zingzing bar near Baralacha Pass.

Elizabeth writes, "...rock carving at Zingzingbar – a remote uninhabited place near the source of Bhaga River" and translates it as: "Jesus said, I am the resurrection and the life: he that believeth in me though he were dead yet he shall live, (St. John II, xxv)," (Elizabeth, A.S. 1991: 73).

c. From Beeling:

Translation: For the welfare of you all much wealth is needed. The wealth produced from the earth is consumed as soon as it is produced. The thieves also dig out from the earth to steal. Therefore you should save wealth in the sky, (courtesy Mangal Chand).

Part B - Areas Surrounding Lahul

7 Zanskar

a. Zanskar – Phugthal Boyig, Register of Phugthal, Chhukutsi (Chhos-sku-tse) gonpa, c. C.E. 1450.

Crook has given photograph of a piece of text from the Boyig from Phugthal monastery in Zanskar which relates to the monastery of Chhukutsi in Lahul, (Crook and Omaston, 1994: Pl. 80).

Translation: The king of Kullu offered ..... Zho-gling, Gye-mur, Tshan-dre-mos(?), the division of Gzhi (bZhi), the whole valley, from its head to the end, - upto the monastery of Chhukutsi.

Note: The incident occurred in around C.E. 1450. It indicates that the Gelug sect was founded in Lahul early in the time of Sherab Zangpo (1380-1457), born at Thigse in Ladak. Here the offerings made by the king of Kullu indicates that the upper part of Lahul, i.e. the whole of Bhaga valley was under the domination of the Raja of Kullu.

In this text the geographical places of Chhos-sku-tse, Zho-gling, Gemur and gZhi are known villages in the Bhaga valley.

Francke translates the same text as, "As an offering of the king of Ñuṅ-ti (Kulu) were given the region up to the Chos-sku-tse monastery; Žo-gliṅ on the narrow road, Gye-mur; Gre-gri-mos(?) and the upper and lower part of the Ži-bde valley," (Francke, 1926-2:160).

b. i. Zanskar, Decree by the King Nyima Namgryal (1694-1720) of Ladakh, C.E. 1701.

Translation: The present decree is addressed to all the Teachers, the men [common men], ministers, the eminent ones, village chiefs, the holders of managers' duties, managers of horses, and specially the Teacher-Managers of Phugdal [monastery], of the whole valley of Zanskar, from the inner head of the valley to the lower end. The [area of] khrang-nag Jo-mo Ras-cheng Dong-ri belongs since early times to the astrologer of Aen-mu.

The benefits of water and grass from the interiors of [the valley of] Surla had been harvested in common [by the astrologer and the public] since early times. This tradition should be maintained according to the former customs. Moreover whatever the Uncle [the Astrologer] has instructed should be followed.

The others should allow the tradition to continue, and none should say any bad words and should make no complaint. It is essential that the tradition of the turn for grazing the cattle [common pool of the cattle of all the villagers] had not fallen [on the astrologer] since old times for which the villagers envied and it is important that this custom should be maintained, like the junior astrologer and physician who are exempted from the turns for such kind of works.

It must be understood that if one does not consider these orders even by seeing the decree, he will be punished severely.

The solicitors [the makers of the document] are Sonam Lohundup and Kunga. It was issued on 25th day of 6th month of Iron-serpent year, from the mansion of pleasure, the great palace of Leh, (C.E. 1701), (Internet source).

b.ii. Zanskar. Decree by the King Tshe-dbangr Nam-rgyal (1753-1782) of Ladakh, C.E.1766.

Translation: This decree is addressed generally and specially, to all the inhabitants of the kingdom, those under the reign, the leaders of the class of the gods and men, the ministers, eminent ones, officers of the castle, village chiefs, chiefs among the inhabitants, and the holders of duty of manager; in short all those coming and going to diverse directions, the representatives and the spokesmen; small and great all.

The astrologer of Aen-mu had been religious manager of the chiefs of Padum from old times. They have been looked upon by Ladak and Padum with kindness ever since. The firm decree ordains that the Dong-ri of Jo-mo Ras-chhen has been looked upon by the chiefs of Ladak and Padum with kindness.

The benefits of harvest of water and grass from the interiors of the valley of Surla can be shared in common [by the astrologer and the other inhabitants] and, therefore like old traditions they [the people] need not go to Monyul [Padar, Pangi?] and Jangthang [for grazing their cattle]. The tradition should be maintained according to the contents of the earlier decrees.

The tradition [of paying the cess] of carrying of the harvested [fire]-wood, [supply of] ponies for carrying the grains to watermill, the turns for supplying beer and cattle, and [supply of] the required services of horses, all the items of revenue, to the astrologer and Namkha, in the lineage of father and son, should be maintained without difference of even of a hair's breadth. This decree has been issued for enforcement looking at them with kindness.

It will not be good for you, as stated above, to make any complaint, even to the extent of a hair's breadth, and it is essential that the tradition should be maintained. You must understand that whosoever does not follow this flawless decree will be pursued and punished severely.

The decree was issued in the year of fire-dog from the high palace of Leh, the capital, the really high place of the two traditions [of gods and men], (C.E. 1766). (Internet source).

Note: This decree was issued by Tshewang Namgyal (1760-1780), the king of Ladakh, in C.E. 1766.

8 Spiti (Piti)

i. Decree of Dechhog Namgyal, (sDe-mchhog rNam-rgyal) king of Zanskar and Spiti (c. 1642-1694), C.E. 1671.

This (decree) is addressed to our own subjects. The houses and fields of two households of Phi-ba sTud and dPang-byor, of village sTod-nam (in Pin) have been allocated (to the astrologer). The great prayer (festival of) Tshe-chu (tenth day of the first/fifth month, the day of birthday of Guru Padmasambhava) is being celebrated since the time of Urgyan (Padmasambhava). For the assembly of the monks of the sa-ngags snying-ma (monastery) the levy of mule, sheep and paper have been charged (from the other households).

All should bear in mind that anybody who defaults in the payment will be recovered from him without discrimination from the beginning. Kharpon (Castle Officer), Zongpon (Fort-officer), old men, the public, soldiers, the manager, the officer for the external tasks, hunters and other important persons of other villages, none will have any objection. It should be left undisturbed.

None will have any concern. Anybody doing so will be punished with the harsh thrashing. This order was issued on the 12th day of the 3rd month of iron-female-pig year at the great palace of Yang-mkhar-rtse (= Dankhar), (C.E. 1671).

Petitioner: mKhar-dPon, Nam-mkha' rGyal-mtshan.

ii. Documents, Ancient literary compositions, from Buchhens, Pin Valley, Relating to the marriage of king Srong-btsan sGam-po (569-650) of Tibet with the Chinese princess Kongjo.

The first document is the Royal Decree of king Srong-btsan sGampo. The second contains answers to the supposed three questions that would have been asked by the King of China from the Bridal party coming from Tibet. The party was sent by the king Srong-btsan sGampo to ask the hands of the princess of China as queen of Tibet. The wise minister mGar of the king guessed before hand the questions that would be asked by the king of China and he had prepared the answers before meeting with the king.

Translations:

a. Messages of Srong-btsan sGam-po, the King of Tibet, to the king of China c. C.E. 636:

Then, again, the Minister mGar went before the king and requested to order him to go to China and bring the princess. The king sent seven gold coins and told him to offer them as present. A cloak, studded with seven hundred precious stones and a jewel of *padmaraga,* was also sent. The king instructed that this may be presented as the gift of marriage. One *dre* full of gold grains was sent for miscellaneous expenditure. The king's instructions were collected in three different paper-rolls, and the minister was advised to present them one by one at appropriate moment. The king gave many articles of urgent need like clothes, ornaments, etc. loaded on camels and mules. The king bade to offer prayers day and night to goddess Tara on the way and wherever needed. mGar took whatever the king had sent. The minister together with one hundred horsemen set out at the auspicious moment on the 8th day of 4th month in fire-male-monkey year (C.E. 636) on journey to China. Then they reached at Tashi Khrigo, the main palace of the King Thang rDsung in the capital city in China. There were one lakh men and dogs there. Each side of the palace was equal to a day's walk in width and there were four big gates. They appeared wonderful and awful to look. There the hundred horses of the king of India were present who had come to take the princess Kongjo. The king of Gesar, king of soldiers....; the king of Tazig (Persia), king of wealth,....; the king of Bhata Hor (Turkistan), ...; the king of Tibet, of the borderland,....; people of different races and five hundred camels and mules, had assembled before the king at one time. The Indians came through the eastern gate. The people of

Gesar came through southern gate. Tazig... The people of Hor.... The Minister and men from Tibet stayed on the direction of north-east. Then the other Ministers made presentations of their gifts.

b. Three Letters from the King of Tibet, presented by mGar, Minister of the king of Tibet, to the king of China, c. C.E. 636.

mGar (d. C.E. 667) was Minister of the king Srong-brtsans Gampo. As we have seen above he is supposed to have gone to the city of Khrang-An, in China, and brought Wun-shing Kong-jo, princess of king Tha-e Tsung, of China in marriage with the prince Srong-brtsans Gampo in C.E. 636. The princess of Nepal was brought in C.E. 634. Other sources give the dates of marriage of the king slightly later.

Here are given the three bK'a-shog, letters, containing the statements of the Minister mGar containing the probable questions that would have been asked by the king of China from the party sent by Srong-brtsan sGampo asking for the hands of the princess in marriage and answers thereto. Each successive letter discloses the answer to the question contained in the previous letter. The answers were prepared beforehand by the Minister as he had prophesied the questions. The answers were devised for each of the three occasions and placed before the Emperor of China as if these were the answers given by the king of Tibet himself. The letters express the ingenuity of the Minister of the Tibetan King.

b.i. First Paper Roll, Letter

On presenting the first paper-roll to the king of China, the king looked on it and opened the blue sheet on which was written in golden letters in the Chinese character. "You possess the Doctrine. O! king of China. I, king of Tibet, have no tradition of Dharma. O king, you have the tradition of the ten royal virtues, so you may be pleased to give your daughter to me.

I will turn my body to the incarnated five thousand miraculous forms and I can establish the Law of the ten virtues in one day's time. If you don't give your daughter in this manner, I will send five thousand miraculous soldiers who will kill you and bring seizing your worthy daughter, and capture whole of your kingdom."

The king became greatly frightened. Even though he was frightened, he pretended as if not to be so. "You, the king of Tibet, speak too high. Do you have power to construct viharas in your country? If you possess the capacity, I will give my daughter. Go and bring the massage," ordered the envoy.

b.ii. Middle Paper Roll, Letter

Then the middle paper-roll of mGar was presented in the king's hand. One cannot go to Tibet for one and only one massage. O King, look for the answer to your query. The king was surprised and looked in the manner:

"You have Dhamma and have got constructed viharas in your country. I the king of Tibet have no strength to construct viharas. O king, becoming happy to construct viharas thus, you could also extend the hands of your princess. I turning my body to five thousand forms, will construct one hundred and eight viharas and show all their doors towards you. Will not curse you. If you don't give your daughter in this way, I will send five thousand fantom soldiers, who will kill you, snatch your daughter and destroy your kingdom."

The king becoming extremely frightened yet pretended not to be so. "The mouth of your king is very loud. Is there the practice of five *kámaguha* in your country? If there is, I will give my daughter, otherwise not. This time go and bring the answer."

b.iii. The Last Paper Roll, Letter

Then the Minister mGar again handed over the last roll of paper stating that, for each massage one cannot be sent from China to Tibet. For this, O King, see the answer to your question.

"O! king of China, you are wealthy. I am not so. If you are pleased with your wealth, give the hands of your daughter to me. I will multiply my body miraculously to five thousand times and accumulate wealth of grain, silk, cloth, jewellery, in your front."

c. Messages of the Parents, Advices, to the Princess.

c.i. As advised by father (the King) pray do go to Tibet. Go far off from before the father. Go in or go out, pray go anyway. The great mother of the world is Dro-mo (?). The running horse carries the Three Jewels. This is the key which opens the gate to Tibet. We offer pure salutations, thrice. I don't have the turquoise of the kind a-bzhag-'khyil for presenting to you.

Making the big white turquoise the central jewel, there are turquoises with names in thousands and thousands. There are innumerable turquoises without name. Father's superior horse pa-ba is covered with gold. Men have to be invited with mother horse and golden cows. The barren land of Jangthang is a long walk.

O daughter, you not having amassed merits, and not having experience of walking on foot, we request, you will have to take trouble to walk on foot. The Law of the Lord Buddha has not spread in Tibet. You should see whether the Law of the Buddha has spread there well. Even if the Law of the Lord has not spread, O girl, the Revealer Shakya Muni is your Tutelary Deity for your own benefit.

c.ii. Ae ma ho! Oh great Princess Kongjo, you are wonderful. Please listen to my suggestions. The discourses amuse the thoughts. In the kingdom of Tibet there grow jewels from the earth. In the palace resides Srong-btsan sGampo, the king, the son of god, the Lord of Men. He is the brilliance of prosperity of the six kinds of beings. As one looks at him one is attracted to him. He is greatly kind, and rules the kingdom righteously.

The subjects obey his commands. The ministers and attendants sing in merry. There rises the sun of the Law. They light the lamp of prosperity. There grow all kinds of trees. The land is vast. Grains of five kinds grow over the lands, as one crosses the boundaries. There are gold, silver, copper, iron, etc. in plenty. Cattle, horse and sheep expand here to a great number. The land is filled with so much happiness and pleasure. Ae ma ho, great wonder! Listen oh, Princess Kongjo! So was sung for the recreation of the Princess.

The Princess thought, it is true, the land is just like my own country. So thinking, wiping her tears, followed the minister.

c.iii. The king is possessed of skillful knowledge of kindness. Having discarded the ten non-virtues, he follows the Law of the ten virtues. The king is powerful and prosperous, enjoying by fulfilling all the desires of pleasure. Son of god, the king is possessed of a mass of knowledge. Any gracious and beautiful girl would like to go there. O daughter, you must go to the country like this.

Oh beautiful daughter, the Lord of Men is the Protector as a result of your accumulated merits. The image of the Revealers is the object of my worship. Lord Indra is the owner. Wishes are fulfilled by five kinds of jewels. Visvakarma is its creator. The consecration of this image was done by all the Buddhas. This is the kind of image of the Jina, incomparable.

By merely seeing, hearing, remembering, touching and worshipping the image of the Jina, one would soon gain the view of the Buddha, so the Jina said. O daughter you are so good and helpful to me and extremely close to my heart, it will be a great loss to me. O you beautiful daughter, even then I am sending you, afar.

The store of jewels and the store of wealth, even though many jewels are dear to me, O beautiful daughter, I send them all with you.

Objects greatly satisfying to the heart like gold, turquoise, etc. satisfying and 360 kinds of yi-se(?) of Vihars, and many kinds of ornaments of gold and turquoise, many kinds of dresses, I send with you. .....

Twenty thousand women, decorated with dresses of many colours, will be sent in your company.... Beautiful in lineage and appearance..... Women congenial and helpful at the time of trouble..... twenty-five will be attending you. Oh, daughter I cannot separate from you. These are words of love from my heart, keep it in mind.

d. Zang-yig (mdsangs-yig), Wise Sayings – Dialogue between the Princess of China and her parents and brother.

This is a dialogue between the princess on the one side and on the other side are her parents – father, the king of China, mother, the queen, and the younger brother. The princess explains the difficulties and problems in going to Tibet and the others advise her to go to Tibet because it is the custom everywhere that the daughters cannot live in the houses of their parents.

Translation: Ae ma ho! Wonderful! India and China are prosperous countries. India, the white, is like the land where the sun rises. China is like an elephant lying astride. Those who speak wisely reside in the middle of Nepal.

In the holy palace of the king of wealth, there was born a godly king of medicines, actually a flower of ornament of the kingdom, the (princess Kongjo?) in Tashi Khrigo, palace of the king of China. There is the long path across the vast desolate plains of Jangthang.

The religious king of Tibet in the Himalaya administers the worldly religion in fair manner. Outside the court there is the practice of the Law and inside live the council of ministers. The king is judicious and there is the golden rule. The noble lady (Kongjo) is wise and possesses the book of Wise Sayings written in turquoise ink. The king and the ministers are miraculous. There is the holy book composed by the wise minister dGos. The kings holding lineages are merciful. It is like the sermons of the king Srong-btsan sGam-po. (2) It is like a heart held in hand. It is also like the pronouncements made by the wise ministers. This is the capital of good medicines.

Request of the Princess: This is the petition presented before the parents. Over the head it is like a white canopy and a soft mat is spread on the ground. The two, the sky and the earth, making a charm box are like clothes. The parents, the king and the queen of China, are miraculous.

Their daughter like pibang, a musical instrument of strings, has become the cymbal of the gods. It is a prayer for keeping stationed the gods above. It is an invocation for drawing up the she-serpents from the below. It is a cymbal for pleasing the god bTsan in the middle of the world, between the heaven and the earth. It is a place where the kind parents console (their daughter). Wings are useful in the vast deserted plains of Jangthang. The memory of the kind parents are unforgetable. Days and nights are spent in the memory of the parents. It is like the daughter has not amassed the merits of religion. There are people of the kind who have amassed merits and those not.

(3) The paths are of two kinds, the one having strong impressions of foot (by constant treading) and the other not being so, sinless and sinful. Amassing merits by noble norms one obtains the human life. Even the energy is egg, a woman is worried for the body. Even though young in age, she has to come paving the path through (the vast plains of) Jangthang. Before the completion of the age of fifteen years, she had to get departed from her kind parents. She had to get separated from her kind parents and brother, the four kins, including herself. There is a tradition among the living beings, of separation like the splitting of wood (or from the dead). But the tradition of separation from the living life exists only among the parents. The parents, brother and the princess, they will not meet in a month or two, nor in a year or two. The separation is till the occasion of separation from the spouse. Separation from the spouse and the trade are like as given by the parents.

I, the daughter, feel the white section of the month as blank. Meeting with the parents is like getting thousand lives. The later part of the month is dark. At the end of our life we have a short time of living together with our parents.

(4) The period of fifteen years as desired is short. My birthplace is Tashi Khrigo in China. The hair grown on my head should be done not as is done in my fatherland but it should be plaited on the back. A stranger's land had to be considered like the glass which is white like silver. The parents are kind for having gifted the mind. Any person who came to me, I had to take heed of him and share with him. Parents have gifted precious articles. Although the girl can go with her jewellery but the authority has to be shared with the others.

The sin accumulated has to be carried with oneself likewise. A girl has to share her fortune with the others. When unfortunate, the meal possessed, has to be shared. The life has to be spent in misery.

(5) Upto this is the presentation made by Gyal-za, the wise and beautiful princess, before her parents.

After this is the mother's advice to her daughter. My daughter, whose body was nourished from my blood and flesh, listen to me. I tended you from childhood. I nourished you from the childhood, I cannot separate from you, my daughter, listen to me. Mother swayed you in play. You are extremely dear daughter. Good complexioned and pure, listen. Performing the worldly religion, you are going to Tibet in the Himavata.

The great father of yours is the great king of China. He has not sold his daughter to Tibet considering it a gainful transaction. My daughter you have not been sent to Tibet in happiness. It is also not that your brother is arrogant and he is heir to the throne. It is also not that elder sister is less arrogant and therefore she is going to the distant land. This is the tradition existing since the time of origin of the world. A father adopts a child at his birth even though he may be rolled in rotten patches of clothes, for the sake of his fields and house, even though the child may become rotten and worthless. A daughter may be heroic and good, yet she has to go to a far away land at long distance. Snow falling from the above, cannot obstruct the door. I whose daughter has departed and the son is unsuccessful.

(6) But the snow fallen on the mountain, is still there on the mountain peaks. For us women, our daughters are like secret wealth for others. For a daughter there is no fatherland. Still my daughter is not without fatherland. Tashi Khrigo in China is her fatherland. Yet though her fatherland is good, she has no authority to stay on.

My daughter listen to me, I tell you your age. You having reached four threes, twelve years of age, you are in right age. Having reached five threes, fifteen years, you are in the age of a householder. At six threes, eighteen you are at the stage of over age. Like the horse of ten having weakened mouth (having loosened the teeth) and a woman having reached the age of twenty, the two, even though the wares of trade are good, but will not attract the buyers.

Therefore listen to mother's advice. A colt attaining the age of maturity and a girl reaching the age of five-threes fifteen, the two on getting the proper measure and colour, if they can be sold at the moment, it is well. Chhang and milk, the two, if finished in proper time, one is wise. In the game of dice and in a quarrel, if one is able to judge the proper time of victory, one is hero. If one is able to know the measure of requirement of the stomach, meal, one is a doctor.

If a good horse is not tested, made to run on the plains, its gait, fast or slow, cannot be known.

(7) If the sword is not touched upon the enemy, it cannot be known whether its edge requires sharpening or not. If a girl is not given when someone has come to ask for her hands and medicine is not given to the one who has requested for it, their qualities cannot be understood. Taking these as examples, my daughter, go to Tibet and accept the king as your spouse.

My daughter listen to me here. I give advice with examples. The wild animals are harming the fields in the high mountains. We need good fencing walls there to protect the fields from the animals. Travellers harm the fields. There is need of good fencing of thorny branches of plants. The water-heads are damaging fields near the watercourses. There is need of good channels. To us women there are many who utter abusive languages. A good spouse is required to reply such utterings. Happiness and sorrows are in the parent's house. Aged at home, thinking of happiness, the disease goes on increasing. From this example think of the king spouse and be happy with him. Daughter on the door of mind you are a bird. If found in the mind bear it. Up to this was said by the mother. Advice of Mother ends.

Princess's Request to her Father, the King of China: Below this is given the petition made by the princess before the great father-king.

(8) Great father, king of China, listen here. I, daughter, have not accumulated merits of the Doctrine. Worried about the worldly religion, I go for relationship to the far distant land. The daughter is getting separated from the good parents and the brother. At this moment of separation, although the voice has to be in suppression, I am worried it is heard at high pitch. Although there are neighbours of my village, but they are jealous like an enemy. Daughter while

combing the hair, although the face is good, skin and blood are felt later on. Louse grows from eggs, yet it is an enemy.

I, Gyal-za, the daughter, even if a small portion of the cloth worn on my body is torn, I may become lower in the eyes of the onlookers. Even if one does not own land even equal to the soles of his shoes, he crosses the mountain passes. When young girls go together, without shoes, they are left behind on the way. Specially when the girl has no food and wealth, people behave with jealousy and treat like an enemy. Even though there are parents and brother, everyone spits and vomits. She may have parents but the officers and attendants behave meanly.

(9) The officers and servants ... The Lama may be good ... Sermons may be deep ... The blessings of empowerment and sermons are not given to a man without wealth. Therefore I am worried of the worldly religion. Not in possession of the required wealth, the householder is worried.

O, miraculous king of China, I the daughter, place before her parents the three words of plea with examples. When the food is not tasty, one is like a sickman. When one is not considered among one's relations one is weak. When one is not considered among the companions one is unhappy. If a meal harms, it is considered as poison. If a kin is not good he is considered as an enemy. A wealthless person is a faulty person. If the mouth becomes weakened it cannot produce saliva. In Tibet there are noble men with lineages and clans. The black headed men are noble men. Among the noble there are good and bad persons. The noble good persons in power is soft like the thread of wool. The bad one is like the bark of the tree.....

(10) On the day when there is no cloud it is hot. The rules without kindness are heavier than the mountains. A man's words without kindness are sharper than stone. If a girl is given in practice of the worldly religion the offering is final. In the time of rain without waiting for the sun to appear it is better to go in the shelter.

Instead of riding a horse which has not been trained in gait, it is better to decide and move on foot. Instead of purchasing chhang which is neither sweet nor strong, it is better to determine and take water from a glacier, and that coming out between the rocks. To go to a king who does not get pleased or is hard to please, it is better to be in the capital of China where a door keeper is pleased. If one is happy not to hear, the girl should see the friend when she is pleased. How can a good spouse be found in Tibet who has not been seen at all. In reality the girl is pleased to a superior religion. Upto this is petition put before the king-father by the daughter.

(11) **Father's Advice:** Below this is the father's advice to his daughter. Dear daughter Gyal-za, listen to me. You for practicing Lha-chhos, the religion of gods the Excellent Doctrine, Saddharma, even though one's mind is not engrossed in the thought, the hair famous as even not having life, keeps on growing. Ordinarily in this manner the girls and boys don't learn the Doctrine. But if a great man desires that his daughter should learn the Doctrine, the woman and the man are not able to complete it.

On the completion of education no remedy can be made. If Saddharma comes by shaving the head, even the droppings of sheep and goats, and the black young cows would become learned in the Doctrine. If one can get the Doctrine by wearing the yellow dress, banks of the lakes far off in the moonlight would have been so. By circumambulation one would not be purified from the sin. If it were so, the whirlpools along the crossings of rivers would become pure of sins. By meditating one would not receive the Buddha. If it were so, yellow spittal will also receive Buddhahood.

(12) Good thoughts and good Doctrine originate together from the Buddha. I ask you to practice the Doctrine from your heart. Keep in the mind and make donations. If your body becomes dull, circumambulate the chaitya. If your happiness dims, give alms to the destitute. If your mouth becomes dull, pronounce the six excellent syllables. There is an example for attaining the accomplishment.

Even if you practice the godly religion you will not be at the edge. If you practice the worldly religion there is no requirement of meditation. Even if you practice the sacred religion it is not required to do so. These are the words of advice of your father. Daughter, keep it in your mind. Upto this it was said by the father to his daughter.

Princess's Petition to her Brother: Below this is said by Gyal-za Kong-jo. I made petitions before the parents. I don't know whether they have heard and pondered over it. Now I have come to you my brother and make a petition. I have come before the loving younger brother. The elder sister is holding the hands of her brother. The elder sister's face is white like the mirror of silver.

(13) Now the drops of tears are falling down in chain of glass beads. Sister's good younger brother worthy of protection, listen to me. The brother stays back in his fatherland. Achi (sister, elder) has not amassed merits and she now wanders and is in worry. The great father, the king of China, has only one prince son. The great queen, mother has no daughter other than me. We two brother and sister are not to be separated. The great father king is comparable with the high blue sky. I and the soft drizzle are comparable. The drizzle may fall on me and the small lake, here, there, or anywhere. As it is so, girl, I see my brother. The body of the great mother is like the lake, high above. The small fish with yellow eyes, is like me, the daughter. I, like her, don't know where I may go, brother see. Sometimes I may be in the hands of those having yellow eyes. Daughter, the body of my brother is similar to the Sumeru mountain. Daughter, my body and the wild animals are alike. This is my condition, look my brother. Anytime she may be in the hands of a hunter.

(14) The body of my brother is like the Sumeru mountain. My body is like that of a wild animal. But I cannot go everywhere like the animals. As I have no power to go anywhere you take care of me. Anytime I may be in the hands of a hunter. I may be in the hands of the wise ministers of Tibet. My body is like Tshe-zang. We both cannot move from here to there. Therefore as I cannot go anywhere take care of me. Achi is likely to go to the country of Tibet. This is known to you. Please help make petition before the great father. And also help me to petition before the great mother. The chest and the heart of both the parents are not warm. They taking out the warm hearts have sold me to Tibet. Sister's brother, now it is upto you for speaking to the great kind parents, so saying help me to petition before the parents. Help me to petition before

the people of China. Help me to have a talk with the wise ministers of Tibet.

(15). Help me to say them to go back to Tibet. My little brother you are well aware. Specially the father, mother and the brother, the three may have an assembly. Tell them not to send Achi to Tibet. Upto this is the petition made before the brother.

Brother's Reply

After this is the reply to the petition given to the brother. My good sister Bhattarika Dolma, listen to me here. Good sister, daughter of god, princess, listen to me here. I, brother, has become free. Sister, there is none other than you in my thought. The ears of the two parents are thinner than silk. The spouts of the ministers of Tibet are sharper than rdsong. Thin silk and spout of rdsong have made exchanges. For this reason sister you should go to Tibet.

Petition has been made here to the great king-father. The king's advice is higher than the sky. In the beginning I come to the sky of my brother from where I will not return. I placed petition before the mother. Mother's advices are like the rock rolling down along the sharp inclinations of the precipices.

(16) Even though the rolling stones are falling down my brother is not stopping them. I make petitions before the gods and men of China. But the gods and men of China are under the authority of the father and mother. I have a talk with the wise ministers of Tibet. They are similar to the wind. The wild winds are not able to touch the feet of the brother. I place my petition before my sister. In the garden of the prince there are grown three flowers. One is the flower of saffron, the second is the Halo, and the third is the Ser-chhen. They are grown in the garden. Although they have grown up in the garden, they don't have the luster. Ordinarily they become the ornaments of monasteries, they are like the objects of sacrifice in the prayer rooms. I offer petition with these examples. My sister's country is Tashi Khrigo of China. She was born in a palace which is nine storeys high.

(17) Although she was born there, she has no authority to stay there. Even though she was born in the palace of nine storeys, she

has no authority to keep staying here. Therefore, Achi, you should go to Tibet as an ornament of it. You should go for the welfare of the king Srong-btsan sGampo. Taking it as example Achi you should go to Himavata. You meet the king, the spouse. This is my prayer. Achi, if you have felt it bad kindly speak. Upto this was said by the brother.

Princess's Petition to the mother and relatives: Below, this is the petition made by the princess before the king, the queen, relatives and the companions. Great father, sitting on the golden throne listen to me. Great mother sitting on the throne of turquize listen. Younger brother, worthy of protection, sitting on the throne of conch, listen. Good companions of the medicine of the Doctrine and the medicine of Rabjor, and the memorables, the three; and those sitting on the throne of the singing peacocks, listen.

(18) The wise ministers of Tibet sitting on the red mat of tiger, listen here. I, an unhappy girl, sitting on the seat of eight petalled padma, I appeal to you. O great father, king of China, I am going to Tibet in order to practice the worldly religion. I, the daughter, like a small mugpo and a fawn go crossing nine mountain ranges and nine valleys. May the wishes of the great father be fulfilled. Great mother queen listen. I, your daughter, like the small fish with golden eyes will jump into the river, and will fulfill the wishes of my mother. O younger brother, listen. I, like the bird gongmo, will go to the peak of the mountain and will fulfill the wishes of the younger brother. The three friends like three brothers, listen. I, a woman like the aged useful yak stuck up in the mud, may your wishes be fulfilled. The wise ministers of Tibet, listen to me. The wonderful knife stuck in my waist, is given by my father with his own hands. Its handle and jewels have been given by my mother.

(19) The yellow golden knife, with the silver handle and red beads, it is as if I acquired it myself, I who has acquired no merit. Daughter, this is the killer knife, with which one can cut one's own heart by oneself.

When piercing the heart, strike the tip of the knife on the left side of the chest above the nipple. Daughter, I am cutting my life myself, fulfilling the wishes of the king of Tibet. Your Ministers are determined. The parents let them do the bad talk. Daughter, I have not amassed merits. I will end my life and turn the body into a corpse. So saying, she struck the knife on her heart. The parents and the brother, the three, were wonder struck.

The other Ministers were accompanying each other. The wise ministers sitting before raised a caution.

(20) Addressing Gyal-za, they appealed to her like this. Wise Gyal-za, listen, even though the officer will not go to Tibet, it is possible that one can take one's life oneself. By the difficult task of daljor one can take a human life. After that one can take one's own life. Even though it is possible, there is an example that one will be born in the hell but will not be able to cross the hell even after five hundred births. Specially you belong to the lineage of the king of China. On the side of the monastery it is like peas have been spread. For holding the lineage of Gyalza, thereafter one can cut one's life oneself. If one kills oneself, like the mug-chhung baby of a deer, one can cross nine mountains and nine valleys. Thus the wishes of the great king father can be fulfilled. The Minister cannot make final verdict. (The matter is incomplete and the translation may be fualty at places).

iii. Karchhags.

a. Karchhag, village of Kyis, King of Ladakh, Tshe-dbang rNam-rgyal, 1575-1595.

Introduction: The present document belongs to Kyis village in Spiti. It was composed on the occasion of death ceremony of a person in the village during the reign of the Ladakhi king Tshe-dbang rNam-rgyal. Dangkhar (Brag-mkhar-rtse) was then the seat of the government of Spiti. Here resided the Kharpon, Castle Governor, the representative of Ladaki king, named sTan sKyong rGya-mtsho. It names the monastery of Dankhar as Norbu Gephel (Nor-bu dGe-'phel) where there resides the chief lama bLo-bsang Don-grub. Then it describes the prosperous and happy village of Kyis where the occasion is being celebrated. The tenor of the document is Gelug which reveals that Dankhar at this time was Gelug. We discern from the document that the literary name of the monastery of Dankhar is Norbu Gephel.

Translation: *Aum swasti siddham*! Tsongkha-pa introduced the vehicle (of the Law, Gelug) in the Snowy Land. rGyal-mtshab-rje holds the power of foreknowledge; and mKhas-grub-rje is the holder of knowledge of sutra and mantra. I bow reverentially to the three Jinas, the Teacher and the pupils.

At the high and extensive Palace, of dPal mKhar-rtse in the great capital of Leh, resides the great righteous king Tshe-dbang rNam-rgyal. May his crown be held high and may the kingdom expand. The good public here is under his reign.

Here at the high and strong palace at the capital of Dankhar resides the great Castle Governor (mKhar-dpon) bsTan-skyong rGya-mtsho. May his life be long and may his kingdom expand.

At the well developed monastery of Norbu Gephel, resides the great Acharya bZang-don-'grub. May the crest of his Faith be held high and may the number of monk-disciples expand. Here is situated the joyous and prosperous village of Kyis. At the head of the valley the stores of essences (snow) spread and many kinds of grains ripe at the end of the valley.

Tshering Chhos-zin, of the well founded lineage of the great clan of Khyung-po, is donor. He for the sake of emancipation of his deceased spouse, from the path of liberation, got made three small and large copies of the specially developed Dorchhod, Vajrachhedika, of the well developed Doctrine. The donations made for the accumulation of the virtues are wonderful. The respectable father [of the donor]...

The account of the offerings received:... From the monastery of Norbu Gephel..; Kibbar (Kyid-par), Tashi Gang, Rangrig, Khyurig (Khurig), Hall ('Al), Pha-ldar, Kyoto (Kyo-dro), Chichim (sPyi-khyim), sTeng-rgyud, rGya-te, sKyis and Chig-zar. They presented one meal (gung-tshigs), tea and chhang for *tshogs*, the worship ceremony.

b. Karchhag, village Gyete, king Tshepal Namgyal of Ladakh (1802-1837), c. C.E. 1830.

Text: gling gi mchhog gyur lho-yi 'dsambu'i gling. dgra bchom bzhugs gnas ti-si gangs gyi mgul. ma-gros gzhus gnas ma-spang gyu-yi mtsho. seng-ge kha-babs 'brug pa'i g-yas phyogs 'dir. pho-grang chhen-po 'dir. ble-chhen dpal mkhar rtser chhos-rgyal chhen-po mi -'gyur tshe-dpel snam-rgyal gyi a-u rmog mtho gyur chig. khong gi mnga' zhabs bzang-po spyi-ti 'dir. rdsong mtho brtsan rgyalsa grang mkharr tser. rdsong-dpon chhen-po ga-ga khan yab-sras kyi sku-tshe bstan gyur chig. dgon-pa khyad du 'phags-pa nor-bu dge-'phel nas. dpon-slob chhen-po ye-shes rnam-rgyal kyi chhos btsun mtho zhing 'phrin-las rgyas chig. xxx g-yang chhags skyidpa'i rgye-te 'dir. phu-ru rtsa chhu'dsom zhing mdoru'brusna smin. mi rigs khungs btsun rus chhen rgya-shing rgyud. dad ldan yon gi bdag-po dkon-mchhog gixxxxkyen bar-chhad zhi phyir dang. 'chhi-ma rgyal-ba'i go-'phang thobp hyir du. dam-chhos khyad 'phags rdo-rje gchod-pa dang pha-yon dang sdig-bshags bchas ma-bu sum xxx sdigs grib kun 'byoms. pyi gshegs. khyon mdos snanga tsam bzhengs. bsags-pa chhos phyir btongba ngo-mtshar chhe.

dad ldan yon gi bdag-mo dpal mdses.....

Translation: On the right side of the river Sindhu, as it flows, here is situated the great palace of Leh. Here resides the great religious king Tshepel Namgyal. May his crown be held high. Spiti is under his good reign. At the capital Dankhar there is the high and strong fort where there resides Ga-ga Khan, the Fort Officer, and his son, may their life be strong. Yeshe Namgryal, the great Abbot of the well developed monastery of Nor-bu Ge-phel, the monastery of Dankhar, may the fame of his knowledge be higher and may his activities increase.

Gyete is a happy and prosperous village. May there be abundance of grass and water at the head of the valley so that there may be abundance of crops in the valley and the grains may ripe. Konchhog, the great faithful donor, having the lineage of noble origin, belongs to the great clan of rgya-shing. He for the purpose of removing the obstacles and with the objective so that in the next life he may get the stage of the Boddisattva, the works belonging to the well developed Doctrine rDorje-chodpa, Pha-yon and sDig-shags, the three small and large works, were raised and the impurities were washed. There were numerous donors for the welfare of the Doctrine. The lady donor Pal Zes served excellent meal.

Summaries: The donors mostly belonged to Dankhar and the other villages are Gyudpar, Gyete, Sumling, Kyi, etc. They were: Monks = 17 and Others = 10.

They offered: gSolja, tea (11). Solja and dokar, Lunch (1). Chhang tshos, one lot (4). Nyin-gang chhang tshos, chhang full day (5). Chhang tshos and dokar (2). Chhang tshos and solja (3). Ge'u? (3).

Both the above two karchhags name the monastery of Dankhar as Norbu Gephel.

iv. The roll of Ladaki Kharpons, Castle Governors, stationed at Dankhar.

During the medieval period Spiti was ruled by Ladakh. The representatives of the kings of Ladakh who were designated as Kharpon, Castle Governor, resided at Dangkhar, the capital of Spiti. Here we give their list gathered from different sources.

List of the Kharpons at Dankhar

Name of the Ruler	Name of the Kharpon	Remarks	Authority (=Auth.)
Tashi Namgyal (1555-1575)	bsTan-pa rGya-mtsho	do	Thubs-bstan Kharpon in Pin
Tshe-dbang Namgyal (1575-1595)	'Bum-pa-lde (Minister, as per Petech)	do	sTan-skyong rgya-mtsho
Tshe-dbang Namgyal	Tanzin Namgyal	--	
Sing-ge Namgyal (1616-1642)	Tanzin Namgyal, continued.	do	Chhering Namgyal (Son of Tanzin Namgyal?)
Dechhog Namgyal 1671	Namkha Gyaltshan.	--	

Name of the Ruler	Name of the Kharpon	Remarks	Authority (=Auth.)
Dechhog Namgyal	Namkha Gyaltshan	He is now designated as Kahlon, c. 1680.	
Francke (Authority).	Sonam (?)	--	
Trebeck (Auth.) 1816.	Rabgey	--	
Trebeck (Auth.) 1822.	Sultan Begh	Gaga Khan, (Chief = Kharpon?) (Manager= Zongpon?)	
Gyete, Colophon c. 1830	Gaga Khan	--	(Tashi Dondub)
C.L. Datta. (Auth.) 1841.	Rahim Khan	Kiladar, Kharpon,	
J.D. Cunningham (Auth.) (Tobdan, 2015: 134-135).	Son of Gaga Khan 1843		

9 Kinnaur (Khunu)

i. Inscription on Stone, village Roghi, near Kalpa, C.E. 1706.

A rare inscription in an unknown Indian script was found in village Roghi, near Kalpa, in Kinnaur. It is in a script resembling Sharda written on a stone block placed in the retaining wall in the field. This was reported by Ashwani Negi and photographed by Tanzin Phuntshok. Devendra Handa, a renowned numismatist, (2016) remarks that, "The inscription is in an unknown script. I can only hazard to guess that it is dated to Samvat 1763 (=C.E. 1706)."

ii. Tsha-par Inscription, c. 11th-12thcentry C.E.

There is a tsha-par, a small stucco image produced by stamping, containing the image of Manjushri with an inscription, said to have been found in an excavation. It belonged to the period of Rinchhen Zangpo. It is about three inches in height made of white soil which is found locally.

The inscription in Bhoti on both sides of the object reads the famous Sanskrit *shalok*: *"ye dharma hetuprabhava..."* complete on the reverse side and visible partially on the obverse side, (courtesy Roshan Lal Negi).

iii. a. Kamru Image inscription, 11th-12th c. C.E.

Text: paṇ-bri-ta byi-rya ba-dras phyag-len mdsad. smer blon-čhe klu-mgon mčhed yum-sras kyis yon-bdag bgyis nas. tshes-'das-pa smer blon-čhe śes-pyan gyi bsod-nams su. rigs gsum gyi sku bžeŋs-su gsol-bas. tshe 'das la dad-pa 'byas pa'i sems-čan thams-čad sgrib-pa byaŋ-bar gyurd-čig. (Amy Heller, Internet 29 July, 2023).

Translation: Panḍita Viryabhadra attended the work (of ritual ceremony). kLu-mgon, the great Minister of sMer, brother (of the deceased), mother (spouse of the deceased) and son (of the deceased) becoming donors the statue of Lokesvara, Avalokiteśavara, with the three peaked crown was raised for the welfare of the deceased Shes Chan, the great Minister of sMer. May the impurities of sins of all those beings be removed who possess faith in the deceased.

Rahul Sankrityayana discovered the statue and had read the inscription.

iii. b. Kamru, Rahul: Rahul reads an inscription at the same place on another statue of the size of three inches on which it is written: "rgyal-ba 'bar-r-b-n-mkh'irdo-rje la n-mo," and he says that the person in the statue belongs to some saint named Namkha Dorje belonging to the Bon faith, (Rahul, 1956: 243).

It is difficult to expect to find an object of a different faith mixed up among the objects of worship of one's own faith anywhere. The inscription gives the person a high status as *rgyal-ba* i.e. Jina. There has been a great siddha named gNam-mkha' rDo-rje (1077-1161) in Tibet, (Roerich, 1949: 297).

iv. Karchhags gathered by Rahul Sankrityayan

Rahul Sankrityayan colleceted several karchhags from Kinnaur and put them in his book.

a. Raja Vijay Singh, Bashahar, (1696-1719).

The Doctrine has spread in Guge and Zhang-zhung. The Lord of men, self-born, has done unlimited amount of virtuous tasks, is much famed and revered by many. This place of pilgrimage was treaded by Rinchhen Zangpo. The prosperous country of Mo-na, here, where there has assembled the ten virtues, ... The Lord of the Sky and the Earth Bi-dir Singh, this place is subject to him. A-si, ... and the faithful Lady donor Go-phul, ...They donated wonderfully for the sake of the Doctrine. .

Note: Rahul writes that the handwritten Bhoti version of the Sanskrit book Suvarnprabhas-sutra contained the dedication with the name and detail about the donors in its beginning. During the time of king Bi-dir Singh the government officials A-si, A-sol, O-mol, etc. got the book copied at Mo-ne. Bi-dir Singh is the corrupt form of Vidya or Vijaya Singh. Vijay Singh lived in the later half of seventeenth century and was successor of Kehar Singh.

The text clarifies that the names listed here are those of the donors. They were the kins of the household who got the book copied.

b. Raja Ugar Singh of Bashahar, 1844-1878.

The excellent Revealer spread the Doctrine in the north of Vajrasana. Himvanta is the pilgrimage place where the Docrrine has spread. Mount Tise is like a chhorten where there reside the Arhatas. Ma-bang, the Turquise Lake, is accomplished lake of bathing. This is the land treaded by Rinchhen Zangpo. Here has spread the Doctrine of bLo-bsang Grags-pa (Gelug). The great river Satluj originates from the mouth of elephant. There is the vast river valley, the valley of gods which is inhabited. The Khyung-dsongs and the sPur-rgyal mountains are like heaps of jewels. Mo-ne (sMon-gnas), the self-born.... The king, Lord of the Doctrine, resides at Sarahan (So-ra-rang). This place Chhit-kul is under his sway and here ten virtues have assembled. Of the clan of Chha-na, having pure origin, the faithful donor is Zo-gu. Si-tson the daughter. La-te like a flower, Arjun, the excellent son, and Po-ti the Lady donor. ..... Ashtasaharsarika, the book was copied. ... At Mo-nye the king Ugar Singh (Ubur Singh) ....

c. Raja Shamsher Singh, 1907-(?).

d. Possessed of two houses, the religious king Shamsher Singh. The great Lord of men, reverence to him. May his kingdom expand. The Minister Ran Bahadur, reverence to him.

10 Kullu

i. Bhoti Inscription on stone, Dhomya Rishi Temple, Jagatsukh, c. first quarter of twentieth century C.E.

In the village of Jagatsukh there is a small dehri, shrine, still in practice, dedicated to Dhomya Rishi. In the corner of the room of the shrine there is placed a small pink slate with inscription on it in Bhoti, (Courtesy Kirit Mankodi and Tara Chand).

Translation: Lord! Here in this world, if somebody among the gods, human beings, non-gods (Asura) and others, desires to acquire the knowledge of the Doctrine, by enquiring, upholding, explaining, studying, obtaining perfection and practicing, it would be unexplainably wonderful.

The Lord, like a teacher, stopped wherever possible. Ayushmaan Subhuti asked from the Lord, Oh Lord, what is the name of this kind of Doctrine. How it should be held? So he asked. The Lord Tathagat explained to Ayushman Subhuti in this manner. Oh Subhuti! The name of the Doctrine is Pragyaparmita. This should be held like this. This is so because, Oh Subhuti, the Lord Tathagat when he explained the Pragyaparmita, at that time the beings were benefitted. Therefor it is called Pragyaparmita. Subhuti you ponder over it as much as you can. Has the Lord told the Doctrine without leaving anything?

Subhuti said, nothing is left after whatever the Lord has explained about the Doctrine. The Lord told, O Subhuti think over it as much as you can. In the great world, among the three thousand worlds, as much as there are particles of the earth, is it more? Subhuti said, those told by the Tathagat are more. This is so because Tathagat has said more than there are particles of the earth. Therefor they are the particles of the earth.

In the fields where the Lord has told the Doctrine they are more than there are fields in the world. Therefore they are known as fields of the world.

The Lord told Subhuti to think over it as much as he could. The Great being with thirty-two marks, with these, Tathagat, Arhat, may they attain the status of Samyak Sambuddha!

Note: Along the small shrine of Dhomya Rishi there is a wild bushy pomegranate tree over which was placed apair of horns of ibex. These denote to its antiquity. Jagatsukh is situated near to Naggar where once there lived the renowned scholar Nicholai Roerich and his family. His son George N. Roerich was a great scholar in Tibetan.

The composition appears to be unlike the texts in the traditional sacred scriptures.

ii. Colophons to Tankri manuscripts, Tandi, Lahul, C.E. 1824

The following are two colophons from the manuscripts in Tankri script, consisting of two different chapters of Ramayana. The author of both the works is the same Bragi (Brāgī) Ram, Negi from the village Khakhnal, near Jagatsukh, in Kullu. He completed both the works in the same year in sambat 100 of Shri Sam. equivalent to C.E. 1824. The first one mentions Sobha Ram, the Minister of Kullu, of the time of Raja Ajit Singh, whom Moorcroft also mentions in his travelogue. Here Sobha Ram is designated as 'Sampuran Vazir' – Full Minister. Bragi Ram was perhaps Hakim, the head, as Moorcroft calls, of the official of Kullu posted in Lahul. These are:

a. बालकांड समाप्त शुभ शुभ खखनालीनेगीब्रागीरामेलिखीपझणे वदणे दे अर्थबालकांड लिखीअ .. सं० 100 रेजेठ प्र० 15 सम्पूर्ण वजीरसोभरामजीजस्त्री दीतुरीलीखीकल्यारी अस्थानेनरजणे।

Transcription: *bālkāṇḍ smāptashubhshubhkhakhnālīnegībrāgīrāmel ikhīpajhaṇevadaṇe de arthbālkāṇḍlikhīa .... saṃ. 100 re jeṭhpra. 15 sampū rṇvajīrsobharāmjījastrīdīturīlīkhīkalyārīasthānenarajne.*

Translation: Bal Kand, a chapter from the Ramayana, was finished. It was written by Bragi Ram, the Negi from Khakhnal. ...On Jeth 15 of Sam. 100, C.E. 1824... Sobha Ram, the full Minister, was written, at Kalyari.

b. कथा खखनालीनेगीब्रागीरामेलिखीश्री सं० 100 री भाद्र प्र० 25 लहुलरी वजीरी पीछे तंदीकोठीलिखी।

Transcription: *kathākhakhnālīnegībrāgīrāmelikhīśrīsaṃ. 100 ri bhādrapra. 25 lahulrivajīrīipichhetandīkothīlikhī*

Translation: The story was written by Bragi Ram, Khakhnali Negi, at Tandi in Waziri Lahul on Bhadra 25, of sam. 100 equivalent to C.E. 1824.

11 Bhramaur and Pangi

a. Bhramaur, inscription on stone in Sharda script

At Naugraon, in Bhramaur, there is an inscription on a stone slab in Sharda script. The big stone slab is about six feet long, three feet wide and six inches thick. The slab lies flat on the ground and face containing the inscription is turned downwards therefore it is on the underside of the slab. It is rested on some round stones at different points with a space of about four inches at places between the surface of the earth and the face of the slab. But much of it is filled up with moving soil and growth of weed. A few letters could be photographed with mobile which could bring only a pair of letters. The letters appear to be large and clear. May be that it contains inscriptions in two scripts. Yeshe Dorje tells two more inscriptions in the area. All have been brought to the notice of the concerned authorities.

The slab is located about 100 meters away from the edge of the main road, where there is a newly constructed temple. It is situated on a very narrow ridge, extending from the edge of the road, which is precipitous on both sides. Here there are also trees of chil around it making the going safer. There is also a narrow path running along it used by the villagers. For a common man, an outsider, it is difficult to reach here. The place is known as Naograon. The Chamba to Bhramaur road turns at Kharamukh to left from where Holi is 25 kms and from there Naograon is ten kms. At Naograon on the curve there is a newly constructed temple dedicated to a devi named Laka-vali.

b. Pangi, inscription in Tankri script on a metal plate, Devi Mindhal, C.E. 1909.

In Pangi there is a metal plate said to be with devi Mindhal which contains an inscription in Tankriscript which reads as follows:

Text: थल 1 तोल 80 मा० दाश्रीदेवीमींधला के सतीजीदा सं० 1966 कती प्र० 6।

Transcription: *thala 1 tola 80 mā. dāśrīdevīmīṃdhlākesatījīdāsaṃ. 1966 katī pra. 6,* (courtesy C. Dorje).

Translation: This plate [of metal with gold] of weight 80 ma[sha] was offered to Shri Devi Mindhal in sambat 1966, Katik 6, equivalent to C.E. 1909.

12 Mandi and Riwalsar

i. Mandi. Agreement-Devata, Tankri script, C.E. 1946.

Below is given Nagari transcription of a text of Agreement written in Tankri script, as far as it could be read.

1. आजश्री सं० 2003 वास्य सं० 22 चैत्र 30 लीखततसभहा
2. राजीनमाश्रीदेव्रताचयाणेरेदेओलुकारकून वा कार
3. दारप्री द ओसम ने देवता पूछकर के आपस में
4. सलुक आंए दाकोबकाए आहेपीछेआजतकमदर
5. जग के दीन मे वे आदमी की थी आं एदाकोमतेहारी व
6. कारकूनेकारदारेगुरेकमेरे चाए ते कमेटी मे
7. जाहे मेलापकररकीकारदार त दुइसल्योणी
8. ----- मी का ------ ह दोकारदारसाताहारी
9. गेमजेर की हेआएंदा-----श्रीदेवताकोदोनोमलाप से
10. के रे दे ओरामेभादी का रर्य इ ऐकसालकरमसीध करे
11. ऐकसालनरगुकरेगुरकरमसिघ के साथ भदरगुर
12. कामकरेनरगु के साथ गुरनरोतमकोमकरेगुरकामसो
13. की लीनकनहीहे स० 2003 के जेठ मे कारदारकरमसीध
14. गुरभदर कम करे आंएदीसालकार दारनरगुगुरनोरोतम
15. का कम करेइसीतराबरसप्ररमणआपआपलभीता
16. के मतावकचलतेरहेपुजारी का हकवरावरनीसभता
17. मलाहारनहराहारजओलहारलमाहार न ह छ धारा ग होइपजारी
18. परसा वी झर हरकुरमाहार माख हारलमारमै दे - धारलगढे -
19. - त ला र ता क धरमु का हासा शरीदेवता का रसममें खुल्याणे

20. -एक साल का काढा मे पुले एग सालसाल धाढ मे हलमदर

21. से वरणेजाताहे जो देवता-करजात शावहारी मत होरबोल

22. मे लाहारहे

23. जेकोए हार र ओलीमेकरपाल ह चलेकारदारकमेटी

24. दार का कत्यारइोगादेवता का चलणेकारसेमपढी जढी के वासत

25. रखा जीसका सधलुपहलेहला के इस कोमीलेवाकीप

26. जयारी का भीरेहीमल-- मी वरातरओलाी के मतवक

27. हारीहारी--इस वसा--कों-हारी मे नचणे

28. पो ज '-मनेकारदार----- क ता एक शरतनामासनद

29. रहे

30. नीलरहारसीदअव--- त

(स्टाम्प पेपर बेचने वाले का लेख। उर्दू लिपि और भाषा में।)। न० 92 सजेरामबलद---जातकनैत धडोगी व अमल पैमाईज़करने-- पूरचूरनी के अमईमुस्तफीवासतेदियागयावाराय मलकीयत खानगीसादर-- कीमतकागजतहरीर--- 21-10-94

Note: Below the end of the text are given signatures of the office bearers of the devata who are parties to the agreement. These are about twenty in number of which two signs are in Nagari and the rest are in Tankri.

Summary of the Agreement: This Agreement was made among the officials like the gur, kardar, pujari, karkun, kamere, etc. after duly obtaining consent of the devata Chyālu on Shri sambat 2003, accordingly Chaitra 30 of Vāsya sambat 22, equivalent to C.E. 1946 for the future conduct of duties, from year to year, by the various office bearers The document was written by the professional scribe.

This Agreement was made on a Stamp Paper issued in the State of Mandi. On the front page at the top about a quarter part of it is printed with usual design of a stamp paper. In the centre of it is given picture of the Raja, of the State of Mandi. Above it is written in Roman script as 'Mandi State Panjab' and the same legend is given below in Nagari script. On the four corners of the picture are written the cost of the paper as eight annas, in four languages in respective scripts of Roman, Nagari, Urdu and Tankri.

According to the text of the Agreement the document was executed in the year Shri samvata i.e. Vikrim Samvata 2003, equivalent to C.E. 1946. The document gives another date as Vāsya year 22. Vāsya is a new term of era but it coincides with the Sapta Rishi system of the cycle of 100 years. All systems agree to one year of C.E. 1946. The document bears another date. As seen above the Stamp Vendor gives date of sale of the paper as 21-10-94 i.e. 21st October, 94. This date cannot be 1994 because the paper was used before this. The other possible date is 1894, which is the correct year.

Thus according to the Stamp Vendor the paper was sold to Saje Ram for the purpose of some deal in 1894. Its cost was eight annas. The deal failed and the paper being of high cost remained preserved safe in a coffer.

In the present Agreement Saje Ram, the purchaser of the paper, is not party to the Agreement and the purpose is also different from that for which it was purchased. It is not a registered document. Therefore no question was raised about the validity of the stamp paper.

ii. Riwalsar Prayer Offerings (gSol-'debs), to the Great Pilgrimage place of Lotus-Lake (mTsho Padma) of Zahor Country, c. C.E. 1643(?).

It was faintly known that there existed any gsol-'debs, gnas-yig or gnas-bshad, guidebook, about the famous pilgrimage place of mTsho Padma, Riwalsar, Mandi, Himachal. The officials at the monastery had no idea at all. Tashi Paljor a scholar from Lahul tells to have seen it once. Incidentlly a very faint photostated copy of the Prayer Book was found with a person unconnected with the affairs. It was a print from a wood block. Thus it also came to be known that there also existed a wood block of the work. The blocks from which this print was obtained too appears to have had become much faded.

A copy of the prayer book was given to the management of the monastery, renowned as rich, with the offer of full service.

On enquiry later they appeared least concerned about it and even whereabouts of the copy of the prayer book was not known.

The copy was difficult to read. I tried to take help from several persons like Sonam Angdui Pankharpa, Norbu Kukuji, etc. Ultimately Thinlay Shashni, a scholar in CIHTS, Varanasi, gave the full reading and also gave a translation in Hindi. It was done in collaboration with Lama P. Ogyan Tenzin, a scholar of Nyingma, who heads the Uddyan Dharmakaya Vihar, Sarnath, Varanasi, and is also Director and Head Lama of Lhundub Tobgye Ling, Yog-Sadhna Kendra, in Arunachal Pradesh. P. Ogyan, belonging to Arunachal, is said to have been very much appreciative of the highly scholastic composition of the gsol-'deb.

The author of the gsol-'debs dedicated the book on the tenth day of the first month of the water-hare year, the day of birthday of the Guru, which day is still celebrated, at Rewalsar. Unfortunately date in the text is incomplete. Roughly we place it at 1643, the latest.

This gsol-'debs is dedicated to the holy and miraculous place of Zahor, where there is the lake which was turned from the heap of fire by miracle attributed to Padmasambhava. This Zahor is also identified in belief with the native place of Princess Mandarva, the spiritual Indian consort of Padmasambhava who in the iconography is shown accompanying the Guru. But Mandarva has a historical evidence having connection with Mandi. There is a well named Khuha Rani (Well of Queen) in Mandi town which according to O.C. Handa represents Mandarva. Handa writes, "To cap all these evidences and traditions, a subterranean temple in the heart of Mandi town enshrines a black stone syambhu [self-born] image of a goddess. That temple is known as Khuā Rani. That Khua Rani is none but Mandarva, the daughter of king Arshadhar of Sahor and the spiritual partner of the Vajracharya Padmasambhava. What was the birth name of that Vajracharya we don't know. However, after having emerged out of the lake Padmasambhava at Sahor on a fully blown lotus, he became Padmasambhava," (O.C. Handa, 2008: 128). There also visit some Buddhist pilgrims. In this connection Prakash Chander Dhiman writes that, "Sometime between 8th and 14th c. A.D. Usandara, the Raja of Mandi of the time, built the temple in the memory of his daughter princess Mandarva. The statues are established in a well. Among them one is that of Mandarva who since long time is known as Khuhā Rani (=Queen Well), Mother, Devi Tara. It is told that Mandrava considered Baudh Tantrik Teacher Padmasambhava as her Teacher. She used to visit him in the caves at Riwalsar. People told this story in another way and it reached the ears of the Raja. The Raja with the fear of shame of the public buried Mandarva live in this well and on the other hand buried Padmasambhava at Riwalsar. It is told that the area was filled with smoke for a week long. At last it turned into water which is now known as Riwalsar lake and is revered. Mandarva was worshipped as a goddess", (Dhiman, P.C. 2019:79).

The gsol-'debs relates to mTsho Padma, Riwalsar, the existing place of pilgrimage. This is an authentic and perhaps the only such evidence showing Zahor situated in the north-west India. The environment strengthens the evidence.

Translation: Prayer for Lake Padma the great Pilgrimage Place of Zahor Country

aum a'ahh'um!

1. Samantabhadra, the Teacher, resides in the state of dharamkaya in yab-yum form in the incomparable palace of dharamdhatu adorned with the rainbow of five colours, in the uppermost region of heaven, surrounded by the companions and attendants of numerous gods in their existence of dharamkaya.

   O! incarnate Teacher of Uddyan, look at us with kindness. We, all the beings living between the earth and the sky, who are greatly tormented, pray with great reverence, that we may be able to meet the Teacher and become identified with him like the god Abhasvara, whose two divisions, mother and son, meet inseparably.

2. Lord Amitabh, in red padmarag colour, decorated with thirty-two good signs and eighty marks, resides in the supreme castle in the western region, in the dominion of

great happiness, surrounded by innumerable companions of the Buddhas of the ten directions.

Pray, bless us so that we may be able to be born in the region of great bliss.

3. Avalokiteśvara, clear white, the lord of voidness and of benevolence, adorned with the excellent ornaments of the celetial existence, resides in the great holy palace of Potalaka, surrounded by the companions of the Bodhisattvas of the tenth stage.

   Pray, bless us, may we be able to generate the feeling of kindness in us in the natural way.

4. Padmasambhava, Lord of the world, who has discarded the nature of birth and death, appearing from the centre of the rainbow of the collective manifestation of the three forms, resides on the lotus plant, in the middle of the lake which he transformed from the heap of fire, and is surrounded by the innumerable vidyadhars - the translators of India and Tibet.

   Pray, bless us, may we be able to convert the beings of the world with the four kinds of deeds.

5. Ye-she mTsho-rgyal, the incarnate of the Great mother (Prjnyaparmita), resides in the middle of lakhs of dakinis in their existence of dharamkaya. Princess Mandarva, the beloved incarnate of Tara, is surrounded by the companions of crores of knowledge-dakinis.

   Pray, bless us, may we by excelling in the four kinds of powers be able in manifesting the four kinds of bodies.

6. The root teacher, possessed of the three forms of kindnesses, carrying the three kinds of traditions and lineages in a single form, resides in the palace of the indestructible spot, in the centre of the heart, surrounded by the innumerable excellent practicing deities of knowledge in peaceful and wrathful forms.

   Pray, bless us, may the self-liberation of the self-identity of four kinds become manifest.

7. The great house of seed and drop (veins and the vital fluid), the body, is home of aggregate of the three roots – the root Teacher, personal deity and the dakini. They send messages in symbols to the mother (Ekjati), the Lord (Mahakal), Rahul, the Vajra, and the lord of the cemetery, the five brothers, all possessed of the eyes of knowledge, the perfect guardians of the Doctrine.

   Pray, bless us with the rain of accomplishments of the fulfillment of the deeds.

8. The lotus-lake is like the lake of dirtless nectar, possessed of eight beneficial attributes, where live varied coloured birds of white, yellow, red and blue making sounds of ur-ru-ru like that of the sermons of the four branches of Mahayana, and are adorned with the various kinds of flowers of the Wish-granting tree.

   Pray, bless us, may we be able to attain perfection in our efforts in obtaining the three well known branches of knowledge.

9. The sky over the lake is covered by the cloud of the crowded assembly of the teachers of the three traditions. In the middle region there is the rain of the assembly of the guardian deities. A lightning of the guardian deities in protection of the lake flows on the margins. The mountains around it are similar to the copper coloured Shriparvat situated in the fabulous continent of Chamar-dvipa.

   Pray, bless us, may we be born in the pure land of the Buddhas.

10. By merely remembering, hearing about and visiting the holy place, all the sins that have been accumulated during the numerous previous lives become cleansed and the Buddha, in three Bodies, becomes manifested, in this my very life. By remembering it even for a moment all the difficulties are removed.

    Pray, let the doors of birth of six kinds of beings be shut.

11. By the power of blessings of this prayer, the beings existing to the extent of the expansion of the space from the top of the world down to the hell, all of them may be able to go to the chief city of the Premordial Lord Smantabhadra.

    Pray, bless us. May we be anointed with the blessings of two kinds of accomplishments.

12. May the essence of the body of the Teacher be blessed into our body so that all of us, the beings existing between the earth and the sky, be able to accomplish our tasks like your Vajra body, O Guru! May the essence of voice of the Teacher be blessed into our voice so that all of us, all the beings existing between the earth and the sky, be able to get our voice perfected like the voice of Brahma.

    May the essence of the heart of the Teacher be blessed into our heart so that all of us, the beings existing between the earth and the sky, be able to identify our minds with the Dharmkaya.

13. May I be able to attain the source of the knowledge which is like the sea of the Buddha deeds. O! Guru Padmasambhava, Guru of Oddiyan, I pray that I may be able to accomplish without delay, in this very life, just like you, the multitude of accomplishments, the source of all knowledge, which is like the sea of the Buddha deeds, while also working for the welfare of all beings. May I be able to accomplish the tasks of my life and get liberated.

    With the power attained on the accomplishment of the Three Precious Ones, which is without illusion, and the blessings of the group of the personal deities, and the powers granted by the airborne Dharmpalas, whatever prayer I make, may all be accomplished soon.

14. This prayer offering to the great and important pilgrimage place of Zahor, where there exists the Lake of water caused to have formed from the heap of fire by Vidyadhar Padmasambhava, was pronounced by sMang-sKyong Rig-'dsin Padma Kun-bzangr Gya-mtsho, at the time of great

offering ceremony on the occasion of pilgrimage to the place, not declining the instigation of the religious companions, on the 10th day of first month, in the year of water hare. May there be wellness and auspiciousness.

13 Guge

i. Colophon to Dorchhod, king Tashi Dagpa De, capital Tsarhang.

This is a karchhag from the book Dorchhod which is wholly written in gold ink.

Translation: The Buddha, excelling in (fulfilling) the objectives of the two kinds, the Excellent Doctrine which protects by removing the two kinds of sins, the Noble Congregation which liberates the two classes, I bow to the three incomparable Rare Ones reverentially. Ae ma ho! Jambudvipa in the south is the best among the continents. On the north of Vajrasana, where the Doctrine originated, is situated the mount Tise and the lake Mansarovar. On the left of the Satluj (Ganga), as it flows, is situated the great palace at the capital town of Tsa-hrang (rTsa-hrang). The king, is descended from the clan of 'Od-gsal whose white lustre does not fade. The great religious king, bKra-shis Grags-pa lDe, may he conquer all the unfriendly kingdoms. The pleasant village of Sha-'ang is under his vast reign.

...mang-yer-gur-ldog clan....,,,, Konchhog Palzang .... the deceased....

The lady donor younger sister dPal-zom mixed the nectar of the gods in the meal of men.

The excellent Vajrachhedika, Dig-shags, Ser-gi-pu-dri and Rin-chhen-ser were raised,. ...Lobzang Tashi, the excellent son and daughters Samdub, Khykug may they too become dear to the Doctrine like their parents. Moreover, relatives, the villagers and the neighbours doing, excellent services, may all the beings go to and be born in the heaven of Sukhavati.

Note: Here the capital of the king Tashi Dags-pa lDe is named as rTsa-hrang. Dorje from Spiti quotes the name from Sumpa Khanpo, and says that the monastery of rTsa-hrang Rag-rig was held by Rinchhen Zangpo. (Dorje, 1978: 80.). Tucci in his work on Rinchen Zangpo identifies Tsa-rang with Tsaparang in Guge, (Tucci, 1988: 57). The name also appears in the Namgya Document which has been identified by Petech with Tsaparang, (Petech, 1947: 196, 198). Tashi Dagpa does not appear to figure in the mNgaris rGyal-rabs.

ii. Guge, Karchhag, Ga-ga Sonam, capital Khartse.

Translation: Ga-ga Sonam, capital Khartse. Karchhag to the book: *'phags-pa 'jam-dpal gyi mtshan yang dag- par brjod-pa.*

Arhats reside at Tise, the neck of snow. Khartse, the capital, situated on the left side of the great river Sindhu (Sindhava), i.e. Satluj, is like an engraving on the earth. There resides Gaga Sonam whose crown is held high. Under his excellent rule, is the village of Ling-khyim where there has assembled the ten virtues. There live the lineage holder, belonging to the clan of bLon-chhos of the ancestors, the donor Sonam Palzin; the faithful donor Chhosjor Tshering and Lady donor Zang-kyid.

Book II
Texts in Bhoti

Part A - Lahul (Garzha)

1 Pattan (Manchhad), Chandrabhaga Valley

ii. Margul (Udaipur), Inscription on stone, Bhoti script, c. 17th-18th century C.E.

རྒྱན། ཨོཾ་སྭ་ཏི། ལྷ་རྒྱན་གྱིས་མ་གོས་སྐུ་འདོགས་དཀར།

ཛོགས་སངས་རྒྱས་ཀྱིས་དབུ་ལ་རྒྱན། ཐུགས་རྗེའི་སྤྱན་གྱིས་འགྲོ་ལ་

གཟིགས། སྤྱན་རས་གཟིགས་ལ་ཕྱག་འཚལ་ལོ། དྲི་མེད་རྒྱན་བྲལ་པད་

མའི་གདན་ལ་བཞུགས། ཞལ་གཅིག་ཕྱག་དྲུག་ཞབས་གཡས་གར་

སྟབས་མཛད། འགྲོ་དྲུག་འཁོར་བའི་གནས་ནས་འདྲེན་མཛད་པའི་རང་

བྱུང་འཕགས་པའི་སྐུ་ལ་ཕྱག་འཚལ་ལོ། ཅོམ་ལྡན་འདས་མ་རྡོ་རྗེ་ཕག་མོའི་

འཕགས་མ་ནི་དུས་ གསུམ་རྒྱལ་བའི་ཡུམ་མཆོག་དྲག་མོའི་གཟུགས་ཅན་མ།

སྨུགས་བྱེད་རེངས་བྱེད་སྨོས་བྱེད་དགག་ལ་རྣམ་རྒྱལ་བའི་དངོས་གྲུབ་རྣམས་གཉིས་

སྩོལ་ལ་ཕྱག་འཚལ་སྟོད། རླུང་སེམས་དབང་ཐོབ་རྣལ་འབྱོར་མ་གཅིག་ངའི་

བཞན་རྣམས་དགེ་བསྐུལ་ཕྱིར་ཐོག་ཐ་བར་གསུམ་མ་ཆི་སྟོང་ཕྲག་གསུམ་མི་འགྱུར་

ཇོ་ལ་བཞེངས་ཡོད། ཨེ་མ་ཧོ།།

གཞན་ཡང་རི་ཕག་འཕགས་པ་མར་སྐུ་ལ་གཉིས་ཀའི་བསྐོར་ལམ་དུ་མ་

ཆེ་འི་འཁོར་ལོ་ཅས་ཚང་ཡང་བཞེངས། མར་སྐུ་ལ་དགོན་པར་གསར་

བཞེངས། དགེ་འདི་འི་འགྲོ་ཀུན་སངས་རྒྱས་ཐོབ་ཤོག།། བཀྲ་ཤིས།།

iii. Triloknath (Rebag).
b. Karchhag, mDo, Lal Chand, Thakur of Triloknath, c. C.E. 1900.

ཀྱེ་ལགས། གླིང་གི་མཆོག་གྱུར་ལྷོའི་འཛམ་བུ་གླིང་། དམ་ཆོས་དར་བ་གནས་མཆོག་འཕགས་པའི་གླིང་། ས་ལ་འབུར་ཐོ་རྒྱལ་ས་རི་འཕགས་གླིང་། མི་དབང་ཆེན་པོ་ཇོ་བོ་བླ་ལ་སྤྱན་རྒྱ་དང་། སྐོར་གཉེར་འཛམ་དཔལ་ཆོས་རྒྱལ་གཉིས་ཀྱིས་སེམས་ཅན་གྱིས་འགྲོ་དོན་དུ། གསུངས་རབས་མདོ་མང་འདི་ལ་དག་ནས་ལྷན་དྲངས་པ་ཡིན།།

vii. Village Shansha (Śānśā, Shang)-1, Household of Bir Singh, Karchhag, Rai Dilip Singh (1869-1892), c. C.E. 1880.

ཨོཾ་ས་སྟི་སིད་དྷི་ཧྲ་(ཕ་)ལ་ཧོ། ཀར་ཆགས་བཞུགས་སོ།། རྒྱལ་ས་ཆེན་པོ་སུར་བརྟན་པུ་རི་ཛེ། ཆོས་རྒྱལ་ཆེན་པོ་དྷི་ལིབ་སེངྒེ་བཞུགས། ཆབ་སྲིད་ཡར་ངོའི་ཟླ་ལྟར་རྒྱས་པར་ཤོག། དེང་

སང་ས་ལ་དབང་བསྒྱུར་ཕྱི་གླིང་དུས། བསླབ་གསུམ་རྒྱན་མཛེས་ཆོས་འཁོར་ཨོ་ཐང་དགོན། ད་ལྟའི་ཞལ་བཞུགས་བློ་བཟང་ཉི་མ་བཞུགས། ཞྭ་སེར་བསྟན་པ་དར་ཞིང་རྒྱས་པར་ཤོག། ཁྱེད་ཀྱི་ཆབ་སྲིད་བཟང་པོའི་མངའ་འོག་འདིར། ཡུལ་གཡང་ཆགས་སྐྱིད་ཡུལ་ཤང་བསྐོད་ན། ལས་འབྲས་ཆོས་ལ་དགར་བའི་འཇིག་རྟེན་པ་མི་རྟག་སྒྱུ་མར་ཤེས་པའི་དད་ཅན་མ། མི་རིགས་ཁྱུངས་བཙུན་པ་མེའི་ཐོ་སུའི་བརྒྱུད། དད་ལྡན་ཡོན་གྱི་བདག་མོ་མ་ནེ་དང་། ནོ་མོ་ཆུང་བ་སོ་ནེ་དེ་ཉིད་ཀྱིས། སྤྱིར་དུས་སངས་རྒྱས་བསྟན་པ་དར་ཕྱིར་དང་། རྗེའི་ཆབ་སྲིད་མངའ་ཐང་མཐོ་ཕྱིར་དང་། མཐའི་དམག་དཔུང་ཐམས་ཅད་བཟློག་ཕྱིར་དང་། ཡར་འདྲེན་བླ་མ་རྣམས་ཀྱི་དགོངས་རྫོགས་དང་། འདྲེན་ཅན་པ་མ་རྣམས་ཀྱི་སྒྲིབ་སྦྱོང་དང་མཁའ་མཉམ་འགྲོ་བའི་རྣམ་མཁྱེན་ཐོབ་ཕྱིར་དང་། འཇིག་རྟེན་འདི་ནས་པ་རོལ་སྐུ་བཤེགས་ནི། སྐྱེ་དམན་གཉིས་ཀྱི་བདག་པོ་ཧྲི་ལི་རམ། ཧྲི་ལི་རམ་གྱི་པ་ནི་རག་དས། ཆུང་བ་ཨ་ཁུ་གྱི་ཤན་འདི་ཉིད་ཀྱང་། ཆོས་ཡི་དུས་བྱེད་བུ་ལས་ཕྱི་མ་ཡིན། སྲིད་པའི་མཚོ་ལས་བསྒྲལ་བའི་ལྟུང་(རླུང་)བཤགས་ཀྱི། བདེ་ཆེན་ཐར་པའི་ལམ་མཆོག་བསྒྲོད་ཕྱིར་དུ། ཆོས་ཕུང་བརྒྱད་ཁྲི་ནང་ནས་ཟབ་བསྡུས་པ། དམ་ཆོས་ཁྱད་འཕགས་རྡོ་རྗེ་གཅོད་པ་བཞེངས། གསུང་གི་རྟེན་ལ་ཐེག་གཤགས་གཟུངས་ཐོར་དང་། སྐུ་ཡི་རྟེན་ལ་ཆོས་སྐུ་སྣང་བ་མཐའ་ཡས། སྤྲུན་རས་གཟིགས་དང་ཚྭ་ཚ་གྲང་མང་བཞེངས། འཛངས་དྲུངས་ལྡན་ཞིང་གཉེན་འདྲེལ་མཐའ་ནས་སྐྱོང་། གཡོ་སྒྱུའི་ཕུང་གོས་ཕུད་སེར་སྣའི་མདུད་པ་གྲོལ། བདད་ལྡན་སྦྱིན་པའི་བདག་མོ་མ་ནེ་དང་། སྐྱེ་དམན་ནོ་མོ་སོ་ནེ་འདི་ཉིད་ཀྱིས། མི་ཡི་ཟས་ལ་ལྷ་ཡི་བདུད་རྩིར་སྒྱུར། བླ་དཔོན་ཞལ་དུ་གྲངས་པ་ངོ་མཚར་ཆེ། བློ་གྲོས་ལྡན་ཞིང་བྱམས་པའི་གོ་ཆ་གོས། དཀོན་མཆོག་མཆོད་ཅིང་དཀར་པོའི་དགེ་ལ་སློབས། པ་མ་བཞིན་ཆོས་ལ་དགར་བ་དང་། ཚེ་རིང་ནད་མེད་བདེ་སྐྱིད་ལྡན་པར་ཤོག། ཨ་ལ་ལ་ཧོ། དམ་ཆོས་འདི་ལ་དགེ་རྩེ་འབྱུང་ཐོ་ནི། ཐོག་མར་ཕ་རི་མག་པ་སུག་གུ་རམ་ཨུ་ཁྲི་ཚང་དང་ལག་ཤ་རྟེན། གོ་མཛིང་ཧྲི་ག་དང་ནོར་བུ་ཤ་ལག་པ་ཨ་རག་རྟེན། ཐྲ་ད་ར་བག་ནན་ཧྲ་ཨ་རག་རྟེན། ཡོད་ཏུབ་ཧྲ་ས་ཨ་རག་ཕྱེ་མར་བྱུང་། རྣམ་རྒྱལ་ཨ་རག་རྟེན། རང་བེ་ནོར་འཛོམ་དང་མ་ནུ་དངུལ་ཕྱེད་རྟེན། མཆོད་ནོར་འཁྱོར་ཨ་རག་ཕྱེ་མར་རྟེན། ཤང་ཤེ་བུ་ཨ་རག་རྟེན། དུ་ཙ་ཨ་ན་གཉིས། ཟུ་ཧྲ་རམ་ཨ་རག་ཕྱེ་མར། བྲམ་ཟེ་ཧྲ་ནི་ཨ་དངུལ་ཕྱེད། ས་ཟེ་རམ་ཨལ་(ཏལ་)ཧོ་ཆང་། གོ་གི་ཨ་ན་གཉིས། ཁོ་གུ་ཨ་རག། ཧྲ་ནི་ཨ་ན་བཞི། སུན་ཧྲུ་ར་ཨ་ན་གཉིས། ལྷ་པ་དོམ་པར་ཨ་རག་ཕྱེ་མར། སྒོ་རོམ་ཨུ་བརྒྱན་ཚེ་རིང་དང་ནོམ་ཅུང་ཨུ་ཁྲི་ཚང་དང་ར་པོ་རྟེན། གླིང་སྟོད་ཁོ་གུ་དང་ཚེ་རིང་བུ་ཁྲི་ཨུ་ཁྲི་ཚང་ཕྱེ་མར་རྟེན། ཕུར་པ་ཚེ་རིང་ར་པོ་རྟེན། ཚོགས་མཛིང་ནོ་ཚེ་རིང་དངུལ་རྟེན། ཡོབ་རང་ཏར་ཧྲ་ས་དངུལ་རྟེན། དགོན་པ་ནས་སྟོབས་ལྡན་ཨུ་ཁྲི་ཚང་ཕྱེ་མར་རྟེན། ཕུ་ར་ནས་རམ་ས་ཡི་དང་སྒྲོལ་མ་ཟ་མི་གཉིས་ཀྱི་ཨུ་ཁྲི་ཚང་ར་པོ་རྟེན། ར་གླིང་ནས་ལྷ་བབས་སྐྱི་བུ་ཨ་ན་བཞི་ཨ་རག་ཕྱེ་མར་རྟེན། ཆོས་འཛོམས་ཨ་རག་ཕྱེ་མར་རྟེན། ཕ་རི་ནས་པ་ཏུའི་དངུལ་གཅིག། ཡོད་ནས་ཧྲས་ཏའི་དངུལ་

གཅིག་། ཐྱ་གླིང་ཐྲ་ག་ཏ་ཨ་ན་གཉིས། ཡ་རྣམས་འཕེལ་ནས་ཅིང་ག་ཨ་ན་གཉིས། སྒོ་རོམ་ནས་སུ་ཀུ་ཨ་ན་བཞི། འཚོད་འབྲུག་ཨ་ན་བཞི། ཡོ་ཐྲ་རང་གཏྲ་ཨ་ན་བཞི། ཤང་སྨད་གཏྲ་རམ་དངུལ་ཕྱེད།།

རབ་གནས་ཀྱི་རྒྱུ་ཞིག་ཐོ་ལ། འབྲུ་ཁལ་ལྔ་བཅུ་ནས་ཆང་ལ་སོང་། ཁུ་ར་ལ་བག་ཕྱེ་ཁལ་སུམ་བཅུ་སོ་གཉིས། བྲམ་ཟེ་ལ་ཁལ་དགུ་སོང་། ཕེ་ལ་ནས་ཁལ་ཉི་ཤུ་སོང་།། ཏ་གིར་ལ་བག་ཕྱེ་ཁལ་བཅུ། ཁུ་ར་ཆུང་ཅེ་ལ་ཁལ་གཅིག་བག་ཕྱེ་སོང་། མར་ནག་མ་ཏ(ན་)ཕྱེད་དང་བཅུ། ལུག་བརྒྱད། རས་དངུལ་རིན་གཉིས། རྡོ་རྗེ་གཙོད་པ་དང་སྲིག་པ་གཤགས་ལ་སྐུ་ཡོན་ལ་དངུལ་ཕྱེད་དང་བཞི། སྤྱན་རས་གཟིགས་ཕྱག་བཞི་པ་ལ་དངུལ་ལྔ་བཅུ་ང་གཉིས། རབ་གནས་ཡོན་ལ་དངུལ་བདུན་སོང་། ནང་པ་ཕ་རི་སུ་ཀུ་རམ་དང་ཨོ་ཐང་ནོར་དཔལ་གཉིས། ཤ་པ་ཡང་ཕ་རི་སུ་ཀུ་རམ་དང་ཨུ་རྒྱན་ཚེ་རིང་གཉིས། ཆང་མ་ཕ་རི་ཏ་ས་རམ་དང་ཚེ་རིང་བུ་ཁྲིད་སློམ་ཚུང་སུམ་གྱི་མིའི་ཟས་ཏེ་ལྟའི་བདུད་རྩིར་སྦྱར་ནས་དཔོན་ལ་ཞབས་ཏོག་ལེགས་པར་བསྒྲུབས་པའི་དགའ་སྟོ་ལེགས། བཀྲ་ཤིས་དཔལ་བར་འཛམ་གླིང་རྒྱན་ཏུ་ཤོག།། ཅིག་ཞུས།།

viii. Shansha (Shang)-2, Household of Khinu, Karchhags.

a. Khinu, Shansha-2, Rai Dilip Singh (1869-1892), c. C.E. 1880.

རྒྱལ་ས་ཆེན་པོ་སུར་བསྟན་པུ་རི་རྗེ། ཆོས་རྒྱལ་ཆེན་པོ་རྡི་ལིབ་སེཾཧ་བཞུགས། དེང་སང་ས་ལ་དབང་སྒྱུར་ཕྱི་ལིང་དུས། ·····ཆོས་བློན་ཆེན་པོ་ཏ་རི་ཙན་ད་བཞུགས། ·····ཆོས་འཁོར་འོ་ཐང་དགོན་བླ་མ་ངག་དབང་དམ་ཆོས་བཞུགས། ཞྭ་སེར་བསྟན་པ་དར་ཞིང་རྒྱས་པར་ཤོག། བྱིན་བདག་ཐྲ་ཡི་དང་ཁོང་གྱི་བུ་གུར་ཚེ་རིང་། ·····ཕུན་སུམ་ཚོགས་པ་རྒྱལ་བ་རྒྱ་ཚོ་

ཡིས། ཕུན་སུམ་ཚོགས་པའི་ཡུལ་ཤང་སྟོད་ན། ཕུན་སུམ་ཚོགས་པའི་མདོ་

མང་ཀུན་བཞེངས།།

b. Shansha, Khinu, Thakur Hari Chand and Rai Megh Singh-i, (1892-1921), C.E. 1885.

དཀར་ཆགས་རྒྱལ་ས་ཆེན་པོ་སུར་བཏན་པུ་རི་ཞེས། ས་སྐྱོང་གདུང་

འཛིན་མི་ལྷ་སེང་ག་བཞུགས། དེང་སང་ས་ལ་དབང་སྒྱུར་ཕྱི་ལིང་པ་བཀའ་

བློན་ཆེན་པོ་ཧ་རི་ཙནྡ་ད་ཞེས། ཆོས་འཁོར་འོ་ཐང་དགོན། བླ་མ་བློ་བཟང་

བཞུགས། བྱིན་བདག་དོམ་དཔལ།འདི་ནས་ཕ་རོལ། སྐུ་གཤེགས་པ་ཕ་ཡི་

མཆོག་ཏུ་ཨ་གུ་ལྷ་ཏ་དང་བུ་རྣམས་ཀྱིས་ཟབ་མོ་འི་མདོ་འདི་བཞེངས། རབ་

གནས་རབ་བྱུང་བཅོ་ལྔ་ཤིང་མོ་བྱ་ལོ་ ཟླ་བ་བཅུ་གཅིག་ལ་རབ་གནས་བྱས་

སོང་།།

c. Shansha, Khinu, Thakur Amar Chand and Rai Megh Singh-ii, (1892-1921), C.E. 1910.

རྒྱལ་ས་ཆེན་པོ་སུར་བཏན་པུ་རི་ཞེས། ས་སྐྱོང་གདུང་འཛིན་མི་ལྷ་སེང་

གེ་བཞུག། དེང་སང་ས་ལ་དབང་སྒྱུར་ཕྱི་ལིང་པ། བཀའ་བློན་ཆེན་པོ་ཨ་

མར་ཙནྡ་དར་བཞུགས། ཆོས་འཁོར་འོ་ཐང་དགོན། བླ་མ་ནི་ལྷུན་གྲུབ་བཀྲ་

ཞིས། སྐྱིད་ཡུལ་ཤང་སྟོད།ཁྲིན་བདག་ཇོ་ཐྐ་ལ་དང་བུ་འི་མཆོག་གྲུར་སྦུ་ཁི་ར་མ། རབ་གནས་འདི་ལ་རྒྱ་སོང་གི་ཐོ་ལ། ནས་ཁ་རི་ལྔ་སོང་། མར་ནག་མ་ན་བརྒྱད་སོང་། མར་མ་ན་གཅིག་སོང་། སྔོར་བཅོ་ལྔ་སོང་། རས་དངུལ་བཅུ་གཉིས། འགྲུས་ཁལ་གསུམ། ཛ་དངུལ་བཞི་སོང་། ལུག་ལྔ་སོང་།།

d. Shansha, Khinu, Thakur Amar Chand and Rai Megh Singh-iii (1892-1921), C.E. 1921.

ཀར་ཤགས་བསལ་བའི་མི་ལོངས་བཞུགས་སོ། རྒྱལ་ས་ཆེན་པོ་སུར་བཏན་པུ་རི་ཞེས།ས་སྐྱོང་གདུང་འཛིན་མི་གྷ་སིང་གྷ''ག་བཞུགས། དེང་སང་ས་ལ་དབང་སྒྱུར་ཕྱི་ལིང་པ། བཀའ་བློན་ཆེན་པོ་ཨ་མར་ཙན་དར་བཞུགས། ཆོས་འཁོར་འོ་ཐང་དགོན། བློ་བཟང་དོན་འགྲུབ་བཞུགས། ཁྲིན་བདག་ཇོམ་ཐྐལ། རབ་བྱུང་བཅོ་ལྔ་ལྕགས་མོ་བྱ་ལོ་ཟླ་བ་གསུམ་པའི་ཚེ་བརྒྱད་དགེ་བ་འདི་བྱུས།།

e. Shansha, Khinu, Thakur Abhe Chand and Rai Bhagwant Singh-i, (1921-1947), C.E. 1924.

རྒྱལ་ས་ཆེན་པོ་སུར་བརྟན་པུ་རི་ཞེས། ས་སྐྱོང་གདུང་འཛིན་བྷ་གའན་སེང་གེ་བཞུགས། དེང་སང་ས་ལ་དབང་སྒྱུར་ཕྱི་གླིང་པས། བཀའ་བློན་ཆེན་པོ་ཨ་བྷེ་ཙན་ད་བཞུགས། ཆོས་འཁོར་འོ་ཐང་དགོན། ད་ལྟ་འི་ཞལ་བཞུགས་བླ་མ་ཚེ་རིང་དོན་གྲུབ་མཚན། ཞྭ་སེར། ཡུལ་ཤང་སྡོད། དད་ལྡན་ཡོན་བདག་སུ་ཁ་ར་མ་དང་བུ་སོ་བྷ་ར་མ། འདི་ག་རྟེན་འདི་ནས་ཕ་རོལ་སྐུ་བཞེངས་པ་ཨ་བྷ་རྫོམ་བྷལ། སྲིད་མོ་སུ་ག་དྷ་སི། རབ་བྱུང་བཅོ་ལྔ་འི་ཤིང་ཕྱི་ཟླ་བ་བཅུ་པའི་བཅོ་ལྔ་ལ་རབ་གནས་བྱས་སོང་གཟའ་པ་སང་།།

f. Shansha, Khinu, Thakur Abhe Chand and Rai Bhagwant Singh-ii, (1921-1947), C.E. 1928.

རྒྱལ་ས་ཆེན་པོ་སུར་བརྟན་པུ་རི་ཞེས། ས་སྐྱོང་འདུལ་འཛིན་བྷ་སྭན་སེང་གེ་བཞུགས། དེང་སང་ས་ལ་དབང་སྒྱུར་ཕྱི་གླིང་པས། བཀའ་བློན་ཆེན་པོ་ཨ་བྷེ་ཙན་ཌ་བཞུགས། བསླབ་གསུམ་རྒྱན་མཛེས་ཆོས་འཁོར་ཐང་དགོན། ད་ལྟའི་ཞལ་བཞུགས་བླ་མ་ཡེ་ཤེས་བཟང་པོ་བཞུགས། ཞྭ་སེར་བསྟན་པ་དར་ཞིང་རྒྱས་པར་ཤོག། སྐྱིད་ཡུལ་ཤང་སྡོད་འདིར། མི་རིགས་ཁྲངས་བཙུན། ཕ་མི་ལྷ་བེ་རྒྱུད། དད་དན་ཡོན་གྱི་བདག་པོ་སུ་ཁ་ར་མ་དང་

བུ་འི་མཆོག་གྲུར་སོ་བྷ་ར་མ།   རབ་བྱུང་བཅོ་ལྔ་ས་འབྲུག་ཟླ་བ་བཅུ་པའི་ཚེ་བཅུ་ལ་རབ་གནས་བྱས་སོང་།།

g. Shansha, Khinu, Thakur Abhe Chand and Rai Bhagwant Singh-iii, (1921-1947), c. C.E. 1930.

རྒྱལ་ས་ཆེན་པོ་སྲུར་བརྟན་པུ་རི་ཞེས།   ཆོས་རྒྱལ་གདུང་འཛིན་བྷ་གན་སེང་ག།   དེང་སང་ས་ལ་དབང་སྒྱུར་ཕྱི་གླིང་དུས།   ཆོས་བློན་ཆེན་པོ་ཨ་བྷེ་ཙན་ད་བཞུགས།།

h. Shansha, Khinu, Thakur Pratap Chand and Rai Bhagwant Singh-iv (1921-1947), C.E. 1933.

རྒྱལ་ས་ཆེན་པོ་སྲུར་བརྟན་པུ་རི་ཞེས།   ཆོས་རྒྱལ་གདུང་ཛིན་བྷ་གན་སེང་ག་བཞུགས།   དེང་སང་ས་ལ་དབང་སྒྱུར་ཕྱི་གླིང་དུས།   ཆོས་བློན་ཆེན་པོ་པར་འཏབ་ཙན་ད་བཞུགས།   ཆོས་འཁོར་འོ་ཐང་དགོན།   ད་ལྷ་ཞལ་བཞུགས་བླ་མ་བློ་བཟང་དོན་གྲུབ།   ཡུལ་ཤང་སྟོད།   སྦྱིན་པའི་བདག་པོ་སུ་ཁ་ར་མ་བུའི་མཆོག་གྲུར་སོ་བ་ར་མ།   རབ་བྱུང་བཅོ་ལྔ་ཆུ་བྱའི་ཟླ་བ་བཅུ་པའི་ཚེས་བཅུ་ལ་རབ་གནས་བྱས་སོང་།།

i. Padma Thangyig copied from the wood blocks made at Tayul (Te-yur) monastery, Tashi Tanphel, C.E. 1885, Karchhag.

དཀར་ཆགས།ཐང་ཡིག། བཀྲིས་བསྟན་འཕེལ། ཨུ་རྒྱན་གུ་རུ་པདྨ་འབྱུང་གནས་ཀྱི་སྐྱེས་རབས་རྣམ་པར་ཐར་པ་རྒྱས་པར་བཀོད་པ་པདྨ་བཀའ་འི་ཐང་ཡིག། སངས་རྒྱས་ཀུན་འདུས་པདྨ་འབྱུང་གནས་ཀྱི་རྣམ་པར་ཐར་པ་ལ་མི་ཕྱེད་པའི་དད་པ་ཐོབ་པ་ཤད་འོ་བཟང་དུ་འཁྲུངས་པ་ཏེ་མི་དགོན་གྱི་མཛོད་ཟུར། བསོད་ནམས་ལྷུན་གྲུབ་དང་། ''''''ནོ་བསོད་ནམས་རྡོ་རྗེ་སྐུན་གཉིས་ཀྱི་ཕ་གཡང་འཛིན་དང་མ་མཚོ་མོ་གཉིས་ཀྱི་གཙོ། '''གསུང་འབུམ་སོགས་གྲུབ་པོད་མང་པོ་དང་། ལྷག་ཏུ་གུ་རུ་པདྨ་འི་རྣམ་ཐར་གྱི་པར་གསར་སྒྲུབ་པའི་ཐུགས་བསྐྱེད་བཟང་པོ་རྨད་དུ་བྱུང་བའི་མདུན་པ་དྲག་པོས། རབ་བྱུང་བཅོ་ལྔ་ཆུ་ལུག་ལོ་ཟླ་བ་བརྒྱད་པར་མཛོད་ཟུར་བསོད་ནམས་ལྷུན་གྲུབ་རང་ཉིད་གར་ཞ་རུ་ཕེབས་ནས། གར་ཞ་རྡོ་གསུམ་ལ་པར་ཞིང་སྒྲུབ་པའི་ས་གནས་གཞན་དུ་མེད་སྟབས་ཀྱི་ཞུ་བ་ཡིན་པར། དམ་པ་རྣམས་ཀྱི་མགོ་འདྲེན་ཐོག་འདི་ཁ་གར་ཞ་རུ་པར་སྒྲུབ་དགོས་སྐན་མགྲོན་ཞུས་རྗེན་མཁར་གསར་མཁར་གྱི་རྡོ་མི་དཔང་

ཞྭ་ཟེར་ཏ་རི་ཙནྡྲ་ཡི་པར་ཤིང་ཡོངས་རྫོགས་དང་གཅིས་མ་མན་ཧྲ་སི་ལྷན་རྒྱས་ནས་དངུལ་གྱིར་མོ་ཉེར་ལྔ། ཕོ་ལར་གྱིར་མོ་གཅིག་གི་རིན། པར་པ་སོགས་ལ་ཕར། སྐུ་མགྲོན།ཡང་འབྲས་ཁལ་གཅིག། ཤ་ཁོག་གཉིས། ཙོང་ཕླ་ཏྲི་གཅིག། འབྲུ་ཁལ་གསུམ། མཁར་གསར་གཅིས་མ་ནོར་འཛིན་ནི་འབྲུ་ཁལ་གསུམ། དཀུང་རང་ཇོ་མི་དབང་ནོ་ནོ་དེ་ཕླི་ཙནྡྲ་ཡིས་ཛ་ཕླ་ཏྲི་གཅིག། མར་ཕླ་ཏྲི་གཅིག་དང་སེར་བཞི། མར་ནག་ཕླ་ཏྲི་གཉིས། ཤ་གོག་གཉིས། ཕེ་ཁལ་བཅུ་གསུམ། བག་ཕེ་ཁལ་གཉིས་བྲེ་བཅུ། འབྲས་ཁལ་གཉིས། ལྩམ་ཁལ་གཅིག་བྲེ་བཅུ། གཅིས་མ་ཆེན་མོ་ཚེ་རིང་དཔལ་འཛོམ་གྱི་མར་ཕླ་ཏྲི་གཉིས་དང་སེར་གསུམ། ཇོ་ཇོ་དཔལ་འཛོམ་གྱི་ཕེ་ཁལ་གསུམ། ཚེ་རིང་བསོད་ནམས་གྱི་མར་སེར་བཞི། ཏེ་ནན་ཇོ་ཏ་རི་ཙནྡྲ་དང་གཅིས་མ་ཚེ་རིང་སྒྲོལ་མ་ལཏ་ཡས་ནི། མར་ཕླ་ཏྲི་གཅིག། གྲོ་ཁལ་དགུ།ཕེ་ཁལ་གསུམ། ཤ་གོག་གཅིག། འབྲས་ཁལ་འབྲུག། ལ་དྭགས་རྒྱལ་མོ་ཚེ་འཛིན་དཔལ་མཛེས་སྒྲོལ་མ་བུ་ཁྲིད་དབང་མོ་ཡིས་འབྲུ་དང་སྤྱ་གཅིག། བླ་མ་བཀྲ་

ཞིས་སྟན་འཕེལ་གྱི་གྱིར་མོ་ཉེར་ལྔ། གུས་ཀྱུར་དཔལ་བཟང་གི་ཇ་སེར་ཕེ་དང་གསུམ། ཀྱ་ལང་གོང་ཀྱུག་ཀྱུག་གི་མར་ལྷ་དྲི་གཅིག། མ་དགོན་ནོ་ནོ་ཏརི་ཧོད་དང་གཅེས་མ་དཔལ་འཛོམ་བུ་ཁྲིད་གཉིས་ཀྱི་ཞབ་ཁལ་གཉིས་། འབྲུ་ཁལ་གཅིག་གི་སྣེམ། མ་དགོན་ཧོ་མོ་རྣམ་རྒྱལ་བུ་ཁྲིད་ཀྱི་ཁལ་གཅིག་གི་ལྷུམ། དགུང་གླིང་འཚོ་བྱེད་དཔལ་བཟང་གི་འབྲུ་ཁལ་གཅིག། གྱོར་ཧོ་མོ་ཚེ་སྐྱིད་ཀྱི་ཁལ་གཉིས་ལྷུམ། གསོལ་དཔོན་ཚེ་སྐྱིད་ཀྱི་ཁལ་གཅིག་ལྷུམ། ཕྱི་གླིང་ཧོ་མོ་བསོད་ནམས་སྒྲོལ་མའི་བྲི་བཅོ་ལྔའི་ལྷུམ། ལྷབ་ཅང་དབང་ཕྱུག་དང་སྒྲོལ་མ་གཉིས་ནི་གྲོ་ཁལ་གསུམ། འབྲུ་ཁལ་གསུམ། ཀ་རིང་སྤྱང་རིང་དབང་དྲག་རྡོ་རྗེ་དང་བསོད་ནམས་ཆོས་འཕེལ་ནང་ཚང་ནི་གྲོ་ཁལ་གཉིས། བུ་ཕོད་ཆོས་གྲགས་ཀྱི་གྱིར་མོ་གཅིག། མོ་ཞི་དྣ་ཡ་ལུ་ཡི་གྱིར་མོ་གཅིག། གྱོར་མ་དགོན་དགུང་གླིང་སོགས་ཀྱི་པར་པ་རྣམས་ལ་ཞབས་ཏགས་ལེགས་པར་ཕུལ། པར་འདི་ཡི་ལས་ཀྱི་འགན་ཁུར་ནི། མར་ཁ་བ་མེ་ཉག་གདོང་དམར་པོའི་རིགས་སུ་སྐྱེས་པ་དེ་མིས་གྲྭ་སྟག་སྟ་ཟླ་མ་བཀྲ་ཞིས་

སྟན་འཕེལ་གྱི་དབུ་མཛུག་གི་ཟླ་འབྲིས། ཤོག་གྲངས་གཅིག་ནི་བརྒྱ་དོན་
ཅིག། ཉིས་བརྒྱ་གྱ་ཅིག་ནི་མཛུག་རྫོགས་པར་པར་ཡིག་ཀྱང་རང་ཉིད་ཀྱི་
བྲིས། བརྒྱ་དོན་གཉིས་ནི་ཉིས་བརྒྱ་བརྒྱད་བཅུ་བར་པར་ཡིག་ཀྱ་ལང་
འོག་ཐར་པ་ཙུག་ཤི་ཆེ་དབང་། པར་ཞུས་ཀ་ཡ་རྒྱས་བདག་བཙུན་པ་
མཆོད་གནས་ཕུན་ཚོགས། རྐོས་མཁན་མར་ཁ་འུམ་ལུང་བ་སྐྱབ་པ་
དཔལ་འབྱོར་ཕུན་ཚོགས། ཆུ་ཤོད་མི་ཕམ། ཟང་མཁར་པི་བུ་ཚེ་རིང་
དབང་ཕྱུག། སྟོད་དགེ་སུར་དགོན་ནི། ནོ་ནོ་དཀར་རྒྱུད་རིག་འཛིན།
བསྟན་པ་ཚེ་རིང་། ཏི་ནོ་དགོན་མཆོག་བཟོད་པ། ཡོ་ཅེ་བསྟན་འཛིན་
དོན་གྲུབ། ཡར་གཞི་བསྟན་འཛིན་ཆོས་འཕེལ། ཟླ་རོང་རྡོ་མོ། ལྷ་རྗེ་
ཚོས་སྐྱིད། པུ་ནན་མཁས་སྐྱབ་ཟླ་མ་ཚེ་དབང་རིག་འཛིན་དང་དབུ་མཛབ་
ཕྲིས་གཉིས་ཀྱི་གྲྭ་བུ་སློབ། བང་བཀར་སྟོང་། བསོད་ནམས་རྡོ་རྗེ། ལྷ་
རྗེ་ཚེ་རིང་།ཁྲིམས་བརྩེས་ཚེ་རིང་།ནོར་བུ། མ་ཧི་པ་དོན་གྲུབ། ཞོ་གླིང་
རིག་འཛིན། དཔལ་ལྡན། ཀླི་གླིང་ནོར་བུ། བསོད་ནམས་རིག་འཛིན།
ཨ་ནུ་ཅེ། འཇིགས་བྱེད། ཀྱི་ཅེ།ཀྱ་ལང་འོག་ཅེ་པ། འབྲུག་རྡོ་རྗེ།

རིག་འཛིན། ནོར་བུ།ཀྱཱ་ལང་གོང་ནི་ཀླུ་ཀར་རིག་འཛིན། བར་ཅི་ན་མོ། གློ་རོམ་འབྲུག་ཆེ་རིང་། ནག་ཚ་དང་པར་ཡིག་གི་ཤོག་རྫུ་ལ་མི་ཏེ་ཡུད་དཀོན་གཉེར་ཀུ་ལུ། གཉེར་དོ་དམ་སྐྱབ་པ། གསོལ་དཔོན་ཇོ་མོ་བསོད་ནམས་ཆོས་སྒྲིད།།

གཞན་ཏེ་ཡུར་དགོན་གྱི་ཆོས་མཛད། ཇོ་མོ་འབྲུག་འཛོམ། མ་དགོན་ཨ་ནེ། དཔལ་འཛོམ་གཉིས། ཨུ་རྒྱན་སྒྲོལ་མ། བགྲིས་བཅས་ཀྱི་པར་པ་སོགས་ལ་དགེ་རྗེས། ཤིང་རྩུ་རྒྱུ་ལུས་ཀྱི་ཞབས་རྟོག་སྐྲོ་གསུམ་གྱུས་པ་ཆེན་པོའི་སྐྱབ་པའི། གནས་ཏེ་ཡུར་དགོན་ཨུ་རྒྱན་ཆོས་འཁོར་གླིང་དུ། རབ་བྱུང་བཅོ་ལྔ་ནང་གི་ཤིང་བྱ་ལོ་འདི་སྐབས། རྣམ་འདྲེན་ཤ་ཀྱའི་རྒྱལ་པོ་སྲིད་ཞིའི་མགོན་ཤར་ནི་འདས་ལོ་ཉིས་སྟོང་བདུན་བརྒྱ་གྱ་དྲུག། གྲུབ་ཐོབ་སྟག་རས་འཁྲུངས་ནས་ལོ་གསུམ་བརྒྱ་བཅུ་གཅིག། ཏེ་སི་དགོན་ས་གཞི་བྱིན་བརླབས་ནི་ལོ་ཉིས་བརྒྱ་རེ་དྲུག། ཏེ་སི་མཛོད་ཁྲིའི་བཞུགས་ངག་དབང་ཆོས་བཟང་གི་ཞལ་འདེབས་གྱིར་མོ་ཉེར་གཅིག།

ལ་དྭགས་སེང་པའི་དབང་དུ་སོང་ནི་ལོ་ང་ཅིག། ཤི་ཧྣི་མ་ཧླ་རླ་ཛ་

ནྡ་ཀྲི་ར་སེང་མངའ་ཐང་རྒྱས་ཤིང་། ལ་དྭགས་སྐྱོང་བ་སྟོཾས་རྣམ་རྒྱལ་རྡོ་རྗེ་ཁྲི་

ལ་འཚོ་གཞིས་དུས། འཕགས་ཡུལ་པའི་སན་སྟོང་དང་དགུ་བརྒྱ་ཞེ་གཉིས་

ཧི་དུ་ཏན་སོགས་ལ་དབང་བསྒྱུར་བའི་རྒྱལ་མོ་གོ་ཡི་ཀླི་ག་ཏུ་རི་ཡཱ་ཀི་སར་

ཧིན་དི། དེ་ཡི་ཆབ་སྲིད་གར་ཞ་འདི་ཡི་འཁྲིས་ཀྱི་བྱེད་པོ། ཁར་སར་ཛོ་མི་

དབང་ཕྱ་ཟེར་ཧ་རི་ཅན་དར་དབང་བསྒྱུར་བའི་དུས་སུ་བསྒྲུབ་པའི་གར་ཆགས་

འདི་བཞིན་བླ་མ་བཀྲིས་བསྟན་འཕེལ་གྱིས་བྲིས་པ་སྐྱེ་དགུ་རྣམས་དགེ་བཅུའི་

དཔལ་ལ་སྤྱོད་པར་གྱུར་ཅིག།

ix. Village Rwaling (Rāllṅ, Rwāllṅ), Household Srangpa (Ṣāñpā).

a. Rwaling, Srangpa, mDo-mangs, c. 17th-18th century C.E.

ཡོན་བདག་ཀུན་ཟ་མི་གཉིས་ཀྱང་། ང་རེའི་སྡིག་སྒྲིབ་མ་ལུས་དག་

ཕྱིར་དང་། དྲིན་ཅན་ཕ་མི་དྲིན་ལན་བསམ་ཕྱིར། ཚེ་འདས་ཨ་མ་ཧླ་གྱུ་ལ་

དང་སྤུ་བ་སྐྱིད་གཉིས་བདེ་ཆེན་ཐར་པའི་ཞིང་དུ་འདྲེན་སྒྲོད་ཕྱིར་དུ། དམ་

ཆོས་ཁྲིད་འཕགས་སྟང་རྒྱུད་དང་། སྐྱུན་ཏུ་བཟང་པོའི་སྨོན་ལམ་དང་།

གཙུག་ཏོར་ནག་མོ་སྡིག་བཤིགས་གསེར་གྱི་སྤྱུ་གྲི། དབྱངས་ཡིག་རྟེན་

འབྲིལ་སྟིང་ལ་སོགས་བཞིངས། བསགས་པ་ཆོས་ཕྱིར་གཏོང་བ་ཨ་ལ་ལ། ངོ་མཚར་ཆེའོ།།

b. Rwaling, Srangpa, c. 17th-18th century C.E.

ཨོཾ་སྭ་སྟི །གསུང་རབ་འདི་ལ་དགེ་རྩིས་འབྱུང་གྲངས་ལ། ཨ་པ་ཞུན་ནུ་སྐྱོག་ཞབས་ཅིག་ཏེན། ཀ་ཆེན་བློ་བཟང་མཁས་གྲུབ་གསོལ་ཛ་སྐྱོག་ཞབས་རྒྱས་པ་འབྱུང་། གྲུབ་པ་དཀོན་མཆོག་རང་གྲོལ་གསོལ་ཛ། གྲུབ་པ་མཉ་ཧུ་ཕུ་དེབས་གཅིག། ལག་ཐག། ཨ་ཅི་ཛོ་མོ་ཕྲིས་རོ་ལ་མ་ཆང་ཅིག་ལག་ཕྲ་སོགས་ཞན་ཡང་དཔོན་རྣམས་ལ་སྙིན་ཀུར་ལེགས་པར་མཛད་པ་ཨ་ལ་ལ། ར་པེ་ན། ནང་བློན་ར་མགོ་ཟ་མི་གཉིས་ཀྱིས་མཆོ་བ་གདན་ནོན་ཆང་གཅིག། ཅེ་པ་ཟ་མི་གཉིས་ཆང་ཆོ་བ་གདན་ནོན། རྒྱམ་ཆོ་ཟ་མི་གཉིས་ཀྱི་མཆོ་བ་གདན་ནོན་ཆང་ཨ་རག་ཁྲུ་ར་ཏེན། ངག་དབང་བསམ་གཏན་ཆང་གཅིག་ཁྲུ་ར། ར་སྤྲེལ་ན། བསོད་ནམ་བཀྲིས་ཆང་གཅིག་ཁྲུ་ར། བསམ་འགྲོར་ཆང་གཅིག་ཁྲུ་ར། མར་རིལ་ཅིག། ཕྲ་ལག་པ། ལག་ཕྲ། ནང་ཕྲ།

ཞ་དལ་མོ། ལིང་ཐུང་། གཡོ་འབྲང་། གྲོ་ཟིང་། མང་ལང་། རང་ལྡེ། ཀེ་ ལང་འོག། ནང་སྔོན་སྔོད། ཤ་རི། འོ་ཏ་མ་ན།།

c. Rwaling, Srangpa, mDo., Raja Tedhi Singh (1742-1767), c. C.E.1760.

ཨོཾ་སྭ་སྟི་སི་དྡྷཾ། ཨེ་མ་ཧོ། གངས་ཅན་གྲོ་བའི་མུན་སེལ་བཀའ་བརྒྱུད་འདི། དགྲ་བཅོམ་བཞུགས་གནས་ཏི་སེ་གངས་ཀྱི་འགུལ། དེ་ནས་རི་བརྒྱུད་མ་ཆད་པ་འབྲེལ་བ་ལས། ཡུལ་ལ་ཡངས་ཆགས་གར་ཞ་མཁའ་འགྲོའི་གླིང་། སྟོད་ནས་གནས་ཆེན་ཁྲུད་འཕགས་དྲིལ་བུ་རི། བཅོམ་ལྡན་བདེ་མཆོག་འཁོར་ལོའི་ཕོ་བྲང་དུ། རྒྱལ་བ་རྣམས་ཀྱིས་ལུང་དུ་བསྟན་པའི་གནས། མདོ་ན་རྡོ་རྗེ་ཕག་མོའི་ཐེ་བོང་བཞུགས། ཡུལ་ཆེན་ཉེར་བཞི་ཡ་ཁལ་མཁའ་འགྲོའི་གནས། དཔའ་བོ་མཁའ་འགྲོ་ཚོགས་རྣམས་འདུས་པའི་ཞིང་། བར་ན་གནས་ཆེན་རི་བོ་པོ་ཏ་ལར། ཁམས་གསུམ་འགྲོའི་དཔལ་མགོན་སྤྱན་རས་གཟིགས། ཐུགས་རྗེ་ཆེན་འགྲོ་དྲུག་འགྲོལ་བཞུགས། ས་ལ་འབུར་ཡ་ཕློ་ཡི་རྒྱལ་ས་ཆེན་པོ་སུར་ཏན་པུར། ཆོས་རྒྱལ་ཆེན་པོ་མཛེས་སེང་གེ་དང་སྤྱུལ་པའི་རྒྱལ་མོ་ཝླ་ཀུ་ཏྲེ་བ་གཉིས། དབུ་དམོག་མཐོ་ཞིང་ཆབ་

སྲིད་དར་བའི་དུས། ཁྲིད་ཀྱི་ཆབ་སྲིད་བཟང་པོའི་མངའ་འོག་འདིར། བླ་མའི་གདན་ས་ཆོས་བསྒྲོར་ཨོ་ཏ་མར། བླ་མ་ཡེ་ཤེས་དཔལ་འབྱོར་ཆོས་གཙུག་མཐོ་བ་དང་། དེ་འི་འཁོར་མང་དགེ་འདུན་རྣམས་ལ་བསྟོད། འདི་སྐྱིད་འཛོམ་པའི་སྐྱིད་ཡུལ་གཡོ་བྲང།།'

x. Village Lindoor (gLing-tud, gLing-stod)

a. Lindoor Raja Pritam Singh-i, (1767-1806), c. C.E. 1780.

ལྷའི་ཕོ་བྲང་འདྲ་བ་རྒྱལ་ས་མ་གར་སང་། ཧྣ་ན་སྡུག་པའི་གྲོང་ཁྱེར་ཡིན་ནམ་ཅི། དེར་བཞུགས་མི་ཐུབ་སྡེ་ལ་རྣམ་པར་རྒྱལ། རྒྱལ་པོ་པྲི་ཏམ་སེང་འགྲ་ཡབ་སྲས་རྒྱལ་ཁྲིམས་དར་བའི་དུས། དེའི་མངའ་འོག་གར་ཞ་ཁྲིམས་ཀྱི་ཡུལ། ཡང་ཡུལ་ཁྱད་དུ་འཕགས་པའི་ལིང་ཏུད་འདིར། མི་རིགས་ཁྱུང་བཙུན་ཡབ་མེ་བཟང་པོའི་རྒྱུད་ཡོན་གྱི་བདག་པོ་བསོད་ནམས་དཔལ་ལྷེ་ཀུང་དྲིན་ཅན་ཨ་པའི་དོན་དུ། དམ་ཆོས་རྡོ་རྗེ་བཅོད་པ་མཆར་བདུན་ཞེངས། ཤེས་རབ་སྙིང་པོ་དང་བྱང་ཆུབ་ལྟུང་བཤགས་དང་། མགོན་པོ་གླུ་གྲུབ་སྨོན་ལམ་དང་། རྡོ་རྗེ་ནམ་བཅོ་འཇོམས་དང་། བཟང་པོ་སྤྱོད་པ་དང་། སྡིག་ཤེགས་གསེར་གྱི་སྤུ་དྲི་དང་། མདོ་སྡེ་འཚར་ཙུ་གསུམ་ཞེངས། གཡོན་གྱི་བདག་མོ་འཕགས་པ་སྐྱིད།།

b. Lindoor, Raja Pritam Singh-ii, (1767-1806), c. C.E. 1800.

བླ་མའི་གདན་ས་ཆོས་བསྒྲོར་ཨོ་ཏ་མར། ས་ལ་འབུར་ཐོས་རྒྱལ་ས་སུར་སྟན་པུར་ཆོས་རྒྱལ་ཆེན་པོ་པྲིས་ཏེ་སེང་ཐྭ་དབུ་མོག་ཐོས་པའི་དུས། ཀ་བློན་ཆེན་པོ་མི་ཨཱ་རྩ་རན་ཧྣ་ས་ལ་སྟོད། དེའི་ཆབ་སྲིད་

བཟང་པོས་མངའ་འོག་འདིར། ཡུལ་ལ་ཡང་ཚགས་སྐྱིད་པའི་གར་ཞྭ་མཁའ་འགྲོའི་ཡུལ། ཀྱི་ལེགས། དགེ་བཅུ་མཛོམ་པའི་སྐྱིད་ཡུལ་ལྷིང་ཏུད་འདིར། མིས་རིགས་ཁྲུངས་བཙུན་པ་མི་རྒྱན་ཤིང་རྒྱུད། དད་ལྡན་ཡོན་གྱིས་བདག་པོ་ནན་ཀུ་བླི་དང་ཡོན་གྱིས་བདག་མོ་སེར་མཛོམ་ཉིས་ཀྱིས་ཚེ་ལ་འདས་པ་ཨ་ཕྱ་ཚེ་རིངས་ལེགས་པ་ཨ་མ་བསམ་བུ་སྒྲིད་ཉིས་དོན་དང་ཚེ་འདས་དབྱར་མཛོམ་ཞུང་ཧྲི་ལྷ་ཐོག་ཏུ་ལུག་གསུམ་བཅུ་སོ་སུམ་ཤེས་བའི་དེ་རྣམས་ཐམས་ཅད་ཀྱི་དོན་དུ་དམ་ཆོས་ཁྱད་འཕགས་ཆོས་པགས་མེད་མ་བུ་སུམ། རྡོར་བཅོད་ཕྱིག་ཤེགས་བར་རྡེ་རང་སྒྲོལ་ནང་རྒྱུད་དང་འཛོམས་ན་འདུན་ཞིངས།།

c. Lindoor, Rai Megh Singh (1892-1921), c. C.E. 1910.

རྒྱལ་ས་ཆེན་པོ་སུར་བརྟན་བུ་རེ་རྗེ། ཆོས་རྒྱལ་ཆེན་པོ་མེགྷ་སེངྒེ་བཞུགས། དེང་སང་ས་ལ་དབང་སྒྱུར་ཕེ་གླིང་དུས། རྗེའི་བཀའ་བཞིན་སྒྲུབ་པའི་བློན་ཆེན་ནི་ཨ་སྲ་ཙནྡྲ་ཞེས་པ་ཡབ་སྲས་བཞུགས། ཡུལ་ལ་གཡང་ཚགས་སྐྱིད་ཡུལ་གླིང་སྟོད་འདིར། མི་རིགས་ཁྲུངས་བཙུན་རྒྱ་ཤིང་རྒྱུད། དད་ལྡན་ཡོན་གྱི་བདག་པོ་ཞྱོ་ན་ཚེ་རིང་དང་འཛིག་རྟེན་འདི་ནས་ཕ་རོལ་སྐྱུ་གཤེགས་རྣམས། ཚེ་འདས་མེ་མེ་ནན་དེ་རམ། དང་ཨ་ཕྱ་བག་མན་དང་ཨ་མ་ཚེ་རིང་ཀུན་འཛོམ་དང་།ནོ་རྫོང་གུ་རུ་དང་སུན་ཁྲ་གཉིས། མནའ་མ་སེར་འཛོམ་དང་། ཡང་མནའ་མ་སེར་འཛོམ།

ཚེ་འདས་དེ་རྣམས་ཐར་ལམ་ཐོབ་ཕྱིར་དུ། དམ་ཆོས་མཆོད་འབུམ་བཞེངས།།

ནང་པ་ཨོ་ཐང་ཐྲ་ར་དང་། མ་ལང་ཤི་བུ་དང་། ཀོ་ཐི་གུར་དས་དང་གསུམ། ཚང་མ་ཆེ་རིང་འཛོམ་པ་དང་ཚེ་རིང་སྐྱིད། ཤ་པ་ཐྱེམ་ཅནད། གནས་ཁ་རི་གཅིག་དང་ཁལ་༥། ཚང་ལ་གཞན་ནས་ཁ་རི་གསུམ་དང་ཁལ་༡༠། དངུལ་བཅུའི་འབྲས། ནས་དངུལ་བརྒྱད་ན་ཟ་དང་ཐེ་བ་ཡིན། མར་ཀྱང་དངུལ་༡༠། མར་དངུལ་གཉིས་བརྒྱའི་སོང་། ལུག་བཅུ་སོང་། ཛ་དངུལ་༡། མནྜལོ།།

xi. Tholong (Ṭholoṅ, mChhod), Household of Som Dev, Karchhags.

a. Tholong, Raja Pritam Singh (1767-1806), c. C.E. 1790.

ཀྱཻ་ལགས། བླ་མའི་གདན་ས་རི་བོ་སྤན་རྫོ་ལ། ས་དང་མཁའ་འགྲོའི་སྤྲིན་ལྟར་སྟུ་བའི་གནས། དཔལ་ལྡན་འབྲུག་པའི་སེང་ཁྲིར་ལེགས་བཞུགས་པའི་དཔོན་སློབ་ངག་དབང་------གསར་གླིང་མཁར་སྟོད་མཚུང་རྒྱལ་ས་གསུར་བསྟན་སྲུར། གེ་བསར་དང་མཚུང་ཆོས་རྒྱལ་ཕྲི་ཏེམ་སེང་། ཕྱི་འགྲ་འདུལ་ཞིང་ནང་འབྲན་བུ་བཞིན་ ------ ཡུལ་ལ་གཡང་ཆགས་ཚོད་ཡུལ་ཞེས་བྱ་འདིར། མི་རིགས་ཁྱུང་བཙུན་པ་མས་དར་པའི་རྒྱུད།

དད་ལྡན་ཡོན་གྱི་བདག་པོ་སུ་ཁི་བདེ་བ་དང་། ------ པའི་མཆོག་འགྱུར་ཁྲི་ནི་ཞེས་བྱ་དང་། པད་མ་སྟོང་ལྡན་བུ་མོ་སུ་ཁི་དང་། ལྷ་ཕྲུག་གཞོན་ནུ་འཕགས་པ་དོན་གྲུབ་དང་།

ཡུམ་སྲས་འཁོར་བཅས་བཀའ་གྲོས་------ དམ་ཆོས་འདི་ཡི་མཐུ་དང་བྱིན་བརླབས་ཀྱིས། ལས་དང་སྡིག་སྒྲིབ་མ་ལུས་ཀུན་བྱང་ནས། ཚེ་བསོད་དཔལ་འབྱོར་ཡར་ངོའི་ཟླ་ལྟར་རྒྱས།------ རྟེན་འདི་ནས་ཕ་རོལ་ཚེ་ལས་འདསཱ།སུར་ཐ་ན་དང་སུར་ཐ་ནི་མིང་སྲིང་གཉིས། བདེ་བ་ཅན་གྱི་ཞིང་དུ་སྐྱེ་བར་ཤོག།། ཀྱཻ་ལགས། པཎྜའི་མཚོ་ལ་ངང་པ་འདུ་བ་------ བྱུང་གྲངས་འདི་ལྟར་རོ། ཐོག་མར་ཕག་རྟེས་ཆང་ཞུ་ཊི་དང་ཤ་ཁོག་བཅས་བྱུང་། ཁྲིམ་ནང་དཔོན་པོའི་ལག་ཤ་བྱུང་། རི་འཕགས་པ་སྐུ་གཉེར་གྱི་དངུལ་གཅིག་བྱུང་། དང་བཀྲིས་དབྱང་འཛོམ་ཟ་མིས་------། བཀྲིས་རྣམ་རྒྱལ་དང་ལེགས་སྐྱིད་ཟ་མིས་ཨ་རག་ཙོ་ལི་དང་ལག་ཤ་བཅས་བྱུང་། ཧྲར་ད་ས་ཆང་ཇ་------ མིས་ཆང་ཇ་མ་དང་ལག་ཤ་བྱུང་། རྫ་མོ་དང་ཚེ་རིང་འཛོམ་ས་ཟ་མིས་ཆང་ཇ་མ་དང་ལག་ཤ་བྱུང་། ཙཾ་དས་དང་དཔའ་མོ་ཟ་མིས་ཆང་ཇ་དང་དཔའ་ལག་ཤ་བྱུང་།།

b. Tholong. Raja Vikram Singh (1806-1816), c. C.E. 1810.

ཨོཾ་སྭསྟི་སིདྡྷི། ཀྱེ་ལགས། བླ་མ་མ་ལིག་ཞུགས་དགའ་ལྡན་གནས་ཚུངས་མ་བཞེངས་ལྷུན་གྱི་གྲུབ། ཕོ་བྲང་ཆེན་པོ་རྒྱལ་ས་སུར་བསྟན་པུ་རི་ཏེར། མི་དབང་ཆོས་རྒྱལ་བྷི་ཀྲིམ་སེ་དགེ་ཞེས་དབུ་མོག་ཐོ་ཞིང་ཆབ་

སྲིད་དར་བའི་དུས། དེའི་མངའ་ཞབས་གར་ཞྭ་འི་གནས་ལུང་འདིར། དགེ་འཛོམས་པའི་གྱིད་ཡུལ་མཆོད་འདིར། དད་ལྡན་ཡོན་གི་བདག་པོ་མཁྱེན་ཏུ་དང་ཡོན་གི་བདག་མོ་པོ་མི་དང་ནོ་མོ་དང་བུའི་མཆོག་འགྱུར་སུ་ཀུ་རམ་དང་མན་ས་རམ་དང་སུ་ཀུ་ནན་ཧ་དང་གསུམ་གྱིས་བུ་ཙུ་བ་ཙན་ཧ་དང་། མཁྱིམ་ཧ་ས་དང་ཞ་ག་བདེ་བ་དང་ཐྲེ་མི་ར་མ་དང་ཁྱེད་གུ་ཏུ་དང་ལྷ། པདྨ་འགྲོ་མ་དང་། ནའི་མཆོག་འགྱུར་ཐོ་བེ་ལི་དང་ཆེར་དགྱིད། ནོར་པ་མོ་དེའི་ན་མ་ཏན་འགྲོ་མ་དང་། ཆེ་འདས་མེ་མེ་འཕག་ཙེ་དང་ཨ་ཕ་སུ་ཀུ་བདེ་བ་དང་ཨ་མ་ནོར་བཛོམ་དང་ཨ་བཙོ་དགྱི་ནུ་དང་། སྐྱུ་མ་ནོར་ལ་སྙིང་པོ་མེད་གཟིགས་ནས་བསགས་པ་ཆོས་ཕྱིར་གཏོང་བ་ངོ་ཚར་ཆེ།།

c. Tholong, Raja Ajit Singh (1816-1841), c. C.E. 1830.

ཨེ་མ་ཧོ། ཡུལ་ལ་ཡང་ཚགས་སྐྱིད་པའི་ཆོད་ཡུལ་འདིར། ཆོས་རྒྱལ་ཆེན་པོ་ཛྱེ་ཏ་སེནྒྷེ་ཡི།དེའི་ཞབས་འོག་མཆོད་སྦྱིན་བདག། ཁྱེན་དུ་དང་བསྦྱིན་བདག་མོ་ཆེར་སྐྱིད་དང་དེའི་ནོ་མོ་ནོར་པ་མོ་བུའི་མཆོག་འགྱུར་མན་ས་རམ་དང་སུག་ནན་ཧྲ་གཉིས། དེའི་བུ་ཚ་ཏུ་པུ་ཙནྡྲ་དང་ཁྱིམ་ད་ས་དེའི་ནོ་བོ་ཧྲག་ག་དེ་བ་དང་བེཧྲེ་རམ། དེའི་ནོ་བོ་ཧྲེ་ལི་རམ། ན་མའི་མཆོག་གྱུར་བསྟན་འཛིན་འགྲོ་མ་སྲིང་མོ་སུར་ཏེ་ནོ་མོ་ཆེ་པ་མོ་སྦྱིན་བདག་མོ་རྣམས་ཀྱི་རྣམ་དགའ་དགེ་བརྩིས་འབྱུང་གྲང་ལ། ཁྱིམ་ངང་ནས་ཙོ་ལི་ཨ་རག་ལག་ཤ་གཅིག་གུས་ནས་སོ་ནུ་ཤ་ལག་པ་ཨ་རག་

ཞ་རི་སུ་ཀི་ཤུ་ཊི་༡་ཚང་། སུ་དར་ཤན་ཤ་ལག་པ་ཨ་རག། མ་ཧ་ན་དང་ སོ་ནི་ཤ་ལག་པ་ཧཙུ་༡། ཕྲ་ན་ཕྲ་ས་ཧི་ར་མ་ཤ་ལག་པ་ཨ་རག། ཙན་ཏྲའི་ཤུ་ཊི་ཚང་།-----ཁྱད་པར་དུ་གྲོགས་སུ་ཀུ་རམ་ཆེ་འདས་ཀྱི་དོན་དུ་སྐུའི་རྟེན་ཆེ་དཔག་མེད་ཀྱི་སྐུ་གསུང་རྟེན་རྗོར་གཙོད་ཚར་གཉིས། ཐུགས་རྟེན་དུ་བྱང་ཆུབ་ཆོད་རྣམས་བཞེངས། ཆེ་འདས་ཀྱི་དོན་དུ་ཆེ་སྐྱིད་ནས་ཁལ་ཉི་ཤུ་འཕགས་པ་ཐུགས་རྗེ་ཆེན་པོའི་དྲུང་དུ་མར་མེ་རྒྱ་ཚ་ཚར་བདུན།།d

d. Tholong, Rai Gyan Singh (1852-1869), c. C.E. 1860.

དཀར་ཆག་དགོས་འདོད་ཀུན་འབྱུང་བཞུགས་སོ།

ཀྱཻ་ལེགས། ཆོས་རྒྱལ་ཆེན་པོ་ཕེ་ལིང་པ་ཆ་དང་ཤུང་ཧིའི་རྒྱལ་པོ་རྡེ་ཞན་སེང་།ཚབ་སྲིད་མངའ་ཐང་དཔལ་འབྱོར་ཕུན་སུམ་ཚོགས་པའི་དུས། མི་རིགས་ཁུངས་བཙུན་དད་པ་ཅན་དང་། དད་ལྡན་སྦྱིན་པའི་བདག་པོ་རུབ་ཙན་རྣ་དང་། ཁྱིན་རྣ་ས་དང་ཧག་རྣེབ་དང་། སྦྱིན་པའི་བདག་མོ་བསྟན་གྲོ་མ་དང་བུ་ཡི་མཆོག་གྱུར་ཆེ་པ་དང་། རིཾ་དང་ཤེ་ཧྲེ་རིཾ་དང་ཤེ་བ་རྣ་ས་གསུམ། བུ་མོའི་མཆོག་གྱུར་བསོད་ནམས་འཛོམ་སོགས་དང་། ན་མའི་མཆོག་གྱུར་ཆེ་རིང་བུ་ཊི་དང་། ཆེ་ལས་འདས་པ་སུ་གུ་རམ་མན་ས་རིཾ་དང་། ཁྱི་ཀུ་ཧུ་དང་ནོ་མོ་དང་སུར་ཧེ་དང་། དེ་རྣམས་ཀྱི་དོན་དུ་ཚོགས་སོགས་སྦྱིན་པ་རྒྱ་ཆེན་པོ་བཏང་བ་ཡིན་ལགས། ཡང་དགོས་སུ་

འོད་དཔག་མེད་ཀྱི་སྐུ་རྟེན་བཞེངས་པ་ཡིན། སྦྱིན་པའི་བདག་པོ་ཏུབ་ཚནྡ་དང་ཁྲིན་ཧྡ་ས་ཧྲག་ཧྡེབ་གསུམ་གྱི་ཨ་མ་ཚེར་སྐྱིད་ཀྱི་འགལ་རྐྱེན་སྡིག་སྒྲིབ་དག་ཕྱིར་བསོད་ནམས་ཐོབ་ཕྱིར་རྒྱལ་བའི་སྐུ་རྟེན་ཁྲིད་དུ་འཕགས་པ་འོད་དཔག་མེད་ཀྱི་སྐུ་བཞེངས་པ་ཡིན། འོད་དཔག་མེད་སྐུ་བཞེངས་པའི་རྐྱེ་རྗེས་བྱུང་གྲང་གི་ཐོ་ལ་ཐོག་མར་ནོར་པ་མོ་དང་སུ་ཀུ་ནན་ད་གཉིས་ཀྱི་ཨུ་ཏྲི་གཅིག་ཡང་ཨ་རག་ཚོ་ལི་གཅིག་ཤ་ལག་པ་གཅིག།།

2 Gandhala

Gandhala monastery, Register (tho-yig) c. C.E. 1830.

ཐོ་ཡིག །

འཕགས་པ་ཐུགས་འཇེ་ཆེན་པོའི་ཀུ་ཟུགས་ཕུལ་ཐོ་ལ། ཏེ་ནན་ཁར་ནས་ཕུལ་ཉེ། ཤེ་མ་ཡང་ཤེན་འཛ་༡། ཤེ་མ་ཀྲ་ཤི་ཡང་མཛོཾ་འཛ་༡། གོ་ར་ནས་ཙེ་ལི་འཛ་༡། པུ་ཏྲིད་འཛ་༡། ཚང་ལྷ་མོ་འཛ་༡། ཁྲིམ་ནང་ནས་ཕུལ་༡། ཁང་སར་ནས་xxxx ཕུལ་༡། སྐར་ལ་རྡོ་རྗེ་རྣམ་རྒྱལ་ཕུལ་༡། གྲ་ལིང་ནས་ཚེ་རིང་སོ་རྣམ་ཕུལ་༡། རྡོ་རྡོ་རྩེ་འཛ་ཉེ། ཨ་ནས་འཛ་༡། གོ་ར་པས་ཀྲ་ཤི་ཀུ་འཛོཾ་གྲི་འཛ་༡། ཏུར་པ་རྣམ་རྒྱལ་བུ་ཏྲིད་འཛ་༡། ཡོ་ཏར་ནོ་མོ་པེ་ནེ་ཞི། ཡོན་སར་པ་(ཡོ་སར།ཐོ་རང་)x་ཏུ་ར་མ་ཕུལ་ཕྱེ། གྲི་ལིང་ཀྲ་ཤི་ཚེ་རིང་འཛ་༡། ཐོ་རང་འེ་ཀྲ་མ་ནུ་འཛ་༡། པུག་ཏལ་སྐུ་ཏུ་འཛ་༡། ཐོ་རང་ནས་ཚེ་རིང་རྣམ་རྒྱལ་འཛ་༡།

ཀར་མ་ཚེ་རིང་འཛ་༡། སོ་ནམ་ཀྲ་ཤི་འཛ་༡། བླ་མ་ཚུལ་ཁྲིམ་བཏན་འཛིན་ཕུལ་༡ག་ཨ་རག། ཉེར་པུན་ཚོགས་ཀྱི་སྤྱ་མོ་འཛམ་༡། གསོལ་ཇ་༡། གསང་མ་༡། ཇོ་ར། ཕྱི་དྲོའི་གསང་མ་དང་ཆང་ཞུ་ནར་༡། དང་བཅས་པུལ། གྲ་པ་སྤྱིའི་ཕུལ་༡། རྡ་ནུའི་དངུལ་ལྷ་དྲང་ནས། ཕུལ་༡། ཨ་གར(རག)། སྐ་རའི་གྲ་ཀུར་པེ་ར་གང་། མཆོད་མེ་ལ་ཕུལ་༡། དཔལ་འཛོམ་ཆང་ཙོ་ལི་༡། སིལ་ལའི་བླ་མ་ལྷུན་གྲུབ་ཀྱི་ཨ་རག་ཙོ་ལི་༡། ཡང་

ཧང་ཧེ་ནས་ནང་ལོན་ཅན་རྣའི་རེས་བུབ་༡་སྲུལ་༡། སྣ་རའི་གྲ་ཀུར་པེ་ར་གང་། ཚོད་སེ་ལ་སྲུལ་༡། ལྷ་རྗེ་ཁམ་པ་ཚལ། ཧང་ཧེ་ལྷའི་རྒྱུ་རུ་གྲ་ཀ་ལྷ། རུབ་རྣས་སྲུལ་༡། སྙེ་རི་དང་ཨ་རག མ་ནེ་རམ་གོང་མེའི་རས་སྲུལ་༡། ཧེ་ཡིང་སྲུལ་ཉེ། ཀུ་ནའི་རས་ཆི་ཧྲ་སྲུལ་སུཾ། ལས་མ་ནེ་རས་ཆི་ཧྲ་སྲུལ་སུཾ། གསུམ་རྣམ་ནས་སོ་ནམ་ཚེ་རིང་སྲུལ་༡་གྱི་རས། འཕགས་ཚེ་རིང་ནས་ཁལ་བྱེད། ཡམ་ནམ་འཕེལ་ནས་ཡེ་ཤེས་བུ་དྲིད་བྲུ་རུ་སུཾ་ཡུ་༡། ཡང་ལོད་ནས་སྣ་ར་རས་སྲུལ་ཉེ། ཙེ་ནེ་དང་ཨ་མ་སྐྲོ་གྲི་དང་ཁྲི་ནེ་དང་གསུཾ་གྱི་ནས་ཁལ་བྱེད། སྦུ་སའི་སྲུལ་༡། རང་སྦེ་སྣག་ནན་སྐྱེའ་སྲུལ་༡། ལོད་ནས་ཙེ་ནའི་ཇ་ཝུ་༣། རང་པེ་སུག་བདེ་བའི་ཡུ་ཆག་པོ་གསུཾ། བྲང་ལྷང་སྙེར་ཧེ་འཛའུ་ཉེ་xx་ཉེ། ཕྲ་རི་ཙུ་རུང་གྱི་སྲུལ་༡། བྲུ་རུ་གཉིས། རིན་པོ་ཆེ་༡། ཡུ་༡། གྲོ་ཟིང་ནོ་ཙེའི་ནོམ་ཙུང་གཉིས་གྱི་དངུལ་བཙུ་གསུམ། མ་སླང་ནས་སྡོམ་པར་སྲུལ་༡། ལྷ་རྗེ་གཙེ་པ་སྲུལ་༡། སྙེར་པལ་སྲུལ་བྱེད་གྱི་སེར། ཚོད་པ་བསྟན་འཛིན་གྱི་སྲུལ་༡། བགྲིས་སྲུལ་༡། སྦུ་ཙུང་གྱི་སྲུལ་༡། ཁར་པོན་སྣ་ལི་རམ་མ་ནེ་ཐུན་སྐྱེན་ཤུ་གུ་མི་ཀུར་ཉེ་ཁྲུར་ལ་དངུལ་ཉེ། ཧ་གམ་སུག་སྟེའི་སྲུལ་༡། ཨམ་ཙེ་ཙེ་བས་མ་ཊེ་ཐུན་སྐྱེན་ལ་ནས་ཁལ་བཙུ་ཉིས། མལ་བར་ས་མན་འཛའུ་ཉེ། ཕྲ་རི་ནས་ནང་ལོན་མ་ཊེ་ར་མ་དངུལ་༡། ལོད་ནས་འབུ་སེ་སྲུལ་༡། དང་ཤུ་ནུར་༡། སྣ་ར་ལྟོལ་པོ་གསུམ་པ་༡། ཁྲུ་ཁྲུ་སྲུལ་༡། ཆེ་རིང་ཐ་ལི་༡།

ལྷ་རི་ཙུ་ལུད་འབྲས་སྨུལ་ཀ་འབྲ་བ། ནན་རྙིའི་འབྲས་དངུལ་ཀ། འབྲང་དར་པ་མན་ཧྲ་ས་སྨུལ་ཀ་འབྲས། ཏ་གསན་སྨུལ་ཀ་འབྲས། ཧོ་ཟེང་ནས་ཕེ་ལེ་སྨུལ་ཀ། སྨེ་རྙན་པྲ་ཀ་གུད། མ་ལང་ནས་རྙོན་པར་ར་སྨུལ་ཀ། ལྷ་པ་ཐྲིལ་ཐྲར་སྨུལ་ཀ། ཡང་མ་ནི་ཐུན་སྐྱེན་ལ་ཏང་ཏེ་བཙན་རྙེའི་དངུལ་ཉིས། གོང་མེ་མ་ནི་ར་མ་དངུལ་ཀ། ཡང་མ་ནི་ར་མ་ཡོག་མེ་དངུལ་ཀ་གི་བལ། ཡང་གསུམ་རྣམ་གོང་མའི་སོ་ནམས་ཚེ་རིང་གྱི་དངུལ་ཀ།ཡང་སྨུ་ལིང་ནས་ཟང་ཀར་སྡོའི་གྲོས་པེ་ཁལ་ཉིས། མན་ཧྲས་དངུལ་ཀ། མ་ཊེ་ཐུན་སྐྱེན་ལ་ཚོད་པ་མན་ཧྲས་དངུལ་ཀ། ཐྲེ་ཏ་དངུལ་རིན་ཀ་ནས། བགྲིས་དངུལ་ཀ། མང་དེ་དངུལ་ཀ། ཅེ་པ་ཚེ་རིང་དངུལ་ཀ། ཚེ་གྱུ་དངུལ་ཀ། ལྷ་རང་ནས་མ་ཞན་དངུལ་ཀ། ཞུང་ཏེ་ཁམ་རྣམས་གྱི་མ་ཊེ་ཐུན་སྐྱེན་ཐོག་མ་སྨོན་ལམ་བཟང་མོ་དངུལ་ཀ། འབྲུག་ཕུན་ཚོགས་དངུལ་ཀ། དུན་འགྲུབ་དངུལ་ཀ། རིག་འཛིན་འགྲོལ་མའི་དངུལ་ཀ། ཨ་པེ་བློ་བཟང་དངུལ་ཀ། པང་འགེ་རྫོ་མོ་དངུལ་ཀ། རྒང་འཛོམ་འཛ་ཉེ། ཚེས་འདས་ཀན་ཙུན་དངུལ་ཀ། གོར་རེ་ལ་དངུལ་ཀ།།

iii. Village Shashin (Ṣa-ṣin, Sra-srin): (Sissu-2).

a. Shashin, Shashin Jo (The Household of the Thakurs of Shashin).

a.i. Shashin, Shashin Jo, Silla gonpa, 17th-18th century C.E.

པའི་ཆོས་གསོལ་ལ་མཆོད་མི་དུག་པ་སངས་རྒྱས་གཞི"

a.ii. Shashin, Shashin Jo, Ka-ka Gyatsho, c. C.E. 1750.

ཨོཾ་སྭ་སྟི་སིད་དྷཾ། དགེ་བཙུ་ཕུན་ཚོགས་གར་ཆག་མཁན་འགྲོ་ཡུལ། རྒྱབ་རི་སེང་ཆེན་འགིང་འདྲ། འདུན་རི་རིན་ཆེན་སྤུང་འདྲའི་འདུན། ཆུ་བོ་ཆེན་པོ་གྱུང་གྱུལ་འགྱུག་སྡིང་། ཡང་ཡུལ་ཁྱད་པར་འཕགས་པའི་ཞབས་ཞེན་འདིར། རྟུས་ལ་ཁྱད་པར་འཕགས་པ་འབྱམ་ཞེས་རིགས་སུ་འབྲུངས། ཀྱེ་ལེགས། དད་བརྩོན་ཞེས་རབ་ལྡན་པས་ཀ་ཀ་རྒྱ་མཚོའ་ཀྱང་། ཡར་ལ་དཀོན་མཆོག་མཆོད་ཅིང་མདོ་སྡེ་སྡོམ་ཚིགས་བཞེངས། བསགས་པ་ཆོས་ཕྱིར་གཏོང་བ་ངོ་ཚར་ཆེ། ཞེས་རིགས་རྒྱས་པས་དཔའ་རྩལ་གཉིས་དང་ལྡན། འཛང་ཞེས་གཉིས་ལྡན་ནང་གིས་གཉེན་རྣམས་སྐྱིངས། དད་གུས་ལྡན་པའི་

ཆོས་ལ་མོས་ཀུན་གྱིས་ཡིད་འོང་བློ་གྲོས་ལྡེ་དང་། དཔལ་སྡེ་གཉིས་ཀྱི་ཀྱང་། དམ་པའི་ཆོས་ལ་བསྐུར་སྟི་ཞབས་ཏོག་བྱེད་པ་ངོ་མཚར་ཆེ། དེ་ལྟར་ཡབ་ཡུམ་བཅད་རྣམ་ཀྱིས་ཀྱང་། ཁྱད་ཡབ་ཡུམ་སྲས་བཅས་སྐུ་ཚེ་རིངས་པའི་ཕྱིར། དམ་ཆོས་ཁྱད་པར་འཕགས་མདོ་ནི་སྟོམ་དང་ཀ་ཆོམ་གཞེངས། བསག་པ་ཆོས་ཕྱིར་གཏོང་བ་ངོ་མཚར་ཆེ། ཀྱེ་ལེགས། ཡོན་གིས་བདག་མོ་བློ་གྲོས་སྒྲོན་གྱིས་ཀྱང་། སྲས་མོ་བཀྲ་ཤིས་བཟང་མོ། ཐ་ཙོ་ཤ་ན་བི་སྣ་མ་རྣམས་ཀྱིས་ཀྱང་། ཞབས་ཏོག་ལུག་བཞིན་བྱེད་པ་ངོ་མཚར་ཆེ། ཡི་གེ་པ་ནི་རྡོ་རྗེ་སེམས་དཔའ་བྲིས། ནོར་འཕྱུལ་འཆིས་ན་བཟོད་པར་གསོལ། ཉེ་དྲུང་རྣམ་ཀྱིས་གེ་སི་སྟེག་པ་ལ། སྒྲོ་ན་མ་ཆེ་བསྟན་བཟང་མོ་བཟའ་མི་གཉིས། དགོན་གཡུང་སྲུང་སྐྱིད་བཟའ་མི་གཉིས། ཨ་ཛོ་སོ་ན་བ་སྐྱིད་བཟའ་མི་གཉིས། བཟུངས་སྐྱབས་དཀར་རྩ་སྐྱིད་བཟའ་མི་གཉིས། མ་ཚོ་གེའི་མ་བུ་གཉིས། སེང་སི་སོ་བསོད་ནམས་སྐྱིད་བཟའ་མི་གཉིས། འདི་རི་སྐྱིན་དག་བཟའ་མི་ཉེ།།

b. Shashin, Shashin Jo, Lhun-grub of Shashin and Raja Tedhi Singh (1742-1767), c. C.E. 1760.

ས་ལ་འབུར་ཐོན་རྒྱལ་ས་སེ་བསྟན་པུར།   ཆོས་རྒྱལ་ཆེན་པོ་ཏྲི་དྲུ་སེང་གེ་ཡི།   དབུ་རྨོག་མཐོ་ཞིང་ཆབ་སྲིད་རྒྱས་གྱུར་ཅིག།   དེ་འི་མངའ་འོག་གར་ཞ་རང་ལོ་འདིར།   བླ་མའི་བདུན་ས་ཀུ་ཞིལ་སྤྲིང་འདིར།   རབ་འབྱམ་སློ་བཟང་དོན་གྲུབ་ཆོས་བཙུག་ཐོར་གྱུར་ཅིག།   སེ་སྐྱིད་འཛོམ་པའི་དབྱང་གླིང་འདིར།   ཡུལ་གྱི་ནང་སློན་བགྲིས་རབས་ལར་སྐུ་ཕྱེད་སྐུ་ཚེ་བསྟན་གྱུར་ཅིག།   དགེ་འཛོམ་པའི་གཡང་ཡུལ་སྲ་སྲིན་འདིར།   མི་རིགས་ཁུངས་བཙུན་འོད་གསལ་ལྷའི་བརྒྱུད།   དཀོན་མཆོག་མཆོད་དང་སྦྱིན་པ་བཏོང་ལ་རྒྱས།   དད་ལྡན་སྦྱིན་པའི་བདག་མོ་ལྷུན་གྲུབ་སྐུ་ཚེ་བསྟན་གྱུར་གཅིག།   ལྷ་བུ་འདད་ཚུངས་ནོ་ནོ་ཆེ་དབང་སྐུ་ཚེ་བསྟན་གྱུར་གཅིག།   སྦྱིན་པའི་བདག་མོ་ ཛོ་ཛོ་ནམ་རྒྱལ་མཚོ་མོ་སྐུ་ཚེ་བསྟན་པར་ཤོག།   སྲས་ཀྱི་མཆོག་གྱུར་ལྷ་སྲས་དང་ཚུངས་ནོ་ནོ་མཛོ་གོ་རམ་དང་ནོ་ནོ་སོ་ནམས་རྒྱལ་མཚན་གཉིས།   སྲས་མོའི་མཆོག་གྱུར་སེར་ཆེན་མི་ཏོག་དང་ཚུངས་རྒྱལ་ཆོས་མཛོམ་དང་།   ཡེ་ཤེས་ཆོས་མཛོམ་དང་།པ་དྨ་ཆོས་མཛོམ་དང་།   ཉི་མ་སྒྲོལ་མ་ཞི་ལ་སྟོད།།

ཨ་མའི་མཆོག་གྱུར་ལགས་མཛོམ་དང་ཅ་ཏྲི་རི་གཉིས་ལ་སྟོད།
བག་མའི་མཆོག་གྱུར་ཀུ་འཛོམ་ལ་སྟོད།ཡོན་གྱི་བདག་པོ་ནོ་ནོ་ལྷུན་གྲུབ་དང་ཛོ་ཛོ་ནམ་རྒྱལ་མཚོ་མོ་གཉིས་ཀྱི་ནི། ད་ལན་སྦྱིན་པའི་བདག་མོ་ཛོ་ཛོ་རྣམ་རྒྱལ་ཚོ་མོ། བྲིལ་དཀར་པོའི་དགེ་རྩེ་བྱུང་དྲངས་ལ།།

གྲོག་མར་རང་བློའི་བླ་མ་བློ་བཟང་དོན་གྲུབ་དགེ་རྩེ་ལགས་པར་སྣང་བྱུང་། སྔགས་རམ་པ་ཡེ་ཤེས་ཚོས་ཕེལ་དགེ་རྩེ་ལེགས་བྱུང་། ནང་བློན་བཀྲིས་པལ་ལྷེ་མ་བུ་གཉིས།ཤུར་ཐང་།ཀོ་ཐལ། ཏེ་ནན་ཁང་སར་ནས་ནོ་ནོ་རྟ་འཛིན་བཟང་པོ་དང་ལགས་སྐྱིད་སྟིང་ཞལ། ཏུར་པ། དབྱང་ཀར། སྟར་ཀྱི། རོབས། སྐྱུ་རད་ཕར་མ། སྐྱུ་རད་ཚུར་མ་། ཁྱིམ་ནང་ཡར་ཀྱི། མར་རྒྱེད། མར་རྒྱེད་ཡོས་། ཤུག་ཐལ། ཡང་སྐྱང་། ཡང་གླིང་ཕར་མ། སྤྲོབ། ཤུ་གླིང་གོང་། སྐྱེ་བག། ནང་པ་དང་ཚང་མ་ཤ་པ་ལ་སོགས་ཏེ་འཁོར་བྱུས་བྱེད་ལག་བདེ་ཐམས་ཅད་ཀྱིས། ཤ་ཚང་འདོད་ཡོན་རོ་བརྒྱའི་ཚོགས་རྣམས་ཀྱིས། འགྲོན་རྣམ་འཆམ་ཞིང་མཉེས་པ་། ཨེ་མ་ཧོ།།

iv. Khyinang (Khyīnaṅ), the Village and Household.

a.Khyinang, Nam-kha-rgyal-po, the Thakur of Gundhla, c. C.E.1350-1375 (?).

ཨོཾ་སྭ་སྟི་སི་དྡྷཾ། བདུན་ས་ཁྲི་འདུང་དཔོན་རྣམས་ལ་དགེ་སི་བྱུང་བའི་གྲངས་ལ། ཇོ་བོ་ནམ་མཁའ་རྒྱལ་པོ་དང་། བག་མ་ཉི་ཟླ་སྐྱིད་གཉིས་ཛེ་ཞལ་གཉིས། ཇོ་ཙོ་བཟང་མོ་དེ་བ་འགོ་གོ་བཟའ་མི་གཉིས། ཨ་གུ་གསང་རྡོར། བླ་མ་གྷི་གུང་པ། ཡོན་པོ་ནོར་བུ། ཡོན་པོ་སྣ་རང་ང་། ཆོས་སྐོར་ར་པད་མ་བཟང་པོ་དང་། སྲོང་པོ་གཉིས། ལྔེ་རེ་ཙུན་ཆུང་། བསོད་ནམས་བསྐྱིད། ཏུ་ཏུ་དང་། ཆོ་ཁྲུམ་གཟའ་མི་གཉིས། འབིར་མི་མར་དགེད་པོ་སེ་བསོད་ནམས་སེང་། ཤི་གོ་པ་གང་ལ་སྐྱབས། ཉིར་ར་ལིང་ནོར་བཟང་། པུ་རང་ཏ་ལ་ག། གུད་ལ་ཡི་ གློན་པོ་བི་ལྷ་དགོན། བཀྲ་ཤིས་བཟང་པོ། ཇོ་བོ་ཙ། བཟང་པོ་ཇོ་པོ། པུ་རད་ཏའི་བཟང་པོ་ཙ། ཁར་གི་དགེའ་དུན་འབུམ། སུ་ལིང་ང་ཀོའོ་ཙ་ནྡ། དེ་རྣམས་ལ་དགེ་སི་ལུག་བཞིན་བྱས་པ་ངོ་མཚར་ཆེ། གསུང་རབས་འདི་ཐུགས་རྗེ་ཡིས། ཡོན་ཆོད་རྫོ་བྱས་འགྲོ་དྲུག་སེམས་ཅན་རྣམས་བདེ་བ་ཅན་དུ་འཇལ་བར་ཤོག། བུ་མོ་ལྷ་མོ་ཙ་བཟང་པོ་མོ་ཙ་དང་སར་ཀར་འགོ་ན་ཙ་དེ་ལ་སོགས་པ་ཐམས་ཅད་ཀྱི་སི་ལུག

བཞིན་ངོ་ཚར་ཆེ། ཀ་རྡོ་རྗེ་གཙོད་པ། འབྲུག་"སྒྲུངས་ཐང་བདེ་ཆེན་གྱི་པར་མ་ལ་འདྲ་ཞུས་བྱས་པའི། བྱིན་པའི་བདག་པོ་དཀར་རྒྱུད་ཕུན་ཚོགས་དང་། ཡོན་གྱི་བདག་མོ་འཛོམས་སྐྱིད་ཞེས་བྱ་བ་གཉིས། རྐོས་ཀྱི་འདུ་བྱེད་དམ་ཆོས་དབང་པོ་དང་སྐལ་བཟང་ཚེ་རིངས། ཀྱི་ལེགས་བསྒྲུབས། ཡི་གེ་པ་ནི་དཀར་རྒྱུད་ཕུན་ཚོགས་ཡིན།།

b. Khyinang, 16th-17th century C.E.

གཟུངས་ཆེན་གྲལ་ལྔ་བཞུགས་སོ། ཧེ་ཧེ།།

དགེ་ལེགས་སུ་གྱུར་ཅིག།། ཀྱི་ཡི་ལགས། གནས་ ལ་ཁྱད་འཕགས་ གནས་ ཆེན་དྲིལ་བུ་རི་འི་འགྱུལ། ཡུལ་ལ་གཡང་ཆགས་ཧེ་ནན་ཁྲིམས་ཀྱི་ཡུལ། ས་ལ་འབུར་དུ་ཐོ་བའི་སྐུ་མཁར་ནལ་ཟེའི་ཁར། ཀྱི་ལགས། བདན་ས་ཁྱད་འཕགས་པ་ཁྲི་འདད་འདིར་མི་རིགས་ཁྱུངས་བཙུན་ཡབ་མེས་དོལ་ཆེན་ཉི་མ་རིས།།

ཡོན་གྱི་བདག་པོ་དྲུང་པ་བསོད་ནམས་བཟང་པོ་དང་། ཨོན་པོ་བསོད་ནམས་གྲགས་པ་དང་སྒྲུ་ཆེད་གཉིས་ཀྱིས། ཐུགས་དགོངས་ ལེགས་

པར་བཏང་བས་དགེ་སྡིག་ཤན་ཡང་ཕྱེད། ཡབ་དྭང་པ་མཁན་པོ་དང་ཨ་གུ་འཇམ

་དཔལ་གྱི་དོན་དུ་སྐུ་གསུང་ཐུགས་ཀྱི་རྟེན་རྣམས་བཞེངས། བླ་མའི་སྐུ་

འདྲ་དང་། བཟུང་ཆེན་གྲལ་ལྷ་དང་། མཆོད་རྟེན་དང་། དེ་རྣམས་

བཞེངས་པ་ངོ་མཚར་ཆེ། བསགས་པ་ཆོས་བཞིན་ཧོང་དེ་ཀུན་ཀྱང་སྨོན།

ཨོན་ཇོའི་རྣམ་སྤྲུལ་འཛངས་དྭང་གཉིས་དང་ལྡན། བུད་མེད་ལུས་ལ་

གཡའི་རྒྱུར་བ་སྤྱངས་པའི། ཡོན་གི་བདག་མོ་ཇོ་ཙོ་རྒྱལ་མོའི་མིའི་ཟས་

ལ་ལྷའི་བདུད་རྩིར་སྒྱུར། མཆོད་གནས་གཉིས་པའི་ཞལ་དྲངས་པ་ཀུན་

ཀྱང་སྨོན། འཁྲུལ་ཡིག་འབྲི་བའི་ཨོན་པོ་ལྡོག་ལྡན་དང་། ཇོ་བོ་སྨྲ་ཅན་

གཉིས་ཀྱིས་བླའི་སྐུ་འབྲ་མཆོད་རྟེན་རྣམས་ལགས་འབྲིས་ཞིང་བཞེངས་པ་

ལགསོ། མི་འགྲུག་དང་། བཟང་མོ་ལ་སོགས་རང་གི་བུ་མོ་རྣམས་ཀྱིས།

དཔོན་ལ་ཞབས་ཏོག་བྱས་པ་ངོ་མཚར་ཆེ།།

c. Khyinang, Vajrachhedika, 16th-17th century C.E.

རྡོ་རྗེ་གཅོད་པ། བྱིན་པའི་བདག་པོ་ཀར་རྒྱུད་ཕུན་ཚོགས་དང་།

ཡོན་གྱི་བདག་མོ་འཛོམས་སྐྱིད་ཞེས་བྱ་བ་གཉིས། ཀོས་ཀྱི་འདུ་བྱེད་དམ

ཆོས་དབང་པོ་དང་སྐལ་བཟང་ཆེ་རིངས།ཀྱི་ལེགས་བསྒྲུབས། ཡི་གེ་པ་ནི་

དཀར་རྒྱུད་ཕུན་ཚོགས་ཡིན།།

v. Tinan (Gundhla) Khar (mKhar), the House of the Thakurs of Gundhla (Gundhlā).

a. Tinan Khar, Karchhags of Gundhla Kangyur. The following are karchhags from the set of books known as Gundhla Kangyur belonging to Tinan Khar which were mostly copied here at Tinan.

a.i. Tinan Khar, Gundhla Kangyur, 2/12, 3/3, p. 685, Ra-na-pa-la of Gundhla, c. C.E. 1275-1300 (?).

འབུམ། རི་བོ་གངས་དང་འབྲིལད་པའི། ཡོན་ཏན་འབྱུང་གནས་ལྷན་ཧྲ་ལ།

ཡན་ལག་བརྒྱད་ལྡན་ཆུ་འབྲུག་པས། བགྲེས་སྒོམ་སྡུག་བསྡལ་དེ་ན་མྱེད།

དགྲའ་དང་འཚོམ་པོའི་འཛིགས་པ་ནི། དེ་ན་གང་ཡང་མྱེད་པ་ཡིས། བྲོ་

བདེང་ཉམས་སྤྱོད་སྐྱུང་པ་ར། དེ་འདྲའི་གནས་ཀྱི་གཡོན་ལོགས་སུ། དད་

མོས་གཉིས་དང་ལྡན་པའི། ཡོན་བདག་ར་ན་པ་ལ་ཡིས། དུས་གསུམ་

རྒྱལ་བའི་ཡུཾ་མཆོག་བཞེངས། ཡོན་ཏན་བྱུང་གནས་གུ་གེའི། རིག་པའི་

འབྱུང་གནས་འཕགས་པ་ཛྫེ། དེ་འི་རྒྱུད་པ་ཟེན་པའི། རྒྱ་བྲག་ཡིག་དཔོན་

ཕྱེ་བས་བྲིས། འདི་འིས་སྤྱི་ཕྲིས་ཟེར་ནས་ཡང་XX.XXསྔོད་ཅིང་བཞུང་བའི་
སྤྱི་རྣམས་ནི། རང་རྒྱུད་ཕྲག་དོག་མེའིས་བསྲེག། དཔེར་ན་ཤིང་གི་མེ་
བཞིན་ནོ། ཡ་སྣ་གྱུག་འཁྲིང་ཆག་པ་རྣམས། རྒྱལ་བའི་ཡུམ་ལ་བཟོད་
པར་གསོལ། འདི་ཡིས་བདག་དང་འགྲོ་བ་ཡོངས་ལ་བསྔོལ། པོ་ཧྲི་འདི་ལ་
འབྲི་མཁན་གཉིས། སྔོད་ནི་གཟིམས་མལ་སྐྱི་ལ་ཕྱུག་ཟླ་བ་ཕྱེའིས་བྲིས།
སླད་ནི་ཤེས་པ་ཡུག་ཙུག། བསླབས་པའི་རྒྱ་བྲག་བདག་གིས་བྲིས།།

a.ii. Tinan Khar, Gundhla Kangyur, 6/12, 1/2, P. 533, Dorje Pala, c. C.E. 1300-1325 (?).

དཀོན་བཅོགས།

རི་མཐོའ་ས་ཅང་སྤྱུ་རྒྱལ་བོད་ཀྱི་ཡུལ། གནསཆེན་བརྒྱད་ཀྱི་ཡན་
ལག་ཬྷན་དྷ་ལ། རི་དེ་ལ་ཧྗེནད་པའི་ཧྲི་ནན་འདིར། ཡ་རབས་ཆོས་སྐྱོང་
རྡོ་རྗེ་པ་ལ་ཁྲུངས། འབངས་རྣམས་ཞི་བས་བཅིས་པས་ཆབ་སྲིད་རི་བས་རི་
བས་བརྟན། དཀོན་མཆོག་དབུའ་དཔངས་བསྟོད་པས། ཕྱི་མ་བྱུང་ཆུབ་ཐོབ།
ནོར་ཟས་སྐྱུ་མར་གཟིགས་པས། མདོ་སྡེ་འགྱུར་འོད་བཞེངས། མཆོད་

གནས་འདིགས་པའི་རྗེ་ཕྱ་བཟང་གཉིས་དང་། དམ་ཆོས་རྒྱས་པར་བྱེད་པའི་

ཡིག་མཁན་རྡོ་རྗེ་རྗེ།།

a.iii. Tinan Khar, Gundhla Kangyur vol. 15 p. 492. Dorje Pala, c. C.E. 1300-1325(?).

སའི་སྙིང་པོ་འཁོར་ལོ་བཅུ་པའི་མདོ་བཞུགས་སོ།།

ཉི་སེ་གངས་ལས་རི་རྒྱུད་མ་ཆད་པ་གཡུང་རུང་འགྱུར་མེད་རི་བོ་ག

ནད་ལ། རི་དེ་ལ་གནས་པའི་ཏི་ནན་འདིར། ས་དེའུ་ཆུང་ནལ་ཟེའི་སྐུ་

མཁར་ཆགས། འཁར་དེ་འི་རྒྱནད་དུ་རྡོ་རྗེ་པ་ལ་ཁྲུངས། དཔའ་བརྗིད་

ལུས་ལ་ལྡན་པས། སོག་རུ་ཟེལད་ཀྱིས་ནོནད། གསུང་སྙན་མོལ་པ་

མཁས་པས། རྒྱལ་ཁམས་མོས་པ་སྐྱེ། ཐུགས་རླབས་ཤིནྡུ་ཆེ་བས།

མགོ་ནག་དབང་དུ་བསྡུས། སྤྱོད་བཟང་ངེས་དང་ལྡན་པས་འབངས་རྣམས་

འཁོར་བར་སྐྱོ། འབྲུས་དང་གཙང་སྦྲ་ཆེ་བས། རྒྱལ་པོའི་སྤྱོད་པ་འདྲ།

གློག་ལྷར་དྲན་བ་བསལ་བས། ཉེས་ལེགས་ལྷར་ཕྱ་འཛིནད། ཤིནད་དུ་

དྲག་བརྩན་ཆེ་བས། སྡང་བའི་སྒྲ་ཡང་འདུ་ལ། ངན་པའི་བྱ་བ་ཅུང་བས་

བཞུགས་པའི་བདན་ཐུབ། རྣམ་སྨིན་དགེ་སྡིག་འཛོམ་པས་འབངས་ནམས་

དགེ་ལ་བཀོད། འདི་འདྲའི་ཡོན་བདག་དད་ཅན་དང་། ཚོགས་སྐྱུན་ཞབས་
སྡེ་གས་འབུལ་བའི་རིན་ཅེན་བསོད་ནམས་དང་། ཆོས་ལ་བཀུར་སྡེ་སྐྱོ་རས་
མྱེད་པའི་ཀྲ་ཤིས་ལྡན། སུག་ ནས་སྤྱུལ་སྐྱུ་འབྲུལ་བའི་དམག་ཕྲུག་རྡོ་རྗེ་རྩེ།
འདི་རྣམས་ཆེ་རབས་གར་སྐྱེས་ཀྱང་། སའི་སྙིང་པོའི་ཞལ་ཁྲུམས་ཤོག།
སའི་སྙིང་པོའི་ཞལ་ཁྲུམས་ནས། སའི་སྙིང་པོས་ལུས་ལུང་བསྟན་ཤོག།
ཞུས་ཏེ་དགེ་གོ།།

a.iv. Tinan Khar, Gundhla Kangyur, 1/12, 6/6 p. 6, lDe-ljam rGyalpo of Tinan Khar and Raja Parbat Singh (1575-1608), c. C.E. 1590 (?).

ཆོས་རྒྱལ་ཆེན་པོ་རྒྱལ་པོ་སྲོང་བཙན་སྒམ་པོའི་འཕགས་པ་ནམ་
མཁའི་སྙིང་པོ་སོགས་ཕྲན་འགའ་བཞུགས་སོ།

གངས་རི་འི་རྒྱལ་"པོ་ཏི་སེ་དང་། དངོས་གྲུབ་ཆབ་འཁྱིལ་མ་པང་
མཚོའི་ནུབ། ཆུ་དེ་ཆེན་པོ་གང་འགའ་འབྲུག་པའི་བྱང་། གནས་ཆེན་བརྒྱད་
ཀྱིས་ཡན་ལག་གན་དྷ་ལ། མཁའ་འགྲོའི་དུས་གནས་ནས་ཆེན་དྲི་ལ་བུའི་
མགུལ། ཡུལ་ལ་གཡང་ཆགས་ཏི་ནན་སྐྱིད་ཡུལ་འདིར། ས་ལ་འབུར་
མཐོ་སྐྱུ་མཁར་ནལ་ཟེའི་མཁར། དཔལ་སྤྱོར་རྒྱ་མཚོ་ལྷ་བུའི་གྲོང་ཁྱེར་དེར།

རིགས་བཟང་ཁྲུང་བཙུན་བུ་རམ་ཤིང་པའི་བརྒྱུད། ཀྱེ།ལེགས། ཆོས་རྒྱལ་ཆེན་པོ་པར་བད་སེང་ཕྲ་དང་། ཆོས་རྒྱལ་ཆེན་པོ་བདེ་འཛམས་རྒྱལ་པོ་དང་། བློན་ཆེན་ར་ཙུ་ལ་དང་། ཡོན་གྱི་བདག་པོ་ཁར་ཀོ་དང་། སོད་ནམས་རྒྱ་ཚོ་དང་། བཀྲ་ཤིས་རྒྱལ་པོ་དང་།། "'

a.v.i. Tinan Khar, Gundhla Kangyur, Miscellaneous 1/12, 1/6. Tashi Paljor of Tinan Khar and Raja Pritam Singh (1767-1806).

ཨུ་རྒྱན་གུ་རུ་པ་དྨ་བྱུང་གནས་ཀྱི་སྐྱེས་རབས་རྣམ་ཐར་རྒྱས་པ་གསེར་གྱི་ཕྲེང་ཞུགས་སྐྱོ།

ཨོཾ་སྭསྟི་ཧཱུྃ། སྤྲ་མཁས་ཡིད་ཡོང་ཞོན་ཚུལ་སྤྱར་ཙལ་ལྡན་པའི། ཆོས་རྒྱལ་ཆེན་པོ་པིར་ཏིམ་སེང་ཕྲ་དབུ་སྙོག་ཐོ་བའི་"དུས། དགེ་བཙུ་ཁྲིམ་གཉིས་ལྡན་པའི་གནས་སྐུ་ཁར་ནལ་རྩེ་འདིར། མི་རིགས་ཁྲུང་རྩུན་འོད་གསལ་ལྷའི་རྒྱུད། ལྷ་བུ་ཡིད་ཡོང་སྤྲ་མཁས་སྤྱར་ཙལ་ཅན། སྦྱིན་པའི་བདག་པོ་བཀྲ་ཤིས་དཔལ་འབྱོར་གྱི་སྐུ་དྲིན་ཅན་གིས། ཡབ་ཀྱི་དགོངས་པ་རྫོགས་ཕྱིར་དུ། སྙིན་བཞངས་འདི་ལ་ཞབས་རྟོག་ཡང་དག་བྱས། ཡོན་གདགེ་མོ་མེ་ཆུང་མནང་དཀའ་དཔལ་མོའི། ཞིང་གཤེགས་འགྲོགས་ཀྱིས་

དགོངས་པ་རྫོགས་ཕྱིར་དུ། སྐུའི་རྟེན་དུ་གསེར་ཟངས་ལ་ཨུ་རྒྱན་དང་གཙུག་ལག་ཁང་དང་གསུང་གིས་རྟེན་དུ་པདྨ་ཐང་ཡིག་དང་ཐུགས་རྟེན་བྱང་ཆུབ་མཆོད་རྟེན་བཞེངས། བསགས་པ་དོན་ཅན་གྲུབ་ངོ་མཚར་ཆེ། ཀྱེ་ལགས། ནོ་མོ་སུམ་པའི་དང་བློ་གྲོས་རྣམ་གཉིས་ཀྱིས། རྟེན་བཞེངས་འདི་ལ་བཞབས་རྟོག་ལེགས་པར་གྲུབས། ལྷ་བུ་ཡིད་ཡོང་པ་ཊེ་དང་སྲས་ཕྱོགས་གྱུར་ཏེར་ཏེ་རྣམས། ཡབ་མེས་བཞིན་དུ་ཆོས་ལ་དགར་བར་ཤོག། སྲས་མོའི་ཕྱོགས་གྱུར་བཀྲ་ཤིས་དཔལ་མོའི་སྒྲིན་ཞངས་འདི་ལ་ཞབས་རྟོག་ལེགས་པར་གྲུབས། པདྨ་མཚལ་དུ་བདབ་ཆགས་འདུ་བ་བཞིན་དུ་དགེ་ཨུ་བྱུང་བ་ལ། ཀྱཻ། ཀྱེ་ལང་སྐྱ་ཁར་གྱིས་གྱོགས་ཞབས་ཡང་དག་སྣང་། མ་མགོན་ནས་ཨ་མ་རྒྱལ་མོའི་གྱོགས་ཞབས་རྩལ། ཁྱིམ་ནམ་ནས་བླ་མའི་གྱོགས་ཞབས་རྩལ། བར་ སློག་ནས་ཁར་ནས་གྱོགས་བརྩལ། ལྕུག་དྲ་ནས་ཆེ་རིང་རྒྱལ་པོ་སྟེང་ཞལ་གཉིས། སྲ་སྲིན་ནས་ཇེ་བོ་ཧུ་བུ་སྟེང་ཞལ་གཉིས། ཇོ་བོ་དཔལ་འབྱོར་སྟེང་ཞལ་གཉིས། ཏི་གླིང་ནས་ཇོ་བོ་ནོ་ནོ་སྟེང་ཞལ་གཉིས། མཐོ་རང་གླིང་ནས་པད་མ་སྟེང་ཞལ་གཉིས། ནོ་རི་དི་སྟེང་ཞལ་གཉིས།།

a.v.ii. Colophon to the same book on the last page number 754.

སྐུ་གསུང་ཐུགས་ལ་རྒྱུ་ཡོན་སྦྱོར་བ་ཡི། འོད་གསལ་ལྷའི་རྒྱུད་ག་ག་

བཀྲ་ཤིས་དཔལ་འབྱོར་དང་ཡོན་བདག་མོ་མཐང་དཀའ་དཔལ་མོ་སྲས་ཡུམ་

གཉིས་དང། དམ་ཆོས་དེ་ཕྱིར་ཐུན་སྐྱེན་སྒྲུབ་བྱེད་དང་། ཇོའ་རིགས་ཀུན་ལ་

ཐོགས་མེད་དཔོན་དགའ་དོན་གྲུབ་ལ་སོགས་པའི་མ་ནམ་མཁའ་ཐའ་ཉམས་

པའི་ཕ་མ་སེམས་ཙན་རྣམས་ཤུ་རྒྱུན་གྱུ་དུ་པདྨའི་དགོངས་ཐོབ་ནས་། སེམས་

ཙན་ཐམས་ཙད་དོན་བྱེད་པར་ཤོག།།

a.vi. Gundhla, Gundhla Kangyur, 1/12, Book 2/6. P. 3-4. Pārī and Sinsau sKum-mjed of Gundhla, and Raja Pritam Singh (1767-1806) of Kullu, and King Sing-ge Namgyal of Ladakh, c. C.E. 1790.

འབྲོམ་སྟོན་བརྒྱལ་བའི་འབྱུང་གནས་ཀྱི་སྐྱེས་རབས།

བཀའ་བསྟམས་བུ་ཆོས་ལེ་ཨུ་ཉེ་ཤུ་པ་བཞུགས་སྷོ།

ཀྱེ་ལེགས། འཕོ་བྲང་ཆེན་པོ་བརྒྱལ་ས་མ་ཁར་སྣ། ཆོས་བརྒྱལ་"

པིརྟམ་སིང་ཕྲ་དབུ་རྨོག་མཐོའ་བའི་དུས། རྒྱལ་སྣ་ཆེན་པོ་བླེ་ཆེན་སྐྱུ་

མཁར་བརྩེར། སེང་གེ་གནམ་བརྒྱལ་དབུ་རྨོག་ཐོ་ཞིང་ཆབ་ཁྲིད་དར་བའི་

དུས་ཡུལ་དང་གནས་ཀྱི་སྐབས་ནས་ཞལ་ཡང་མ་མཇལ་རུང་། ལས་དང་སྨོན་ལམ་འབྲེལ་པས། ཐོས་པའི་མཚན་ལ་རྟེན། ཉི་ཟླ་མཁའ་སྤྱོར་འདྲ་བའི་དགོངས་དབྱིངས་སུ་འཁྱིག། ཕན་ཚུན་བརྩེ་སེམས་གྲོགས་ཀྱིས་ལོངས་སྤྱོད་བསྐྱེས་སུ་འཕུལ།།

བརྒྱ་བོད་མཚམས་ཀྱི་ཧྣ་ར་ལ་སེ་ལ་གློག་དམར་ཁྲུག་ཆེན་འཁྲ་བའི་རྟ་ལམ་དམར་པོ་སྐྱངས། བསྐྱུན་ཚིགས་སྐྱ་མོ་འདྲ་བའི་ལུག་ལམ་དཀར་པོ་སྐྱངས། སྐྱུ་དཀར་འཛོམས་པོ་འདྲ་བའིབུ་བྲན་སྐྱིད་ལ་སྐྱེལ། དེ་འཁྲའི་ཡབ་སྲས་གཉིས་ཀྱིས། ཆབ་ཁྲིད་དར་བའི་དུས། ཡུལ་ལ་དབྱངས་ཆགས་གར་བྱ་མཁའ་འགྲོའི་ལིང་། ས་ལ་འབུར་དུ་མཐོན་བའི། བསྟི་གནན་སྐྱུ་མཁར་ན། ལྷ་ཆེན་རིགས་བཟངས་སྐན་པའི་གྲགས་པ་ཅན། གདུང་རུས་རིགས་བཟངས་འོད་གསལ་ལྷ་ནས་ཆད། དཔའ་རྒྱལ་ཁྲོལ་དང་ལྡན་པའི་ཇོ་ནོ་ཧྣ་རི། སེན་སྟོ་སྐྱུམ་མཛེད་གཉིས་ཀྱིས་ཀུང། དམ་ཆོས་ཁྲིད་འཕགས་ཀ་བམ་ལགས་པོ་དང་། པ་ཆོས་བུ་ཆོས་ལ་སོགས་དུ་མ་བཞེངས།།

b. Tinan Khar, manuscripts containing genealogical lists of the Thakurs of Gundhla.

b.i. Tinan Khar, The Chronical called Golden Mirror, Raja Bahadur Singh (1532-1559).

གསེར་གྱི་མེ་ལོང་ཞེས་པའི་རྒྱལ་རབས།

ཕོ་བྲང་ཁྲིད་འཕགས་རྒྱལ་ས་མ་གར་ས། ཆོས་རྒྱལ་ཆེན་པོ་བི་ཧྲུར་སིང་གི་བུ་རྨོག་མགོ་བའི་དུས། ཡུལ་ལ་ཁྲིད་འཕགས་སྐུ་མཁར་ནལ་ཛེ་འདིར། ཀྱེ་ལགས། མི་རིགས་ཁྲུང་རྩུན་འོད་གསལ་ལྷ་ནས་ཆད་ཚུལ་ནི། ཀུན་དེ་(ཀུ་གེ)ལྷུགས་མཁར་ནས་ཆད། མི་དབང་ཆེན་པོ་ར་ཊ་ཕ་ལ་དང་། དེའི་སྲས་རྡོ་རྗེ་ཕ་ལ། དེའི་སྲས་ཉི་མ་ཕ་ལ། དེའི་སྲས་ནང་ཀ་རྒྱལ་པོ། དེའི་སྲས་བསོད་ནམས་དཔལ་སྡེ། དེའི་སྲས་བསོད་ནམས་རྒྱ་མཚོ། དེའི་ནོ་བཀྲ་ཤིས་རྒྱལ་པོ། དེའི་ནོ་ཚེ་རིང་རྒྱལ་པོ། དེའི་སྲས་བཀྲ་ཤིས། དེའི་སྲས་པའ་རི་མཁན། དེའི་སྲས་ལྷ་སྦ་མན་ཧྲ། དེའི་སྲས་ཧ་རི་ཡ། དེའི་ནོ་རྒྱལ་པོ་དང་། དེའི་སྲས་དཔལ་འབར། ཆབ་སྲིད་ཡར་ངོའི་བཙུ་ལྟ་སྟར་འཕེལ་བར་ཤོག། ཀྱེ་ལགས། ཡོན་གྱི་བདག་པོ་རྒྱལ་པོ་དང་བློ་དྲོས་ཀྱིད་གཉིས་དང་། ཡུམ་གྱི་མཆོག་གྱུར་དང་དབང་གྲོ་མ་གསུམ་གྱིས་སྐུ་གཞེགས་ཧ་རི་འི་དོན་དུ་བྱང་ཆུབ་མཆོད་རྟེན་བཞེངས། གསུང་གྱི་

ཧྲེན་དུ་རྒྱལ་རབས་གསེར་གྱི་མི་ལོང་བཞེངས།།

(A.H. Francke, 1926, II: 212).

b.ii. Tshebang Rabtan, death ceremony, Raja Tedhi Singh (1742-1767), c. C.E. 1760.

དྲིལ་བུ་རི་དང་རི་བོ་ཀླན་རྡོ་ལ། ཏུད་རྩེ་སྨན་གྱི་སྒྲོལ་མའི་ཆུ་རྡོང་ཡོད། ཁྲིད་པར་ནལ་རྩེའི་སྐུ་མཁར་དམ་པ་རུ། གླང་པོའི་རྡུང་དང་ཕག་མོའི་ཕྱུག་སེན་བཞུགས། དེ་ལྟར་གནས་ཡིག་འདི་ནས་གཟུར་ཙམ་ཡིན། །དགའ་ལྡན་གནས་མཆུངས་སུར་བསྟན་པུ་རི་ཞེས། ཆོས་རྒྱལ་ཆེན་པོ་ཏྲེར་སིང་ག་དབུ་སྨོག་མཐོ་བའི་དུས། དེའི་མངའ་ཞབས་ཏི་ནན་ཁྲིམས་གྱི་ཡུལ། ལྷུན་འགྲུབ་ས་ལས་འབུར་དུ་ཐོན་པའི། མཐོང་ན་མཛེས་པའི་སྐུ་མཁར་མཐོ་ལ་རྟེན། ཕོ་བྲང་ཆེན་པོ་རྣལ་རྩེ་སྐུ་མཁར་འདིར། བུ་རམ་ཤིང་པའི་གདུངས་རྒྱུད་ལེགས་འཛིན་པའི། ཡབ་མི་གོང་མ་འོད་གསལ་ལྷ་ནས་ཆད། གུག་གེ་ལྷུགས་མཁར་ཁྲུང་ནས་མཆད་རྩལ་ནི། མི་དབང་ཆེན་་པོ་ར་ཊ་ཕ་ལ། དེའི་སྲས་རྡོ་རྗེ་ཕ་ལ། དེའི་སྲས་ཉི་མ་པ་ལ། དེའི་སྲས་ནང་ཀ་རྒྱལ་པོ། དེའི་སྲས་བསོད་ནམས་དཔལ་བདེ། དེའི་སྲས་བསོད་ནམས་བརྒྱ་མཚོ།

དེའི་སྲས་བཀྲཤིས་རྒྱལ་པོ། དེའི་སྲས་བཀྲ་ཤིས་དཔལ་འབྱོར། དེའི་སྲས་པ་རི་ཁན། དེའི་སྲས་ཧ་རི་ཡ། དེའི་སྲས་བཀྲ་ཤིས་དཔལ་འབར། དེའི་སྲས་ཆོས་བཟང་དབང་པོ། དེའི་སྲས་ཚེ་རིང་དར་རྒྱས། དེའི་ནུ་བོ་ཚེ་དབང་རིགས་འཛིན། སྲས་ཀྱི་མཆོག་གྱུར་ཚེ་དབང་ནོར་བུ་དང་། ཡབ་སྲས་ཀྱི་ཆབ་སྲིད་ཡར་ངོ་ཟླ་ལྟར་གོང་འཕེལ་ཤོག། དད་ལྡན་ཡོན་བདག་པོ་ཚེ་རིང་དར་བརྒྱས་དང་། ཚེ་དབང་རིགས་ འཛིན། གཉིས་དང་། ཡོན་གྱི་བདག་མོ་ཚེ་རིང་ཆོས་འཛོམ། ཁོང་གསུམ་གྱིས་སྐུ་གཤེགས་ཚེ་དབང་རབ་སྟན་ལ་ལམ་སྒྲོད་ཕྱིར་དུ། སྐུ་ཡི་བསྙེན་དུ་ཚེ་དཔག་མེད་ཀྱི་སྐུ། རྡོ་རྗེ་སེམས་པ་ཡབ་ཡུམ་ཀྱི་སྐུ། དཔའ་བོ་ཧྲ་གྲིན་ཀྱི་སྐུ། དགོན་པོ་ཕྱག་དྲུག་པའི་སྐུ། གསུངས་ཀྱི་རྟེན་དུ་རྡོ་རྗེ་བཅོད་པ་ཚར་ཉི་ཤུ་རྩ་གཉིས་དང་། ཐུགས་ཀྱི་རྟེན་དུ་བྱང་ཆུབ་མཆོད་རྟེན་ལ་གཟུངས་འཛུགས་ཁྱད་པར་ཅན་དང་བཅས་པ་དེ་རྣམས་བཞེངས།།

b.iv. Tinan Khar, Gundhla – Sultanpur document written by Bilchhung of Barbog Khar, c. C.E. 1900.

ནག་སེ་ཙི་ཀ་བའི་བ་སྒུ་ཛུ་བ་ན་སྒུ་ནེ་ལམ་བར་ཀ། བ་བ་ཏ་ཧི་མི་ན་གར་པ་ན། གོ་ཁྲི་གུན་ད་ལ། ཡུལ་གུན་ད་ལ།།

ར་ཏན་པལ། རྡོ་རྗེ་པལ། ཉི་མ་པལ། ནག་རྒྱལ་པོ། (ཛ་ཏ་ཁྲ་ཀ་ར། འདུང་རུས་གུ་རམ་ཞིང་པ།)སོ་ནམ་པལ་དེ། སོ་ནམ་"རྒྱ་ཚོ། ཀྲིས་རྒྱལ་པོ། གྲོང་སོང་། ཚེ་རིང་རྒྱལ་པོ། བྲ་ཤིས་དལ་བྱོར། པ་རི་ཁླུ། ཐླ་ག་མན་ཏ། ཏ་རི་ཨ། པལ་བར། ཆེ་ཛ་ཡོན་པོ། ཚེ་རིང་ནམ་རྒྱལ། ཏོ་རུག་ནམ་རྒྱལ། ཚེ་རིང་རྒྱལ་མཚན། ཚེ་རིང་ལྷུར་གྱི། རུབ་ཅན་འདད། སེ་བ་"འདས།གྲོང་སོང་། ཐླག་ཅན་འདད། ལྷར་མ་ཅན་འདད། རུ་མོ་དར་ཅནད། གྲོང་སོང་། ཧེར་ཅན་འདད། ཛླན་ཅནད།། ཨོ་དྲི་དང་བར་བོག་ནོ་ནོ་བི་ལ་ཙུང་ཉིས་བྲིས།།

c. Tinan Khar, Karchhangs, Records prepared at the time of celebration of some social functions in the household.

c.i. Account of receipt of offerings at dge-rtsi, a death ceremony, at Nal-tse mKhar, Tinan c. C.E. 1860.

དཀར་པོ་གྱིས་ཅེས།།

དེ་ནན་ནས་ཟེས་ཁར་ཀྱི་དཀར་པོ་གྲིས་ཅིས་བྱུང་གྲངས་ལ།། བར་འབོག་ཁར་ནས་གྲག་༡༣། སིང་གེ་ར་མའི་གྲག་ག་༡༠། ཡོ་ཏར་ཀྱིས་གྲག་༡༠་དང་དམར་ཏོ་གོར་༡། ཉུ་ཀུར་ནང་མའི་ཨ་རག་ཙོ་ལི་༡་དང་དམར་ཏོ་གོར་༡། ཡོན་སར་ཆེ་རིང་དོ་བ་ལྡན་གྱི་ལག་ཡ་གཅིག་ཤ་ཨ་རག་ཙོ་ལི་༡། ཕུག་ཏུ་ལ་ནང་མའི་འབོ་དོ་ལ་༡་ཨ་རག་དམར་ཏོ་གོར་༡། གྲི་ལིང་ཆེ་རིང་དྲུག་རྒྱའི་གྲག་ཀ་༥།། རམ་བུ་གྲི་འི་ཨན་ན་༩། ཕུ་རད་ནང་མའི་ཨ་རག་ཙོ་ལི་༡་དང་ཤ་ལག་པ་༡། སུམ་རྣམ་ནམ་གང་ཆེ་རིང་དངུལ་༡། གུང་རང་ཀུ་མཁར་ན་ཨ་རག་ཙོ་ལི་༡་དང་ཤ་ལག་པ་༡། སྤྲང་བར་པའི་ཨ་རག་ཙོ་ལི་༡། གྲི་ལིང་གུར་འདས་འི་ཨ་རག་ཙོ་ལི་༡་དང་ཤ་ལག་པ་༡། གྲི་ལིང་གོ་བཀལ་འི་ཚང་ཟམ་༡་དང་ཚ་ཤ་༡། ཏར་ཀྲུམ་པའི་གྲག་ཀ་༥། ཐོ་རང་བོ་དོའི་ཨ་རག་ཙོ་ལི་༡་དང་དམར་ཏོ་གོར་༡། དགུན་ལ་ཡར་ཙོ་ལི་༡་དང་ཤ་ལག་པ་༡། ཁྲིམ་ནང་པའི་ཨ་རག་ཙོ་ལི་༡་དང་དམར་ཏོ་གོར་༡། ཕུག་ཏལ་བསོད་ནམས་ཙའི་ཨ་རག་ཙོ་ལི་༡་དང་ཕེ་དམར་ཏོ་གོར་༡། རྟུར་པ་ཕྱི་མ་ཨ་རག་ཙོ་ལི་༡་དང་ཕེ་དམར་ཏོ་གོར་༡། ཚོད་པ་ཁྲིམ་འདས་འི་དངུལ་༡། ཀོ་རའི་པའི་

ཨ་རག་ཚོ་ལི་༡། མ་ནེའི་པའི་གྲག་ཀ་༩། གུན་ལ་ཀུན་དགའི་གྲག་ཀ་༩། ཡང་དཀར་ཆེ་རིང་གི་གྲག་ཀ་༩། གར་གྲུར་འདྲསའི་པའི་ན་༥། ཕུ་རད་རྟག་ཏུམ་པའི་ཨ་རག་ཚོ་ལི་༡་དང་ཚ་ཤ་༡། ར་ལིང་མང་ཞའི་དམར་ནོ་གོར་༡་དང་པའི་ན་༡༣། ཅུ་ཀུར་ཕྱི་མ་འི་ཆང་ཟམ་༡་དང་ནོ་གོར་༡་ཐེ་མར། མི་མི་ཁམ་པའི་གྲག་ཀ་༧། གར་མ་ནྟུའི་གྲག་ཀ་༣། གུས་པ་བལ་འདྲསའི་དྲུལ་༡། གུས་པ་ནང་རློན་་གྲག་ཀ་༡༣། ཞུ་ལིང་ཡོག་མའི་ཆང་ཚོ་ལི་༡་དང་ཤ་ལག་པ་༡། སྲོབ་ན་སོ་རྣམ་དཏག་པོའི་གྲག་༡༧། ཕུ་རད་ཕྱི་མའི་ཨ་རག་ཚོ་ལི་༡་ཚ་ཤ་༡། སྨུ་ལིང་བོ་དོའི་ཨ་རག་ཚོ་ལི་༡། ཧི་ནན་ཁང་སར་ནེ་ཨ་རག་ཚོ་ལི་༡་དང་ཤ་ལག་པ་༡། སྲྀ་སྲིན་ཇོའི་ཨ་རག་ཚོ་ལི་༡་དང་ཤ་ལག་པ་༡། མང་དགོན་པ་གྱུང་རང་གཉེར་པའི་གྲག་ཀ་ཞི་དང་པའི་ས་༡། དཀར་དང་དཀར་པའི་ཨ་རག་ཚོ་ལི་གཅིག། ཞུ་གྱུ་པའི་གྲག་ཀ་༩། ཕུག་ཏལ་དྭག་ཆེ་དབང་གི་གྲག་ཀ་༩། ཇག་ལེ་སྲུ་ནྟུའི་གྲག་ཀ་༣། དར་རྩེའི་ཨ་ནྟུའི་གྲག་ཀ་༦། སུ་ནམ་པའི་ན་༦། མར་རྒྱིད་པའི་པའི་ན་༧། ཡང་

དཀར་ཕྱི་མ་འི་པའི་ན་༥། ཀྱང་རྩེ་པའི་པའི་ན་༧། མེ་མེ་ཀྲེ་ལོང་གྱི་
གྲག་ཀ་༥། རང་ལོ་དབང་ཆེན་གྲག་ཀ་༨།།

c.ii. Karchhag prepared on the occasion of celebration of a death ceremony, c. C.E. 1880-85.

གྱེ་ཅི། གྱེ་ཅི་ཡོང་བའི་གྲང་ལ། ཐོག་མར་བླ་མ་གྲིས་བརྟན་པེལ་
དངུལ་༡། ཧོད་ཁང་སར་ཁར་ནས་དངུལ་༡། དགུང་རང་ཁར་ནས་དངུལ་
༡། དཀར་ལྷང་ནང་ལོན་གྱི་དངུལ་ཕྱེད། ཀྱེ་ལང་ཐའ་ཚུག་ཤི་དངུལ་ཕྱེད།
ཀླེ་ལིང་ཡུར་ནད་པའི་དངུལ་༡། བར་སྐོག་སྒྲོ་མའི་ཚང་ལྷ་རི་༡་དང་ཨ་རག་
སྐོ་ཏལ་༡། ཤ་ཤིན་པའི་དངུལ་༡། སྒྲོབ་ནས་ཡོ་ཏར་ནང་མའི་དངུལ་༡།
ཡོ་ཏར་ཕྱི་མའི་དངུལ་༡། ཤུ་ལིང་ཡོག་མའི་ཨ་ན་༤། ཏི་ནན་ཁང་སར་
ཨ་རག་ཙོ་ལི་༡་དང་ཤ་ལག་པ་༡། ས་རང་ཕུན་ཚོགས་ཀྱི་ཨ་ན་༤། གྲི་ལིང་
ཚེ་རིང་འབྲུག་རྒྱའི་ཨ་ན་༥། རྩུར་པ་ནང་མའི་དངུལ་ཕྱེད། སོ་ནམ་རིན་
ཆེན་གྱི་ཨ་ན་༢། ཁོག་སར་འབལ་ཀ་ཛ་སའི་དངུལ་༡། འབར་སྐོག་ནོ་
ནོའི་དངུལ་ཕྱེད། སྐོ་ཀར་མེ་མེ་ཚེ་དབང་རིག་འཛིན་གྱི་དངུལ་ཕྱེད། ནོ་
ལིང་རིག་འཛིན་གྱི་ཨ་ན་༤། འབར་སྐོག་པེ་ཅེ་ནོ་ནོའི་ཨ་ན་༤། ཚོད་ན་

སོ་ནམ་ནོར་ཕེལ་ཨ་ན་༤། ཀོ་ར་པའི་སོ་ནམ་ཚེ་རིང་ཨ་ན་༣། ཚེ་རིང་
དགའ་འི་དདུལ་ཕྱིད། བྲ་ཀུ་ནམ་རྒྱལ་གྱི་ཨ་ན་༤། སྨུར་ཧེ་ཙེ་ནམ་རྒྱལ་
གྱི་ཨ་ན་༤། ཡང་པེ་ཀྱི་ཚེ་རིང་གྱི་ཨ་ན་༤། སོ་ནམས་རབ་འཛིན་གྱི་ཨ་
ན་༤། སི་ལ་ལྷ་མའི་ཨ་ན་༣།སྨུར་ཧེ་ཙེ་འབྲུག་ཆང་གྱི་ཨ་ན་༤། སླབ་བྱུང་
ནོར་བུའི་ཨ་ན་༤། ཡོ་ཧར་ཀྱི་ཆང་ཕེད་པ་༧་དང་མར་ཧོ་གོར་༧། ཐོ་རང་
ནང་མའི་ཨ་རག་ཙོ་ལི་༧་དང་ཞ་ལག་པ་༧། ཧར་ཀྲུམ་པའི་ཨ་རག་ཙོ་ལི་༧་
ཕྱི་མར། ཏུར་པ་ཕྱི་མའི་ཨ་རག་བོ་ཧལ་༧་ཚ་ཞ། ཕུ་རད་ཧག་ཏུམ་པའི་
ཨ་རག་ཙོ་ལི་༧་དང་ཞ་ལག་པ། ཕུ་རད་ནང་མའི་ཨ་རག་ཙོ་ལི་༧་ཞ་ལ་ག་པ།
ཐོ་རང་བློ་ཏོའི་ཨ་རག་ཙོ་ལི་༧་ཚ་ཞ། དཀར་བདང་པའི་ཨ་རག་བོ་ཧོལ་༧།
ཀྲི་ལིང་གོང་མའི་ཨ་རག་ཙོ་ལི་༧་ཞ་ལག་པ། འབྲུ་བདུ་རམ་གྱི་ཨ་རག་བོ་
ཧོལ་༧། ཡོ་སར་པའི་ཨ་རག་ཙོ་ལི་༧་ཚ་ཞ། ཁྲིམ་ནང་ལྷ་མ་འི་ཨ་རག་ཙོ་
ལི་༧་དང་མར་ཧོ་གོར་༧། ཕུག་ཧལ་འབྲུག་ནང་གྱི་ཨ་རག་བོ་ཧོལ་༧། ཀྲི་
ལིང་སྒྲོ་ཀ་ལི་ཨ་རག་བོ་ཧོལ་༧་ཞ་ལག་པ། ཕུག་ཧལ་རྫོའི་ཨ་རག་བོ་ཧོལ་

༡་ཤ་བྲང་༡། དགུན་ལ་ཡར་གྱི་ཨ་རག་བོ་ཧྡོལ་༡། སྤུ་རད་ཕྱི་མའི་ཨ་རག་ཙོ་ལི་༡་མར་ཧྡོ་གོར་ཅིག། རང་བློ་དག་རའི་ཨ་ན།།

c.iii. sha-kan ki dha-nā. Donations received at the Auspicious Ceremony, c. C.E. 1940.

ཤ་ཀན།། ཤ་ཀན་གྱི་དྷ་ནཱ།། ཁྲིམ་ནང་གོང་མི་དངུལ་ཕྱེ། ཁང་སར་ནེ་དངུལ་༡། གུང་རང་ཁར་ཡོག་མི་དངུལ་༡། གུན་ལ་ཕྱི་མི་དངུལ་ཕྱེ། སྤུ་རད་ཕྱི་མི་དངུལ་༡། སྤུ་རད་ནང་མི་དངུལ་༡། སྤུ་རད་དག་ཐུང་པའི་དངུལ་༡། གུན་ལ་ཏར་ཁྲུང་པའི་ཨན་༤། གུན་ལ་ནང་མི་ཨན་༤། གུ་ལར་གྱི་ཨ་ན་༤། དྲི་ལིང་སོན་ཏན་འཛིན་གྱི་ཨ་ན་༤། ཡོ་ཏར་གྱི་ཨ་ན་༣། ཅེས་ཆུང་ཕུན་ཚོགས་དཔལ་འདོན་གྱི་དངུལ་༡། བཀྲ་ཤིས་ངོ་གྲུབ་གྱི་ཨ་ན་༤། ཤ་ཤིན་རྡོ་བོ་དངུལ་༡། གུན་ལ་གོ་ར་པའི་ཨ་ན་༤། ཀལ་བཟང་གྲོལ་མི་ཕྱེད། ནོར་འཛིན་གྲོལ་མི་ཨན་༤། གུང་རང་ཁར་གོང་མའི་དངུལ་༡། ཙེབ་ར་སི་མ་ཧི་ཡ་ཨ་ན་༢། སྒྲོབ་པ་བྱུ་དོ་ཨན་༢། ཡོ་སར་པ་དངུལ་༡། བརྡོག་པ་དངུལ་༡། ཤ་ཤིན་སྟན་འཛིན་ཨན་༢། གུང་རང་ཙེ་ཆུང་ཚེ་རིང་དབང་མོ་དངུལ་༡། སྡོད་པ་ཁར་དངུལ་༡།།

c.iv. Tinan Khar Ge-tsi, c. C.E. 1950.

c.iv.i. sha-kan ki dha-na [shagun kā dāna], giftsreceived at the auspicious occasion, c. C.E. 1950.

གསོལ་ཇའི་ཐོ།

ཁྲིམ་ནང་སྟན་འཛིན་རབ་གྲུས་དངུལ་༡། ཁང་སར་པ་དངུལ་༡།

སྤུ་རད་ཏག་ཐུམ་པ་དངུལ་༡། སྤུ་རད་ནང་མ་དངུལ་༡། སྤུ་རད་ཕྱི་མ་

དངུལ་༡། དྲི་ལིང་བསོན་སྟན་འཛིན་དངུལ་༡། ཤ་ཤིན་ནོ་མོ་དངུལ་༡།

ཀྱི་ལང་སོ་ན་དངུལ་ཕྱེད།།

c.iv.ii. bartana. Receipts of Exchange, c. C.E. 1950.

བར་ཏན།། ཡ་ན་ཕེལ་སུག་དེ་བ་དངུལ་༥། ཀྱི་ལང་ཀྱུ་མོ་དངུལ་༡། ཀོ་

ནུ་དངུལ་༡། ཤ་ཤིན་གོ་དཔལ་རྡ་ས་དངུལ་༢། སྟོད་པ་ཁར་ནས་དངུལ་༤།

ཞི་པ་ཐོ་ལག་བའི་དངུལ་༣། ལྷ་རོག་བཀྲིས་ནམ་རྒྱལ་དངུལ་༡། ཕེ་ཚེ་ནོ་ནོ་

དངུལ་༡། དཔལ་ཀྱིད་རིཾ་དངུལ་༡། ཀྱིར་ཧིང་སུར་ཐན་དངུལ་༡། ཀྱིར་

ཧིང་བོ་བུ་དངུལ་༡། ཀོ་ལོང་ཁར་དངུལ་༣། དཀར་དང་གར་པ་དངུལ་༡།

སྤུ་རད་ཏག་ཏུན་པ་དངུལ་༡། རིང་གྲུབ་རྒྱ་དངུལ་ཕྱེད། གྱིའར་ཐང་ཚེ་རིང་

སྟུན་གྲུབ་ཨ་ན་ཀ། ཙུ་ཀུར་ནང་མ་དངུལ་ཀ། རྟོབ་པ་བུ་ཛྲུ་དངུལ་ཀ། གར་པ་སོན་དུ་དངུལ་ཀ། ར་ལིང་ཡོག་མ་དངུལ་ཀ།།

d. gZungs-yig, dhaarni (dhāraṇī) mantra.

d.i. ཨོཾ་བཻ་ཤྲ་མ་ཎྜ་ཡེ་སྭཱ་ཧཱ། ཨོཾ་ཛམ་བྷ་ལ་ཛ་ལེན་དྲ་ཡེ་སྭཱ་ཧཱ། ཨོཾ་ཛམ་བྷ་ལ་ཡེ་སྭཱ་ཧཱ།ཨོཾ་པཱུ་རྞ་བྷ་དྲཱ་ཡ་སྭཱ་ཧཱ། ཨོཾ་མ་ཎི་བྷ་དྲ་ཡེ་སྭཱ་ཧཱ། ཨོཾ་ཀུ་བེ་རཡེ་སྭཱ་ཧཱ། ཨོཾ་སམ་པྲ་ཛ་ན་ཡེ་སྭཱ་ཧཱ། ཨོཾ་གུ་ཧཡ་སྐན་ཡེ་སྭཱ་ཧཱ། ཨོཾ་བི་ཙི་ཀུ་ཎཊ་ལ་ཡེ་སྭཱ་ཧཱ། ཨོཾ་སུ་པྲ་ཏི་ཥྛ་བ་ཛ་ཡེ་སྭཱ་ཧཱ། ཕུ་གུ་ལས་ཚུ་བདག་ཕྲ་རུ་འི་གཙོ་བྱས་ཀླུ་ཆེན་པོ་བརྒྱད་འཁོར་དང་བཅས་པའི་ས་བདག་ལྷ་ཀླུའི"""

d.ii. བསམ་པའི་དོན་ཐམས་ཅད་འགྲུབ་པར་མཛད་དུ་གསོལ། སྐྱེ་བུ་མཆོག་གི་བཀའ་དང་དམ་ལ་གནས་པའི་ཐོག་མེད་རྫུ་ཕྲུལ་མཐུ་སྟོབས་ཀྱི་བདག་པོ་རྣམས་ཀྱི་བདག་ཅག་རྒྱུ་སྐྱོར་འཁོར་དང་བཅས་པ་ལ་བུ་ནོར་ལོངས་སྤྱོད་རྒྱས་པའི་དངོས་གྲུབ་མཆོག་སྩལ་ཡུལ་ལྷ་གཞི་བདག་རྣམས་ཀྱི་གྲིས་ཤོག།

4 sTod, Upper Bhaga Valley

i. Gonpa – monasteries.

a. Chhu-sku-tsi (Chhos-sku-tse) Gonpa, Khangsar.

a.i. Padma Thangyig, bDe-mchhog rNam-rgyal, king of Zanskar, c. fourth quarter of 17th century C.E.

(a). ཁ་བ་ཅན་ལྗོངས་དམ་ཆོས་དར་བས་གནས། དགྲ་བཅོམ་བཞུགས་གནས་ཏི་སེ་གངས་ཀྱི་ནུབ། ཆུ་ཆེན་དལ་གྱིས་འབབ་ པའི་གཡོན། ཆོས་ཁྲིམས་དར་བ་ཟངས་དཀར་ས་ཡི་དབུས། ས་ལ་འབུར་འཐོན་རྒྱལ་ས་སྤྲ་དུམ་འདིར། ས་དེ་དབང་པོ་དཔལ་བརྗིད་མཛེས། ཆོས་རྒྱལ་ཆེན་པོ་བདེ་མཆོག་རྣམ་རྒྱལ་གྱིས། དབུ་རྨོག་མཐོ་ཞིང་ཆབ་སྲིད་དར་བའི་དུས། ལྷ་སྲས་ཡུམ་མཆོག་བསླབ་གསུམ་བརྒྱན་གྱིས་མཛེས། ཟབ་ལམ་གནད་ཀྱི་གདམས་མཛོད་འཛིན་མ། དབང་སེམས་བདག་མོ་ཁྲི་རྒྱལ་མོ་བསྐྱོད། ཁྱེད་ཀྱི་ཆབ་སྲིད་བཟང་པོའི་མངའ་འོག་དུ། རྒྱབ་རི་རིན་ཆེན་སྤུངས་པ་འདྲ་བའི་མདུན། མདུན་ནམ་ཞིང་གཡུ་མཚོ་མེར་བ་འདྲ། ཡོགས་ན་ཆུ་མིག་འབྲ་རལ་མང་བ་ཡོང་། དབུ་ན་གནས་ཆེན་ཁྱད་འཕགས་ཀ་ནི་ཀ་ཞེས་ཞུགས། ཡུལ་ལས་དགེ་བཅུ་འཛོམ་པའི་སྐྱིད་ཡུལ་ས་ནི་ཏཱ། སྔོན་ཆེ་བསོད་ནམས་བསགས་པས་དལ་འབྱོར་མི་ལུས་ཐོབ། ལས་འབྲོ་བསྐལ་བཅུ་ལྡན་པའི་དམ་པའི་ཆོས་ལ་མོས། མི་རིགས་ཁྱུངས་བཙུན་པ་མའི་གབ་ཆར་རྒྱུད། དད་ལྡན་ཡོན་གྱི་བདག་པོ་སྒྲོལ་མ་དོན་གྲུབ་དང་། བུ་ཙ་སྒྲོལ་མ་དཔལ་འབྱོལ་ངག་དབང་བཙོན་འགྲུས་གསུམ་གྱིས་ཀྱང་། དྲིན་ཅན་ཕ་མའི་དྲིན་ལན་བསབ་པ་དང་ ' ' ' ཕྱིར་དུ། དམ་ཆོས་ཁྱད་འཕགས་པདྨའི་བཀའ་ཐང་བཞེངས། ' ' ' ' ' ' དད་ལྡན་ཡོན་གྱི་བདག་མོ་ཚེ་དབང་སྒྲུ་ཙ་བུ་དྲིད་གཉིས་ཀྱིས་ཀྱང་། ' ' ' ' གསུང་རབ་འདིའི་དགེ་རྩེ་གསལ་བའི་གྲངས་ལ། བླ་མ་རྡོ་རྗེ་འཛིན་པའི་ཚང་གསུམ། དགེ་སློང་བཀྲ་ཤིས་དཔལ་འབྱོར་དགེ་སློང་བཀྲ་ཤིས་རྒྱ་མཚོ་དགེ་སློང་བསྟན་འཛིན་སྒྲུ་ཙ་དེ་རྣམས་ཀུན་གྱི་ནང་ཚང་བདུན། སྒྲུཙ་དོན་གྲུབ་ཚང་ཞི་རྟེན་དང་བཅས། ཀུན་དགའ་དཔལ་འབྱོར་ཚང་གཞི་རྟེན་དང་བཅས། བཀྲ་ཤིས་ཚེ་རིང་ཚང་གཉིས་རྟེན། ཚེ་དབང་འབྲུག་རྒྱས་ཚང་གཅིག་རྟེན་ཨུ་པ་རག་དཔལ་འབྱོར་ཚང་གཉིས་རྟེན།-----

(b) About the Book

ཨུ་རྒྱན་ཐྲུ་ཏ་པ་དྨ་འབྱུང་གནས་ཀྱི་ནམ་ཐར་རྒྱས་པ་གསེར་གྱི་ཕྲེང་ཞེས་བྱ་བ། བྱ་རི་ཕུག་མོ་ཆེ་ཤེལ་གྱི་བྲག་ཕུག་ན་ཐྲུ་ཏ་ སངས་རྒྱས་གླིང་པས་གཏེར་ནས་གདན་དྲངས་པ། གཞན་གྱིས་བཅོས་པ་སྣ་གཅིག་ཀྱང་མེད་པའི་གཏེར་མ་བཞུགས་སོ།། འདི་ལ་བཞི་བྱས། ཨུ་རྒྱན་རིན་པོ་ཆེའི་རྣམ་ཐར་མི་ཅིག་པ་ལྔ་བཅུ་རྩ་ལྔ། སྣ་ཚྭ་ར་བ། ནམ་ཁའི་སྙིང་པོ། ཡེ་ཤེས་མཚོ་རྒྱལ་ལ་སོགས་པའི་རྣམ་ཐར། གཞན་ཡང་ལོ་རྒྱུས་ངོ་མཚར་ཆེ་བ་མང་པོ། སྤྲུབ་ཆེན་རིན་ཆེན་དཔལ་བཟང་གི་ཤངས་རྒྱ་མཚོར་ཐ་དད་དུ་གྲིབ་པར་གནང་བའི་རྣམ་ཞབས་འདེབས་གསར་གྲགས་པ། ཐོ་བོ་དང་ཤངས་ལུང་པར་དར་འདི་ཚོརམ་སྤྱི་སླེབ་པ་མ་བྱུང་། རང་རང་གི་ཡུལ་ཡུལ་དུ་སྣ་ཐོས་ཡོད་པ། གཉེར་ཁ་བཤེས་ཆེ་བ་སོགས་ལ་ཡང་ནམ་ཐར་རྒྱས་འབྲིང་བསྡུས་གསུམ་ཡོང་གི་འདུག་པས། ཀུན་གྱི་གཟིགས་རྟོག་མཛད་པ་བཞུ། ཞང་བློན་ཆེན་པོའི་མི་ཟད་པར་བསྐྲུན་པའི་རྣམ་ཐར་རྒྱས་པར་བཀོད་པ་བཞུགས་ལགས་སོ།། དགེ་ལེགས་འཕེལ་བར་གྱུར་ཅིག།།

a.ii. mDo-mangs, Zanskar, king dBang-chhug rNam-rgyal, first quarter of eighteenth century C.E.

ས་འི་ལྟེ་བ་རྒྱ་གར་རྡོ་རྗེ་གདན། གནས་འདི་གནས་དེ་ནས་རི་ནག་དགུ་འདས་ནས། གངས་ཀྱི་རྒྱལ་པོ་གངས་དཀར་ཏི་སེ་ནུབ། ཆུ་བོ་དལ་འབབ་སེནདྷི་འབྲུག་གཡོན། ཡུལ་ལ་གཡང་ཆགས་ཟངས་དཀར་ཆོས་ཀྱི་ཡུལ། ས་ལ་འབུར་དུ་རྒྱལ་ས་པ་དུམ་རྩེར། ཀྱེ་ལགས། ས་སྐྱོང་ཆེན་པོ་ཨང་ཆུག་རྣམ་རྒྱལ་འབུར་རྨོག་མཐོ་ཞིང་ཆབས་སྲིད་དར་བའི་ཁེད་ཀྱི་ཆབ་སྲིད་བཟང་པོའི་མངའ་འོག་འདིར། ཀྱེ་ལགས། གནས་ཀྱི་མཆོག་གྱུར་བཟང་གླིང་ཕུག་ཐལ་འདིར། མཁན་ཆེན་རིན་ཆེན་ཆོས་བཟང་ཆོས་གཙུག་ཐོ་བའི་དུས། ཀྱེ་ལགས། ཡུལ་དགེ་བཅུ་འཛོམ་པའི་སྐྱིད་ཡུལ་ཨང་མུ་རུ། རིགས་རུས་ཁུངས་བཙུན་པ་མི་སྤྱུགས་ཆང་ཞུག་པ་གདུང་གྱི་རྒྱུད། ཀྱེ་ལགས། རང་ལྷན་ཡོན་གི་བདག་པོ་རྡོ་རྗེ་ཚེ་རིང་། དང་ཀ་ཙུ་པ་དང་། ཀ་བཀྲ་ཤིས་དང་།། ཡོན་གྱི་བདག་མོ་མགུ་ཏུ་བུ་ཁྲིད་ཨ་པེ་བློ་བཟང་འཛོམ་བ་ཁོང་རྣམས་ཀྱི་དྲིན་ཅན་ཨ་པ། ཨ་ཕུ་གཉིས་ཐུགས་དགོངས་རྫོགས་ཕྱིར་དང་། རང་རེའི་རྗེག་རིབ་མ་ལུས་དག་ཕྱིར་དང་། མར་གྱུར་འགྲོ་བ་རིགས་དྲུག་སེམས་ཅན་གྱི་དོན་གྱི་ཕྱིར་དང་། སྐུའི་རྟེན་དུ་སངས་རྒྱས་དང་འཇམ་དབྱངས་དང་ཚོང་ཁ་པ་དང་སུང་གི་རྟེན་དུ་མདོ་མངས་དགོས་འདོད་བཞེངས། བསགས་པ་དོན་ཅན་འདི་ལ་ཀུན་ཀྱང་སྨོན། སྒྱུ་མའི་ནོར་ལ་སྙིང་པོ་མེད་གཟིགས་ནས། ཨེ་མ་ཧོ། སྦྱིན་ཆེ་བསོད་ནམས་བསགས་པའི་དམ་པའི་ཆོས་དང་འཇལ། དེ་ཕྱིར་གསུང་རབ་འདི་ལ་དགེ་རྩེ་ཏིག་པའི་གྲངས་ལ། ཕུག་ཐལ་བླབ་རང་གནས་གཉེར་ཚང་བཞི་གྲང་རྒྱས། མུ་ནེའི་སློབ་དཔོན་ཚང་གཉིས། གྲང་པ་གཉིས་ཀྱི་ཚང་གཉིས་རྟེན། དགེ་སློང་དང་རྒྱལ་མཚན་ཚང་གསུམ། ཀ་བཅུ་པ་བློ་བཟང་ཆོས་གྲགས་ཚང་གསུམ། ་ ་ ་ ་།།

b. Gemur gonpa, Gemur, Gyemur.

b.i. Fresh site for construction of the monastery of gSam-btan Chhos-gling, Gemur gonpa, c. C.E. 1885.

Document from the family of Tanzin Paldan of village 'Bog, Gemur gonpa, Tashi Tanphel C.E. 1887.

༄དགོན་བསམ་གཏན་ཆོས་གླིང་གི་ས་གཞིའི་ཆུ་ནོར་དེ་བཞིན་ལ་མོ་ཁག་ལོ་ཐུག་གཉེར་པ་རྣམས་ཀྱི་ས་ལ་མཚམས་བཅད་ཐོ་རྒྱབ་འདུག། དེ་ནས་ཐུར་མ་ས་ཡན་ལ་ཆུ་ཙམ་བཏང་ཐུབ་ཀྱང་། ཕྱུགས་དགོན་པ་ལ་ཕན་ཕྱིར། ཨ་ཙི་དགེ་སློང་ལ་ས་གཞི་དགོན་ལ་གྱུར་ཕྱིར་ཆུ་གཏོང་ཟེར་བས་ཁོང(ཁྱོད་)རང་གི་ཆུ་བཏངས་ས་སོགས་འོལ་རྒྱལ་བ་སོང་ཀྱང་དགེ་སློང་སྐུ་ཚེ་ནམ་བརྟན་བར་དུ་ཐུགས་རྗེ་དགོངས་པ་ཡིན། སྤྱི་ས་གཉེར་སུ་བཞུགས་སོགས་ཀྱི་སྐོར་ཚེར(ཚོར)་མེད་པ་གནས་ཙུག་(བཙུག་)དགོས། རབ་འབྱུང་༡༥ མེ་ཕག་ལོ་ཟླ་༨ཚེས་༢༢ལ་བླ་མ་བཀྲིས་བརྟན་འཕེལ་གྱིས་བྲིས་པ་དགེ།།

b.ii. Prayer to sTag-tshang Raspa, c. C.E. 1880.

Karchhag in the prayer book for sTag-tshang Raspa, Gemur, c. 1880 C.E.

གྲུབ་དབང་ཤྲཱ་མ་ནྟཱའི་འཁྲུང་རབས་རྣམ་ཐར་གསོལ་འདེབས་དཔག་བསམ་འཁྲི་ཤིང་བཞུགས་སོ།།

ཅེས་དཔལ་ལྡན་བླ་མ་དམ་པ་གྲུབ་པའི་དབང་ཕྱུག་ཨོ་ཊི་ཡན་པ་ངག་དབང་རྒྱ་མཚོ་འཁྲུངས་རབས་དང་རྣམ་ཐར་ལ་བསྟོད་པ་དཔག་བསམ་འཁྲི་ཤིང་ཞེས་བྱ་བ་འདི། དམ་པ་དེ་ཉིད་ཀྱི་རྗེས་སུ་བཟུང་བའི་དགེ་སློང་དཀའ་རྒྱུད་འབྲུག་རྒྱས་ཀྱི་བསྐྱལ་ངོར་དགེ་བའི་བཤེས་གཉེན་ངག་དབང་དཀར་རྒྱུད་རྒྱ་མཚོ་ཞེས་བྱ་བའི་འདི་ཡང་ཏེ་མི་བྱང་ཆུབ་གླིང་དུ་སྦྱར་པའོ། ཅེས་པ་ཡང་ཏེ་མི་གྲྭ་ཐུགས་དཾ་པ་ངག་དབང་དགེ་འདུན་གྱི་སྐྱབས་མགོན་རྒྱལ་སྲས་རིན་པོ་ཆེ་གོང་མའི་རྣམ་ཐར་གསོལ་འདེབས་བསྡུས་པ་ཞིག་བྲི་དགོས་གནང་བའི་བཞེད་ངོར་བདེ་ཆོས་ངས་འཛིན་ཡེ་ཤེས་གྲུབ་པས་དད་དང་དྭངས་བས་བཀོད་པ་དགེ། ཆོས་སྦྱིན་མི་ཟད་པར་གྱི་ཡོན་སྦྱོར་ནི། ཏེ་མཛོད་བསོད་ནམ་མཚན་གྱི་བཀའ་མངགས་པས། དང་ལེན་པར་ཡིག་བྲི་བཀོས་མཛད་དགའ་བ། ཏེ་མི་གྲྭ་རིགས་བཀྲ་ཤིས་བསྟན་སྤེལ་གྱི། དད་བརྩོན་ཆེན་པོས་བསྒྲུབ་པའི་དགེ་ཚོགས་ཀྱི། མཁའ་མཉམ་འགྲོ་དྲུག་ཐར་ལམ་ཐོབ་ཕྱིར་བསྔོ།།

b.iii. There is a similar book, as above. The following is colophon to the second book.

བཀྲ་ཤིས་བསྟན་པ་འཕེལ་བའི་ལྷག་བསམ་གྱིས། གཅིག་ལས་དུ་མར་བགྱིད་པའི་ཆོས་སྦྱིན་པར། བྲི་བྱེད་ཕལ་དང་དག་བྱེད་ཁོ་བོའི་འབད། པར་བསྐོས་སྒྲུབ་པའི་དབང་ཕྱུག་འགྱུར་ལྡན་དང་། བྲིས་བསྐོས་འཕྲིན་ལས་ཀུན་བཟང་གཙོ་མཛད་དེ། དཀར་རྒྱུད་རིག་འཛིན་དགོན་མཆོག་བཟོད་པ་དང་། དཔལ་ལྡན་དོན་གྲུབ་བསྟན་འཛིན་ཆོས་འཕེལ་བཅས། ཆོས་མཛད་ཆོས་སྐྱིད་སྒྲོལ་མ་དབྱངས་ཅན་དང་། ཚེ་རིང་བུ་ཁྲིད་ཆོས་སྐྱིད་ཆོས་སྐྱིད་གཉིས། ཆོས་འཛིན་དབང་མོ་སོགས་ཀྱིས་གུས་པའི་སྒྲུབས།།ལས་ཀྱི་བྱེད་པོ་རིན་ཆེན་སེངྒེའི་བགྱིས། གར་ཞ་བསམ་བསྟན་ཆོས་གླིང་དུ། སྒྲུབ་པའི་དགེ་བའི་ལུང་རྟོགས་ཀྱི། བསྟན་པ་ཕྱོགས་བཅུར་རྒྱས་པ་དང་། རྣམ་མཁྱེན་སངས་རྒྱས་མྱུར་ཐོབ་ཤོག།

ii. Karchhags.

a.i. Household of Tenkhang (sTen-khang), village Khangsar, Karchhag, Tashi Wangyal and his son Tashi Wangdag, the Thakurs of Khangsar; Raja Pritam Singh 1767-1806, and his son Bikram Singh c. C.E. 1790.

ཨོཾ་སྭསྟི་སིདྡྷཾ།། ཀྲང་གཉིས་གཙོ་བོ་སྟོན་པ་སངས་རྒྱས། དེ་གསུང་དྲི་མེད་སྐྱོབ་པ་དམ་ཆོས་དང་། ཚོགས་ཀྱི་མཆོག་གྱུར་འཕགས་པའི་དགེ་འདུན་ལ། ལུས་ངག་ཡིད་གསུམ་གུས་པའི་ཕྱག་འཚལ་ལོ། དགོངས་པ་ཆོས་ཉིད་ནམ་མཁའ་ཡངས་པ་ལ། བརྩེ་བའི་ཐུགས་རྗེ་ཉི་ཟླའི་འོད་འཕྲོས་ནས། འགྲོ་ཀུན་བློ་ཡི་མུན་པ་སེལ་མཛད་པའི། རྩ་བརྒྱུད་བླ་མ་རྣམས་ལ་ཕྱག་འཚལ་ལོ། ཀྱེ་ལེགས། ཕྱི་སྣོད་འཇིག་རྟེན་རྒྱ་ཁྲམ་ལྷུང་གི་རྟེག།། དེ་སྟེང་ཆུའི་དཀྱིལ་འཁོར་ཟླུམ་པོ་ཆགས། དེ་སྟེང་མེའི་དཀྱིལ་འཁོར་གྲུ་གསུམ་ཆགས། དེ་སྟེང་སའི་དཀྱིལ་འཁོར་གྲུ་བཞིར་ཆགས། འབྱུང་བ་རིམས་རྩེགས་རི་རབ་དེ་ལྟར་ཆགས། པད་མ་

བཀོད་ལགས་རིན་ཆེན་ས་ཞིའི་སྟེང་། སྣང་བཅུད་སེམས་ཅན་འོད་གསལ་ལྷ་ལས་ཆད།།

ཕྱི་ལྟར་དཀྲ་བཅོམ་བཞུགས་གནས་ཏི་སེ་གངས། འཁོར་ལོ་སྡོམ་པའི་ཕོ་བྲང་གཞལ་ཡས་ཁང་། འགྲོ་ཀུན་སྒྲིབ་སྦྱོང་ཕྱག་མཆོད་འབུལ་བས་གནས། སྡིག་སྒྲིབ་མི་ཙང་མ་ལུས་ཀུན་ཁྲུད་པས། ཁྲུས་ཀྱི་རྫིང་དབུ་མ་ཕང་གཡུ་མཚོ་འཁྱིལ། ཡན་ལག་བརྒྱད་ལྡན་ཆུ་བོ་བཞི་འདུས་མགོ། རི་རྒྱུད་མ་ཆད་གནས་ཆེན་དྲིལ་བུ་རི། རྒྱལ་བས་ལུང་བསྟན་རི་བོ་གན་རྐྱ་ལ། དཔའ་བོ་དཔའ་མོའི་འདུ་གནས་ངོ་མཚར་ཆེ། ཕུ་ན་སྟན་སྦྱུངས་ལྷ་མོ་དྲེ་བཙོན་བཞུག། ཡོག་འདྲེན་འདུལ་བས་སྟན་སྦྱུངས་ངོ་མཚར་ཆེ། མདོ་ན་རྡོ་རྗེ་ཕག་མོའི་ཕྱག་རྗེན་བཞུགས། མ་དང་མཁའ་འགྲོའི་གནས་ངོ་མཚར་ཆེ། བར་ན་འཕགས་པ་འགྲོ་བ་དྲུག་སྒྲོལ་བཞུགས། ཁམས་གསུམ་དབང་སྡུད་སྲིད་གསུམ་ཟིལ་གྱི་གནོན། ཐོང་ཐོས་དྲན་པས་ལྷ་མཆོག་ངོ་མཚར་ཆེ། ཀྱེ་ལེགས། ཡུལ་ལས་དབྱངས་ཆགས་གར་བྱ་མཁའ་འགྲོའི་གླིང་། ས་ལ་འབུར་མཐོ་ཕོ་བྲང་སུར་ཏན་པུརི། ཕྱིའི་དཀྲ་འདུལ་ནང་གི་བུ་བྲན་སྐྱོང་། ཆོས་རྒྱལ་ཆེན་པོ་པིར་ཏིམ་སེང་གེ་སྲས་ཀྱི་མཚན་བྱིར་ཀེམ་ར་ཛེ་དད་སེང་གེ་ཡབ་སྲས་དང་། དབུ་རྟོག་མཐོ་ཞིང་ཆབ་སྲིད་དར་བར་ཤོག། །ཀྱེ་ལེགས། ལྷུན་གྲུབ་ཞལ་ཡས་ཁང་ཆེན་ཁང་སར་རྩེ། ཆོས་སློན་ཆེན་པོ་བཀྲ་ཤིས་དབང་རྒྱལ་སྲས་བཀྲ་ཤིས་དབང་དྲག་ཡབ་

སྲས་ཀྱི། ཞབས་པད་སྟན་ཞིང་རྒྱལ་སྲིད་དར་གྱུར་ཅིག།། ཀྱེ་ལེགས། ས་ལ་བྱིན་ཆགས་སྐྱིད་ཡུལ་སྟེན་ཁང་འདི་ར། མི་རིགས་ཁྱུངས་རྩུན་འབྲུ་ཤ་རྩེའི་རྒྱུད། ཡོན་གྱི་བདག་པོ་འཕྲིན་ལས་བསྟན་སྐྱོང་དང་། ཡོན་གྱི་བདག་མོ་ཚེ་རིང་ཨང་མོ་རྣམས་ཀྱི། མིའི་ཟས་ལ་ལྷའི་བདུད་བརྩི་སྦྱར། དཀོན་མཆོག་མཆོད་དང་སྦྱིན་པ་གཏོང་ལ་འགལ། བུའི་མཆོག་གྱུར་འཕགས་པ་ཐར་ཆེན་དང་ཚེ་རིང་བསོད་ནམ་དྲན་འཛིན་དང་ཀྱུན་ཀུང་ག་བཀྲིས། ན་མ་བསོད་ལགས་འཛོམ། བུ་མོའི་མཆོག་གྱུར་པདྨ་ཆོས་སྐྱིད་དང་བསོད་ནམ་ཆོན་འཛོམ་དང་། བསགས་པ་ཆོས་ཕྱིར་གཏོང་བ་ངོ་ཚར་ཆེ། སྐུ་བཞུགས་བཀྲ་ཤིས་དཔལ་འཁྱོར་དོན་དུ་གསུང་གི་རྟེན་དུ་ན་རག་སྣང་བཞུགས་དང་ན་རག་དོང་སྤྲུགས་གཞེངས། སྐུའི་རྟེན་དུ་རིག་འཛིན་ཚེ་དབང་ནོར་བུ། རྒྱལ་དབང་འབྲུག་པ་དཀར་བརྒྱུད་བསྟན་པའི་རྒྱལ་མཚན་གྱུར་མེད་ཡུང་འབྲུག་དམ་ཆོས་ཉི་མ། རྒྱལ་སྲས་རྡིལ་བ་རྡོ་རྗེ་ཚེ་རིང་ཆེས་ལྷ་མགོན་པོ་ལྷམ་དྲལ་གསུམ། གསུང་གི་རྟེན་དུ་ན་རག་སྣང་ཞགས་དང་ན་རག་དོང་སྤྲུགས་བཞེངས། ཐུགས་ཀྱི་རྟེན་དུ་བྱང་ཆུབ་མཆོད་རྟེན་བཞེངས། སྐུ་གསུང་བླ་མ་རྣམས་ལ་ཕྱག་འཚལ་ལོ། རྟེན་འདི་ལ་རྒྱུས་པ་རྩིས་འབྱུང་དྲང་ལ། མཐོག་མར་ཁར་ནས་ག་ག་བཀྲིས་དབང་རྒྱལ་ཚེ་དབང་དབྱངས་སྐྱིད་གཉིས་ཀྱི་སང་མ་གསོལ་བྱ་ཆང་བྱས་བྱུང་། ཡང་ཁར་ནས་ཆང་མས་ཏ་ཅིག་དང་ཤ་ཚ་བྱུང་། ཀེ་སྨུར་མཻ་གྲུབ་པའི་གསོལ་བྱ་དང་སང་མ་བྱུང་། ག་ག་དཀར་བརྒྱུད་གི་

གསོལ་ཇ་དང་རྫོན་གྱིར་འབྱུང་། ཚེ་དབང་དམ་ཆོས་ཀྱི་ཆང་མས་ཧ་ཅིག་དང་ཤ་ལག་པ་ཅིག་བྱུང་། སྤང་ཞི་ན་རིན་ཆེན་ཆང་མས་ཧ་ཅིག་དང་ལག་ཅིག་བྱུང་། ས་རང་ཨྱུན་ཚེ་རིང་གི་ཆང་མས་ཧ་ཅིག་དང་ལག་ཤ་ཅིག་བྱུང་། སྟོག་ན་ག་ག་སྐྱེར་པའི་ཆང་མས་ཧ་ཅིག་དང་ལག་ཤ་ཅིག་བྱུང་། ལྷུག་ཁྲ་ན་པདྨའི་ཆང་མས་ཧ་ཅིག་དང་ལག་ཤ་ཅིག་བྱུང་། ཚར་ཇོ་ནས་ཚེ་དབང་ཆང་མས་ཧ་ཅིག་དང་ལག་ཤ་ཅིག་བྱུང་། བུངས་ནད་ནས་བསོད་ནམ་བཟང་མོའི་གསོལ་ཇ་འབྱུང་། མི་ཕམ་ཆོས་བཟང་གི་ཆང་མས་ཧ་ཅིག་དང་ལག་ཤ་བྱུང་། སྲང་བར་ནས་སྐྱིད་ཚེ་རིང་གི་ཆང་མས་ཧ་ཅིག་དང་ལག་ཤ་བྱུང་། ཚེ་རིང་སན་གྲུབ་གི་ཆང་མས་ཧ་ཅིག་དང་ཚ་ཤ་བྱུང་། བསོད་ནམས་རིན་ཆེན་གྱི་ཆང་ཅིག་དང་གསོལ་ཇ་འབྱུང་། ཨ་བི་བསོད་ནམ་བུ་ཏྲིད་གསོལ་ཇ་བྱུང་། དཔལ་བཟང་གི་ཆང་མས་ཧ་ཅིག་བྱུང་། ས་རང་དཔོན་པོ་ཧན་འཛིན་དབང་ཕྱུག་ཆང་མས་ཧ་ཅིག་དང་ལག་ཤ་བྱུང་། ཀྱེ་ལང་བླུག་ཕུན་ཚོགས་གི་ཇ་ཞུ་ཅིག་བྱུང་། ཧེ་ནོ་གུང་རང་པའི་ཚོན་མཛོམ་གི་ཆང་མས་ཧ་ཅིག་དང་ཚ་ཤ་ཅིག་བྱུང་། ཀར་པ་བཀྲིས་རྒྱམ་མཚོ་ཆང་ཅིག་ལག་ཤ་བྱུང་། བཀྲིས་ སཏ་མནྡ་ལམ།།

Name of the book: ནརག་ངན་སོང་དོང་ནས་སྤྲུགས་པའི་ཚོ་ག་བཤགས་འབུམ་རིན་ཆེ་སྤུངས་མདོ་སྣ་མང་བཅུ་བཞི་བ

a.ii. Jispā (gZhi, gZhis) household of Melāg, Thakur Tara Chand of Khangsar, Raja Ajit Singh (1816-1841), c. C.E. 1840.

གཞན་ཡང་གནས་རིས་གྲངས་མ་ཆོད། ཙ་རིས་གནས་ཆེན་དྲིལ་བུ་རི། ཡི་དམ་མཁའ་གྲོ་བཞུགས་གནས་བཟང་། རྒྱལ་བའི་ལུང་བསྟན་གན་རྫོ་ལ། དཔལ་ལྡན་འབྲུག་པའི་ཕོ་བྲང་དུ། བླ་མ་གྲགས་པ་རྒྱ་མཚོའི་དུས། ཆོས་གཙུག་མཐོ་ཞིང་བསྟན་པ་འཛིན། ཆུ་གསུམ་འདུ་བས་གནས་ཆེན་དེར། མ་མོ་མཁའ་འགྲོ་རྒྱུ་བའི་གནས། ཀུ་ལུ་ཏ་དང་མ་ལུ་ཏ། མཁའ་འགྲོ་རྣལ་འབྱོར་བཞུགས་གནས་བཟང་། སྐྱིད་ཡུལ་གར་ཞ་ནགས་མའི་ལྗོངས། ཁྱད་འཕགས་ཡིད་བཞིན་ནོར་བུ་ནི། རང་བྱུང་འཕགས་པ་དངོས་སུ་འབྱུངས། དུས་གསུམ་སངས་རྒྱས་ཞུགས་པའི་ས། ངོ་ཚར་ཅན་ལ་སྐྱབས་སུ་མཆིས། ཐུགས་རྗེ་ཆེན་པོའི་འོད་ཟེར་གྱིས། སྨན་པའི་གླིང་དུ་འགྲོན་མེ་བཞིན། ཐུགས་རྗེ་བྱིན་བརླབས་རྒྱུན་མི་ཆད། སྐྱབས་སུ་འགྲོ་ཚང་སངས་རྒྱས་ས། བསྐལ་པ་སྟོང་གྱིས་སངས་རྒྱས་ཉིད། དམ་པ་མཆོག་ལ་སྐྱབས་སུ་མཆིས། ཕུ་ན་ལྷ་མོ་དྲེ་ཞོན་བཞུགས། ཤ་ཟ་མཁའ་འགྲོའི་འཁོར་དང་བཅས། གཞན་ཡང་གནས་གྱིས་གྲངས་མ་མཆིས། དེས་རྣམས་ཀུན་ལའང་སྐྱབས་སུ་མཆིས། ཀྱེ་ལགས། ས་ལ་འབུར་མཐོ་རྒྱལ་ཁབ་གསུལ་འཐན་ཕུར། ཆོས་རྒྱལ་ཆེན་པོ་ཇོ་བདེ་སེང་གེ་དུས། དབུ་རྫོག་མཐོ་ཞིང་ཆབ་སྲིད་དར་ཞིང་རྒྱས། ཀྱེ་ལགས། དཔལ་མཁར་བཀྲ་ཤིས་ཁང་སར་དུ། ཆོས་ལོན་ཆེན་པོ་ཧྣར་སེངགེ་ཡིས། ཡུམ་སྲས་རྣམ་གསུམ་དབུ་རྫོག་མཐོ་ལ་ཆབ་སྲིད་དར་ཞིང་རྒྱས། དེའི་མངའ་འོག་བཟང་པོའི་ཆབ་སྲིད་དུ། བཀྲ་ཤིས་གཡང་ཆགས་སྟང་

གཞིའི་ཀར་སྒོ་ཏུ། རིགས་ཏུས་ཁྱུངས་ལྡན་ག་ཕུར་ཁ་ཏིར་བརྒྱུད། མི་དབང་དཔོན་ཆེན་ལས་ཀྱི་དབང་བསྒྱུར་ནས། ཁྲིམས་གཙོད་ཆོས་བཞིན་སྐྱོང་བའི་མཛད་པ་ནི། བྱང་ཆུབ་སེམས་དཔའ་ལྷ་བུའི་ངོ་མཚར་ཆེ། བསོད་ནམས་དཔག་མེད་བསགས་པའི་ཞིན་ཤུགས་ཀྱིས། རྩ་བའི་བླ་མར་བོད་ནས་ཕེབས་ལུགས་དང་། རང་གིས་མདུན་པ་བཟང་པོའི་སེམས་སྐྱེད་གཉིས། སྒོ་གསུམ་གུས་པ་ཆེན་པོས་གསོལ་བཏབ་པས། དགེ་བའི་ལས་བྱེད་རྒྱལ་བའི་ལུང་བསྟན་སྒྲུབས། ཐར་པའི་དོན་ཆེན་གྲུབ་པར་ངོ་མཚར་ཆེ། དེ་བཞིན་ཞལ་འགོད་མཛད་པའི་གཙོ་ཆེན་ནི། དད་ལྡན་ཐོ་ནུ་རང་གིས་འབད་འགྲུབ་ལ། ཐོག་མར་མདོ་མང་མགོ་ཤོག་གསེར་ཡིག་ནས་བརྩམས་ནས། བྱམས་པའི་དབུ་མཛད་དཔོན་ཆེན་དཀུ་དང་ལྡན། ནོ་ནོ་བདེ་མཆོག་བཀའ་ཐང་སྔེར་ལྷ་འཐོན། འཇམ་དཔལ་རྒྱ་མཚོ་ཡི་པདྨ་ཐང་ཡིག་ཧོག་གཟུང་མདོ་གཉིས་འཐོན། ཇོར་གཙོད་མཚར་ལྷ་མི་ལོ་གཉིས་སུ་མདོ་སྡེ་ཚར་ལྷ་གྲུབ། དད་བརྩོན་ཆེ་བའི་ཆོས་ལྡན་ཐོ་ནུ་ཡིས། གསུང་རབ་རྣམས་ལ་ཡོན་འབུལ་བསྔོམ་རྩིས་ཀྱིས། ཕྱིད་དང་བདུན་བརྒྱའི་དངུལ་ཀྱི་གྲངས་ག་ལ། ཁེང་སེམས་མེད་པར་ཆོས་སུ་སྐྱབས་བཙལ་ནས། དེའི་འབྲས་བུས་དོན་གྱི་རྩ་བ་ལ།

རང་སེམས་གང་མོས་དེ་ཏུ་སྐྱེ་བར་ཤོག། དགེ་བའི་མཆོག་ཏུ་བསྔལ་མེད་བསོད་ནམས་བསགས། སྐྱེ་བ་ཕྱི་མར་དྲན་པའི་ཚེ་འདི་ཀར། དེ་ཙམ་མཛད་པའི་ངོ་མཚར་ཤིན་ཏུ་ཆེའོ། ཨ་ལ་ལ་ཧོ། དད་ལྡན་ཡོན་གྱི་

བདག་མོ་ཚེ་རིང་བཟང་མོ་དང་ཚེ་དབང་ཆོས་སྐྱིད་གཉིས་གྱིས། ནོར་བུ་
སམ་པས་རྒྱུ་ལ་གསེར་བསྒྱུར་རྩེ་ཡི་བདུད་རྩིས་དྲངས་པ་ངོ་མཚར་ཆེ།
ནོ་ཡི་མཆོག་འགྱུར་འདོམ་དང་བུ་ཡི་མཆོག་འགྱུར་ཏར་ལྷ་ས་ཁོང་
གཉིས་ཀྱིས་ཀྱང་ཕ་མའི་མཛད་བཟང་དགེ་བའི་ལས་ལ་ཡིད་རངས་ཏེ་
ཐོག་ནས་ཞབས་ཏོག་མཐུན་རྐྱེན་ལེགས་པར་འབྱོར་བ་བཀའ་དྲིན་ཆེ།
མནའ་མའི་མཆོག་འགྱུར་ཚེ་དབང་དཔལ་འཛོམ་དང་ཀུ་གུ་མ་གཉིས་
ཡང་ཞབས་ཏོག་ཕུན་སུམ་ཚོགས་པ་ངོ་མཚར་ཆེ། གཞན་ཡང་བུ་མོས་
མཆོག་འགྱུར་ཨ་ནུ་དང་སུ་མིས་དང་གསུམ་རབས་རྟེན་སོགས་ལ་གཞི་
མ་ནང་འཁོར་གཙོ་བྲུས་གཡུལ་མི་ཁྱིམ་ཙོའི། གཞན་ཡང་འགྲེལ་པས་
འབྲེལ་པ་ལ་སོགས་ལག་ཤེས་སྟུག་གྲི་ལ་སོགས་འབྲེལ་ཐོགས་པ་ཐམས་
ཅད་ཀྱང་། གསུང་རྟེན་ཆེན་པོའི་བྱིན་བརླབས་སྟོབས་ཀྱིས་བདེ་ལྡན་
སངས་རྒྱས་ཞིང་དུ་སྐྱིན་པར་ཤོག། ཀྱེ་ལགས། གསུང་རྟེན་འདི་ལ་དགེ་
རྩིས་ཏེག་ཐོ་གྲངས་ལ། ཐོག་མར་གུང་རང་མཁར་ནས་གསོལ་ཇ་སྐྱེམས་
ཤུན་ར་དལ་མོ། ཁང་གསར་མཁར་ནས་གསོལ་ཇ་སྐྱེམ་ལག་ཤ་རྟེན་
ཁང་ནས་འཕགས་པ་ཐར་ཕྱིན་མི་ཏ་ཤ་དལ་མོ། འབོག་པ་ནོ་ནོ་ཚང་མི་
ཏ་ལག་ཤ་སྤྲང་འབར་པ་ཚང་མི་ཏ་ལག་ཤ་ས་རང་མན་བླའི་ཚང་མི་ཏ་
ལག་ཤ་པག་པའི་ནོ་ནོ་ནས་ཚང་མི་ཏ་ལག་ཤ། བར་སྒྲོང་པ་ཚང་མི་ཏ་
ལག་ཤ་ཚང་མི་ཏ་ལག་ཤ། དཀར་པ་ནོ་ནོ་ཚང་་་་། ཉི་ནོ་ནས་རྣམ་རྒྱལ་
ཚང་་་་། ཡོ་ལག་པ་གུ་ལུ་ཚེ་རིང་ཚང་་་་། རིན་ཆེན་ཚེ་རིང་ཚང་་་་། གུང་

རང་པ་དང་ལྷུ་གྲུབ་ཚང་མི་ཧྲ་ལག་ཤ། དགོན་པ་པའི་བཀྲ་ཤིས་ཚང་མི་ཧྲ་ལག་ཤ། བཀའ་རིང་པང་རོང་ནོ་ནོ་ཚང་མི་ཧྲ་ལག་ཤ། བཀའ་རིང་ཡུལ་པའི་འཇའ་གཉིས་ལག་ཤ། གསུམ་དོ་དགྲ་པ་པེ་རྩེ་ཚང་མི་ཧྲ་ལག་ཤ། རང་ཡོ་ནས་སྐྱིད་པ་སོ་ཚང་མི་ཧྲ་ལག་ཤ། སྨིན་གླངས་ནས་ཟླ་ལུ་ནས་ཨ་རག་མི་ཧྲ་གཅིག་དང་མར་རིལ་གཅིག་ལག་ཤ། གྲོང་བསྐོད་བཀྲ་ཤིས་ནས་ཚང་མི་ཧྲ་ལག་ཤ། ཡང་གོ་ལོང་པདྨ་ཡང་འགྱུར་ནས་ཟ་མི་གཉིས་ཀྱིས་ཚང་མི་ཧྲ་གཉིས་དང་དལ་མོ། ཆོས་སྐྱུ་ཙེ་ནས་མཆོག་བུ་གྲིད་གྱིས་གསོལ་ཇ་ཚང་མི་ཧྲ་ལག་ཤ། སྤང་གཞི་ག་དགའ་རིན་ཆེན་ནས་སྐྱེམ་ཤུ་ན་ར་གཅིག་དང་ལག་ཤ་དངུལ་གཅིག། ཡང་དཔོན་རྣམས་ལ་དགེ་བའི་འབྲེལ་ཕྱེད་དུ་བར་བར་ལ་སང་མ་གསོལ་ཇ་ཉིན་ཐུབ་རེ་ལོ་གཉིས་མ་གྲུབ་བར་དུ། ཁང་གསར་མཁར་ནས་ཡང་ལོ་གཉིས་སུ་བར་སྟོན་མཛད་དབུ་རས་གསོལ་ཇ་སྐྱེམ་དང་སང་མ་བཅས་འབྱུང་། འབྱུང་གནད་ནོ་ནོ་འབྲུག་ཚེ་དབང་ཚང་ཤུ་ན་ར་གཅིག་དང་ལག་ཤ་དངུལ་གཅིག་རྣམ་རྒྱལ་ཚང་ཤུ་ ན་ར་གཅིག་དང་ལག་ཤ་དངུལ་གཅིག། ཡར་གཞི་ནོ་ཆེ་བ་ཚང་ཤུ་ན་ར་གཅིག་དང་ལག་ཤ་དངུལ་གཅིག། ཡང་གྲོང་པ་བཞིའི་བར་དུ་བསང་མ་གཅིག། ནོ་ནོ་འཕགས་པ་དོན་གྲུབ་ཚང་མི་ཧྲ་གཅིག། སེ་ལྕོར་འབྲས་བྲེ་བཞི་དང་ལག་ཤ། བླ་མ་འཇམ་དཔལ་རྒྱ་མཚོ་ནས་འཇའ་གཉིས། ཤུག་གླིང་དགོན་ནས་དངུལ་གཅིག། ཀོ་གཉེར་ནས་ཚང་མི་ཧྲ། རྡོ་རྗེ་ཚང་མི་ཧྲ་ལག་ཤ། འདོམ་པ་ཚེ་རིང་

ཚང་མེ་ཏྲ། མེ་ལག་པ་བཀྲ་ཤིས་རྒྱལ་མཚན་སྐྱེམ་ཤུ་ན་ར་བསང་མ་དང་དངུལ་གཅིག། རང་ཡོ་ནོ་ཆེ་བ་སྐྱེམ་ཤུ་ན་ར་གཅིག་ལག་ཤ་འབྱུང་གྲངས་ལེགས་བཀྲ་ཤིས།།

མདོ་མང་འདི་ལ་དཔོན་ཆེན་མང་སྐབས་ཀྱིས་མཁྱེན་པ་རྣམས་ཀྱི་ཐུགས་གྱིས་མ་འཕོམ་ཞིང་གཤིས་མེད་ལྷུན་པོ་བདག་གིས་ལག་ཏུ་ལྷུང་། དབང་ཆེན་དཔོན་པོས་དཀའ་ཡི་མ་བཟོད་པར་རང་གིས་བྱས་ཚེ་ཚིག་མེད་དེབས་མེད་ཅིང་། མཛོན་པར་གཟིགས་ཚེ་ཐུགས་འཁྲིལ་མི་མངའ་བཟོད་པ་གསོལ། མཧྐཡོ།།

iii. Inscriptions:

a.Khangsar (Kolong), inscription on manye stone, Manye-Ringmo, Srangbar, Khangsar c. C.E. 1800.

ༀ་སྐྱོན་གྱིས་མ་གོས་སྐུ་མདོག་དཀར།

ཛོགས་སངས་རྒྱས་ཀྱི་དཔལ་རྒྱན། ཐུགས་རྗེ་སྤྱན་གྱིས་འགྲོ་ལ་

གཟིགས། སྤྱན་རས་གཟིགས་ལ་ཕྱག་འཚལ་ལོ། ཡུལ་ལ་ཡངས་ཆགས་

གར་བྱ་མཁའ་འགྲོ་འི་གླིང་། ས་ལ་འབུར་ཐོ་བ་ཁང་སར་འདིར་མི་རིགས་

ཁྱུངས་བཙུན་དར་བའི་རྒྱུད། དད་ལྡན་ཡོན་གྱི་བདག་པོ་འོད་ཟེར་གི་གསུང་

གྱི་རྟེན་དུ་མ་རྒྱ་རྫ་ཞེངས།།

b. Gemur, inscription on stone, Raja Bikram Singh, (1806-1816), c. C.E. 1810.

ཚུངས་རི་བོ་ཕླནྣ་ལ། ཡ་མཚན་སྙད་བྱུང་དཔལ་གྱི་དྲི་ལ་བུ་རི། སངས་

རྒྱས་རྣམས་གྱིས་བྱིན་གྱིས་''''དཔལ་གྱི་ཚུ་བར་འདུ། ཐམས་ཅད་ཚང་བ་

རྫ་རི་རྫ་གོང་འདུ། གནམས་ལ་ལྷས་ན་འཁོར་རྟེབས་བརྒྱད་འདུ། སྐྱེས་

ཐམས་ཅད་ཁྲོའི་འདུ། '''བོ་སུར་དེན་པུ་རི་ཡི་རྒྱལ་པོ་ཆེན་པོ་ལྷེར་ཁྲིམ་

སིནྡྲེ་འི་དབུ་མོག་ཐ་བའི་འདུས་ཡུལ་དབྱངས་ཆག་གར་ཤ་མཁྲོའི་གླིང་།།

c. Gemur Gonpa, Thakur Dharm Singh of Khangsar, c. C.E. 1820.

''''''ཕོ་བྲང་ཆེན་པོ་ཁང་སར་ན་དྷརྨ་སིང་གི་ཡུམ་སྲས་དབུ་མོག་ཐོ་ཞིང་

ཆབ་སྲིད་དར་བ་འི་དུས་དགེ་བཙུ་འི་ཁྲིམས་ཡོན་གི་བདག་པོ་འབྲུག་རྒྱ་ཚོ་དང་

ཡོན་གི་བདག་མོ་རྐན་འཛོམ་གཉིས་། དེ་འི་སྲས་བསམ''''དབང་དང་པདྨ་བུ་

དྲིད་གཉིས། ནང་དྲོང་ཐམས་ཅད་དགེ་བ་འི་བསམ་པ་ཅན་དགེ་བ་འི་ལས་ལ་

འབྲས་བུ""དགེ་བ་དཔག་མེད་མཛད་ཁྱད་པར་ཡིག་དྲུག་སྟོང་རྩུ་ཙན་གཅིག་

དང་བརྒྱ་གཅིག་བཞེངས།།

d. Gemur-'Bog, inscription on stone c. C.E. 1850.

བང་ཕོ་བྲང་ཁྱད་པར"""བོར་འབངས་འདུལ་མཛད། སྡིག་བསྒྲུག""""། """

བོའི་མཆོག། དེའི་མངའ་འོག་འབོག་གི་གཡུལ་མཆོག། """ར་དང་ནོ་

འབྲུག་ཆེ་དབང་གཉིས་ཀྱི་བཙུན་མོ་བསྟན་འཛིན་འདྲ་དང་ནོ་མོ་ཨ་ནུ་གཉིས།

ཡང་སྲས་བསྟན་འཛིན་ཆེ""""བའོ། སྦྱོན་ཆེ་བསོད་ནམས་བསགས་པའི་མཐུ་

སྟོབས་ལས་ཆེ་འདིར་བད་སྐྱོད་མི་ཟད་ཆར་བབ་ཅིང་། ཕྱི་མའི་དོན་དུ""དོན་

དུ་སྡིག་བསམ་རྣམ་པར་དག་པའི། གོ་ནས་མཛད་པ་ངོ་ཚར་ཆེ་ཆེ།།

5 Punan (Gāhar), Lower Bhaga Valley

a.i. Household of Tharbas, Kyelang, capital at village Kardang, Rana Prayota and Raja Parbat Singh (1575-1608), c. C.E. 1590.

ཨོཾ་སྭ་སྟི་སི་དྡྷཾ། ······ དགེ་བཅུ་ཁྲིམས་གཉིས་ལྡན་པའི་གར་བྱ་འདིར། ཀྱེ་ལགས། དཔའ་བོ་དཔའ་མོའི་འདུ་གནས། ངོ་མཚར་ཆེ། ཨེ་མ་ཧོ། ཆོས་རྒྱལ་ངོ་མཚར་ཆེ། པར་བ་ཏ་སིང་ཧྥ་གངས་ཅན་མགོན་པོ་སྐུ་མཆེད་དབུ་རྫོག་མཛོ་བའི་དུས། དེ་འདྲའི་འབང་ཆེན་ཕྲ་ཡོ་ཏ་དཀོན་མཆོག་རྣམ་གཉིས་ཀྱིས། ཆོས་རྒྱལ་རྣམ་གཉིས་ཐུགས་གོངས་དབྱེར་མེད། བུ་བློན་བདེ་ལ་སྐྱོང་བའི་བཀྲ་ཤིས་ཤོག།། ཨེ་མ་ཧོ། ངོ་མཚར་ཆེ་།

ས་ལ་འབྱུར་དུ་མཐོའ་བའི་རྒྱལ་ས་དཀར་དང་འདིར། ཁུངས་བཙུན་དཀར་དང་ར་ནའི་རྒྱུད། ཡོན་གྱི་བདག་པོ་སྙིང་སྟོབས་ལྡན་པའི་སྐབས་རྩེ་ཡིས། དྲིན་ཅན་ཡབ་ཀྱི་དགོངས་བཛོགས་ཕྱིར་དུ། དམ་ཆོས་ཟབ་མོ་ཁྲུད་འཕགས་རྡོ་རྗེ་གཅོད་པ་མ་བུ་བཞེངས། སྐྱེས་ན་བུ་རི་ཅིག་འདི་ལ་ཀུན་ཡོད། འཛངས་དྲུང གཉིས་ལྡན་ཕྲུལ་གྱི་བུ་མོ་འདྲ། ཡོན་གྱི་བདག་མོ་མནའ་མ་ཚོ་གེ་ཡིས། མི་ཡི་ཟས་ལ་ལྷའི་བདུད་རྩེར་Xནས་ནས། དཔོན་ལ་ཞབས་ཏོག་བྱེད་པ་ཨ་ལ་ལ། ཀྱཻ་ལགས། ཁོང་གི་མཉེན་དྲུང་གྲག་ཞན་ཉེ་རིང་རྣམས་ཀྱིས་ཀྱང་། དཀར་རྩེ་བྱུང་བའི་གྲངས་ལ་ནི། སྔོན་པའི་ཚུལ་དུ་འདབ་བྱ་འདུ་བ་འམ། སྤྲང་རྩེའི་རོ་ལ་བོང་བ་འཁོར་བ་ལྟར། གུང་རང་གོ་ཁྲི་ནས། ཨོན་པོ་ཀུང་ག་སིང་ཛོ་ཅོ་ལེགས་མཛེས་སྟེང་ཞལ་གཉིས། ཡང་ཡོ་ལག་ནས་སྦྱིན་པ་སིང་འགར་མོ་ལྕམ་མ་བུ་གཉིས། བཟང་སེ་བཟང་མོ་བཟའ་མི་གཉིས། ཀྱེ་ལང་གོང་ནས་མག་པ་སེང་གེ་སྐྱབས་བུ་མོ་སོ་ནམ་ཟང་མོ་བཟའ་མི་གཉིས་ཀྱིས་ཤིན་ཏུ། ངོ་མཚར་ཆེ། ཆེ་གླིང་ནས་སེང་གེ་གྲགས་པ་མཟང་མོ་ཡམ་པ་ཚེ་སོ་ནམ་པལ་མོ་བཟའ་མི་བཞི། དཀར་དང་ནས་ཐོ་ལག་ཁྲི་གུ་ཚེ་རིང་བཟང་མོ་མ་བུ་གཉིས། ཀྱེ་ལང་གོང་ནས་ཆོས་བཟང་པོ། བཀྲ་ཤིས་པལ་མོ་བཟའ་མི་གཉིས། ཀྱེ་ལང་འོག་མ་ནས་ཕོ་ཏུས། ཅན་གྱི་ཚ་བོ་རྡོ་རྗེ་ཨ་ཆེ་སོ་ནམ་ལྡན་བཟའ་མི་གཉིས། གུང་སྐྱུར་ནས་སི་དུ་བཟང་མོ་བཟའ་མི་གཉིས། ཡང་དཀར་དང་ནས་ནོར་བུ་སྐྱབས་ཀུང་ག་པལ་མོ་སེ་ཏུ་སྐྱབ་པ་སྐྱ་པ་བཟང་མོ་བཟའ་མི་བཞི། བསམ་པ་བཟང་པོ་འཛོམ་པ་ཅེ་བཟའ་མི་གཉིས། ཁྲི་སྐྱབ་པ་ཤེ་པི་ལི་བཟའ་མི་གཉིས། གཞན་ཡང་རང་རེའི་ནང་ནས་ཁོང་ངེ་ནོར་བུ་ལེགས་དང་། ཤ་ཕྱོར་གཉིས། སྐྱིད་འཛོམ་ཆོས་སྒྲོལ་མ་ཆོས་འཛོམ་ལ་སོགས་ཚ་བཞུག་རྣམས་ཀྱང་དཔོན་ལ་ཞབས་ཏོག་བྱེད་པ་ངོ་མཚར་ཆེ། ཤ་པ་རྡོ་རྗེ་ནོར་བུ་སྐྱབ་པ་སྐྱབ་སེ།

འཆང་མ་སོ་ནམ་བཟང་མོ་སུ་ནེ་ཆོས་བཟང་པོ། བཟང་མོ་དང་བཞི། བཞན་ཡང་པེ་གླིང་ནས་ནོར་བུ་སྐྱབ་པ་ཟླ་ལ་སྐྱིད་བཟ་མི་གཉིས། ཀྱེ་ལང་འོག་མ་ནས་རིན་ཆེན་བཟང་པོ་ཀུང་ག་འཛོམ་ ཚེ་བཟ་མི་གཉིས།། ||

a.ii. Tharbas, Kyelang, Raja Pritam Singh (1767-1806), c. C.E. 1790.

དགྲ་མཙོམ་བཞུགས་གནས་གང་དཀར་ཏི་སེའི་རྩེ། དངོས་གྲུབ་ཆབ་ཁྱིལ་མ་སྤང་ཡུམ་གྱི་མཚོ། རི་རྒྱུད་མ་ཆད་གནས་ཆེན་དྲིལ་བུ་རི། རྒྱལབའི་ལུང་བསྟན་རི་བོ་གཙྫོ་ལ། དཔའ་བོ་དཔའ་མོའི་འདུ་གནས་ངོ་མཚར་ཆེ། ཀྱེ་ལགས།

རྒྱལ་ས། ཁྱེད་འཕགས་སུ་སྟན་པུ་རི་ན། ཆོས་རྒྱལ་ཆེན་པོ་སྤྲི་ཏམ་སེང་གེར་སྟོད། ཀྱེ་ལགས། འདིའི་མངའ་འོག་སྟང་ནས་སྨུ་མནན་སླུང་པ་ན། སྐུ་ཁར་ཁྱེད་འཕགས་སྐྱུང་རང་ན།དཔོན་པོ་ཆེ་དབང་ཡབ་ཡུམ་སྲས་གསུམ་རྣམས་ལ་སྟོད། ཀྱེ་ལགས། ཡུལ་ལ་ཡང་ཆགས་ཀྱི་(ལང་)འོག་མ་འདིར། མི་རིགས་ཁུང་བཙུན་ཡབ་མེ་བཅེ་པ་པའི་རྒྱུད། ཡོན་གྱི་བདག་པོ་ཕུ་ཏུ་ཁོང་ལ་སྟོད། བུའི་ཕྱོགས་གྲུར་དོམ་བ་ཚེ་རིང་དང་། ན་མ་འབྲུག་འཛོམ་བུ་ཁྲིད་ཉིས་ཀྱང་། ཕ་མ་ཞིན་འདུ་ཆོས་ལ་དཀར་བར་ཤོག། ཚ་འོ་ཚ་མོ་ཚེ་རིང་ནད་མེད་ལོང་སྤྱོད་ལྡན་པའི་བཀྲ་ཤིས་ཤོག། སྦྱིན་པའི་བདག་པོ་ཕུ་་ཏུ་ཁོང་གི་ཀྱང་། ཚེ་འདས་གྲོག་གི་མདོན་དུ་རྡོ་རྗེ་བཙོད་པ་བཞེངས། རང་རེ་ཕྱིག་པ་དག་འཕྱིར་དུ། དྲི་མེད་ཀུན་ལྡན་རྣམ་མཐར་དང་། སྲོང་……… འདི་ལ་ཀུན་ཀྱང་སྟོད། འཛངས་དྲུང་གཉིས་ལྡན་ཕྲུལ་གི་བུ་མོ་འདྲ། ཡོན་གྱི་བདག་མོ་མནའ་མ་དྲུག་འཛོམ་བུ་ཏྲི་ཡིས་མི་ཡི། རྩེར་རབ་སྤྱར་ནས། དཔོན་ལ་ཞབས་ཏོག་བྱེད་པ་ཨ་ལ་ལ། ཀྱེ་ལགས་། ཉེ་རིང་མཉེན་དྲུང་རྣམས་ཀྱི་ཀྱང་། དགེ་ལ་ཟོང་སྲོང་ པ་ལ་ནི། ཐོག་མར།།

b. Thaas, Kyelang, Raja Pritam Singh, 1767-1806, c. C.E. 1790.

༄༅། ། ཀྱེ་ལང་ཐ་ས། མདོ་དབང་།

འཛམ་གླིང་ཡོངས་གྲགས་རྒྱལ་ས་སུར་ཏན་པུ་རི་ཏུ། ཆོས་རྒྱལ་ཆེན་པོ་པིར་ཏེམ་སིང་འགྭ་དབུ་རྨོག་མཐོ་བཞེང་ཆབས་སྲིད་རྒྱས་པའི་དུས། ཡུལ་སྐྱིད་པོའི་ཀྱེ་ལང་འོག་མ་དེར། པལ་བཟང་ཡོན་གྱི་བདག་པོ་ཀྱེ་ལེགས། ཡང་ཡུལ་སྐྱིད་པའི་ཕུ་ནན་ལྷོ་ཕྱོགས་ན། སྐུ་ཁར་གུང་རང་འདིར་ནོ་ནོ་ཆེ་དབང་དང་། ཡུལ་ལ་དབྱུང་ཆགས། མི་རིགས་མ་མནོར་ལོན་ཆེན་རྒྱུད། ཡོན་གྱི་བདག་པོ་པལ་བཟང་དང་། ནོ་འོ་བགྲུག་བསམ་ཏན་དང་གཉིས། མི་ལའི་ནམས་མཐར་དང་རྗེ་རྒོད་ཚང་པའི་ནམས་ཐར་ཞེང། ཤ་དལ་སྒོ་ཅིག་དང་། ཆང་ཤོ་ནོ་རའ་ཅིག།

c. Shashur gonpa, Kyelang, Karchhag with Domang written wholly in gold ink, c. C.E. 1900.

c.i. Shashur, Karchhg No. 1, section i:

དཀར་ཆགས་མེ་ལོང་ཀུན་གསལ།།

མངའ་རིས་བསྐོར་གསུམ་ཆར་རྟོགས་མཁའ་འགྲོའི་ཞིང་། ས་གཙང་དགེ་བཅུ་འཛོམས་པ་གར་
ཞའི་ཡུལ། ཨོ་རྒྱན་པདྨ་གྲུབ་ཆེན་དྲིལ་བུ་སོགས། མཁས་གྲུབ་དུ་མས་ཞབས་ཀྱི་བཅགས་པའི་ས།
བཤད་སྒྲུབ་བསྟན་པ་གཉིས་ལྡན་འཛིན་པ་ཡི། གནས་ལྷ་མཁྱེན་པའི་པཊ་གྲུབ་གང་བའི་གཞི།
གཙུག་ལག་ཁང་ཆེན་བཀྲིས་ཤུགས་གླིང་འདིར། ཐུབ་བསྟན་དར་ཞིང་རྒྱས་པའི་དུས་དེ་རུ། བཤེས་
གཉེན་ཚེ་དབང་རིག་འཛིན་འཕྲིན་ལས་གཉིས། མཁས་མང་འཁོར་གྱིས་རབ་བསྐོར་རྒྱུ་སྐར་དབུས།
རི་བོང་འཛིན་པ་ཇི་བཞིན་ཤར་དེ་བ། སྲིད་ན་འགྲན་ཟླ་བྲལ་ཏེ་ཁྱེད་དུ་ཁྱམས། ས་མཆོག་འབུར་
མཐོ་གུང་རང་སྐུ་ཁར་དུ། ཆོས་སློན་ཆེན་པོ་ནོ་ནོ་[ཚེ་]དབང་གིས། །དབུ་རྩོམ་མཐོ་ཞིང་ཆབ་
སྲིད་དར་བའི་དུས། །དགེ་བཅུའི་ཁྲིམས་ཀྱིས་སྐྱོང་བ་ངོ་མཚར་ཆེ། ཡི་གེའི་མཐའ་རུ་ཕྱིན་པ་དཔོན་
རྣམས་ནི། །སངས་རྒྱས་དོན་གྲུབ་དང་ནི་གཅེས་པ་ཡིས། །ཚེ་དབང་དང་ནི་ནོར་བུ་མཆེད་བཞི་ཡི།
སེར་མོའི་གར་གྱིས་རོལ་པ་ངོ་མཚར་ཆེ། ཆོས་ལས་འགྱུར་བ་མེད་པའི་སྦྱིན་བདག་རྣམས། གང་
དགོས་ལོངས་སྤྱོད་རྣམ་ཐོས་བུ་དང་མཚུངས། ཟང་ཟིང་ནོར་ལ་སྙིང་པོ་མེད་གཟིགས་ནས། ཆོས་ཀྱི་
ཕྱིར་དུ་གཏོང་བ་ངོ་མཚར་ཆེ། ཀྱེ་མ། གྲྭ་པ་ཚེ་རིང་ཚེ་དབང་འབྲུག་རྡོ་རྗེ། གསུམ་གྱིས་གསེར་གྱི་
ན་རྒྱན་ཕུད་ནས་ནི། །དགེ་བའི་བསྐུལ་མ་གཙོ་བོར། བཅས་ནས་ཀྱང་། དེ་ཡི་རྐྱེན་བཅས་རྒྱུ་
སྦྱོརསྦྱིན་བདག་གིས།

།ཐོག་མར་གུང་རང་སྐུ་ཁར་ནས་ག་ག་ཚེ་དབང་གིས་དངུལ་ལྷའི་གསེར། གཅེས་མ་ཚེ་
རིང་དཔལ་འཛོམ་གྱི་དངུལ་༧།

c.ii. Shashur Karchhag No.1, section ii:

ཁུ་ནུ་རོ་ཕགས་པ་ཨང་རྒྱལ་དང་འཇོར་ཏྲ་ས་གཉིས་ཀྱིས་ཧོ་ར་གཅིག་སེར། ཧ་ས་རང་
པ་ཏྲར་མ་ཕུར་གྱི་དངུལ་༧། འདི་རྣམས་བྱུང་བ་ཡིན་པས། ད་རྒྱུ་སོང་བའི་མཐོ་ལ། ཧོར་བཙོ་ལྷ་
གསེར་ལ་སོང་བ་ཡིན། དངུལ་ཏྲུག་རམ་ལ་སོང་བ་ཡིན། དངུལ་གཅིག་ཚལ་ལ་སོང་། དངུལ་
གཅིག་གླེགས་ཐག་ལ་སོང་། དངུལ་བཞི་ཆབ་མ་ལ་སོང་། ན་བཟའ་གསུམ་ལ་དངུལ་ཕྱེད་དང་བཞི་
སོང་། ཤིང་མཁན་ཚེ་རིང་ཡང་འཇོར་གྱི་གླེགས་ཤིང་། ཕུན་ཚོགས་བསྟན་འཛིན་གྱི་གཟི་མ་ཡིན།
ཀྱི། སྐུ་ཡི་སྟེན་དུ་ཤ་ཀ་ཐུབ་རྣམ་པར་གཟིགས་། སངས་རྒྱས་གཙུག་ཏོར་ཅན་དང་ཐམས་ཅད་སྐྱོབ།
གསུང་རྟེན་བསྐལ་པ་བཟང་པོ་པ་ཡི་མདོ། རིན་ཆེན་འཁོར་ལོ་དང་པོར་ལེགས་པར་གྲུབ། དགེ་བ་

འདི་ཡི་བསོད་ནམས་ཀྱིས། །ཕ་མའི་ཐོག་གྲངས་འབྲེལ་ཚད་རྣམས། །སངས་རྒྱས་སྟོང་གི་ཞབས་དྲུང་དུ། འདུས་པ་དང་པོའི་མཆོག་ཏུ་གྱུར་ཅིག་གུ།། གུང་རང་ག་ག་ཚེ་རིང༎

c.iii. Shashur Karchhag, No. 1, section iii:

མདོ་སྡེ་བསྐལ་བཟང་པོ་འདི་ལ་ནོངས་པ་སོང་ནས། ཞིག་གསོས་ཀྱི་ལང་གོང་མའི་དཀར་པ་གཉིས་ཀྱིས་ཇོ་མོ་དཔལ་ལི་དང་ཚེ་རིང་ཀུན་འཛོམ་གཉིས་ཀྱི་ཕུལ་བ་ཡིན་ཞུ།།

6 Ye-shu (Moravians) Inscriptions from

1. Moravian Inscription, Kyelang, c. C.E. 1900.

a. བས་མགོན་ཡེ་ཤུས་གསུངས་པ་ཇི་ལྟར་མི་གཞན་གྱིས་ཁྱེད་རྣམས་

ལ་བྱེད་དགའ་བ་ལྟར་ཁྱེད་རྣམས་ཀྱིས་ཀྱང་མི་གཞན་རྣམས་ལ་བྱོས་ཤིག།

b.Baralacha. ཡེ་ཤུས་གསུངས་གོང་ནི་ཤི་ནས་ལང་པ་ཉིད་དང་གསོན་པ་

ཉིད་ཡིན་ཏེ།སུ་ཡང་ང་ལ་དད་པ་དཤི་ཡང་གསོན་པོར་འགྱུར་རོ།།

(Elizabeth, 1991: 73).

c. Beeling: (Sign of cross. ཁྱོད་རང་རྣམས་ཀྱི་།དོན་གྲུབས་ལ་ནོར་མང་པོ། སའི་ནོར་ནི་ སྣུག་ པ་བང་བཙས་ ཀྱང་ཟ ། ཀུན་མས་ཀྱང་བྲུས་ཧོ་ཀུའོ། འོན་ཀྱང་རྣཾ༑ མཁའ་ལ་ནོར་སོགས་ཤིག། (Courtesy Mangal Chand and Sher Singh Merupa).

Part B - Areas Surrounding Lahul

7 Zanskar

a. Zanskar – Phugthal Boyig, Register of Phugthal, Chhukutsi (Chhos-sku-tsi) gonpa, c C.E. 1450.

ཕུག་ཐལ་བོ་ཡིག་།

ཞུང་ཧྲི་རྒྱལ་པོ་ཕུལ་བ་ལ། ཆོས་སྐུ་ཙེ་གོན་པ་ཡན་མཚོད་ལམ་ཁྲལ་ཞོ་གླིང་གྱི་སྣུར་
ཚན་གྱི་མོས་བཞི་དེ་ལུང་པ་ཕུ་མདོ་དང་བཅས་ཕུལ།།

(Crook and Ommaston. 1994. Plate 80.).

b. i. Zanskar, Decree by king Nyima Namgryal (1694-1720) of Ladakh, C.E. 1701.

༄༅། །ས་སྐྱོང་མི་དབང་ཆེན་པོ་ཉི་མ་རྣམ་པར་རྒྱལ་བའི་བཀའ།།

ཟངས་སྐར་ཕུ་མདའི་བླ་སྡེ་མི་སྡེ་བློན་པོ། གྲག་ཞོགས་གྲོང་དཔོན།
གཉེར་ལས་འཛིན། ཆིབས་དཔོན་རྣམས་དང་། དགོས་སུ་ཕྱུག་དལ་གྱི་
བླ་གཉེར་རྣམས་ལ་སྤྲིངས་པ། ཨད་མུའི་དབོན་པོ་ལ་སྦྱ་སོར་ཁྲང་ནག་
རྫོ་མོ་རེ་ཆེན་གདོང་རི་ཁོ་རང་གི་ཡིན་འདུག་པ་དང་། སུར་ལའི་ཕུ་ལ་
ཙ་པ་དང་སྦྱ་སོར་ནས་རྫ་ཁ་མཉམ་ཟ་ཡིན་འདུག་པས། སྔར་ལུགས་
ལྟར་དུ་གནས་པར་བྱེད་པ་དང་། གཞན་ཨ་གུའི་བཀའ་གང་གནང་སྒྲུབ་
ནས་ཞན་གྱིས་ཁ་དམན་སྐད་གཅོར་སོགས་ཙ་བ་ནས་མ་བྱེད་པ་བདེ་
བར་གནས་བཅུག།། སྔར་ནས་མི་བབ་པའི་བ་གསོས་རེ་ཡུལ་པས་

འགྲན་བྲལ་སྐད་ཀྱི་ཡོད་དག་པའི།མི་བབ་པའི་ཕྲ་དབོན་པོ།ལྷ་རྗེ་དང་ འདྲ་བར་གནས་བཅུག་པ་གལ་ཆེ། གལ་སྲིད་བཀའ་ཤོག་མཐོང་ནས་ རྗེས་འཛོག་མ་བྱས་ཚེ།རྩད་གཅོད་ཡོང་བའི་སོ་སོར་གོ་བ་གྱིས།

ཞུ་བ་པོ་བསོད་ནམས་ལྷུན་གྲུབ་དང་། ཀུན་དགའ་ཡིན། ཅེས་ལྷག་ སྤྲུལ་ཟླ་༧ཚེས་༢༥(ལ་ཕོ་བྲང་ཆེན་པོ་སླེ་ཆེན་དཔལ་མཁར་ནས་བྲིས།།

(Internet source).

b.ii. Zanskar. Decree by king Tshe-dbang rNam-rgyal (1753-1782) of Ladakh, 1766 C.E.

༄༅། །ས་དབང་ཆོས་ཀྱི་རྒྱལ་པོ་ཚེ་དབང་རྣམ་པར་རྒྱལ་བ་ལྷའི་བཀའ།།

རྒྱལ་ཁམས་སྤྱི་དང་བྱེ་བྲག་རང་ཞབས་སུ་གཏོགས་པའི་སྡེ་མོ་བ་ལྷ་ སྡེ་མི་སྡེ། བློན་པོ།ཁྲག་ཤོས། མཁར་དཔོན། གྲོང་དཔོན། རྗོ་ཁ་ཆེ། གཉེར་ ལས་འཛིན། མདོར་ན་ཡར་མར་འགྲིམས་འགྲུལ་གྱི་སྐུ་ཚབ་གསུང་ཚབ་ ཆེ་ཕྲ་མཐའ་དག་ལ་སྤྲིངས་པ། ཨེ་སྨུའི་དབོན་པོ་སྤྲ་སོར་ནས་དཔའ་ གཏུམ་མཁར་གྱི་ཆོས་གནས་ཡིན་ཅིང་། ལ་དྭག་དཔའ་གཏུམ་གཉིས་ ནས་སྤྲར་ནས་ཕྱུགས་རྫེའི་གཟིགས་སྐྱངས་ལ་རྟེན། བཀའ་ཤོག་དམ་པོ་ རྗོ་མོ་རས་ཆེན་གྱི་གདོང་རི་ལ་དྭགས་དཔའ་གཏུམ་གཉིས་ནས་ཕྱུགས་ རྗེས་གཟིགས་འདུག་པ། སུར་ལེའི་ཕྱུ་ལ་བཅའ་བ་དང་རྩྭ་མཉམ་ཟ་ མཉམ་འཕྲུངས་བྱས་ཚོག་པ་དང་། སྤྲར་ལུགས་ལྟར་གྱི་བྱང་ཐང་མོན་ ཡུལ་སོགས་གང་དུ་འགྲོ་མི་དགོས་པའི་བཀའ་ཤོག་སྟོན་མའི་དོན་ བཞིན་གཏུང་འདྲེན། ཤིང་བཅད་གས་འདྲེན། ཕྱི་ཐག་དོད་རྟའུ། ཆང་

སེར་ཕྱུགས་སེར། གོ་ཏྲ་སོགས་ཁྲལ་རིགས་ཆེ་ཕྲ་སྤྱི་ཙམ་མེད་པ་དགོན་པོ་དང་ནམས་མཁའ་ཕ་བུ་བརྒྱུད་བཅས་ལ་བཀའ་ཤོག་རྒྱབ་པ་གནོན་དུ་ཕྱུགས་རྗེས་གཟིགས་པ་ཡིན་པས། ཁྱོད་གོང་འཁོད་སུས་ཀྱང་བརྟད་བརྩེར་ཐོས་མི་བདེར་འགྲོ་བ་སྤྱི་ཙམ་མ་བྱེད་པར་བདེ་བར་གནས་ཆུག་པ་གལ་ཆེ།

ངེས་མེད་བཀའ་ཤོག་འདིར་མ་རྟེས་པའི་རིགས་སུས་བྱུང་ཀྱང་འདི་ནས་བརྩད་གཙོད་བརྗེས་གནོན་དྲག་པོ་གཏོང་ཉེས་ཡིན་པའི་གོ་བར་གྱིས། ཅེས་མེ་ཁྱི་ཟླ་ཚེས་ལ་ལུགས་གཉིས་ཀྱི་མངོན་པར་མཐོ་བའི་མདུན་ས་རྒྱལ་ཁབ་ཆེན་པོ་སླེ་མཁར་རྩེ་ནས་བྲིས།། (Internet source).

i. Decree of Dechhog Namgyal, (sDe-mchhog rNam-rgyal) king of Zanskar and Spiti (c. 1642-1694), C.E. 1671.

ས་སྐྱོང་མིའི་དབང་པོ་ཆོས་རྒྱལ་ཆེན་པོ་སྡེ་མཆོག་མནམ་རྒྱལ་གྱི་བཀའ། རང་རེའི་མངའ་འོག་དུ་སྡོགས་པ་རྣམས་ལ་དཙལ། སྡོད་ནམ་གྱི་ཕེ་བ་སྐྱུད་དང་སྤྲ་འབྱོར་གཉིས། ཀྱི་ཞིང་ཁང་ཐུགས་ལ་སྟགས་པ་ཡིན། ཨུ་རྒྱན་གི་དུས་ཀྱི་མཆོད་པ་ཆེན་པོའི་ཚེ་ཆུ་ལ་སྐུལ། ས་སྟོགས་སྙིང་མའི་དགེ་ཚོགས་ཆེན་པོ་ལ་སྐྱོལ་བ་ཡིན། དེ་རྣམས་ལ་སྟག་སོས་ལུག་སོས་ཐོག་ཁྲལ། འདོར་ན་མཁྲལ་རིགས་གང་ཡང་མེད་པ་ཐུགས་ལ་བསྟགས་པ་ཡིན། བསྐལ་པ་ནམ་གནས་གྱི་བར་དུ་ཐུགས་ལ་སྟགས་པ་ཡིན། མཁར་དཔོན་རྫོང་དཔོན། རྐན་མི་མངས་དམག་མི། གཉེར་ལས་བྱེད། ཕྱིར་དཔོན། ཁྲི་ར་དྲག་གཞན། ཡུལ་མའི། འདི་ལ་ཟེར་རི་སོད་པ་གང་ཡང་མེད། བདེ་བར་གནས་ཙུག། སུས་ཀྱང་སྐྱེར་ཆེར་མེད་པ་ཡིན། སྐྱེར་ཆེར་བྱེད་ན་ཚར་དུ་བཅོད་དྲག་པོ་རྫེས་ལ་ཡོང་། ལྕགས་མོ་ཕག་གི་ཟླ་བ་གསུམ་པའི་ཚེས་པ་

བཙུ་གཉིས་ལ་ཕོ་བྲང་ཆེན་པོ་ཡང་མཁར་རྩེ་ནས་སྐྱུལ་། ཞུ་བ་པོ་མཁར་

དཔོན་ནམ་མཁའ་རྒྱལ་མཚན་ཡིན།། **(Internet source).**

ii. Documents, Ancient literary compositions, from Buchhens, Pin Valley, Relating to the marriage of king Srong-btsan sGam-po (569-650) of Tibet with the Chinese princess Kongjo.

a. Messages of Srong-btsan sGam-po, the King of Tibet, to the king of China c. C.E. 636.

རྒྱལ་"པོའི་བཀའ་ཤོག།

དེ་ན་ཡང་བློན་པོ་འགར་གྱིས། རྒྱལ་པོའི་དྲུང་དུ་ཕྱིན་ཏེ། རྒྱ་ནག་གི་ལྷ་

གཅིག་དེ་ཡང་བདེན་འདྲེན་པ། བཀའ་མནང་བར་ཞུས་སོ། ཡང་རྒྱལ་པོ་

གསེར་གྱི་དོང་ཙེ་བདུན་བཀུར་ནས། འདི་ལ་ཞུ་སྟེན་བརྒྱི་ཅིག་གསུངས་སོ།

རིན་པོ་ཆེ་བདུན་གྱི་ནི་ཁྲབ་ལ་པདྨ་ར་གའི་ཕྲ་རྒྱབ་པ་གཅིག་སྐྱུར་ནས།། འདི་

ལྷ་གཅིག་དེའི་རིན་དུ་ཕུལ་ཅིག་གསུངས་སོ། སེར་ཕྱེ་བྲེ་གང་སྐྱུར་ནས། འདི་

གང་དགོས་སུ་ཐོང་ཅིག། རྒྱལ་པོ་དེ་དཀའ་ལུང་མི་འདྲ་བ་གསུམ་དུ་འདུས་

ནས། དེའི་དུས་སུ་འདི་སུམ་རེ་རེ་བཞིན་གཏོང་ཅིག་གསུང་ནས། བཀའ་

ཤོག་གི་ཤོག་རི་ལ་གསུམ་བསྐུར་རོ། འཕྲུལ་གི་ཡོ་བྱད་གོས་དང་རྒྱན་ལ་

སོགས་པ་ཛ་མོ་དང་། དྲེ་ལ་སོགས་པ་ལ་བཀལ་བ་འི་ཁལ་མང་པོ་རྫངས་སོ།

ཉིན་མཚན་དང་ལམ་ཕྲང་གང་དུ་ཡང་། ཇོ་ཙུན་སྒྲོལ་མ་ལ་བསོལ་བ་འདེབས་
ཀྱིན་གསོང་ཅིག་གསུངས་སོ། དེ་ན་མགར་གྱི་རྒྱལ་པོ་བཀུར་བ་ཐམས་ཅད་
ཁྱིར་ཁལ་རྣམས་དོང་། བློན་པོ་རྟ་བ་བརྒྱ་དང་ལྷན་གཅིག་ཏུ་མི་ཕོ་ཕྲུའི་ལོ་
ཟླ་བ་བཞི་པའི་ཚེ་རྒྱད་ལ་སྐར་མ་རྒྱལ་དང་མཛོམ་བ་རྒྱ་ནག་དུ་ཆེས་སོ། དེ་
ན་རྒྱ་ནག་གི་བཟིམ་ཆུང་བཀྲ་ཤིས་ཁྲི་སྒོ། རྒྱལ་ཇོ་ཐང་ཇོང་བཞུགས་པའི་ཕོ་
བྲང་གི་སྒོ་རྡུང་དུ་སླེབ་བོ། དེ་ན་མི་ཁྲི་འབུམ་ཚོ་ཙམ་ཡོད་པ། ལོགས་དེ་ལ་
ཉིན་ལམ་རེ་ཡོད་པ་སྒོ་མོ་ཆེ་བཞི་ཡོད་པ། མཐོང་བ་ཙམ་ཀྱི་སྣང་ངས་ཤིང་
འཇིགས་པ་ཅིག་འདུག་གོ། དེར་རྒྱ་གར་ཆོས་ཀྱི་རྒྱལ་པོ་རྟ་བརྒྱ་ཐམ་པ།
རྒྱལ་མོ་གོང་འཁྱོར་འདོད་པ་ལ་སླེབ་བོ། གེ་སར་དམག་གི་རྒྱལ་པོ་''''།
སྟག་ གཟིག་ནོར་ཀྱི་རྒྱལ་པོ་''''། ལྷ་ཏ་ཧོར་ཀྱི་རྒྱལ་པོ་''''''།
མཐའ་ཁོབ་བོད་ཀྱི་ རྒྱལ་པོ་''''། མི་རིགས་མི་འདྲ་བའི་སྣ་བོ་ལྷ་ལྷ་རྒྱ།
རྒྱལ་ཇོ་རྡུང་དུ་དུས་གཅིག་ཏུ་སླེབ་བོ། དེར་རྒྱ་གར་བ་རྣམས་ཤར་སྒོ་ཡོངས།
གེ་སར་བ་རྣམས་ལྷོ་སྒོ་ན་ཡོད།སྟག་གཟིག''''''། ཧོར་བ་རྣམས ''''''།

བོད་ལྷོན་ནམ་བྱང་ཤར་ཚམ་སུ་གདད་དོ། དེར་བློན་པོ་བཞན་མ་ནམས་ཀྱི་

ཞུ་རྗེན་འཟལ་ཕྲད་བྱེས་སོ།།

b. Three Ka-shog, Letters, presented by mGar, Minister of the king of Tibet, to the king of China, c. C.E. 636.

b.i. The First Paper Roll, Letter

བློན་པོ་འགར་གི་བཀའ་ཤོག།

ཤོག་བྲིལ་དང་པོ། ཤོག་བྲིལ་དང་པོ་རྒྱལ་པོ་ལ་ཕུལ་བ། རྒྱལ་པོ་

ཁ་ཕྱེད་ས་གཟིགས་པས་ཐེང་ཤོག་ལ་གསེར་གྱི་ཡི་གེར་བྲིས་པ་རྒྱ་ནག་གི་

ཡི་གེར་འདུག་དེ། ཁྱོད་རྒྱ་ནག་རྒྱལ་པོ་ལ་ཁྲིམས་ཡོད། ང་བོད་ཀྱི་རྒྱལ་པོ་

ལ་ཆོས་ཁྲིམས་མེད་དེ། རྒྱལ་པོ་ཁྱོད་དགེ་པ་བཅུ་ཡི་རྒྱལ་ཁྲིམས་ཡོད་པ་

དགའ་ནས་བུ་མོ་སྟེར་ན། ངས་སྐུ་ལུས་ཀྱི་བགོད་པ་ལྔ་སྟོང་དུ་སྤྲུལ་ནས་

དགེ་བའི་ཁྲིམས་ཉིན་གཅིག་ལ་བཅད་ནུས་པ་བྱེད། དེ་ལྟར་བྱས་ནས་བུ་མོ

་མི་སྟེར་ན། ངས་སྤྲུལ་བའི་དམག་ཁྲི་ཕྲག་ལྔ་བཏང་ནས་ཁྱོད་གསད་ལྷ་

གཅིག་འཕྲོག། ཡུལ་ཁམས་ཐམས་ཅད་བཅོམ་ནས་བཞག་གོ། རྒྱལ་པོ་ཤིན་

ཏུ་སྐྲགས་པར་གྱུར་ནས། སྐྲགས་ཀྱང་མི་སྐྲགས་པ་ལྟར་བྱས་ནས། ཁྱོད་

བོད་ཀྱི་རྒྱལ་པོ་དེ་ལ་ཁ་སོ་ཞིན་ཏུ་ཆེ་བ་འདུག། ཁྲོད་བོད་ཀྱི་ཡུལ་ན་གཙུག་ལག་གཅིག་པའི་ནུས་པ་ཡོད་དམ་མེད། ཡོད་ན་བུ་མོ་སྟེར། སོང་ལ་དྲིས་ཤོག། གསུངས་སོ།།

b.ii. The Middle Paper Roll, Letter

ཁ། ཤོག་བྲིལ་བར་མ།

ཡང་མགར་གྱི་ཤོག་བྲིལ་བར་མ་དེ་རྒྱལ་པོའི་ཕྱག་ཏུ་ཕུལ་ནས། འཕྲིན་རེ་རེ་ལ་བོད་དུ་འགྲོ་བ་མི་འོང་བས། རྒྱལ་པོ་ཁྲོད་ཀྱི་གསུང་དེའི་ལན་དུ་གཟིགས་པར་ཞུ།རྒྱལ་པོ་ཁ་ཕྱེད་ནས་གཟིགས་པ་འདི་ལྟར་རོ། ཁྲོད་རྒྱ་ནག་ཡུལ་ན་ཆོས་དང་གཙུག་ལག་ཁང་བརྩིག་པ་ཡོད། ང་བོད་ཀྱི་རྒྱལ་པོ་ལ་གཙུག་ལག་བརྩིག་པའི་ནུས་པ་མེད་དེ། རྒྱལ་པོ་ཁྲོད་གཙུག་ལག་ཁང་གཅིག་པ་ལ་དགའ་ནས་ལྷ་གཅིག་སྟེར་ན། ངས་སྐུ་ལུས་ཀྱི་བཀོད་པ་ལྔ་སྟོང་དུ་སྤྲུལ་ནས་གཙུག་ལག་ཁང་བརྒྱ་རྩ་བརྒྱད་བཞེངས་ནས་སྒོ་ཐམས་ཅད་ཁྲོད་ཀྱི་ཕྱོགས་སུ་བསྟན་པར་བྱའོ། དེ་ངོ་མཚར་མི་ཆེ་འམ། དེ་ལྟར་བྱས་ཀྱང་བུ་མོ་མི་སྟེར་ན། ངས་སྤྲུལ་པའི་དམག་ཁྲི་ཕྲག་ལྔ་གཏང་ནས་ཁྲོད་

གསད་ལྷ་གཅིག་འཁྲོག།   ཡུལ་ཁམས་ཐམས་ཅད་བཙོམ་ནས་བཞག་གོ། རྒྱལ་པོ་དེ་ཤིན་ཏུ་སྐྲགས་པར་གྱུར་ཀྱང་མི་སྐྲགས་པ་ལྟར་བྱས་ནས། ཁྱོད་ཀྱི་རྒྱལ་པོ་དེ་ཁ་སོ་ཤིན་ཏུ་ཆེས་པ་འདུག།   ཁྱོད་ཀྱི་ཡུལ་ན་འདོད་ཡོན་ལྔ་ལ་ལོངས་སྤྱོད་པ་ཡོད་དམ་མེད། ཡོད་ན་བུ་མོ་སྟེར་མེད་ན་མི་སྟེར། ད་ལན་སོང་ལ་དྲིས་ལ་ཤོག།

b.iii. The Last Paper Roll, Letter

ག། ཤོག་བྲིལ་ཐ་མ།

ཡང་བློན་པོ་མགར་གྱི་ཤོག་བྲིལ་ཐ་མ་དེ་རྒྱལ་པོའི་ཕྱག་ཏུ་ཕུལ་པ། འཕྲིན་རེ་རེ་ལ་རྒྱ་ནས་བོད་ལ་འགྲོ་བ་མི་འོང་བ།   རྒྱལ་པོ་ཁྱོད་ཀྱི་གསུང་དེའི་ལན་འདི་གཟིགས་པར་ཞུ། རྒྱལ་པོས་ཁ་ཕྱེད་ནས་གཟིགས་པ། ཁྱོད་རྒྱ་ནག་རྒྱལ་པོ་ལ་ནོར་ལོངས་སྤྱོད་ཡོད།   ང་བོད་ཀྱི་རྒྱལ་པོ་ལ་དེ་བཞིན་མེད་དེ།   རྒྱལ་པོ་ཁྱོད་ནོར་ལོངས་སྤྱོད་ཡོད་པ་ལ་དགའ་ན་བུ་མོ་སྟེར་ན། ངས་སྐུ་ལུས་ཀྱི་བཀོད་པ་ལྷ་སྟོང་དུ་སྤྲུལ་ནས་གསེར་དངུལ་གྱི་ལོངས་སྤྱོད

ཆེ། འབྲུ་དང་དར་ཟབ་གོས་དང་རྒྱན་དང་ཟས་ནོར་གྱི་ལོངས་སྤྱོད་བཞིན་རྣམས་སྣོ་དྲུང་དུ་འདུས་ནས་ལྡན་པར་བྱའོ།།

c. Messages of the Parents, Advice to the Princess.

c.i. ཡབ་ཀྱི་བཀའ་བཞིན་བོད་ལ་འགྲོ་ལགས་ཀྱི། ཡབ་ཀྱི་དྲུང་ནས་རྫོངས་ཞིག། ཞུ་བ་ལགས། རྫོངས་ཕྱི་རྫོངས་ནང་རྫོངས་བར་རྫོངས་ལ་ཞུ། ཆེ་བ་རྒྱ་ཆེར་རོལ་པ་ཞུ། ཆུང་བ་འཇིག་རྟེན་སྣང་བཞག་ཞུ། སྲིད་པའི་མ་མོ་དྲེ་མོ་ཞུ། རྟ་འགྲོ་ནོར་བུ་གསུམ་ཞུ། བོད་ཞིང་འགོ་འབྱེད་པའི་ལྷི་སྒྲིག་ཞུ། ཕྱུག་གསུམ་སུམ་འགལ་སྐར་པོ་ཞུ། གཡུ་ཨ་བཞག་འཁྲི་ལ་གནང་རོགས་མེད།། གཡུ་ཆེན་དཀར་ལ་ཞོག་ཕྱོས་ཐོག་དྲངས་པའི། གཡུ་མིང་ཅན་ཁྲི་དང་སྟོང་དུ་ཞུ། མིང་མེད་ཁྲི་གྲངས་མེད་ཞུ། ཡབ་ཀྱི་རྟ་མཆོག་པ་བ་གསེར་ལྡན་ཞུ། མ་རྟ་དང་བ་གསེར་ལྡན་མི་ཞུ་རྒྱུ། བྱང་ཐང་གྱོམ་ས་ཐག་རིངས་པ། བུ་མོ་ཚོགས་མ་སགས་པ། ཀང་འགྲོས་མེད་པ་དང་། བུ་མོ་ཀང་འགྲོས་ངན་ཞུ་དགོས་གདའ། བོད་ཁ་བ་ཅན་ན་ལྷ་ཆོས་མ་དར་ན་གདའ།

རབ་ཏུ་ལྷ་ཆོས་དར་རམ་ལྷ། ལྷ་ཆོས་ཀྱི་མ་དར་ན་འང་། བུ་མོ་རང་གི་ཡི་དམ་བྱེད་པ་ལ་དེ་སྔོན་ཤཱཀྱ་སྲུ་ནེ་ཞུ།།

c.ii. ཨོ་མ་ཧོ། ངོ་མཚར་ལྷ་གཅིག་གོང་རྗེ་ཁྲིད། བདག་གིས་ཅི་ག་ལ་སན། བཀས་སྐམས་སུ་དགའ། བོད་ཀྱི་རྒྱལ་ཁམས་ན། རིན་ཆེན་ས་ལ་གྲུབ། རྒྱལ་པོའི་ཕོ་བྲང་ནས། མི་རྗེ་ལྷའི་སྲས། སྲོང་བཙན་རྣམ་པོ་དེ། རིགས་དྲུག་དཔལ་གྱི་བརྗིད། མཐོང་ནས་སེམས་ཡིད་འཕྲོག། ཐུགས་རྗེ་ཆེན་པོ་ལེགས་རྒྱལ་སྲིད་ཆོས་གྱིས་སྐྱོངས། འབངས་རྣམས་བཀའ་ལ་སྙོན། རྒྱལ་སློན་འཁོར་འབངས་རྣམས། དགའ་སྐྱིད་གླུ་རུ་ལེན།ཆོས་ཀྱི་ཉི་མ་ཤར། དཔལ་གྱི་སྒྲོན་མེ་ཧེག། དེ་ལ་ཤིང་སྣ་ཚང་། ས་བཞི་ཡངས་པ་ལ། འབྲུ་སྣ་ལྔའི་ཚོགས། གོ་མཚམ་མེད་པར་སྐྱེས། གསེར་དངུ་ལ་ཟང་ལྕགས་སོགས། ནེ་ནེ་དུ་མ་ཡོད། སྟག་ཧྲ་ལུག་དར་སུ་རྣས། དགའ་སྐྱིད་དེ་ལྟར་ཡོད། ཨོ་མ་ངོ་མཚར་ཆེ། ལྷ་གཅིག་གོང་རྗེ་ཁྲིད། སོན། ཅེས་གླུ་བླངས་པས། ལ་གཅིག་གི་གེ་སི་ར་བ་ལ། དེ་ལྟར་བདེན་རང་གི་ཡུལ་དང་འདྲ་བ་འདུག་བསམས་ནས། ཕྱི་མ་ཕྱིས་ཧེ་བློན་པོའི་ཕྱིར་འབྲིང་སོ།།

c.iii. ཐབས་མ་ཁས་ཐུགས་རྗེ་གྱིས་ལྡན་པའི་རྒྱལ་པོ་ཡིན། མི་དགེ་བཅུ་པོང་དགེ་བཅུའི་ཁྲིམ་ལ་གནས། མངའ་ཐང་དཔལ་སྦྱོར་འདོད་དགུའི་དཔལ་ལ་སྦྱོར། ཡོན་ཏན་མཐའ་ལ་རྒྱལ་པོ་ལྷའི་སྲས། དཔལ་འཛོམས་བུ་མོ་ཀུན་བྱུང་བས། དེ་འདྲ་གནས་སུ་བུ་མོ་ཁྱོད་སོང་ཅིག། མ་ཇོ་མ་ཁྱོད་ཀྱི་བསོད་ནམས་བསོགས་པའི་རྟེན། བདག་གི་མཆོད་གནས་རྟོན་པའི་སྐུ་གཟུགས་ཀྱི། ཡོན་བདག་ལྷ་དབང་རྒྱ་བྱིན་ཁོང་གི་མཛོད། རྒྱ་ནི་རིན་ཆེན་རྣམ་པ་ལྔ་ལ་འབྱུབ། འདི་ཡི་འཛོ་བོ་བྱི་ཤོ་སྐར་མི་མཛོད། རབ་གནས་སངས་རྒྱས་ཐམས་ཅད་ཀྱི་འཛད་ལགས། དེ་ལྟར་འདྲེན་མེད་རྒྱལ་བའི་སྐུ་གཟུགས་འདི། ཐོང་ཐོས་དྲན་རག་སོལ་བ་བཏབ་གྱུར་བ་ལ། སངས་རྒྱས་སྱུར་དུ་ཐོབ་པས་རྒྱལ་བ་གསུངས། དེ་ལྟར་ཕན་བདེ་བྱུང་བའི་བུ་མོ་འདི། བདག་གི་སྙིང་དང་འདྲ་བར་ཕངས་ན་ཡང་། མཛེ་བའི་བུ་མོ་ཁྱོད། ལ་བདག་གིས་རྫོངས། རིན་ཆེན་བང་རྫོད་ནོར་ཀྱི་ཏེ་ར། བདག་ལ་ཅེས་བའི་རིན་ཆེན་མང་པོ་ཡང་། མཛེས་པའི་བུ་མོ་ཁྱོད་ལ་བདག་གིས་རྫོངས། གསེར་གཡུ་རྫོགས་ཡིད་ཚང་ཆེན་པོ་དང་། གཙུག་ལག་ཡི་སེ་གསུམ་

རྒྱ་དྲུག་ཅུ་དང་། སེར་གཡུའི་རྒྱན་ གྱི་རྣམ་པ་མང་པོ་དང་། གཡོ་རྣ་ཟས་ཀྱི་རྣམ་པ་མང་པོ་དང་། དང་པོར་གཡུ། ལུག''''། ཚད་འཛོད་རྒྱ''''། རྟ་མ་རྒྱ''''། བྱ་མ་རྒྱ''''། སོན་ཤི་འདུམ་བུ་དེ་ན་རང་གི་བཟེམ''''། དེ་ན་བུ་མོ་ཏུང་བ་ཀ་ཀྱི་སྦྱར་ཐ་ཐ་མང་པོ་དང་། གསེར་གཡུ་ཁ་ལེབ་ཅན་ལ་སོགས།།

མཛེ་བའི་བུ་མོ་ཁྱོད་ལ་བདག་གི''''། བཞི་རྒྱ་རྩ་བཞི་ནད་རྣམས་ཛོམས་བའི་སྨན། སྣག་ཐབས་རྒྱ་དང་སྤྱད་ལྔ་ཐྲ་སྤྱད་དྲུག་དང་། སྦྱོར་བདེ་བཞི་ལ་སོགས་པའི་བདག་གི''''། ཚེ་༧གྲོས་བའི་གོས་དང་ཟ་འོག་སོགས། ཁ་འདོག་སྣ་ཚོགས་ལྡན་བའི་རྒྱན་དགོས་དང་། སྟོང་ཁྲག་ཉི་ཤུ་བུ་མོ་ཁྱོད་ལ''''། རིགས་གཟུགས་ལྷ་ན་སྡུག་ཅིང་མཛེས་བ་ཡི། སེམས་ཐུན་ཀྱོ་རོགས་བྱེད་ པ་བུ་མོ་དང་། ཉི་ཤུ་རྩ་ལྔ་ཁྱོད་ཀྱི་ཁོར་དུ་བཟུང་། ཨེ་མ་འབྲལ་བ་མི་ཡོད་བུ་མོ་ཁྱོད། རྩེ་བའི་སྙིང་དམ་ཡིན་པ་སེམས་ལ་ཞོག།

d. Zang-yig: Dialogue between the Princess and her Parents and Brother.

མཛངས་ཡིག་།།

ཨོཾ་མ་ཧཱུཾ། ངོ་མཚར་ཆེ། སྲིད་པོ་རྒྱ་གར་གླིང་དང་རྒྱ་ནག་གླིང་ན་འདུག། རྒྱ་དཀར་པོ་གང་ལ་ཉི་ཤར་འདྲ། རྒྱ་ནག་གླང་ཆེན་འཕྲེད་(ཕྲེང་)ལ་འཁྱིང་གདའ། མཁས་ སུ་བརྗོད་པ་བལ་པའི་མཐིལ་ན་གདའ།

གནས་རྣམ་པར་རྒྱལ་བའི་ཁང་བཟང་ལ། ཕ་བཟང་པོ་ནོར་གྱི། ང་པོ་ལ། སྨན་རིགས་སུ་བཟང་པ་བླ་སྨན་རྒྱལ་པོ་དབྱུངས། དགོས་སུ་ཅོར་(ཙུན་)ཁྲོམ་རྒྱན་མེ་ཏོག་འབྱུངས། སྐུ་ཁྱུངས་པ་རྒྱ་ནག་བཀྲིས་ཁྲི་སྒོ་(ཁྲིས་མགོ་)ཙམ་དུ་འབྱུངས། ལམ་བྱོན་པ་བྱང་ཐང་སྟོང་པའི་ལམ་ལ་བྱོན།

ཆོས་རྒྱལ་འགྲོ་དོན་ཟབ་མོ་བོད་ལ་ཁ་(མཁའ་)བ་ཅན་མཛད། ཕྱི་ཤོད་(ཤང་)ན་རྒྱལ་རབས་ཀྱི་བཀའ་(ཀ་)བ་གདའ། ནང་ཤང་ན་བློན་རབས་ཀྱི་འགྲུགས་པ་གདའ། རྒྱལ་པོ་བདེ་པ་ལ་སེར་གྱི་བཀའ་བ་གདའ། བཙུན་མོ་མཛངས་མ་ལ་གཡུ་འི་འཛངས་ཡིག་གདའ། རྒྱལ་བློན་འཕྲུལ་དུ་བསྐྱིབས་པ་ལ། བློན་པོ་དགོས་ཀྱི་བསྟན་ཆོས་གདའ། ཕྱི་ཤང་ན་རྒྱལ་རབས་ཀྱིས་སྐྱངས་པ་བྱས་རུང་ཀྱང་། ཕྱུགས་རྗེ་ཆེན་པོ་ཙམ་ཀྱི་ཡང་སྙིང་ཡིན་པ་འདྲ། རྒྱལ་པོ་སྲོང་བཙན་ཀམ་པོ་མཛད་པའི་གསུང་རབས་ཡིན་པ་འདྲ། ནང་ཤང་ན་བློན་རབས་ཀྱི་འགྲུགས་པ་བྱ་རུང་ཀྱང་། (༡)ཕྱུག་ན་རྗེས་ཙོ་མ་གྱི་ཡང་སྙིང་ཡིན་པ་འདྲ། བློན་པོ་རིག་པ་ཅན་གསུང་པའི་གསུང་རབས་ཡིན་པ་འདྲ།

༼མཛངས་མ་བླ་སྲས་རྒྱལ་ཟའི་ཕ་མ་ཡབ་ཡུམ་དྲུང་དུ་ཞུས་པ་ཕུལ་པ།༽

དེ་ཡང་འཛང་བྱེད་ཚངས་པ་བླ་སྨན་རྒྱལ་ས་ཡི། ཕ་མ་ཡབ་ཡུམ་དྲུངས་དུ་ཞུ་བ་ཕུལ་བ་ལ། སྟེང་ན་དཀར་པོའི་གདུགས་ཅིག་ཕུབ་པ་གདའ། འོག་ན་འཇམ་པའི་སྟན་ཅིག་སྟིང་པ་འདྲ། ན་འཇའ་གཞུ་ཁ་སྤྱོར་གཉིས་ཀྱི་སྒྲུམ་ཤེད་ན། ཕ་མ་རྒྱ་ནག་འགྲུལ་པའི་ཆོས་རྒྱལ་ཡབ་ཡུམ་(ཡུཾབ་)མཁྱེན། བུ་མོ་པེ་ཞང་བསྐྱུར་པ་བླའི་རོལ་མོ་ཡིན། སྟེང་ལྷ་ཆེན་འདབས་པའི་ཀ་ཅན་ཡིན། འོག་ཀླུ་མོ་འདེབས་པའི་སྨྱིན་འདྲེན་ཡིན། བར་བཙན་མཉེས་པའི་རོལ་མོ་ཡིན། དྲིན་ཅན་ཕ་མ་གཉེས་པའི་སྐྱོ་རོགས་ཡིན། བྱང་ཐང་སྟོང་པ་ཤོག་པའི་ཤོག་རོགས་ཡིན། དྲིན་ཅན་ཕ་མ་དྲན་འདི་དྲན་རོགས་ཡིན། ཕ་མ་དྲན་ཟེར་ནས་ཉེན་ཀྱང་སྐྱུར་གྱིན་འགྲོ། ཕ་མ་དྲན་ཟེར་ནས་མཆན་×། ཉེན་མཚན་རྟག་དུ་སྐྱུར་གྱིན་འགྲོ་ལེགས་དེ། ཕྱི། སྤྱིར་སྐྱེས་མན་བུ་མོའི་བུ་རྩ་འདི། ཚོགས་མ་བསགས་ཞིག་ཡིན་པ་འདྲ། དགོས་རྒྱལ་པའི་བུ་མོ་ང་ཚོགས་མ་གསགས། ཚོགས་བསག་དང་མ་བསགས་

གཉིས་ན་འདུག །(༣)ལམ་སྒྲིབ་པ་བྱུང་དང་མ་བྱུང་གཉིས་ན་འདུག། ཚོགས་བསགས་པ་དལ་འབྱོར་མི་ལུས་ཐོབ། དབང་པོ་སྒོ་ང་ཡིན་ཀྱང་བུ་མོ་ལུས་ལ་ཆེར། ལོ་གཞོན་པ་བྱུང་ཐང་ཤག་དགོས་འབྱུང་། ལོ་ལྷ་གསུམ་བཅོས་ལྷ་མི་འགྲོ་དེ། དྲིན་ཅན་ཕ་མ་གཉིས་དང་སོ་བྲལ་བྱེད་དགོས་འབྱུང་། ཕ་མིང་ཉེན་བཞི་རྣམས་དང་བཏན་བྲལ་བྱེད་དགོས་འབྱུང་། ཤིང་བྲལ་བྱེད་པ་སེམས་ཅན་ཀུན་གྱི་ལུགས་སུ་འདུག། སོན་བྲལ་བྱེད་པ་ཕ་མ་གཉིས་ཀྱི་ཐོད་ལེགས་བསམ། ཨུ་ཡུམ་ཡབ་སྲས་མོ་འདི། ལོ་གཅིག་ལོ་གཉིས་སོང་པ་འཛལ་རྒྱུ་མི་གདའ་ལ།

ཟླ་ཅིག་ཟླ་ཉིས་སོང་བ་འཛལ་རྒྱུ་མི་གདའ་ལགས། ནམ་བཞག་བཏན་གྱིས་བཏན་བྲལ་ཡིན་པ་འདྲ། བཏན་བྲལ་དང་བཏན་ཚོང་ཕ་མའི་གནང་བ་འདྲ། བུ་མོ་ང་ལ་ཟླ་བ་དཀར་བ་ཟླས་སྟོང་ཡིན་པ་འདྲ། ཕ་མ་འཛོམ་པ་ཚེ་སྟོང་ཡིན་པ་འདྲ། ཟླ་སྟོང་ཟླ་བ་དཀར་བ་གང་ཡིན་པ། ཟླ་འཇུག་མུན་པའི་གླིང་ན་འདུག། ཚེ་སྟོང་ཕ་མ་འཛོམ་པ་གང་ཡོད་པ། ཚེ་འཇུག་འོ་(༤)སྐོལ་ཡབ་ཡུམ་རྣམས་ཀྱི་གྲོགས་ཡུན་ཐུང་པ་ལ། ལོ་བཅོ་ལྔ་བདག་གི་འདོད་ཡུན་ཐུང་ལ། སྐྱེས་པའི་ཕ་ཡུལ་རྒྱ་ནག་བཀྲ་ཤིས་ཁྲིས་སྒོ་དེ། བུ་མོ་འི་མགོ་ལ་སྐྱེས་པའི་སྤྲ་ལོ་མན་ལེགས། ཕ་ཡུལ་སྤྲ་ལོ་བྱིན་དུ་རྒྱབ་དུ་གྲིམ་དགོས་འབྱུང་།

མི་ཡུལ་དང་(ངང་)དུ་དངུལ་དཀར་མེ་ལོང་མེན་ལེགས་སེ། མི་ཡུལ་དངུལ་དཀར་མེ་ལོང་བཞིན་དུ་་ངང་དུ་ལང་དགོས་འབྱུང་། བློ་སྣང་བཙོལ་པའི་དྲིན་ཅན་ཕ་མ་ཡིན་ལེགས་སྟེ། མི་ཅི་ཡོང་ལ་བློ་བཏང་སྙིང་བཙོལ་བྱེད་དགོས་འབྱུང་། ནོར་བཟང་པོ་གཅིག་ཕ་མའི་ཕྱག་ན་སྣང་། གིན་གདའ་ལེགས་སྟེ། བུ་མོ་རང་ནོར་ཁྱེར་ནས་ཕྱིན་རུང་ཀྱང་། ཁ་གཞན་དང་དབང་ཆུད་དགོས་ཀྱིན་གདའ། ལེས་ཅི་ཏུ་བསགས་པའི་སྡིག་པ་དགོསུ་འཁུར་དགོས་ཀྱིན་གདའ། བུ་མོ་རང་སྐལ་གཅད་ནས་གཞན་ལ་གཏིང་དགོས་ཀྱིན་གདའ། གལ་ཆུང་རང་ལ་བྱེད་པའི་སྐལ་མེད་ང་འདྲ་ཅིག། བཟའ་རང་མང་པོ་ཚོགས་པ་ན། སེར་རྣ་འཇུར་བགེགས་དགོས་ཀྱིན་གདའ། མི་ཚེ་སེར་སྣའི་ངང་ལ་འཆི་པ་འདྲ། དལ་འབྱོར་མི་ལུས་ཐོབ་པའི་དཀའ་ལས་ལ། ཡོང་ཏིང་མི་ཚེ་སྟོང་ཟད་འདི་ལ་མ་སྣང་དང་། འདི་ཡན་ཆད་མཇངས་མ་ཟླ་སྲས་རྒྱལ་ཟའི་ཕ་མ་ཡབ་ཡུམ་(༥)དྲུང་དུ་ཞུས་པ་ཕུལ་པའོ།

འདི་མན་ཆད་ཨ་མ་བུ་མོ་ལ་ཞལ་ཏ་སྣང་པའོ། ཨ་མའི་བུ་མོ་ཤ་ཁྲག་ལུས་ཀྱིས་དང་མཚུར་ཉོན་མཛོད། ཨ་མི་ཆུང་ན་བསག་པའི། བྲལ་མིའི་ཐོད་ཁྱོད་ཚུར་ཉོན་མཛོད། ཨ་མིའི་རྗེས་པར་གཡོས་པའི་བུ་མོ་ཚུར་ཉོན་མཛོད། ལེགས་པར་དགོན་པའི་བུ་མོ་ཚུར་ལ་ཉོན། ཁ་མདོག་ལེགས་པའི་རྩང་སྤྲ་ཅན་མ་ཉོན། སྒྱུར་འཇིག་རྟེན་མི་ཆོས་བྱེད་པ་འདི། དགོས་པོད་ཁ་བ་ཅན་དུ་འགྲོ་པ་འདི། ཡབ་ཆེན་ཨ་པ་རྒྱ་ནག་རྒྱལ་པོ་འདི།

ཚོང་ཁྱེས་འཛོགས་བྱེས་ནས་བུ་མོ་བོད་ལ་ཚོང་པ་མིན། ཨ་མ་བུ་སྙིང་ཆེས་ནས་བུ་མོ་བོད་ལ་ཚོང་པ་ཡང་མིན། མིང་པོ་ཁ་དབང་ཆེ་ནས་ཕ་མཁར་འཛིན་པ་ཡང་ཡིན། ཨ་ཅེ་ཁ་དབང་ཆུང་ནས་མི་ཡུལ་ས་མཐར་འགྲིམ་པ་ཡང་། མིན་ཚེ་སྔོན་སྲིད་པ་དང་པོ་འཆགས་པའི་ལུགས་སུ་འདུག། བུ་སྐྱེས་པ་གླན་པ་རྩལ་པ་འབྱུང་རུང་ཀྱང་། ཕ་ཞིང་ཕ་མཁར་བུ་རྩལ་ཡིན་ཀྱང་འཛིན་གྱིན་གདའ། བུ་མོ་འཛངས་མ་གྱེར་མ་འབྱུང་རུང་ཀྱང་། བུ་མོ་གྱེར་ཀྱང་མི་ཡུལ་ས་འཐག་འགྲིམ་གྱིན་གདའ། ཡ་ལེས་ཁ་བ་འབབ་པ་ལ་སྒོ་མི་འགོགས་གདའ། འོ་སྐོལ་སྐྱེ་མིན་བུ་མོ་སོང་བའི། ཕ་མིའི་(༧)བུ་གོ་མི་ཆོད་གདའ། རི་ལ་ཁ་བ་འབབ་པ་རིའི་གོསུ་འདུག།

འོ་སྐོལ་སྐྱེ་མེན་བུ་མོ་མི་འི་ནོར་གསེངས་ཡིན་པ་འདྲ། སྐྱེས་མེན་བུ་མི་བུ་རྩ་ལ་ཕ་ཡུལ་མི་འདུག་པ། ཨན་ཀྱང་ཕ་ཡུལ་མེད་པའི་བུ་མོ་མེན་ལེགས་སྟེ། ཕ་ཡུལ་རྒྱ་ནག་བཀྲ་ཤིས་ཁྲི་སྒོ་ཡིན་ལེགས་ཀྱང་། ཕ་ཡུལ་བཟང་ཀྱང་འཛིན་དབང་མི་འདུག་པ། ཨ་མིའི་བུ་མོ་རང་ལོ་གཞད་ཀྱིན་ཉོན། བཞི་གསུམ་བཅུ་ཉིས་ལོན་པ་བུ་མོ་རང་གི་ལོ་ན་འདུག། ལྔ་གསུམ་བཅོ་ལྔ་ལོན་པ་ཁྱིམ་པའི་ལོ་ན་འདུག། དྲུག་གསུམ་བཅོ་བརྒྱད་ལོན་པ་རྒན་གྱི་ལ་ན་འདུག། བཅུ་ཁ་བུད་པའི་ཏ་རྒན་དང་། ཉི་ཤུ་ལོན་པའི་སྨུ་གཙུན་ཉིས། ཚོང་ཁ་མདོག་དྲིན་དྲིན་འདྲ་ལ་མི་དྲིནོ།

དེ་བས་ཨ་མིའི་ཁ་ཏ་ཉོན། མདོ་ཕྲུག་(༨)པོ་ཕྲུག་སུ་ལོན་དང་ཅིག། བུ་མོ་ལྔ་གསུམ་བཅོ་ལྔ་ལོན་དང་གཉིས། ཚོང་ཁ་མདོག་དྲིན་པའི་དུས་སུ་ཚོང་ན་ལེ་པ་བདའ། ཆང་འོ་མ་གཉིས་ཏོག་ཚད་འཛིན་ན་མཁས་པ་ཡིན། ཤོ་འཁྲུག་པ་ཉིས་ལ་རྒྱལ་ཚོད་ཟིན་ན་དཔའོ་ཡིན། སྨོ་ཚོད་ཟིན་ན་སྨན་པ་ཡིན། ཏ་བདེ་མིའི་ཐང་ལ་མ་རྒྱུག་ན། འགྲོགས་བུལ་ཉིས་ཀྱིས་ཤེན་བྱེད་མི་ཤེས་བདའ། རལ་གྲི་ཚད་(༩)པའི་སྒྲ་ལ་མ་རྒྱབ་ན་ཚོན་དར་ཉིས་ཀྱིས་ཤད་མི་བྱེད་གདག། བུ་མོ་སློང་ཁན་གྲོགས་ལ་མ་ཕྱིན་ན། སྨན་དྲུང་ལེན་གཉིས་ཀྱི་ཤེན་མི་ཕྱེད་གདའ།

དཔེ་དེ་ལ་བསམ་ལ་བུ་མོ་བོད་ཁ་བ་ཅན་གཤེགས། སྟན་གྲོགས་རྒྱལོ་ངང་དུ་ལོང་མཛོད་དང་། ཨ་མིའི་བུ་མོ་ཚུར་ལ་གསན་མཛོད་དང་། ཨ་མིའི་དཔེ་དང་ལྡན་པའི་ཞུས་པ་འབུལ་ལེགས་གྱིས། རི་ཁའི་ཞིང་ལ་རིགས་གངས་སྔང་གིན་གདའ། རིགས་དྭགས་སྲུངས་པའི་ཐོ་ཡོར་བཟང་པོ་དགོས་ཀྱིན་བདའ། བརྒྱ་ལ་ཞིང་ལ་འབྲུལ་མི་རྒྱ་སྔང་གིན་གདའ། འབྲུལ་མི་འི་དསྲུངས་པའི·····ཚེར་ཏགས་བཟང་པོ་དགོས་ཀྱིན་བདའ། ཆུ་ཁའི་ཞིང་ལ་ཆུ་རྣ་སྔང་གི་བདའ། ཆུ་སྣའི་བསྲུངས་པའི་ཡུར་བཟང་པོ་དགོས་ཀྱིན་བདའ། འོ་སྐོལ་སྐྱེས་མེན་བུ་མོ་ལ་མི་ཁ·····སྔང་། མི་ཁ་ཅོག་པའི་སྟན་གྲོགས་བཟང་པོ་དགོས་ཀྱིན·····། སྙིད་དགཔ་མིའི་གོ་ཁ་སྙིད་ལེགས་ཏེ། གོར་རྣས་སྙིད་པ་སེམས་པའི་གནད་དུ་ཆེ་བ

གདའ། དཔེ་དེ་ལ་བསམ་ལ་སྟན་གྲོགས་རྒྱོལ་དང་དུ་ལོང་མཛོད་དང་། བུ་མོ་སེམས་ཀྱི་སྒོ་ན་ཁ་ཏ་ཡིན་ལེགས་སྟེ། ཐུགས་ལ་ཐོབ་འབྱུང་ན་བཟོད་པར་གསོལ། འདི་ཡན་ཆད་ཨ་མའི་གསུངས་པའོ།

འདི་མན་ཆད་ཡབ་(༡)ཆེན་རྒྱལ་པོ་འི་དྲུང་དུ་ཞུ་བ་ཕུལ་བའོ། ཡབ་ཆེན་ཨ་བ་རྒྱ་ནག་རྒྱལ་པོ་ཚུར་བསན་དང་། བུ་མོ་ཚོགས་མ་བསགས་ང་མི་ཆོས་ཀྱི་ཚེར་པ་ལ་ཁྱེད་པར་ཐེགས་རིང་ཉེན་ལ་འགྲོ་བ་སེང་། རྒྱབ་བཟང་བའི་ཕ་མིང་དང་བུ་མོ་དྲལ་གྱིན་གདའ། བཟང་བའི་ཕ་མི་གདོང་ལེགས་པོ་ཡོད་ཀྱང་ཤ་ཁྲག་སྟེང་ན་གཅོར་གྱིན་གདའ། ཤིག་སྲོ་མ་ཡིན་ཀྱང་དགྲ་ཉ་ལྡང་གྱིན་གདའ། བུ་མོ་ལུས་ལ་གོན་པའི་གོས་ཆུང་ཉུལ་ཙ་ན། རྒྱལ་ཟ་ལྷའི་ཤེས་པ་གཞན་ལ་དམའ་བ། གོག་ཤམ་ཁྱི་མོ་ཡིན་ཀྱང་འགྲི་ལོགས་འཚོད་གིན་ཕུགདའ། བུ་མོ་ཁང་ལ་གྲོན་པའི་ལྷམ་ཆུང་རྡོལ་ཙ་ན། ཙ་སྐྱེས་ཙ་ལ་དྲིས་ཙག་འཐོལ་གྱིན་གདའ། རྒྱལ་ས་ང་ལ་ལྷམ་ཐེལ་མེད་ཅིག་ཀྱང་ལ་འཇུག་གྱིན་གདའ།

ན་ཆུང་སྐམ་སྐམ་མང་པོ་འགྲོ་ཙ་ན། ལྷམ་མེད་བུ་མོ་རྡོག་ཐབས་ཤུལ་དུ་ལུས། ཁྱེད་པར་བུ་མོའི་ལེགས་ན་ཟས་ནོར་མེད་ཙ་ན། ནོར་མེད་མི་ལ་དྲག་པོ་སྡང་གྱིན་གདའ། ཕ་མ་སྤུན་ཟླ་ཡིན་ཀྱང་ཁམ་དྲོ་དང་ཀུགས་དྲོ་བྱེད་ཀྱིན་གདའ། ཕ་ཡུན་(༩)མ་བུན་ཡིན་ཀྱང་དཔོན་ཡོག་ཁྱེད་ཙམ་བྱེད་ཀྱིན་གདའ། བླ་མ་བཟང་པོ་ཆུག་པའི་ཉེས་ཀྱིན་གདའ། གདམ་ངག་ཟབ་མོ་ཟས་ནོར་དོ་ལ་གནང་བ་གདའ། ནོར་མེད་མི་ལ་དབང་དང་གདམ་ངག་མི་གནང་། དཔེ་དེ་ལ་བསམ་ནས་མི་ཆོས་ཀྱིས་ཚེར་པ་ལ། ཡང་དགོས་ནོར་མེད་ཀྱིས་ཁྱིམ་ཐབས་ཚར་པ་ལ། བརྒྱ་ནག་དཀྲུལ་པའི་ཆོས་རྒྱལ་ཡབ་ཡུམ་ལྗིན་བུ་མོ་དཔེ་དང་ལྡན་པའི་ཞུས་པ་ཚིག་གསུམ་ཕུལ་ལེགས་ཀྱི། ཟས་མི་ཞིམ་ཙ་ན་ན་བ་ཡིན་པ་འདྲ། ཉེན་མ་རྩེས་ཙ་ན་རྒྱུད་ཡིན་འདྲ། གྲོགས་མི་རྩེ་ཙ་ན་གྱེས་པ་ཡིན་པ་འདྲ། ཟས་ཟ་བ་ནོངས་ན་དུགེ་བཞི་མ་ཡིན། ཉེན་མ་ལེགས་ཤིག་དགྲའི་གཡབ་མོ་ཡིན། ཁ་ཞེན་པ་དབྱལ་བ་ཐར་མེད་ཡིན། །ནོར་མེད་པ་མི་སྐྱོན་ཅན་ཡིན།

ཁ་ཆུས་པ་བུ་བ་སློང་མེད་ཡིན། སྤྱིར་བོད་ཁ་བ་ཅན་གྱིས་ས་ཕྱོགས་ན། གདུང་རུས་པ་མི་བཙུན་ཁ་མདོག་ཐུགས་ཐལ་བཙུན་གྱིན་གདའ། མགོ་ནག་མི་ལ་སོང་རྣམས་བཙུན་གྱིན་གདའ། བཟང་པོ་ཡ་རབ་ཅིག་དང་མ་རབས་གཉིས་ན་གདའ། བཟང་པོ་ཡ་རབས་མི་རྒྱུད་པ་བལ་་ལ་འཇམ་པ་གདའ། ངན་པ་སྐྱི་སྤྱོང་ཅིག་རྒྱུགས་ཤིང་ལ་གློང་པ་གདའ། (༡༠)སྙེས་མ་ལོང་ག་དབུ་ལ་ཐོབ་བ་གདའ། རྣམས་སྤྲིན་མེད་ཀྱི་ང་ར་མདའ་ལ་ཚ་པ་གདའ། རྗེས་དྲིན་མེད་ཀྱི་བཀའ་ལུང་རི་ལས་ཅེ་བ་གདའ། མི་དྲིན་མེད་ཀྱི་ཚིག་ངན་རྡོ་ལས་ནོ་བ་གདའ། ཅི་ཀྱང་བུ་མོ་མི་ཆོས་ཅིག་ལ་སྣང་ཟེར་ན། བུ་མོ་ད་ཕོ་ཐགས་ཚོད་པའི་ཞུ་བ་འབུལ་ལེགས་ཀྱི། མི་

ཆར་ཆར་དུས་ཉི་མ་ལ་དགུག་པ་སང་། སེམས་ཁོ་ཐག་ཆོད་པའི་གྲིབ་སོ་གྲོ་བ་གདའ། བང་འགྲོས་མེད་པའི་རྟ་ལ་ཞོན་པ་སང་། སེམས་ཁོ་ཐག་ཆོད་པའི་རྐང་ཐང་འགྲོགས། མངར་མིན་ཀྱུར་མན་ཆང་ལ་ཉོ་ཚོང་བྱེད་པ་སང་། ཁོ་ཐག་ཆོད་པའི་གཡར་ཆུ་གང་ཆུ་ཁ་བདེ་བ་ཕྱི། མི་ཐེ་ཐེ་རིང་རྒྱལ་པོའི་འགྲོགས་ལ་གྲོ་བ་སང་། རྒྱལ་ས་རང་སེམས་ཐད་པའི་རྒྱ་ནག་ཡུལ་ཀྱིས་གོ་བྲན་ཅིག་ལ་སྣང་བ་བདེ་བ་གདའ། ཅིས་ཀྱང་མི་གསན་མི་ཆོས་ཅིག་ལ་སྣང་ཟེར་ན། བུ་མོ་ཐད་པའི་གྲོགས་ལ་སྣང་བར་ཞུས། བོད་ཁ་བ་ཅན་ད······མིགི་མ་ཐོང་པའི། གཏན་གྲོགས་བཟང་པོ་ཅིག་ག་ལ་ཐོང་། དའོས་བུ་མོ་ལྷ་ཆོས་ཅིག་ལ་སྣང་བར་ཞུ། འདི་ཡན་ཆད་བུ་མོ་ཡབ་ཀྱི་དྲུང་དུ་ཞུས་པའོ།

འདི་མན་ཆད་ཡབ་ཀྱི་བུ་མོ་ལ་ཞལ་ཏ་གསུངས་པའོ། ཨ་པའི་བུ་མོ་ལྷ་ཅིག་རྒྱལ་(༡༡)ཟ་ཚུར་ཉོན་དང་། ཁྱེད་དམ་པའི་ལྷ་ཆོས་བྱེད་པ་ལ། ནྡོ་ཁ་ཚོསུ་མ་སོང་ནས། སྒྲ་ལོ་སྙིང་མེད་གྲགས་ཀྱང་སྐྱེས་ཡིན་གདའ། སྤྱིར་བུ་མོ་བུ་ཙ་ལ་ལྷ་ཆོས་མི་ཡོང་འདུག། ཡང་དགོས་མི་ཆེན་གྱིས་བུ་མོ་ལ་ལྷ་ཆོས་འབྱུང་དགོས་ན། བུད་མེད་བུ་ཚའི་ཆོས་མགོ་མི་ཐོན་འདུག། ཆོས་འཇུག་ཐ་རུ་ཁྱོལ་དོགས་མེད། མགོ་བོ་རིལ་རིལ་བྱེས་པ་ལ་ན྄་ཆོས་ཡོང་དག་ན་རིལ་མང་བ་ནག་ཆུང་ཁོ་ལ་ན྄་ཆོས་ཡོང་འདུག། ལུས་སེར་པོ་གྱོན་པ་ན྄་ཆོས་ཡོང་དག་ན། ཚོ་ཐའི་དད་པ་སེལ་ལྡན་ཁོ་ལ་ན྄་ཆོས་ཡོང་བར་འདུག། སྐོར་བ་སྐོར་ཚད་ཀྱིས་སྒྲིབ་པ་མི་དག་འདུག། སྐོར་བ་སྐོར་ཚད་གྱིས་སྒྲིབ་པ་དག་ཟེར་ན། ཆུ་རབས་ནག་ཆུང་ཁོ་ཡང་སྒྲིབ་པ་དག་པ་འདུག། བསྒོམ་རྒྱབ་ཚད་ཀྱི་སངས་རྒྱས་མི་ཡོང་འདུག། བསྒོམ་རྒྱབ་ཚད་ཀྱི་སངས་རྒྱས་ཟེར་ནས། ཕྱིལ་བ་ལགས་གསེར་ཁོ་ལ་ཡང་སངས་རྒྱས་འོང་པ་འདུག། བསམ་(༡༢)པ་བཟང་པོ་དང་ཆོས་བཟང་པོ་གཉིས།། སངས་རྒྱས་ནས་མཉམ་པོར་རྒྱས་པར་འདུག། ཁྱོད་སྙིང་ན་ལྷ་ཆོས་བྱེད་ཟེར་ནས། རྐོ་ལ་བཞོག་ལ་སྦྱིན་པ་གཏོང་། ཁྱོད་སྙིང་ན་ལྷ་ཆོས་བྱེད། ལུས་དལ་ན་མཆོག་རྟེན་ལ་བསྐོར་བ་རྒྱབ།

ལེགས་དལ་ན་དབུལ་ཕོང་ལ་སྦྱིན་པ་གཏོང་།

ཁ་དལ་ན་གསུང་མཆོག་ཡིག་དྲུག་ཐོངས།

ཕོ་རབ་མོ་རབ་ཉིས་སྐྱེ་འོག་ན་སངས་རྒྱས་པའི་དཔེ་ཅིག་འདུག། ནྡོ་ཆོས་བྱས་ཀྱང་ཟུར་ན་མི་འདུག་པ། མི་ཆོས་བྱས་ཀྱང་སྨོན་རྒྱུ་མི་འདུག་པ། ན྄་ཆོས་བྱས་ཀྱང་དེ་ཀ་མན་ལེགས་སོ།། ཡབ་ཀྱི་ཁ་ཏ་ཡིན་པ་བུ་མོ་སེམས་ལ་གཞོག། བསླབ་ཉེར་ཡིན་པ་སློ་(ནྡོ)ལ་བཟུང་།

འདི་ཡན་ཡབ་ཀྱི་བུ་མོ་ལ་གསུངས་པའོ།

འདི་མན་རྒྱལ་ཟ་བཀོང་འཛོར་གྱིས་གསུངས་པའོ། ཕ་མ་ཡབ་ཡུམ་དྲུངས་དུ་ཞུ་བ་ཕུལ་ཀྱང་སན་དགོངས་ནི་མ་འབྱུང་། རྒྱལ་ཟ་ཐུགས་དགོངས་ཅིག་གདང་པ། ད་ནི་མིང་པོ་ཡི་

རྩར་ཕྱིན་ནས་ཞུ་རོགས་ལ་སྐན་སྟེ་ཞུ་བ་ཅིག་ཨེ་སྒྲུབ་བསམ་ནས། མིང་ཆུང་སྐྱབ་ཕྲུག་ལེགས་པའི་དྲུངས་དུ་ཕྱོན་ནས། མིང་པོའི་ཕྱག་ན་འཇུས་ནས་ཨ་ཕྱི་ཞལ་རས་དཔལ་དཀར་མེ་ལོང་འདྲ་པ་དེ་(༡༣)ན་སྨྱུན་ཆབ་ཤེལ་ཕྲེང་བལྡ་བུ་གསིལ་ཞིང་ཞུ་བ་འདི་ལྟར་ཕུལ། ཨ་ཅེ་མིང་ཆུང་སྐྱབ་ཕྲུག་ལེགས་པ་ཚུར་སན་དང་། བུ་མོ་མིང་པོ་ཕ་ཡུལ་འཛིན་པ་གདའ་ལེགས་སྟེ། ཨ་ཅེ་ཚོགས་མ་བསགས་ད་མི་ཡུལ་ཁྱམ་པའི་ཚེར་པ་ལ། ཡབ་ཆེན་ཨ་བ་རྒྱ་ནག་རྒྱལོ་ལ། ཕྲེ་རྒྱལ་བུ་ཅིག་ལས་མི་འདུག་པས།

ཡུམ་ཆེན་ཨྣ་མ་ཁྲི་ལྷམ་རྒྱལ་མོ་ལ། ཕྲེས་མོ་ང་ལས་མི་འདུག་པ། འོ་ཀོལ་ལྷམ་སྲིང་གཉིས་མིང་ཅིག་སྲིང་ཅིག་འདི། དཔྲལ་པའི་མིག་ཅིག་མན་ལེགས་སེ། ཡབ་ཆེན་རྒྱལ་པོ་དང་དགུང་གནམས་སྔོན་མོ་འདྲ་འདུག་། བུ་མོ་ང་དང་སྤྲང་ཆར་གཟིམ་ཕྲུག་འདྲ་བ་འདུག་། སྤྲང་ཆར་གཟིང་བུ་ང་ལ་གར་འབབས་དང་འདིར་འབབས་མི་འདུག་པ། གར་འབབས་འདིར་འབབ་མེད་བུ་མོ་ཡི་མིང་པོ་གཟིགས་ལེགས་སྟེ། ནམ་འཇུག་སྤྲང་ཆར་དོག་མི་ས་ལ་ལྷུང་ཉེན་འདུག་། ཡུམ་ཆེན་ཨ་མའི་ལུས་དང་ཚོ་སྟོད་ཐོན་པོ་འདྲ་བ་འདུག་། བུ་མོ་ང་ཡི་ལུས་དང་ཉ་ཆུང་སེར་མིག་འདྲ་བ་འདུག་། ཉ་ཆུང་སེར་དམིག་ང་ལ་གར་འགྲོ་དང་འདིར་འགྲོ་མི་འདུག་པ། གར་འགྲོ་དང་འདིར་འགྲོ་མེད་པ་བུ་མོའི་མིང་པོ་གཟིགས་ལེགས་སེ། ནམ་འཇུག་སེར་མིག་ཅིགི་ལག་ཏུ་འཚོར་པ་འདུག་། བོ་ངའི་(༡༤)མིང་པོ་འི་ལུས་དང་རི་རྒྱལ་ལྷུན་པོ་འདྲ་བ་འདུག་། བུ་མོ་ང་ཡི་ལུས་དང་རི་དྭགས་འདྲ་བ་འདུག་། རི་དྭགས་ང་ལ་གར་འགྲོ་དང་འདིར་འགྲོ་མི་འདུག་པས། གར་འགྲོ་འདིར་འགྲོ་མེད་པ་ཕྱོའི་མི་ངོ་གཟིགས་ལེགས་སེ། ནམ་འཇུག་ཕོན་པ་ཁྱིར་ར་པ་ཅི་གི་ལག་ཏུ་འཚོར་པ་འདུག་། བོད་བློན་རིག་པ་ཅན་དང་ཟ་འདྲེ་གདུག་པ་ཙན་དང་འདྲ་བ་འདུག་། བུ་མོ་ང་ཡི་ལུས་དང་ཚེ་ཟང་ཅིག་དང་འདྲ་བ་འདུག་། ཚེ་ཟང་ང་ལ་གར་འཆིས་དང་འདིར་འཆི་མི་འདུག་པ།

གར་ཆིས་འདིར་འཆི་མེད་པ་ཕྱོ་འི་མིང་པོ་གཟིགས་ལེགས་སེ། ཨ་ཅེ་ང་བོད་ཀྱིས་ཡུལ་དུ་འཆི་བ་འདྲ། ཨ་ཅེ་མིང་ཆུང་སྐྱབ་ཕྲུག་ལེགས་པའི་དྲུང་ནས་ཁྱེན། ཡབ་ཆེན་རྒྱལ་པོའི་དྲུངས་དུ་ཞུ་བ་འཕུལ་གྲོགས་མཛོད། ཡུམ་ཆེན་ཨ་མའི་དྲུང་དུ་ཞུ་བ་འཕུལ་གྲོགས་མཛོད། འོ་ཀོ་ལྷམ་སྲིང་གཉིས་ལས་སོན་བྲལ་མ་སྟོང་ཞུ་གྲོགས་མཛོད། ཡབ་ཡུམ་ཕ་མ་ཅིགི་ཁོག་སྙིང་དྲོན་མོ་མན་ལེགས་སེ། ཁོང་སྙིང་དྲོན་མོ་སྟོན་ནས་བོད་ལ་ཚོང་པ་ཕོང་ལེགས་སམ། ཡབ་ཡུམ་མཁྱེན་ནོ་གསུང་ཞིང་བུ་མོའི་མིང་པོ་ཞུ་གྲོགས་མཛོད། རྒྱ་ཡི་མི་རྣམས་ལ་ཞུ་བ་འཕུལ་གྲོགས་མཛོད། བོད་བློན་རིག་པ་ཅན་ལ་གཏམ་ཅིག་ལབ་(༡༥)གྲོགས་མཛོད། བོད་ཀྱི་ཡུལ་ལ་ལོགས་ཅིག་གསུངས་གྲོགས་མཛོད། ཨ་ཅེ་མིང་ཆུང་སྐྱབ་ཕྲུག་ཡ་ལེགས་པའི་

བྱུངས་ནས་ཁྱེན། ཁྱེད་པར་ཡབ་ཡུམ་སྲས་གསུམ་བཀའ་གྲོས་བྱེད་པ་ལ། ཨ་ཅི་བོད་ལ་གནང་བའི་བཀའ་གྲོས་མ་དཔེ་ཅིག། འདི་ཡན་ཆད་མིང་པོའི་བྱུང་དུ་ཞུ་བ་འཕུལ་པའོ།

འདི་མན་ཆད་མིང་པོའི་ཞུ་ལན་གནང་པའོ།

ང་ཡི་ཨ་ཅི་མཛངས་བྱེད་རྗེ་བཙུན་སྒྲོལ་མ་ཀྱུར་བསན་དང་། མིང་ཚོག་ལྷ་ཡི་སྲས་མོ་ཀྱུར་ཉོན་མཛོད། བདག་མིང་པོ་རང་དབང་དུ་སོང་ན་དག། བདག་ལ་བསམ་རྒྱུ་ཨ་ཅི་ཁྱེད་ལས་མེད་ལེགས་སྟེ། ཡབ་ཡུམ་གཉིས་ཀྱིས་སྣན་ནི་དར་ལས་སྲ་པར་དུག། བོད་ཀྱིས་བློན་པོ་ཡི་མཆུ་ནི་རྫོང་ལས་རྣོ་བ་གདའ། དར་སྲབ་རྫོང་མཆུ་བདེབས་སྡེབས་ནས། ཨ་ཅི་བོད་ལ་གཤེགས་དགོས་ཡོད་པ་འདྲ། ཡབ་ཆེན་རྒྱལ་པོའི་བྱུང་དུ་ཞུ་བ་འབུལ་ལེགས་རྟེ། ཡབ་ཀྱི་བཀའ་ནི་ནམཁའི་ཐོག་དང་འདྲ་བ་འདུག།

ཐོག་མ་ལ་འབབ་པ་ང་མིང་པོའི་གནམ་དུ་མི་ཐོག་འདུག། ཡུམ་གྱིས་བྱུང་དུ་ཞུ་བ་འཕུལ་ལེགས་སྟེ། ཡུམ་གྱིས་བཀའ་ནི་རི་གཟར་སྲབ་དང་འདྲ། སྲབ་ཐུར་ལ་ཡོང་པ་ང་(༡༤)མིང་པོའི་གྱེན་ལ་མི་ཐོག་འདུག། རྒྱ་ནག་ལྷ་བདེ་དང་མི་བདེ་ཞུ་བ་ལ་སྨྲན་ལེགས་ཀྱང་།། རྒྱ་ནག་ལྷ་བདེ་དང་མི་བདེ་འི་གཉིས་པ་ཡང་། ཕ་མ་ཡབ་ཡུམ་གཉིས་ཀྱིས་དབང་བ་འདུག། བོད་སྟོན་རིག་པ་ཅན་ལ་གཏམ་ཅིག་ལེབས་ལབ་ལེགས་སྟེ། བོད་བློན་རིག་པ་ཅན་དང་སྙིད་སེར་ནླུང་པོ་འདྲ་པ་འདུག། ནླུང་པོ་སྟོང་པ་ལ་ང་མིང་པོའི་ཞབས་པ་མི་ཐེབས་འདུག། ངའི་ཨ་ཅིའི་བྱུང་དུ་ང་མིང་པོའི་དཔེ་དང་ལྡན་པའི་ཞུ་བ་འཕུལ་ལེགས་ཀྱིས། རྒྱལ་བུའི་ལྷམ་ར་སྐྱེས་པའི་མེ་ཏོག་གསུམ་ཙམ་གདའ། གུར་ཁུམ་མེ་ཏོག་དེ་དང་ཅིག། ཧྭ་ལོ་མེ་ཏོག་དེ་དང་གཉིས། སེར་ཆེན་མེ་ཏོག་དེ་དང་གསུམ། ཁྲུངས་ས་ལྷུམ་ར་ཡིན་ཕ་པར་འདུག། མེ་ཏོག་ལྷུམ་རའི་ནང་དུ་ཚར་ཙང་ཀྱང་། ཁྲུངས་ས་ལྷུམ་ར་ཡིན་ཀྱང་སྡང་དབང་མི་འདུག་པ། སྤྱིར་གཙུག་ལག་ཁང་གི་རྒྱན་དུ་ཆེ། དགོས་ཆོད་མཆོད་ཁང་ཕྲ་མའི་སྒྲུན་གཟིས་ཡིན་པ་འདྲ། དཔེ་དེ་དང་ལྡན་པའི་ཞུ་བ་འཕུལ་ལེགས་ཀྱིས། ངའི་ཨ་ཅིའི་ཡུལ་རྒྱ་ནག་བཀྲིས་ཁྲི་སྒོ་ཡིན་པ་འདུག། འཁྲུངས་ས་སྐྱ་མཁར་དགུ་རི་དགུ་ཐོག་ཡིན་པར་འདུག། སྐྱེས་པའི་(༡༥)ཕ་ཡུལ་རྒྱ་ནག་བཀྲིས་ཁྲི་སྒོ་ཡིན་ཀྱང་བཞུགས་དབང་མི་འདུག་པ། འཁྲུངས་ས་སྐྱ་མཁར་དགུ་རི་དགུ་ཐོག་ཡིན་ཀྱང་འཛིན་དབང་མི་འདུག་པ། ཨ་ཅི་སྤྱིར་བོད་ཁ་བ་ཅན་གྱི་རྒྱན་དུ་ཆེ་པ་འདུག། དགོས་རྒྱལ་པོ་སྲོང་བཙན་སྒམ་པའི་དཔལ་དུ་ཆེ་བ་འདུག། དཔེ་དེ་ལ་བསམ་ལ་ཨ་ཅི་བོད་ཁ་བ་ཅན་ལ་གཤེགས། བཏན་གྲོགས་རྒྱལ་པོ་དང་དུ་བཞེས་མཛོད་གཅིག། ང་མིང་པའི་ཁ་སྟེས་སྟེན་དཀར་ཡིན་ལེགས་སྟེ། ཨ་ཅི་ཐུགས་ལ་ཐོག་པར་བྱུང་ན་བཟོད་པར་གསོལ་མཛོད་ཅིག།། འདི་ཡན་ཆད་མིང་པོའི་གསུང་པའོ།།

འདི་མན་ཆད་རྒྱལ་ཟའི་ཡབ་ཡུམ་གཉེན་འཁོར་རྣམས་ལ་ཞུ་བ་འཕུལ་པའོ།།

ཡབ་ཆེན་ཨ་བ་གསེར་ཁྲི་ཁ་ན་ཀྱུར་བསན་དང་། ཡུམ་ཆེན་ཨ་མའི་གཡུ་ཁྲི་ཁ་ན་ཀྱུར་བསན་

དང་། མིང་ཆུང་སྐྱབ་སྐྱུག་ལེགས་པ་དུང་ཁྲི་ཁ་ན་ཚུར་བསན་དང་། མ་གྲོགས་རབ་སྟན་སྨན་
དང་རབ་འབྱོར་སྨན། དྲན་པའི་གསེར་འཛིན་མ་དང་གསུམ། ཁྲི་རྨ་བྲ་འཛོམ་མའི་ཁ་
ན་ཚུར་གསན་དང་། བོད་བློན་རིག་པ་ཅན་སྟག་སྟན་དམར་པོའི་ཁ་ན་གསན་མཛོད་གཅིག།
བུ་མོ་(༡༨)ཚོགས་མ་བསགས་ང་ས་པདྨ་འདབ་བརྒྱད་ཀྱི་ཁ་ན་ཞུ་བ་འཕུལ་ལེགས་ཀྱིས། ཡབ་
ཆེན་ཨ་བ་རྒྱ་ནག་རྒྱལ་པོ་ལེགས། བུ་མོ་ང་འཛིག་རྟེན་མི་ཆོས་བྱེད་པ་ལ། བོད་ཁ་བ་
ཅན་དུ་འགྲོ་པ་ལ། བུ་མོ་ཤ་བ་སྨུག་ཅུང་བཞིན་དུ་ལ་དགུ་ལུང་དགུ་རྒྱབ་ནས་འགྲོ་ལེགས་
ཀྱི། ཡབ་ཆེན་རྒྱལ་བའི་ཐུགས་དགོངས་ཇོགས་པར་མཛོད། ཡུམ་ཆེན་ཨ་མ་ཁྲི་ལྷམ་
རྒྱལ་མོ་ཚུར་གསན་དང་། བུ་མོ་ང་ཉ་ཆུང་སེར་མིག་བཞིན་དུ་ཆུ་བོའི་ཞུང་ལ་ཞྒེབས་
ལེགས་ཀྱིས། ཡུམ་ཆེན་ཨ་མའི་ཐུགས་དགོངས་ཇོགས་པར་མཛོད། ཨ་ཅེའི་མིང་ཆུང་
སྐྱབ་ཐུག་ལེགས་པར་ཚུར་གསན་དང་། ཨ་ཅེ་ང་ལྷབ་བྱ་གོང་མོ་བཞིན་དུ་རི་བོའི་རྩེ་ལ་འགྲོ་
ལེགས་ཀྱི་། མིང་ཆུང་གཉིས་ཀྱི་ཐུགས་དགོངས་ཇོགས་པར་མཛོད། ཨ་གྲོགས་
དཔུན་གསུམ་ཚུར་ཉོན་དང་། བུ་མོ་ང་གཡག་རྐན་རོག་པོ་བཞིན་དུ་འཛམ་ལ་བྱིང་ལེགས་
ཀྱིས། ཨ་གྲོགས་སྤུན་གསུམ་གྱི་ཐུགས་དགོངས་ཇོགས་པར་མཛོད། བོད་བློན་རིག་པ་
ཅན་ཁྱོད་ཚུར་ཉོན་དང་། ང་ཡི་སྐྱིད་ལ་གཟེར་བའི་གྲི་བུ་ཡ་མཚན་ཅན། ཡབ་ཆང་
རྒྱལ་བའི་ཕྱག་ནས་གནང་་ཡིན། ཁྲ་དང་བཟུང་པ་ཡུམ་ཆེན་ཨ་མའི་གནང་བ་ཡིན།
(༡༩) གསེར་པོ་གསེར་ཀྱིས་གྲི་བུ་ལ། མ་ཁམ་པ་དངུལ་གྱི་ཡུ་བ་ཅན། དམར་པོའི་བྱེ་
རུའི་ཟུང་པ་ལ་གཡུ་ཆུང་ཁྲུག་དམར་གྱིས་ཁྲ་ལེགས་རྒྱབ། དེ་འདྲའི་གྲི་བུ་ཡ་མཚན་ཅན།
བུ་མོ་གནས་དུས་སོ་ལ་ཡོད་པའི་ཡའི་དུས། ཚོགས་མ་བསགས་ང་ཡི་འཕྱོར་གྲི་ཡིན་ལེགས་ཏེ།
ད་གྲི་གྲི་གུ་ཁྱོད་ལ་འཕྱོར་གྲི་བྱེད་པའི་གཏིང་མ་བགྱི། བུ་རང་གྲོགས་རང་བཙོད་པའི་གཤེད་
མ་གྲི་གུ་ཁྱོད། འཇུགས་ཡང་ན་ཕྱིན་གཡེས་པའི་སྙིངས་སུ་འཇུགས། བུ་མོ་རང་སྲོག་རང་
གིས་གཙོད་ལགས་པ། བོད་ཀྱི་རྒྱལ་པའི་ཐུགས་དགོས་ཇོགས་པར་མཛོད། ཁྱོད་གྱི་བློན་པོ་ཡང་
ཁོ་ཐག་ཆོད་པར་གྱིས། ཕ་མ་ཡབ་ཡུམ་གཉིས་པོ་གཏམ་ངན་གྱི་ཐུང་པར་མཛོད། བུ་མོ་
ཚོང་མ་ཚོགས་བསགས་ང་ཚོའི་ཐུང་པར་བྱེད། ཅེས་གསུངས་ནས་ཐུགས་ཁར་གྲི་གུ་གཙུགས་
སོང་པ་ཡབ་ཡུམ་སྲས་གསུམ་ནི་ཧད་དེ་ཆད་དེས་ལུས་འདུག། བློན་པོ་གཞན་རྣམས་ནི་གཅིག་
སྡོང་ཅིག་ལ་ཆེར་ཆེན་འདུག་པ་དང་། བོད་བློན་རིག་པ་ཅན་དེ་ཀ་པའི་མདུན་ན་ཏོག་
བཞངས་ནས། རྒྱལ་ཟའི་འགྲུལ་ནས་གཟུངས་ནས་ཞུ་བ་འདི་ལྟར་འཕུལ་ལོ། འཇང་
(༢༠)མ་བླ་ཅིག་རྒྱལ་ཟ་ཚུར་གསན་དང་། དཔོན་མོ་བོད་ཁ་བ་ཅན་ལ་མི་གཤེགས་ནས་འང་།
རང་སྲོག་རང་གི་གཙོད་པ་ཐོད་ལེགས་སོ། དལ་འབྱོར་མི་ལུས་ཐོབས་པའི་བཀའ་ལེས་ལ།
ཐོབས་ཧིང་རང་སྲོག་རང་གི་གཙོད་པ་ཐོད་ལེགས་སོ། རང་སྲོག་རང་གི་གཙོད་པ་ཐོད་ལེགས་

ཀྱང་། སྐྱེས་བ་ལྔ་རྒྱ་དགྱལ་བ་ཐར་མེད་དུ་སྐྱེས་པའི་དཔེ་ཅིག་གདའ། ཁྱད་པར་རྒྱ་ནག་རྒྱལ་པོའི་གདུང་རྒྱུད་འཛིན་པ་འདི། ལྷ་ཁང་ལོགས་ལ་སྲུན་མ་གཏོར་བ་དང་འདྲ་པ་འདུག། རྒྱལ་ཟའི་གདུང་རྒྱུད་མི་ཟིན་ཟིན་པའི་གཙུག་ལེག་ལ། ཟིན་ཏིང་རང་སྲོག་རང་གི་གཅོད་པ་ཕོད་ལེགས་སེ། ཅི་ཀྱང་མི་གསན་རང་སྲོག་རང་གི་གཅོད་ཟད་ནས། ཤ་བ་སླུག་ཙུང་བཞིན་དུ་ལ་དགུ་ལུང་དགུ་རྒྱབ་ནས་འགྲོ་ཟེར་ནས། ཡབ་ཆེན་རྒྱལ་པའི་ཐུགས་དགོངས་རྫོགས་ཉེན་ཡོང་། ང་སློན་པོ་ཁོ་ཐག་མི་མཆོད་དོ།།

iii. Karchhags,

a.Karchhag, village of Kyis, King of Ladakh, Tshe-dbang rNam-rgyal, 1575-1595.

གངས་ཅན་ཞིང་རྟའི་སྲོལ་བྱེད་རྟོང་ཁ་པ། མངོན་རྟོགས་རིག་པའི་དབང་ཕྱུག་རྒྱལ་མཚབ་རྗེ། མདོ་སྔགས་བདག་པོ་མཁས་གྲུབ་རྗེས། རྒྱལ་བ་ཡབ་སྲས་གསུམ་ལ་གུས་ཕྱག་འཚལ། ""ཡོ་བྲང་ཆེན་པོ་ཐོ་ལ་ཡང་པའི་ནང་། རྒྱལ་ས་ཆེན་པོ་ཁྲི་ཆེན་དཔལ་མཁར་རྩེར། ཆོས་རྒྱལ་ཆེན་པོ་ཚེ་དབང་རྣམ་རྒྱལ་གྱི། དབུ་རྨོག་ཐོ་ཞིང་ཆབ་སྲིད་རྒྱས་གྱུར་ཅིག། ཁོང་གི་མངའ་འོག་ཟང་པོ་སྐྱི་ དྲི་འདིར། སླུ་མཁར་ཐོ་ལ་རྩན་པ་རྒྱལ་ས་གྲག་མཁར་རྩེར། མཁར་དཔོན་ཆེན་པོ་བསྟན་སྐྱོང་མགྱ་མཚོ་འི། སྐུ་ཚེ་བསྟན་ཞིང་། ཆབ་སྲིད་རྒྱས་གྱུར་ཅིག། དགོན་པ་ཁྱད་འཕགས་ནོར་བུ་དགེ་ཕེལ་ན། དཔོན་སློབ་ཆེན་པོ་བློ་བཟང་དོན་བགྲུབ་ཀྱི།ཆོས་རྒྱུག་མཐོ་ཞིང་གྲྭ་

བརྟན་དར་གྱུར་ཅིག།ཡུལ་གཡང་ཆགས་ཀྱིད་པའི་ཀྱིས་འདི་རུ། ཕུ་རུ་རྩེ་

བཅུད་རྒྱས་ཞིང་། མདོ་རུ་འབྲུ་རྣམས་སྨིན།།

9 Kinnaur (Khunu)

iii. a. Kamru image inscription in Bhoti:

The following inscription is taken from the photo of the inscription in (Amy Heller, 2008: 114, internet source

པན་བྲི་ཏ་བྲི་ཏྲ་བ་དྲས་ཕྱུག་ལེན་མཛད། མཆིར་བློན་ཆེ་ཀླུ་མགོན་མཆེད་

ཡུམ་སྲས་ཀྱིས་ཡོན་བདག་བགྱིས་ནས་ཆོས་འདས་པ་མཆིར་བློན་ཆེ་ཤུས་

པུན་གྱི་བསོད་ནམས་སུ།རིགས་གསུམ་གྱི་སྐུ་བཞེངས་སུ་གསོལ་བས།

ཆོས་འདས་ལ་དད་པའ་བྱུས་པའི་སེམས་ཅན་ཐམས་ཅད་སྒྲིབ་པ་བྱང་གྱུརད་

ཅིག།).

iii. b. རྒྱལ་བ་འབར་ར་བ་ན་མཁའི་རྡོ་རྗེ་ལ་ན་མོ།

iv. Karchhags gathered by Rahul Sankrityayan: Translcription from Devanagari into Bhoti.

a. Raja Vijay Singh (1696-1719).

གུ་གེ་ཞང་ཞུང་དམ་ཆོས་དར་གནས་འདིར། །དཔག་མེད་
བསོད་ ནམས་ལྷུན་གྲུབ་མི་འི་བདག། མང་པོས་བཀུར་བའི་གདར་གྲུད་
ཐྲ་ན་མེད། རིན་ཆེན་(244)བཟང་པོ་ཞབས་ཀྱིས་བཅགས་པའི་གནས།
ཡུལ་ལ་དགེ་བཅུ་འཛོམས་པོའི་དབྱངས་ཡུལ་མོ་ན་འདིར། ---

གནམས་སའི་བདག་པོ་བི་རྡེར་སིང་གི་མངའ་འོག་ན། ཡོན་གི་བདག་པོ་ཨ་སི་དང་། ཨ་སོལ་དང་། ཨས་མོལ་དང་། རོང་མོལ་དང་། ར་མོན་དང་། ཁུ་དུ་དང་། དལ་ལྷན་ཡོ་ནེ་གྱི་བདག་མོ་ཀོ་ཡུལ་དང་། གནས་སའི་མཆོག་གྱུར་ཟུང་མོ་དང་། ས་དཔོན་ནེ་དང་། ས་རོ་ཟེ་དང་། ཧེ་ཕུར་དག་ནོ་ཀྱི་དང་། ཀོན་ཏང་དང་། ཨ་རྫེ་དང་བི་རོམ་དང་། རྙོ་འདའ་ར་དང་། རྒུ་ཙུ་དང་། དགེ་སློང་དང་། གནལ་འབྱོར་དང་། དེ་རྣམས་ཆོས་ཕྱིར་སྟོང་བ་ངོམ་མཚར་ཆེ།། (Rahul Sankrityayan, 1956: 243-244).

b. **Raja Ugar Singh, 1844-1878.** སྟོན་པ་བཆོས་སུངས་རྡོ་རྗེ་གདན་གི་བྱང་། ཁ་བ་ཅན་ལྗོངས་དམ་ཆོས་དར་བའི་གནས། ཏི་སེ་མཆོད་རྟེན་དགྲ་ཅོམ་བཞུགས་པའི་གནས། མ་བང་གཡུ་མཚོ་དངོས་གྲུབ་ཁྲུས་ཀྱི་རྫིང་། ཀྱི་ལེགས། རིན་ཆེན་བཟང་པོའི་ཞབས་ཀྱི་(245)བཅགས་པའི་གནས། བློ་བསང་གྲགས་པའི་བསྟན་པ་དར་བའི་གནས། ཆུ་ཆེན་ང་ལ་འབབ་གླང་པོ་ཁ་འབབ་ཅན། ཆུ་ཡི་གཡང་ར་ཞུང་བཞུང་ལྷའི་ལྗོངས། ཁྱུང་རྫོངས་སྤྱུ་ཕྲོ་རིན་ཆེན་ལྷུན་པོའི་ངོས།---གང་---ནམ་ལྷུན་གྲུབ་ནུས་མཐོང་སྨོན་གནས། སོ་ར་རང་ན། གཏམ་པའི་བདག་པོ་རྒྱལ་པོ་སའི་དཔལ་གྱི་མདང་ངོག་ན། ཀྱི་ལེགས། ཡུལ་ལ་དགེ་བཙུ་འཛོམས་པའི་ཆེད་དཀུལ་འདེར། ནེ་རིགས་ཁྲུངས་བཙུན་ཆ་ནའ་རྒྱུད། དང་ལྡན་ཡོན་གྱི་བདག་པོ་རྫོ་དགུ་དང་། རིག་པའི་གནས་ལང་པ་ལ་

ཁས་པའི་སྲུས་པོའི་ཆག་གྱུར་སི་རྗོན་དང་། ལྷ་ཕྱུག་བཞོ་ནུ་འདད་བང་དགྲོ་མོན་དང་། རྒྱ་གར་པ་སང་འདྲ་བའི་ཨ་ལོ་དང་། པངས་ལ་མེ་ཏོག་འབར་བ་འདྲ་བའི་ཀལ་ཀེ་དང་། སྲུས་པོའི་ཚོག་གྱུར་ཨོ་ཧྲུན་དང་། (246)བསྲིན་པའི་བདག་མོ་པོ་ཧེ་དང་། གནའ་མའི། ཚོག་གྱུར་སེ་མོར་དང་། ---སྲུ---ཅང་དང་གོན་ཙོག་ཚེ་རིང་དང་། མིའུ་རི་དང་། ཧོ་པོ་བསང་མོ་སྐྱིད་དང་ས་བི་དང་། ཧུར་ཟ་དང་གུང་ནི་གཉིས་(གསུམ)་ཀྱི་དོན་དུ་ཕགས་རྒྱ་སྟོང་བཞེང་-p. 244.

--- རྒྱལ་པོའི་ཕལ་ཁལ་མཉིས་ཡེ་བཞི་ཞུང་ཁང་ཡོའ། ...ཆོས་རྒྱ་སྟོང་བ་པྱིས་སྐུལ་ཁུན་ན་ཀེ་འདས་ར་ནས་སྟོས་ཡིན་ནི་ལྷ་ལ་ཙུ་གཉིས་སྟོང་ལ་ཡུལ་རྒྱ་ཙུ་འཛོན་རྒྱལ་ཆེན་པོ་མོ་ཏེ་ཏུ་རྒྱལ་པོ་འུ་བུར་སིང་---སྲིན་འབས་དག་པོ་འཇྲན་མྱོ་ནོར་ངས་ཨ་པ་མིང་པུ་ཅ་མིང་འཇུ་དས་དང་རྨ་ས་འིས་ཡང་ཕྱུ་གུ་མིང་ནི་ཁྲ་ཀུར་འདས་(The language is very bad. . . -Rahul).

c. Raja Shamsher Singh, 1907-(?).

ཁྱིམ་གཉིས་ལྡན་པར་ཆོས་རྒྱལ་སམ་སེར་སིང་།མིའི་དབང་ཕྱུག་ཆེན་པོ་དེ་ལ་བསྟོང་།ཆོས་རྒྱལ་དེ་འི་ཆབ་སིང་བགྲུས་གྱུར་ཅིག། ···ལྷ་མི་ཀུན་གྱིས་མངོན་དུ་དགའ་བ་སྣང་བའི་བཀའ་སློན་ནི་རོན་མ་ཧྲར་ཕོང་ལ་སྟོང་། (Rahul, 1956: 243-245).

10 Kullu

i. Bhoti Inscription on stone from Dhomya Rishi Temple, Jagatsukh, c. first quarter of twentieth century C.E.

བཅོམ་འདོན་ནཏན།

སྟོན་པའི་ས་ཕྱོགས་འདིར་དེ་ན་ལྷ་དང་མི་དང་ལྷ་མ་ཡིན་དུ་བཅས་"པའི་འཇིག་
རྟེན་གྱི་མཆོད་རྟེན་དུ་འགྱུར་བ་ཡིན་ན་སུ་ཞིག་ཆོས་ཀྱི་རྣམ་གྲངས་འདི་ལེན་པ
'དང་། འདྲི་བ་དང་། འཛིན་པ་དང་། འཆད་པ་དང་། ཀློག་པ་དང་།
ཀུན་ཆུབ་པ་དང་། བྱེད་པ་དང་། ཚུལ་བཞིན་དུ་ཡིད་ལ་བྱེད་པ་ངོ་མཚར་
རབ་དང་ལྡན་པར་གྱུར་བ་ལྟ་ཅི་སྨོས། ས་ཕྱོགས་དེ་ན་སྟོན་པའམ་བླ་མ་ལྟ་
བུ་གར་ཡང་རུང་བར་གནས་སོ། དེ་སྐད་ཅེས་བཀའ་སྩོལ་བ་དང་བཅོམ་ལྡན་
འདས་ལ་ཚེ་དང་ལྡན་པ་རབ་འབྱོར་གྱིས་འདི་སྐད་ཅེས་གསོལ་ཏོ། བཅོམ་
ལྡན་འདས་ཆོས་ཀྱི་རྣམ་གྲངས་འདི་འི་མིང་ཅི་ལགས། འདི་ཇི་ལྟར་བཟུང་
བར་བགྱི། དེ་སྐད་ཅེས་གསོལ་བ་དང་། བཅོམ་ལྡན་འདས་ཀྱིས་ཚེ་དང་ལྡན་

པ་རབ་འབྱོར་ལ་འདི་སྐད་ཅེས་བཀའ་སྩལ་ཏོ། རབ་འབྱོར་ཆོས་ཀྱི་རྣམ་གྲངས་འདིའི་མིང་ཤེས་རབ་ཀྱི་ཕ་རོལ་ཏུ་ཕྱིན་པ་ཞེས་བྱ་སྟེ། འདི་དེ་ལྟར་ཟུངས་ཤིག། དེ་ཅིའི་ཕྱིར་ཞེ་ན། རབ་འབྱོར་དེ་བཞིན་གཤེགས་པས་ཤེས་རབ་ཀྱི་ཕ་རོལ་ཏུ་ཕྱིན་པ་གང་གསུངས་པ་དེ་ཉིད་ཕ་རོལ་ཏུ་ཕྱིན་པ་མེད་པའི་ཕྱིར་ཏེ། དེས་ན་ཤེས་རབ་ཀྱི་ཕ་རོལ་ཏུ་ཕྱིན་པ་ཞེས་བྱ་འོ། རབ་འབྱོར་འདི་ཇི་སྙམས་དུ་སེམས། དེ་བཞིན་གཤེགས་པས་གསུངས་པའི་ཆོས་གང་ཡང་ཡོད་སྙམ་མམ། རབ་འབྱོར་གྱིས་གསོལ་པ། བཅོམ་ལྡན་འདས་དེ་བཞིན་གཤེགས་པས་གསུངས་པ་འི་ཆོས་གང་ཡང་མ་མཆིས་ལགས་སོ།

བཅོམ་ལྡན་འདས་ཀྱིས་བཀའ་སྩལ་བ་རབ་འབྱོར་འདི་ཇི་སྙམ་དུ་སེམས། སྟོང་གསུམ་གྱི་སྟོང་ཆེན་པོའི་འཇིག་རྟེན་གྱི་ཁམས་ན་སའི་རྡུལ་ཇི་སྙེད་ཡོད་པ་དེ་མང་བ་ཡིན་སྙམ་མམ། རབ་འབྱོར་གྱིས་གསོལ་པ། བཅོམ་ལྡན་འདས་སའི་རྡུལ་དེ་མང་ལགས་སོ། བདེ་བར་གཤེགས་པ་མང་ལགས་སོ། དེ་ཅིའི་སླད་དུ་ཞེ་ན་བཅོམ་ལྡན་འདས་སའི་རྡུལ་གང་ལགས་པ་རྡུལ་མ་མཆིས་པར་དེ་བཞིན་གཤེགས་པསཧ་སྒྲ་ཁྲི་གསུངས་པའི་སླད་དུ་སྟེ། དེས་ན་སའི་

རྒྱལ་ཞེས་བགྱི་འོ།   འཇིག་རྟེན་གྱི་ཁམས་ལགས་པ་དེ་དག་ཁམས་མ་མཆིས་པར་དེ་བཞིན་གཤེགས་པས་གསུངས་པའི་སླད་དུ་སྟེ། དེས་ན་འཇིག་རྟེན་གྱི་ཁམས་ཞེས་བགྱི་འོ། བཅོམ་ལྡན་འདས་ཀྱིས་བཀའ་སྩལ་བ། རབ་འབྱོར་འདི་ཇི་སྙམ་"དུ་སེམས།སྐྱེས་བུ་ཆེན་པོ་མཚན་སུམ་ཅུ་རྩ་གཉིས་དེ་དག་གིས་དེ་བཞིན་གཤེགས་པ་དགྲ་བཅོམ་པ་ཡང་དག་པར་རྫོགས་པའི་སངས་རྒྱས་སུ་བྱར་ཅིག།

ii. Prayer Offerings (gSol-'debs), to the Great Pilgrimage place of Lotus-Lake of Zahor Country, Riwalsar, c. C.E. 1643 (?).

ཟ་ཧོར་ཡུལ་གྱི་གནས་ཆེན་མཚོ་པདྨའི་གསོལ་འདེབས་བཞུགས་སོ།།

ཨོཾ་ཨཱཿཧཱུྃཿ

(1)འོག་མིན་ཆོས་ཀྱི་དབྱིངས་ཀྱི་ཕོ་བྲང་དུ།།

འཇའ་འོད་ཐིག་(ཐིགས་ལེའི)་ལེ་ལྷ་ལྷུན་གཞལ་ཡས་ལྟར་།།

སྟོན་པ་ཆོས་སྐུ་ཀུན་བཟང་ཡབ་ཡུམ་ལ།།

ཆོས་སྐུའི་ཚོམ་བུ་འབུམ་ཕྲག་འཁོར་(L.2)གྱིས་བསྐོར།།

ཐུགས་རྗེས་(ཐུགས་རྗེ)་གཟིགས་ཤིག་ཨོ་རྒྱན་སྤྲུལ་པའི་སྐུ།།

བདག་དང་མཁའ་མཉམ་(མཉམས)་སེམས་ཅན་(L.3)ཐམས་ཅད་

ཀྱིས(ཀྱི)།། མོས་གུས་གདུང་ཤུགས་(གཤུགས་)དྲག་པོས་(པོའི)་གསོལ་

བ་འདེབས།། འོད་གསལ་མ་བུ་(L.4)རང་ངོ་ཕྲོད་(འཕྲོད་)པར་

ཤོག་།

(2)ནུབ་ཕྱོགས་བདེ་ཆེན་དབང་གི་གཞལ་ཡས་སུ།། འོད་དཔག་མེད་(L.5)མགོན་པདྨ་རྣགའི་མདོག་། མཚན་བཟང་པོ་གཉིས་དཔེ་བྱད་བརྒྱད་བཅུས་བརྒྱན(བཅུའི་རྒྱན)།། (p.1b,L.6)ཕྱོགས་བཅུའི་སངས་རྒྱས་གྲངས་(གྲང་)མེད་འཁོར་གྱིས་བསྐོར།། ཕྱགས་རྗེས་(L.1)x།། བདག་དང་x།། མོས་གུས་x།།བདེ་ཆེན་ཞིང་དུ་སྐྱེ་བར་བྱིན་གྱིས་བས(བརློབས)།།

(3)གནས་ཆེན་རི་བོ་(L.2)ཏ་ལའི་ཕོ་བྲང་དུ།། སྟོང་ཉིད་སྙིང་རྗེ་མངའ་བདག་སྤྱན་རས་གཟིགས།། དཀར་གསལ་ལོངས་སྤྱོད་རྫོགས་པའི་(L.3)རྒྱན་གྱིས་སྤྲས།། ས་བཅུའི་བྱང་ཆུབ་སེམས་དཔའི་འཁོར་གྱིས་བསྐོར།། ཕྱགས་རྗེས་x།། བདག་དང་x།། མོས་(L.4)གུས་x།། བཅོས་མིན་སྙིང་རྗེ་སྐྱེ་བར་བྱིན་གྱིས་རློབས།།

(4)མི་སྤྱུང་(དཔུང་)མཚོར་གྱུར་།(བརྒྱུར་)པདྨའི་སྡོང་པོའི་དབུས།། (L.5)སྐྱེ་འཆི་གཉིས་སྤངས་(སྤང་)འགྲོ་མགོན་པདྨ་འབྱུང་།། སྐུ་གསུམ་རིགས་འདུས་འཇའ་འོད་ཀློང་ན་བཞུགས།།

རྒྱ་བོད་(p.2a,L.6)པཊ་(དཔན་)གྲུབ་རིག་འཛིན་བྱེ་བས་(བྱེ་
བའི་) བསྐོར།། ཐུགས་རྗེས་x།། བདག་དང་x།།མོས་གུས་x ||
འཕྲིན་ལས་རྣམ་བཞིས་(བཞི་)འགྲོ་འདུལ་བྱེད་པར་ཤོག་།(L.1)

(5)ཡུམ་ཆེན་སྤྲུལ་པ་ཡེ་ཤེས་མཚོ་རྒྱལ་མ།།
ཆོས་སྐུའི་མཁའ་འགྲོ་འབུམ་གྱི་དབུས་ན་བཞུགས།།
ཧཱ་རེ་འི་ཐུགས་སྤྲུལ་ལྷ་ལྕམ་མནྡཱ་ར།།　ཡེ་ཤེས་(L.2)མཁའ་འགྲོ་བྱེ་
བའི་འཁོར་གྱིས་བསྐོར།། ཐུགས་རྗེས་x།།　བདག་དང་།། མོས་གུས་།།
དབང་བཞི་མཐར་ཕྱིན་སྐུ་བཞི་མངོན་གྱུར་ཤོག (L.3)

(6)སླིང་དབུས་མི་ཤིགས་(ཤིག་)ཐིག་ལེའི་གཞལ་ཡས་སུ།།
བརྒྱུད་གསུམ་རྩ་གསུམ་རྣམ་རོལ་གཅིག་འདུས་པས།།
བཀའ་དྲིན་གསུམ་ལྡན་རྩ་བའི་བླ་མ་(L.4)ལ།།
རིག་རྩལ་ཞི་ཁྲོ་དམ་པ་རིགས་བརྒྱུས་(བརྒྱའི་)བསྐོར།།
ཐུགས་རྗེས་།། བདག་དང་།། མོས་གུས་།། རང་ངོ་རྣམ་བཞི་རང་གྲོལ་
ངོ་ཤེས་ཤོག (L.5)

(7)རྩ་དང་ཐིག་ལེའི་གཞལ་ཡས་ཆེན་པོ་རུ།། རྩ་གསུམ་བསྡུས་པའི་བཛ་ཡི་ཕོ་ཉ་བ།། མ་མགོན་གཟའ་རྡོར་(རྡོ་)མཆེད་ལྷ་དུར་ཁྲོད་བདག (p.2b,L.6)ཡེ་ཤེས་སྤྱན་ལྡན་ཆོས་སྐྱོང་(སྐྱོངས་)ཡོངས་རྫོགས་ལ།། ཐུགས་རྗེས་x།། བདག་དང་x།། མོས་གུས་(L.1)x།། འཕྲིན་ལས་མྱུར་འགྲུབ་དངོས་འགྲུབ་འཆར་འབེབས་ཤོག

(8)དྲི་མེད་ཡན་ལག་བརྒྱད་ལྡན་བདུད་བརྩིའི་མཚོ།། དཀར་སེར་(L.2)དམར་ལྗང་བྱ་རིགས་སྣ་ཚོགས་ཀྱིས(བཀྱིས)།། ཐིག་ཆེན་ཕྲན་བཞིའི་ཆོས་སྒྲ་འུར་རུ་རུ།། དཔག་བསམ་ལྗོན་ཤིང་མེ་ཏོག་སྣ་(L.3)ཚོགས་བཀྲ།། ཐུགས་རྗེས་x།། བདག་དང་xཀྱིས།། མོས་གུས་x།། སྣང་གྲགས་རིག་(རིགས་)གསུམ་བསྐྱེད་རྫོགས་མཐར་ཕྱིན་ཤོག (L.4)

(9)སྙིང་ན་བརྒྱུད་གསུམ་བླ་མ་སྤྲིན་ལྟར་བཏིབས།། བར་ན་ཡི་དམ་ལྷ་ཚོགས་འཆར་ལྟར་འབེབས།། མཐའ་བསྐོར་ཆོས་(L.5)སྐྱོང་(སྐྱོངས་)སྲུང་མ་གློག་ལྟར་འཁྱུག་།། ཛ་ཡབ་དཔལ་གྱི་རི་དང་གཉིས་སུ་མེད།། ཐུགས་རྗེས་x།། བདག་དང་x།། མོས་གུས་(p.3a,L.6)x།།དག་པའི་ཞིང་དུ་སྐྱེ་བར་བྱིན་གྱིས་རློབས(བརློབས)།།

(10)གནས་དེ་མཐོང་ཐོས་དྲན་པར་(པ་)ཙམ་གྱིས་ཀྱང་།།

ཚེ་རབས་(རབ་)(L.1)གནས་བསགས་སྡིག་སྒྲིབ་ཀུན་དག་ནས།།

སྐུ་གསུམ་མངོན་གྱུར་ཚེ་གཅིག་སངས་རྒྱས་ཐོབ།།

སྐད་(L.2)གཅིག་དྲན་པའི་སྡུག་བསྔལ་ཀུན་ནས་གྲོལ།།

ཐུགས་རྗེས་x།། བདག་དང་x།། མོས་གུས་x།།

རིགས་དྲུག་འཁོར་བའི་(L.3)སྐྱེ་སྒོ་ཆོད་པར་ཤོག་།།

(11)དེ་ལྟར་གསོལ་བཏབ་མཐུ་ནུས་བྱིན་རླབས་ཀྱིས།།

སྲིད་པའི་རྩེ་ནས་ན་རག་ཡན་ཆད་(L.4)དང་།།

ནམ་མཁའི་གར་ཁྱབ་སེམས་ཅན་ཐམས་ཅད་ཀྱིས(ཀྱི)།།

གདོད་མའི་མགོན་པོའི་རྒྱལ་སར་ཕྱིན་པར་ཤོག་།(L.5)

ཐུགས་རྗེ་x།། བདག་དང་x།། མོས་གུས་x།།

དངོས་གྲུབ་རྣམ་(རྣམས་)གཉིས་བྱིན་རླབས་འབྱུག་པར་ཤོག་།།

(12)གུ་རུའི་(p.3b,L.6)སྐུ་ཡི་བྱིན་བརླབས་ལུས་ལ་སྨོལ།།

བདག་དང་མཁའ་མཉམ་སེམས་ཅན་ཐམས་(L.1)ཅད་ཀྱི།། རྡོ་རྗེའི་

སྐུ་ལྟར་འགྲུབ་པར་(པ་)བྱིན་གྱིས་བརླབས།། གུ་རུའི་གསུང་གི་བྱིན་

རླབས་(L.2)ངག་ལ་སྩོལ།། བདག་དང་མཁའ་མཉམ་སེམས་ཅན་ཐམས་ཅད་ཀྱིས།། ཚངས་པའི་དབྱངས་ལྟར་འགྲུབ་པར་བྱིན་གྱིས་བརླབས།། (L.3) གུ་རུའི་ཐུགས་ཀྱི་བྱིན་རླབས་སེམས་ལ་སྩོལ།། བདག་དང་མཁའ་མཉམ་སེམས་ཅན་ཐམས་ཅད་ཀྱིས།། རང་སེམས་ཆོས་སྐུར་རྟོགས(L.4)་པར་བྱིན་གྱིས་བརླབས།།

(13) ཡོན་ཏན་ཀུན་འབྱུང་འཕྲིན་ལས་རྒྱ་མཚོ་ལྟར།།
རིང་པོར་མི་(L.5)ཐོགས་ཚེ་གཅིག་འདི་ཉིད་ལ།།
ཨོ་རྒྱན་པད་འབྱུང་ཁྱེད་ལྟར་གྲུབ་ནས་ཀྱང་།།
མཁའ་མཉམ་(p.4a,L.6)སེམས་ཅན་ཀུན་གྱི་དོན་བྱས་ནས།།
ཚེ་དང་བསྒྲུབ་པ་མཐའ་རུ་ཕྱིན་པར་ཤོག། བསླུ་མེད་དཀོན་མཆོག་(L.1)གསུམ་གྱི་བདེན་པ་དང་།། ཡི་དམ་ལྷ་ཚོགས་རྣམས་ཀྱི་བྱིན་རླབས་དང་།། མཁའ་འགྲོ་ཆོས་སྐྱོང་རྣམས་(L.2)ཀྱི་ནུས་མཐུ་ཡིས།། བདག་གིས་སྨོན་ལམ་གང་བཏབ་མྱུར་འགྲུབ་ཤོག།།

(14)གསོལ་འདེབས་སྨོན་ལམ་འདི་འང་(L.3)ཟ་ཧོར་ཡུལ་གྱི་གནས་ཆེན་རིག་འཛིན་པདྨའི་མེ་དཔུང་མཚོ་རུ་བསྒྱུར་བའི་གནས་ཆེན་ཁྱད་པར་ཅན་དུ་གནས་འབྲེལ་གྱི་སྐབས་སུ།། ཆུ་ཡོས་ཧོར་ཟླ་

དང་པོའི་(L.4)ཆོས་བཅུའི་ཉིན་ཚོགས་འཁོར་རྒྱ་ཆེན་སྐབས་སུ་ཆོས་གྲོགས་རྣམས་ཀྱིས་བསྐུལ་ངོར།། མི་ལྷོག་ཙམ་དུ་སྨང་སྐྱོན་རིག་འཛིན་པདྨ་ཀུན་བཟང་རྒྱ་མཚོས་སྦྱས་(L.5)པ། དགེའོ།། བཀྲ་ཤིས།། (p.4b,L.6).

13 Guge

i. Colophon to Tsarang Dorchhod, written complete book in gold ink, king Tashi Dagpa De, capital Tsarhang. རྡོ་རྗེ་གཅོད་པ།།

ཨོཾ་སྭསྟི་སིདྡྷཾ། དོན་གཉིས་ཐར་ཕྱིན་སྟོན་པ་སངས་རྒྱས་དང་། བསྒྲིབ་ གཉིས་མུན་སེལ་སྐྱོབ་པ་དམ་པའི་ཆོས། རིགས་གྲོལ་གཉིས་ལྡན་འཕགས་པའི་དགེ་འདུན་སྟེ། བླ་མེད་དཀོན་མཆོག་གསུམ་ལ་གུས་པའི་ཕྱག་འཚལ། ཨེ་མ་ཧོ། གླིང་གི་མཆོག་གྱུར་ལྷོའི་འཛམ་བུ་གླིང་། (བསྟན་པ་བྱུང་?)གནས་རྡོ་རྗེ་གདན་གྱི་བྱང་། ཏི་སེ་གངས་དང་མ་པང་མཚོ། (དགང་གའ་གཡར་འདྲན་?)འབབ་པའི་གཡས། ཞོ་བྲང་ཆེན་པོ། ཙ་ཧྲང་རྒྱལ་ས་འདིར། འོད་གསལ་རིགས་ཀྱི་འོད་དཀར་མ་ཉམས་པས། ཆོས་རྒྱལ་ཆེན་པོ་བཀྲ་ཤིས་གྲགས་པ་ལྡེ། མི་ཐུབ་ཕྱོགས་རྣམས་ཀུན་ལ་རྒྱལ་གྱུར་གཅིག། དེ་འདྲའི་ཆབ་སྲིད་རྒྱས་པའི་མངའ་འོག་ན། དགེ་བཅུ་འཛོམ་པའི་སྐྱིད་ཡུལ་ཤ་འང་འདིར། རིག་ཙུས་ཁྱད་འཕགས་པ་ཆེན་མང་ཡེར་གུང་ལྔོག་བརྒྱུད། སྐྱེས་པའི་མི་ལ་གྲགས་པའི་x། བདབ་ཡོངས་པ་བྱམས་རྩེ་ལྡན་པ་གཉེན་དྲུང་སྐྱོང་ལས་མཁས། ལམ་སྣ་ཟིན་གཞོན་ནུ་རབ་བྱུང་ཚུལ་ཁྲིམས་ལྡན་པ་ཡིས་ཤ་ཀྱ་དགེ་སློང་དོན་གྲུབ་དཔལ་བཟང་དང་······དཀོན་མཆོག་དཔལ་བཟང་གི་དྲིན་ཅན་མ་ཛ་

འདིག་རྟེན་པ་རོལ་སོང་། ·········སྐྱེས་མ་ཉེས་དམྱལ་བ་ལྟུང་ང་དོན་ནམ། གསུང་གི་མཆོག་གྱུར་རྡོ་རྗེ་གཅོད་དང་ནི་སྡིག་གཤགས་གསེར་གྱིས་སྦྱུ་གྲི་རིན་ཆེན་གསེར་ལས་བཞེངས། བསགས་པ་ཆས་ཧྲོང་བ་པོ་ཆེ། ཡོན་གྱི་བདག་མོ་ནུམོ་དཔལ་འཛོམ་གྱིས། མི་ཟག་ལྷའི་བདུད་རྩིས་འདྲེས། མཆོད་ནས་གཉིས་པའི་ཞབསརྟོག་དཔག་མེད་བསྒྲུབ། སྲིང་མོ་ཆོས་མཛད་ཀུན་དགའ་དཔལ་མོ། དམ་ཆོས་ཞབསརྟོག་དཔག་མེད་བསྒྲུབ། བུའི་མཆོག་གྱུར་བློ་བཟང་བཀྲ་བཤིས་དང་། བོ་མོ་བསམ་གྲུབ་དང་ནི་ཁྲི་ཀུག་དང་། ཕ་མ་བཞིན་དུ་ཆོས་ལ་དཀར་བར་ཤོག། གཞན་ཡང་གཉེན་དྲུང་ཡུལ་མི་ཁྲིམ་འཛས་རྣམས་ཀྱི་ཀྱང་། དགེ་རྩེ་དཀར་ཏུ་བྱས་པ་དེས་ཡིད་……དགེ་བ་འདིས་མ་གྱུར་སེམས་ཅན་རྣམས་མྱུར་དུ་བདེ་བ་ཅན་དུ་སྐྱེ་ བར་ཤོག།། ཨཾགཡོ།།

ii. Guge, Karchhag, Ga-ga Sonam, capital Khartse.

འཕགས་པ་འཇམ་དཔལ་གྱི་མཚན་ཡང་དག་པར་བརྗོད་པ། དགྲ་བཅོམ་བཞུགས་གནས། ཏི་སེ་གངས་ཀྱི་མགུལ། ཆུ་ཆེན་འབྲུག་པ་སེན་ཧྥ་བའི་གཡོན། ས་ལ་འབུར་ཐོ་རྒྱལ་ས་སྐྱ་ཁར་རྩེར། ག་ག་བསོད་ནམས། དབུ་རྗོག་མཐོ་བའི་དུས་ཁྱིད་ཀྱི་ཆབ་སྲིད་བཟང་པོའི་མངའ་འོག་ཏུ། ཀྱི་ལགས། ཡུལ་ལ་དགེ་བཙུ་འཛོམ་པའི་གླིང་ཁྲིམ་སུ། མི་རིགས་ཁྱུངས་བཙུན་ཕ་མ་སློན་ཆོས་རྒྱུད། ཡོན་གྱི་བདག་བསོད་ནམས་དཔལ་

འཛིན་དང་། དད་ལྡན་ཡོན་གྱི་བདག་པོ་ཚོས་འཁོར་ཚེ་རིང་དང་། ཡོན་གྱི་བདག་མོ་བཟང་སྐྱིད།།

14 Word Meanings and Notes

a-bi = Grandmother.

a-ku (sTod) = Uncle, father's younger brother.

a-khu = See a-ku.

al-to (sTod) = A small pitcher of the capacity of about three to five litres for keeping ghee, a-rag, chhang, etc. This could be earthen, metallic or wooden.

a-pi = See a-bi.

a-rag = Wine.

u-ṭhi, a-u-ṭhi, 'u-ṭhi = A metal container of copper or brass having capacity of about 30 litres for keeping chhang. It is a factory manufactured item and came from Amritsar. Likely of the origin of about early twentieth or last quarter of nineteenth century. It was in common use till sometime after the independence, c. 1980s. It is still in use.

bal-tib (sTod) = Cap used in Lahul of the style of cap used by a Balti or in Baltistan. Also called yo-'ar i.e. Uigur.

bartan = Literally utensil (Hindi). An important term of social exchange in Kullu, etc. and adopted in some parts of Lahul, like Tinan. Culturally it means exchange of the customary gifts between the kins. In sTod it is called *zong* i.e. *gzungs*.

batungru, butungru = Also harkara, messenger.

be-da =One of musician class, the musician class.

bheri (Tinan) = Earthen pitcher of the capacity of about 15-20 litres for keeping chhang.

bhe-ta = See be-da.

big (bi-ga) = Fire made of hay and sheep droppings in the fields.

bra-phye = Flour of buckwheat.

bra-tsag (sTod) = Beer prepared from the flour of buckwheat.

'bru = Grain of any kind, here of *nas*, barley grain.

'brug-pa = This word has been used in the old scriptures in place of the verb rgyug-pa, to run, to flow.

'bub = Length measuring from the tip of the middle finger of one hand to that of the other hand, when the two arms are stretched fully about three meters.

Char (Pattan) = A multi-storied building structure like the castle of Gundhla of Kullu style. Similar structures are told to have existed in Chembak, near Thirot, Goram, Yombe and Gahli near Nalda in Pattan. It is told that there were small windows in them. The wooden beam forming body of the deity Gepang is also called Char.

cha-ra = A village official in olden times. The term is still used in sTod to designate a person functioning as Supervisor in the ceremonies like marriage, etc. Char was an officer heading over the Mandala in Chamba in olden times.

chhag-nas = A ceremony of consecration, consecrated barley grain.

chhang = Locally brewed beer of nas or rice.

chhang-ma = A person in charge for distribution of chhang in a ceremony.

chhang ma-chhu **(sTod), Also chhangnying-khu.** = Chhang juice-pure. The pure liquid of chhang before adding water.

chhatru= Colt. Name of a place in upper Chandra valley.

Chāḷh **(Pattan)** = Chaukidar.

dal-mo **=** Chest of slaughtered sheep or goat, without limbs.

dangs-ma (Punan) = See chhangma-chhu.

do-pa = See alto.

dothain = Son of a Raja. The heir-apparent is called Tika. The younger brothers of the Tika are called dothain, in the language of the lower hills like Suket.

mdun-pa = Good thoughts.

'don-sing (sTod), hon. ('don-che, hon. = to drink) = A drink, cold, like chhang and a-rag.

ga-ga, hon. = Elder brother.

Gandha-la = Name of the mountain at the junction of rivers Chandra and Bhaga. Name of the monastery which has been brought down to Tubchiling and is presently called Gandhala-Tublchiling. Later it corrupted to Gandhola.

ga-ru = In Pattan the class formed after marriage between a Brahmin and Nangpa.

gha-ra, **mgar-ra, ga-ra** = The artisan class, a person of the class. Iron smith.

grol-ma chhu-gdong = Dolma of water pit. Name of the image of goddess Tara found carved on stone near the old monastery of Gandhala.

gu-dal (Punan) = See dal-mo.

gu-lu and ma-lu-ta = This pair of the names of two sacred places in Lahul are found in two documents related to Thonu, the great Kharpon. These two are corrupt forms of Ku-lu-ta, that is Gushal near Tandi, and Maru or Margul, Udaipur.

Gyab **or** *rgyab* (Shashur) = Back. A man load.

gyir-mo = Rupee.

gyus-mtshan = Information, knowledge.

dge-ba = Virtue, auspicious ceremony. The ceremony held after the death of a person.

dge-rtsi **or** *dge-tsi* = Celebration of merriment. Virtuous task. It appears that the term used for the famous annual festival of go-tsi held in Punan comes from this term of dge-tsi. Although the tradition must be much older.

dgu-dal = See gu-dal.

rgam-pha = bskal-pa, bskal-mchhod. Worship.

rgyal- or rgya-bza' = A woman from China.

harkārā (Pattan) = Messenger.

ja-'u, ja-oo = A brick of tea. The word also appears used to mean a coin, which is unknown.

kar-chhag, dkar-chhag(s) = Sometimes also named as tho-yig or bo-yig. In modern times it means register, index or inventory. Traditionally, when these objects were not there, it meant an epilogue.

khar-pon **(mkhar-dpon)** = Castle-authority, a fort-supervisor. An employee of Kullu Raja belonging to Lahul and posted at Tandi. He was second to Hakim.

khu-ra = Snacks. Used for local item of food, cake cooked in oil.

kun-dga' ra-ba (sTod) = A rack of pigeon holes for keeping statues, books, etc.

kunnū (Pattan) = Hannū, (Hindi = hāndī). See al-to

ko-ook, kronk, se-ok (Pattan) = Chowkidar, guard.

kyar (Tinan) = The Tower castle of Gundhla.

bskal-mchhod = Auspicious offering. It is pronounced as kal-chhor.

dkar-rtsis (sTod) = White paint; to paint white, white-washing.

skyang = skyang-pa. Single, only, pure.

skem (sTod), hon. = Cold drink like chhang and arag.

skyem = See skem.

skye-rtags (sTod) = Birth-signs. Birth-examination. A forecast by a priest as to the kind of the species in which the deceased person will take birth like bird, animal, human, etc. in the next life. Symbols of the next birth are collected through a customary practice. This also suggests the books to be copied, statues of the particular deities to be raised, etc.

lag-sha = Hand-meat. One limb of meat.

lakh (Kullu) = Same as khal in Lahul.

lhum = Yeasted, nas, barley or rice ready for preparing chhang. Cooked nas or rice mixed with phab, yeast, is kept in bed warm for three days, then it becomes lhum.

lhye-ki (Pattan) = Lower, the lower, of the lower.

likir = ?

bla-brang = Labrang. Old designation for a temple or monastery. In Tinan the monastery at Khyinang was known as Labrang.

The monastery of Tinan situated near the castle, at Shelting, is described as Labrang.

bla-bris, **(Pronounced lab-ri)** = Painting, drawing.

mahāṅ-gī (Pattan) = Upper, upper side.

makar- ?

me-rta = See al-to.

mo-me (mes-mo) = Grandmother.

mun-tsi (Punan) = A small field.

myug-gri = Knife for sharpening reed pen.

nang-lon (blon) = Lambardar. A village official representing a cluster of villages or a kothi.

nang-pa = Here the Supervisor in charge looking after the overall arrangements of a ceremony like death ceremony. A Buddhist.

Nautor = Newly broken land. Piece of a government wasteland allotted to a cultivator is called nautor.

no = Younger brother.

no-no, **hon.** = Same as *no*..

no-mo = Younger sister.

pung-ying, pu-nya = A death ceremony like dGe-ba, performed by a social class named Songla in Pattan.

phe (phye) = Flour of any kind. Here for bra-phye, flour of buckwheat.

phe-mar **or** *phye-mar* = Tsampa, sattu, mixed with ghee and sugar.

phye = Same as *phe*.

pi-rī = Fields in Lahul are all irrigated and land is generally slopy. Yu-ra, water channel, runs at the higher or upper edge of the field. Between the boundary of the field and the line of the yu-ra there is a small stretch of uncultivable land. But it being generally wet due to the water flowing in the cahnnel, there have flourishing growth of grass and also contains growth of some valuable medicinal plants. This stretch of land is called pi-rī.

spa (Ladakh) = pā. A preparation of tsampa, mixed with salty tea, buttermilk or chhang.

spar-tsal = dpa'-rtsal. dpa' dang rtsal. Powerful and efficient.

rab-nas = A ceremony of consecration.

ram = Colour made from natural objects.

ri-bong 'dsin = One holding rabbit, the Moon.

ru-ma, sru-ma = Beer made from buckwheat flour.

sha brang-go,sha brang-gog = See dal-mo.

sha-kog, sha-gog, sha-khog = The skinned full body of slaughtered sheep or goat with four limbs.

sha lag-pa = See lag-sha.

sha-pa = In charge of distribution of meat in a ceremony.

shel-bum = Bottle of glass.

shelṭu (Tinan) = The open place usually above the village where the villagers bring their sheep and cattle in the morning and collect in the evening. The village shepherd collects and leaves the cattle here after grazing them in the day. (This applies to whole Lahul, each having varying term.) In Gundhla it is name of the place where there stands the castle and the monastery.

she-ma = The married lady of a Thakur family.

shem-chung = Young lady of a Thakur family.

shu-na, shu-nar, shu-na-ra (Pattan) = Pitcher.

srum, hon. = Curry of meat.

sru-ma = See bra-tsag.

Suraḷī = The Ranas or Thakurs of the lower Lahul are said customarily to marry with the gaddi or Rana families. But those marrying with any other family was known as suraḷī.

bsang-ma, hon. = Meal.

gsol-ja, hon. = Brewed tea.

gches-ma = See she-ma.

tsag-mo (Punan) = Beer prepared from flour of nas. It is considered as superior to bra-tsag.

tso-li = see al-to.

tsug-shi **(Punan)** = Concerning something. Barbog, a household, makes contribution in its own name. Dolma of the same household makes contribution additionally in her personal name. So the entry is 'Dolma Barbog tsugshi,' Dolma belonging to Barbog house.

tsha-tsha **or** ***tshva-tshva*** = It is an object prepared of earth painted white, at the time of raising of a chhorten and placed in it as gzungs. It is like a mtshogs, a conical ball, of weight of about 250 gms.

tshal = A kind of stone of different colours used for making colours.

mtshe-srung, phyogs-srung = Protector of life, a charm.

rdsa-ma (sTod) = Pitcher.

to-gor = Here a ball of butter or ghee of about a seer.

Tubchiling (folk) = Name of the plateau above the highway at the junction of the rivers Chandra and Bhaga where Gandhala monastery has now been shifted down. Earlier there was residence of lamas of Gandhala and was a resting place for the pilgrims coming to visit Gandhala monastery.

Tu-ki-gling = Same as Tubchiling. This name is found written in the literary documents.

yo-'ar (sTod) = See bal-tib.

zhib, hon. = Tsampa, flour of parched nas.

gzhi-rmad (sTod) **=** Wife, reference.

zong, zung, ***gzungs*** = Sanskrit dhāraṇī. A sacred object placed in the structures like a house or chhorten, etc.

gzims-khang hon. = Sleeping room, (gzims-che, hon. = to sleep). Here 'place of residence.'

Bibliography

Books in English

Crook and Omaston. 1994. *Himalayan Buddhist Villages,* Motilal Banarsidass, New Delhi.

Datta, C.L. 1973. *Ladakh and Western Himalayan Politics, 1819-1848,* Munshiram Manoharlal, New Delhi.

Elizabeth, A.S. 1991. *Rediscovering Western Tibet* (A Thesis Submitted for the degree of Doctor of Philosophy of the Australian National University), not published.

Francke, A.H. 1926. *Antiquities of Indian Tibet,* Vol. II, S. Chand & Co., New Delhi, reprinted.

Lyall, J.B. 1874. *Final Report on the Revised Settlement of Kangra District.*

Punjab Govt. 1918. *Ruling Princes and Chiefs, Notables and Principal Officials of the Punjab Native States*, Punjab Government, Lahore.

Roerich, Goerge N. 1949. *The Blue Annals,* Motilal Banarsidass, Delhi, reprinted 1976.

Tobdan. 1984. *History and Religions of Lahul,* Books Today, New Delhi.

Tobdan & C. Dorje. 1996. *Historical Documents from Western Trans Himalaya Lahul, Zanskar and Ladakh,* Book India, Delhi. No. 128. Pp. 21-23.

Tobdan & C. Dorje. 2008. *Moravian Missionaries in Western Trans-Himalaya: Lahul, Ladakh and Kinnaur,* Kaveri Books, New Delhi. Pp. 144-146.

Tobdan. 2015. *Spiti: A Study in Socio-Cultural Traditions,* Kaveri Books, New Delhi.

Tobdan. 2023. *Mahakappina: the King of Kuluta and the Kinnaras of Himalaya*, Kaveri Books, New Delhi.

Tucci, Giusseppe. 1988. *Rinchen bZangpo and the Renaissance of Buddhism in Tibet Around the Millenium,* Aditya Prakashan, New Delhi.

Vogel, J. Ph. 1911. *Antiquities of Chamba State*, Part I, Archaeological Survey of India, New Delhi, reprinted 1994.

Hindi

Handa, O.C. 2008. In *Guru Padmasambhava,* Ed. Banarsi Lal, Guru Padmasambhava Monastery, Riwalsar, Mandi.

Rahul Sankrityayan. 1956. *Kinnara Desh Me,* Kitab Mahal, Allahabad.

Bhoti

Donyod Dorje, sKyab-rje sTag-sna Rin-po-chhe. 2011. *dPal La-dwags sTag-sna dGon ma lag dang bchas pa'i chhags-rabs gsal bar bkod-pa bdon gtam rnaba'i bdud-rtsi zhes bya ba,* Khenpo Shedup Tanzin, Kathmandu.

Dorje, Gelong, Spiti. 1978. *lotstsha-ba rinchhen bzangpo'i rnam-thar dad-ldan dge-'phel,* Author, Spiti (Himachal Pradesh).

Journals, English

Amy Heller. Observations on an 11th century Tibetan inscription on a statue of Avalokiteśvara, *Internet source,* 29 July, 2023.

Petech, L. 1947. *The Tibetan-Ladakhi Moghul War of 1681-83,* The Indian Historical Quarterly Vol. XXIII, No. 3, September 1947, pp. 169-199.

Index

Plates

Plate 1 : Village Tindi. Metal drum in the temple of Mrikula Devi, with inscription in Sharda script, C.E. 9th century.

Plate 2: Margul, Udaipur, Mrikula Devi, inscription in Sharda script, 16th century C.E., (see Vogel, 1911: 249-251).

Plate 3: Margul, Udaipur. Inscription in Tankri script on a wooden board (courtesy O.C. Handa).

Plate 4: Triloknath, Inscription on stone in Sharda script, C.E. 9th century, (picture, anonymous).

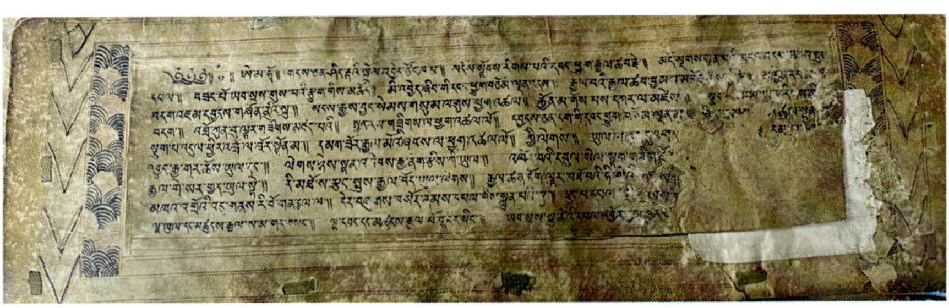

Plate 5: Village Rhape. A page from a karchhag containaing the name of Raja Bahadur Singh (1532-1559), bottom line, earliest of the kind in Lahul.

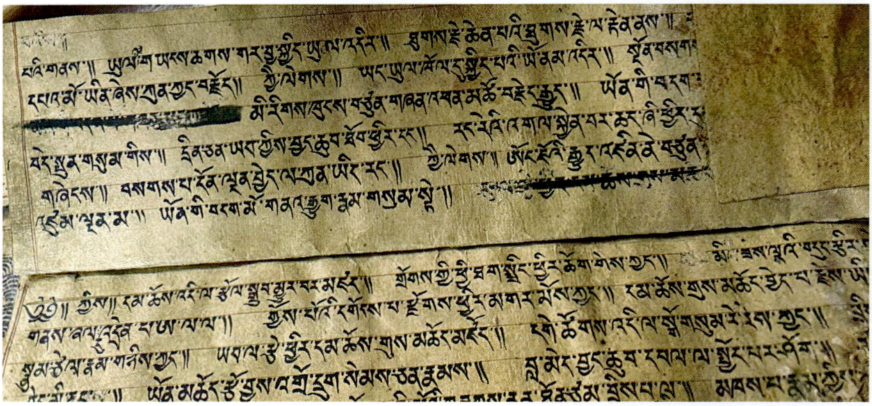

Plate 6: Rhape, a page from a karchhag mentioning the term Kholl, top two lines.

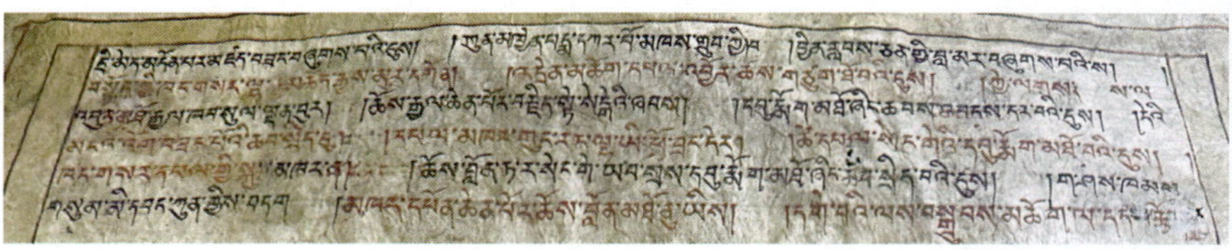

Plate 7: Village Jahlma. A page from a Karchhag describing Ajit Singh, Raja of Kullu (1816-1841), Thakur Tshe-dpal Seng-ge of Gungrang, Thakur Tara Chand (Singh) of Khangsar (Kolong) and Thonu, the Great Kharpon.

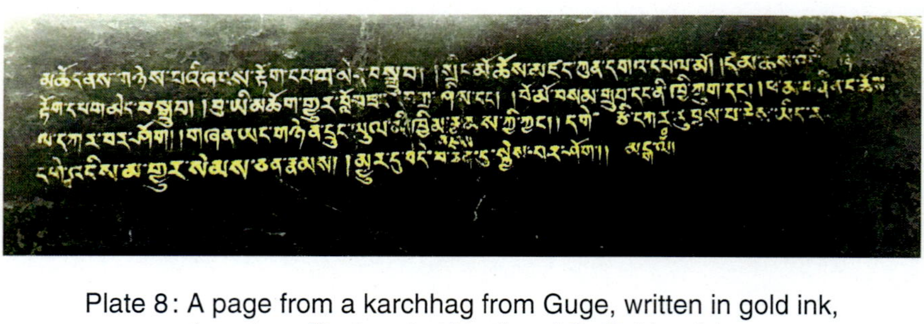

Plate 8: A page from a karchhag from Guge, written in gold ink, (courtesy Roshan Lal Negi and O. C. Handa).

Plate 9: Kinnaur. Village Roghi, Inscription on stone in an unknown script, c. C.E. 1766, (courtesy Ashwani Negi and Tanzin Phuntsok).

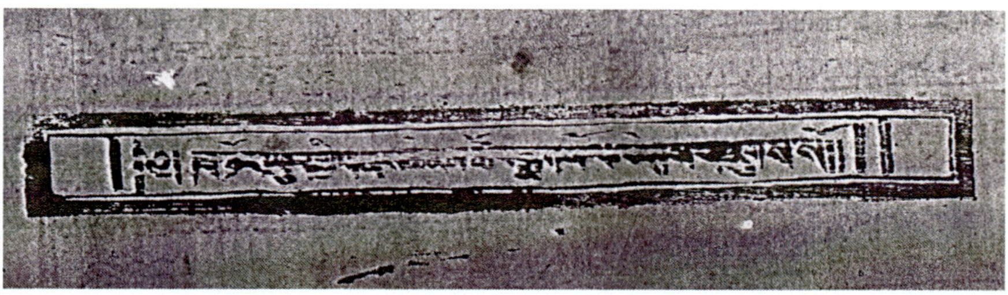

Plate 10: Riwalsar. Title Page of gsol-'debs, Prayer Book, which reads: "za-hor yul gyi gnas-chhen mtsho padma'i gsol-'debs bzhugs-so." 'Here begins the Prayer Book of the great pilgrimage place of mTsho Padma of the Zahor country.' It gives the name of the area as Zahor.

Plate 11: Village Rwaling, metal mohra of devata Naunath with inscription in Tankri script mentioning the name Tedhi Singh, Raja of Kullu, (C.E.1742-1767).

Plate 12: Village Lindoor, Kankani Chhorten, c. C.E. 18th-19th century.

Plate 13: Lindoor, mChhod-khang, Worship Room, inside the monastery.

Plate 14: Lndoor, tsha-tsha, from the gZungs of the dismantled Chhorten.

Plate 15: Lindoor,Temple of Buhaari devata.

Plate 16: Gemur inscription on stone, c. 1800, Thakur Dharam Singh of Khangsar. The two stone slabs containing inscriptions, kept on a large platform of manye stones, located at the old site of Gemur gonpa, are lost.

Plate 17: Chhukutsi gonpa, Khangsar. Image named Khyung, Garuda, Eagle, of mixed metal.

Plate 18: Chhukutsi gonpa, Khangsar. Thanka on a metal base of Mi-khrug-pa (Mithukpa), Akshobhya.

Plate 19: Khangsar Khar, the castle of the Thakurs of Khangsar (Kolong) whose construction was completed in c. 1895, photograph c. 1975. The front extensions have been demolished.

Plate 20: Srangbar, Khangsar, Manye Ringmo, the Long Manye, between two chhortens.

Plate 21 : Srangbar, Khangsar. Ancient monument Dankhar, Watch Tower.
It was situated at the edge of the plain of Khangsar village.
Now replaced by a Community Centre.

Plate 22: Chhokhor, monastery. Impression of the inscription in Sharda script on a stone image in the monastery, c. C.E. 9th-10th century (courtesy C. Dorje).

Plate 23: Srasrin, Sissu. Carved Fountain Stone Slab, in the tradition of Pangi and Chamba and Kishtwar

Plate 24: Tinan Khar, the castle of the Thakurs of Gundhla, both Kyar and Nal-ze built in two different traditions, located at Shelting (photo courtesy Prem Lal Yotarpa).

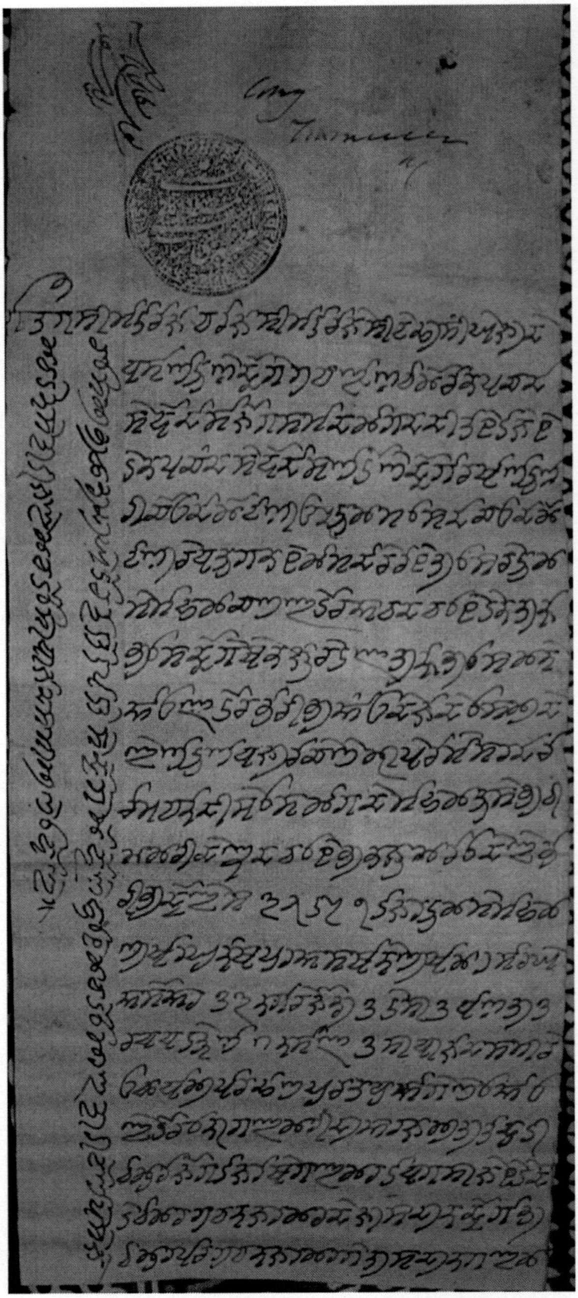

Plate 25: Tinan. Decree issued by Raja Tedhi Singh, C. E. 1760, Tankri script, appointing Rup Chand-Seva Das, the Thakurs of Gundhla, as Daroga of whole Lahul.

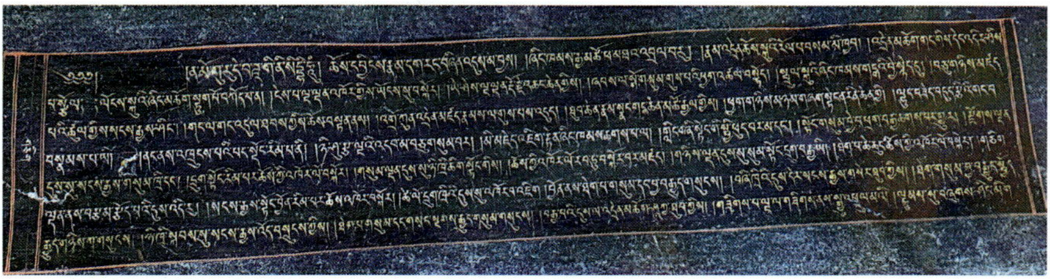

Plate 26: Shashur gonpa. A page of the karchhag forming part of mDo Kalzang, written in gold ink c. C.E. 1900, (courtesy Urgyan Tshering Melagpa).

Plate 27: Village Beeling. Inscription on stone, Moravians, Missionaries, c. C.E. 1900, (courtesy Mangal Chand).

Plate 28: Pangi. Inscription in Tankri script on a metal plate, C.E. 1909,Village Mindhal, temple of devi Mindhal Vasini, (courtesy C. Dorje).

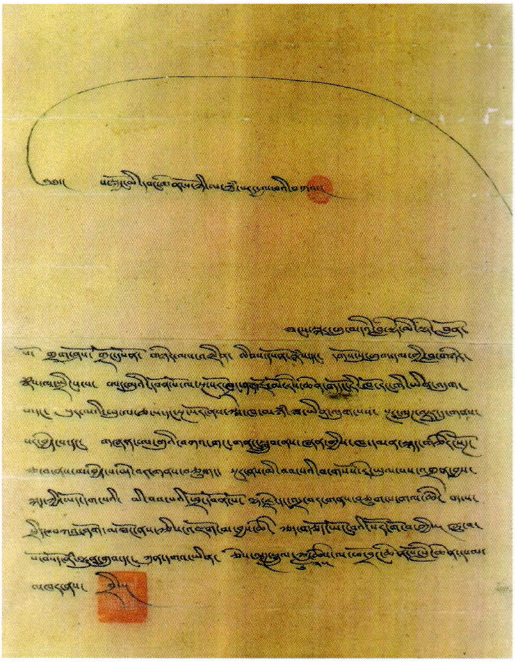

Plate 29: Zanskar. bKa'-shog, Decree of Nyima Namgryal, C.E. 1701.

Plate 30: Spiti, bKa'-shog, Decree of Dechhog Namgyal, C.E. 1671, on silk cloth

Plate 31 : Bhanodi, Chamba.Old manye inscription, Bhanodi monastery (see Tobdan, 2023:108-126).

Plate 32 : Chhukutsi. Pre-title page of the book Padma Thangyig decorated with paintings. It reads 'a-u-rgyan skad du 'In the Language of Uddiyana.' The names of the figures are L-R :Chhos-sku kun-tu bzang-po (Samantabhadra), Man-dha'r-ba, dBu-rgyan (Urgyan) Padma, Ye-shes Tsho-rgyal and Chhos- sku sNang-ba mTha'-yas (Amitabh).

Plate 33: Jagatsukh, Kullu. Temple of Dhomya Rishi,inscription in Bhoti (courtesy Kirit Mankodi and Tara Chand).

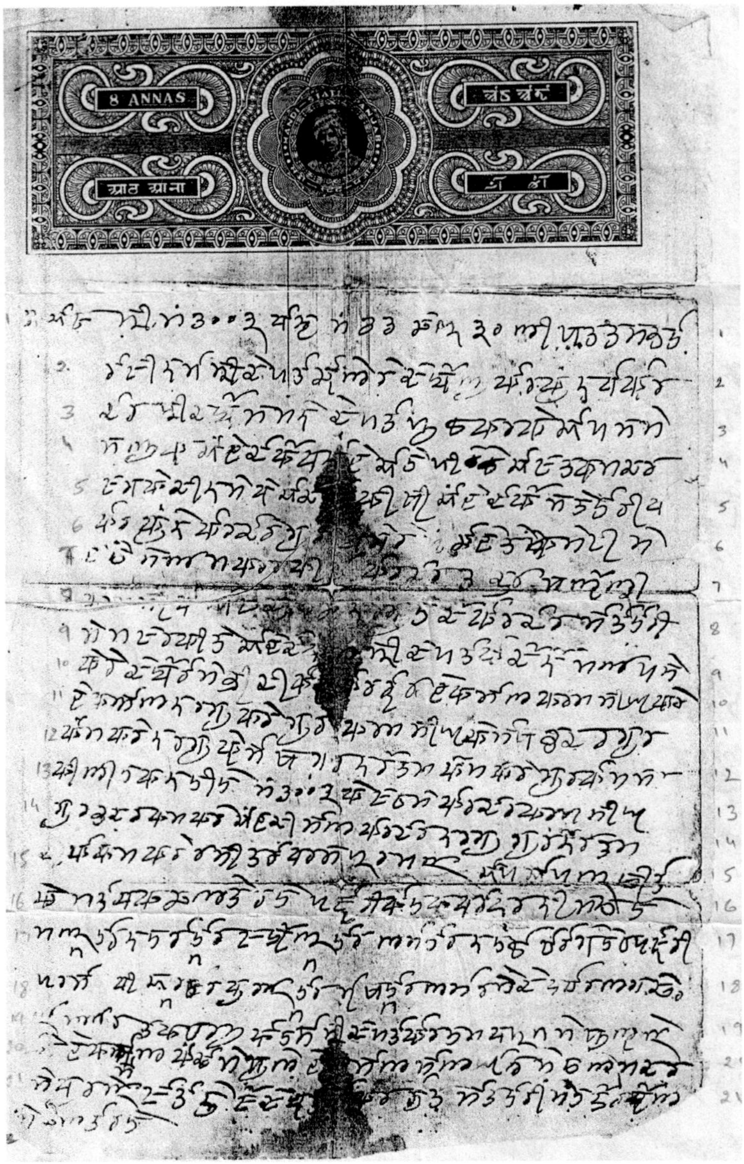

Plate 34: Mandi. An Agreement in Tankri script, on a stamp paper purchased in C.E. 1894 and the document executed in 1946.

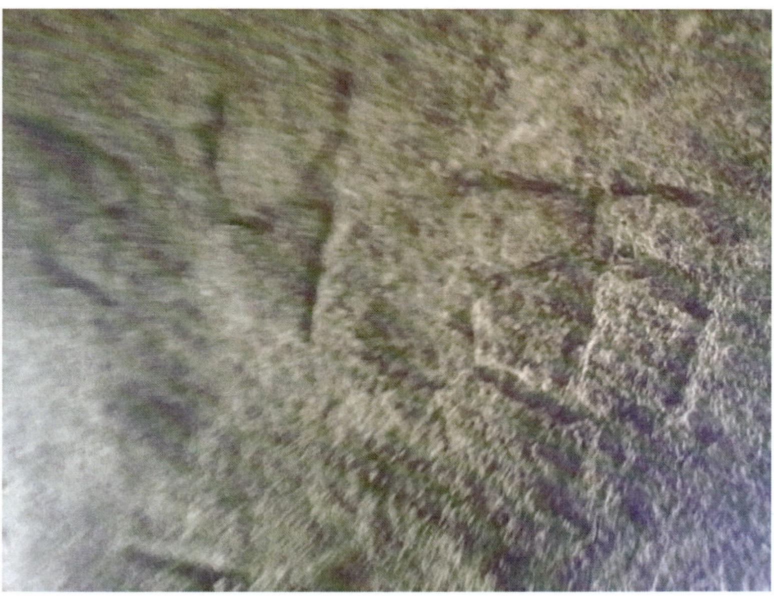

Plate 35-36 : Naograon, Holi valley, Bhramaur. Inscription in Sharda script, (courtesy Yeshe Dorje).

Plate 37: Kinnaur, Tsha-par. Image of Manjushri, with inscription of a sloka in Sanskrit, Bhoti script. Inscription visible partially, c. C. E. 11th-12th century.